The Triumph of the Will

The Journey of My Experience

Jamal Sanad Al-Suwaidi

Dedicated to my beloved country,

the United Arab Emirates

First Published in 2017

ISBN 978–9948–10–377–6 Paperback Edition
ISBN 978–9948–10–397–4 Hardback Edition
ISBN 978–9948–10–382–0 Electronic Edition

All correspondence should be addressed to:
United Arab Emirates
PO Box: 114898, Abu Dhabi
E-mail: dr.jamal.sanad@gmail.com

 jamalsanadalsuwaidi | jamal_sanad | jamal_sanad |  Jamal Sanad Al-Suwaidi

Contents

Preface

It occurs to me that this autobiography would not have come to light had it not been for my battle with cancer and suffering with treatment for more than 10 years since the end of 2003. By God's mercy and grace, I have recovered from my condition and have been able to continue my normal life equipped with this experience. I have almost been born again. Perhaps it is this experience that has convinced me I have something to offer my readers outside the academic and research fields to which I have devoted my life and effort.

Documenting my experience with cancer has opened a door for me to reflect on my entire life and contemplate its stages and transformations in light of a new experience, completely different from anything I had previously faced. My main goal of writing this autobiography is to show all cancer patients, their relatives and society that I am a former cancer patient who now writes, speaks, performs his job, deals every day with new duties and complicated tasks, and directs a large institution with all the pressure and physical and mental exhaustion that it entails.

I would like to say to every cancer patient that after 10 to 20 years, they too could be in their homes with their children and loved ones facing life with determination and willpower as I personally do, and continue their mission of enriching humanity as God commands us to do. I would like to say, based on a real case, that cancer is not an irrevocable death sentence that cannot be resisted. In fact, it is a disease that can be beaten by treatment, provided that you do not surrender to it. This is the core message of this book.

In addition, this autobiography includes the essence of my experience and a success story built on hard work, perseverance and loyalty to the country and its leadership. The child who was born in 1959 to a modest family and illiterate parents, never thought that in the coming years of his life he would become one of the elite thinkers in his home country. He never thought that hardship would turn into ease and prosperity, by the grace of God. He never thought he would lead large successful institutions. He never thought that he would stand on platforms of honor in his country and in the most prominent countries in the world, and would receive a lot of material and moral appreciation. If this child had been told then that meeting with world leaders would become a matter of familiar routine for him when he grew up, he would have thought that to be an impossibility or an excessive stretch of imagination.

Although I was not enthusiastic to write my autobiography, I discovered that recollection of past events and evocation of old memories stir indescribable feelings in one's heart and soul, relieve the heart from the agonies of the past and rekindle the flames of nostalgia. Faces of loved ones show up from behind the realm of the unseen, relieving some of the pain we feel from their absence. Childhood friends appear from within the anecdotes and reminiscences, illuminating our days and filling the void with their heartfelt laughs and pure love.

I would like to extend my sincere appreciation and gratitude to His Highness Sheikh Mohamed bin Zayed Al Nahyan, Crown Prince of Abu Dhabi, Deputy Supreme Commander of the UAE Armed Forces and President of the Emirates Center for Strategic Studies and Research (ECSSR) (may God protect him) for all the kindness that His Highness has bestowed on me. His Highness Sheikh Mohamed bin Zayed Al Nahyan (may God protect him) has been behind every success I have achieved. I literally owe him, after the Almighty God, my life and my recovery from cancer, as I will explain in the coming pages.

Finally, I do not want to talk at length in this preface. I hope my readers will find some benefit and useful lessons in this autobiography, and hope to be successful in achieving the goals of writing it.

Prologue

Prologue

"You will die in two weeks."

Those were the words the British doctor told me bluntly in that long-gone evening in December 2003. The doctor said it in an indifferent tone as if he were telling me news of a football match in a local tournament between two unknown teams. I looked at the doctor with a certain composure though I do not know where it came from. I listened to what he had to say about the few remaining days and hours of my life with the same concentration with which I listen to a scientific lecture, or the news of a political event in my field of work and then analyze and scrutinize its every aspect. In what seemed to be a self-developed defense tactic to face this difficult moment, my mind started recalling dispersed scenes from my life revolving around certain moments of my childhood, education and career, in addition to distant and close memories of my mother, my children, my wife, and other people I knew. Scenes with no obvious connection to one another that my subconscious brought out according to its own obscure logic. The subconscious was building a wall of resistance, helping me overcome the shock of the moment and preparing me for the long-term battle that lay ahead.

Although death is the only certain, inescapable fact of life, it always comes as a surprise. People are always astonished by the news of death as if it is against the natural laws of the universe. Contrary to those who see a human contradiction in death, I see it in harmony with the will for life, which the Creator has made the most inherent trait of human beings; it even extends to other creatures whose will for life or survival instinct represents the primary driving force for their behavior. The moment I was diagnosed with cancer, my strong, deeply rooted religious values emerged to support me in facing the earth-shattering news. Nonetheless, the surprise still had its impact. No matter how strong you are, it is not easy to be told you are going to die in two weeks.

One of the elements of surprise in encountering the idea of death in my case was the very limited time available. There were only a few days to deal with the British doctor's prognosis. It seems that the very statement "you will die in two weeks," was enough to invigorate the will for life, the secret weapon implanted by the Creator inside us. The Creator gave us some knowledge of it and entrusted us to use it at the right moment to face the elements of death and mortality.

I do not know how professional that British doctor was, but he gave himself the right to predict my remaining days on Earth. However, what I was able to learn in this field, which is neither comprehensive nor conclusive knowledge, is that it is quite often required to inform a patient of their true condition, no matter how critical, unless there are specific circumstances that prevent that. But specifying the time left to live is not an acceptable behavior. Moreover, in the particular case of cancer patients, they need a doctor who knows how to deal with them psychologically. The two-week period the doctor specified for me affected my psychological state extremely negatively. This incident could have led to serious repercussions had I given in to the feelings of fear and weakness.

I am not aware of the British doctor's whereabouts. I do not know whether he is still alive or whether he met his inevitable fate of death. I do not know whether he still follows the same way of informing his patients of the remaining days he estimates they will live on Earth. I do not know. Nevertheless, what I definitely know is that the two weeks this doctor estimated had passed, as well as another two weeks, followed by more than

600 weeks. By God's grace, I am still alive. I sleep, wake up, write, play sports, have fun with my grandchildren, engage in political and intellectual discussions and participate in stressful activities that continue for long hours.

Was the doctor's tone, which was defiant to my human existence, the driving force that led me to hold on to the

At one of the lecture series titled "ECSSR: The Present and the Future" organized by the ECSSR to develop the professional skills of its employees, November 26, 2015

God-given will for life and get ready for a fierce fight with a deadly enemy? I do not know exactly. But I found myself preparing for the battle. A light inside me – a hunch – told me that this doctor sitting in front of me, equipped with the authority of what he thought was absolute definitive knowledge, was unable to judge a medical situation. I felt there was something wrong with his judgment although he was studying medical analyses and x-ray images as if he was only a conveyor of their mysteries. As I was familiar with hypothesis testing in my professional career, I treated his judgment as a hypothesis that I would test. I decided not to let the smug authority of the white coat shake the principles of the hypothesis testing methodology, which I deeply respect.

As Gabriel Garcia Marquez chose the title *Living to Tell the Tale* for his wonderful autobiography, I have certainly lived to tell the tale of my life. Marquez was unique in writing his autobiography, but I am not a storyteller like him. I am a researcher who has lived through a frightful experience full of pain and hope, and deemed it my duty to narrate this experience in order to help lessen the despair of those who are going through a similar experience or may go through it in the future.

The Reason behind the Change of Mind

It was not easy for me to accept the idea of writing my autobiography. I received a number of proposals from different people in this respect, containing a variety of perspectives, visions and ideas, but none of them convinced me to write it. Perhaps, the general idea of the previous proposals to write my autobiography was to focus on myself. Such an idea may imply

At the ECSSR, 1997

self-aggrandizement or self-admiration, which I always try to avoid. Everyone who has worked with me knows that even in dealing with national issues that may impose some degree of alignment, I insist on being objective and focus on facts and all aspects of the issue in question. I believe that the strongest way to defend national interest is to acknowledge, understand and analyze the facts before making sound decisions.

I often say that research approaches based on objectivity and structured reasoning are the right way to deal with any issue. Even in books on the lives of UAE historical personalities, I tell those who work with me that excessive praising is not the appropriate way to unveil the aspects of greatness and excellence; instead the focus should be on their achievement in terms of scale, circumstances and context. This is what shows how great a personality is. As such, I will follow the same way when I write my autobiography by recounting the details of what happened without any exaggeration. Sufficient for me as witnesses were my struggle against pain, my hope, and my clinging to life.

Work and only work was the value on which I wanted my autobiography to focus. On several occasions, I felt that I have already been writing my autobiography through continuous work for almost four decades. Actions speak louder than words, and a person's achievements are a much better testimonial than books written about them. Successful projects are more eloquent than successful chapters of publications. A life full of work in research and educational institutions delivers the message more clearly and effectively than written lines.

Delivering my speech at a conference titled "Gulf Security: A National Perspective II," UK, April 29, 1998

Work was the only aspect of life that I considered deserved my time. The months it would take to complete an autobiography could be invested in writing a new book that would benefit people and help fill a worrying shortage in the Arabic library. These months could also be used to establish a new section at the Emirates Center for Strategic Studies and Research (ECSSR) or to improve the existing work flow.

What has changed this time? Maybe it was the focus on benefiting and serving society that made the proposal to write my autobiography more acceptable. There are some people who wish to serve their country in the field of studies and research and they are interested in knowing about my experience, believing it would help them achieve their goals. There are others who are involved in building national institutions and are in need of detailed experiences to help them follow proper ways to avoid mistakes and miscalculations. Others are looking for an inspiring role model to lead them on the pathway to success and are interested in seeing real success stories that would save them from giving in to despair.

At the ECSSR, February 2, 2000

Cancer Does Not Mean Death

My experience of conquering cancer was particularly a divine blessing and writing it down may help cancer patients by convincing them that cancer does not mean the end. There is someone who had suffered cancer just like them but survived the difficult test by mobilizing their inner capabilities implanted by God. My case assures them that death is not the only option for them and chances of recovery are available if they refuse to give in and resist their deadly enemy. As a result, some cancer patients may succeed, today or after one or 100 years, in conquering the disease by relying on God Almighty first and with the help of this autobiography and other means. The intended message, which should be conveyed and rooted in the minds, is that cancer does not mean death as some people may think; that there are previous patients who conquered it; and that causes of death are innumerable, regardless of cancer or any other disease.

Initially, I did not feel the need to write my autobiography, but I started to change my mind. I became convinced that many people may need it and that it was my duty, nationally, religiously and humanly, according to the correct understanding of the pure religion in which I believe and that prompts us to do good and provide everything beneficial to mankind. I felt I was performing a duty and I could shoulder the additional burden for the sake of that mission. Nonetheless, I am used to handling busy schedules loaded with tasks and responsibilities. I felt that this noble objective was worth the effort and may benefit people today and in the future, given the human nature of the experience I went through and its ability to continue to inspire others.

During a signing event of my book *Eternal Imprints: Figures that Made History and Others that Changed the Future of Their Countries*, at the Ministry of Foreign Affairs and International Cooperation, May 9, 2016

The Triumph of the Will

As a lifelong specialist in humanities and social sciences whose way of thinking has been shaped by their methods and approaches, the first thing I thought about was to determine the central idea, the unifying element that would encapsulate the whole story and explain the decisions, achievements and even the transformations I have gone through. It did not take long for me to settle on "The Triumph of the Will" as the central idea and title of the book.

The underlying principle behind what I have achieved in my life is that I have never surrendered to the difficulties and obstacles I faced, no matter how tough they were. If I were the type of person who withdrew out of despair or fear, I would not have managed to take a single step forward since the day I was born, two months premature. Indeed, I was born after seven months of pregnancy and spent the remaining two months in an incubator.

"The Triumph of the Will" epitomizes the essence of my experience. I know that God Almighty has created people and endowed them with unequal levels of endurance, determination, intellect and will. Perhaps, He has blessed me with a good deal of them that enables me to

At the ECSSR January 16, 1998

refuse to surrender. Nonetheless, I am sure that each human being possesses some level of these traits. It is possible, and necessary, to develop the power of endurance and determination. Training oneself in them could be instrumental in achieving goals and resisting any obstacle, even if it is a deadly disease like cancer. I think I would not have recovered from cancer had I not strengthened my determination and willpower to the maximum, by God's grace, and refused to surrender at moments when any collapse of morale would have meant certain death.

As I started the first stage of my cancer treatment, I looked back to the past days of my life, and I discovered that they had been a connected series of triumphs over difficulties, adversities and challenges to which I refused to give in. This had happened throughout each of my educational stages, from primary school to university, leading to postgraduate study for master's and doctoral degrees in the United States of America. I strived to excel among colleagues. I fulfilled the dream of my illiterate parents by receiving the highest academic degree from a prestigious university and started a research career, which has continued to this day.

Also, I did not surrender when I was conspired against by the Muslim Brotherhood that were controlling United Arab Emirates University and scholarships to study abroad. In 1981, after I received my bachelor's degree in political science with distinction from Kuwait University, the late Dr. Izz Al-Din Ibrahim, a Muslim Brotherhood leader, was the

With H.H. Sheikh Mohamed bin Zayed Al Nahyan, Crown Prince of Abu Dhabi and Deputy Supreme Commander of the UAE Armed Forces (may God protect him), during his visit to the ECSSR, April 6, 1994

chancellor of UAE University. The Minister of Education at the time was also a Muslim Brotherhood member and one of its leaders. Members of the group blocked my appointment as an assistant lecturer in the Political Science Department citing ridiculous excuses. Also, the Minister of Education refused to give me a scholarship to do a master's and PhD abroad and excluded me in favor of other students who belonged to the Muslim Brotherhood and who were not academically eligible for scholarship. I was excluded because I stood against the Muslim Brotherhood and gave early warnings about their schemes and devious goals.

I also worked relentlessly during my master's and PhD education when I competed with students selected from around the world, including the United States of America and Europe. I took it upon myself to present a positive example of an Emirati, Arab and Muslim student, both academically and personally. I possessed the same determination and resolve when I was laying the first foundations of the Emirates Center for Strategic Studies and Research (ECSSR) in 1994, and at all stages of expanding the Center and improving its operations, relying on the full support of His Highness Sheikh Mohamed bin Zayed Al Nahyan (may God protect him), who has been President of the ECSSR since its establishment. I had to prove that I deserved the trust His Highness placed in me, which required me

With H.H. Sheikh Mohamed bin Zayed Al Nahyan, Crown Prince of Abu Dhabi and Deputy Supreme Commander of the UAE Armed Forces (may God protect him), during the first honoring ceremony for His Highness's visit to the ECSSR, June 20, 1995

to work for 24 hours every day. The journey of determination and resolve continued as I established the Distinguished Student Scholarship of His Highness the President of the UAE and the Emirates National Schools. I was determined not to let anyone deprive a distinguished Emirati student from their right based on personal or ideological desires, the way I was deprived.

The challenges I faced were enormous and daunting, but I always said to myself: never give up. That was part of what I thought about when I learned I was entering a battle with an even more ferocious challenge whose mere name stirs horror in the heart of anyone. I knew that the battle with cancer was different, but I believed that the same prescription I had throughout the course of my educational, professional and personal life was still the key to victory. I never gave in to adversities.

With a firm will and resolve, I believe everybody can do that. Hence the message of this book is: whatever challenges or adversities you may face, you should fight the battle with determination and the confidence

With H.H. Sheikh Mansour Bin Zayed Al Nahyan, UAE Deputy Prime Minister and Minister of Presidential Affairs; H.E. Ahmed Al-Hemeiri, Secretary-General of the Ministry of Presidential Affairs; H.E. Dr. Abdullah Al-Raisi, Director General of the National Archives; H.E. Mohammed Salem Al Dhaheri, Executive Director of School Operations sector at Abu Dhabi Education Council, and member of the Board of Scholarship Office affiliated with the Ministry of Presidential Affairs; H.E. Dr. Ali Al-Irri, Director of External Scholarships at the Scholarship Office affiliated with the Ministry of Presidential Affairs; and H.E. Dr. Abdullah Maghribi, Director of Studies and Research at the Ministry of Presidential Affairs, during a ceremony for honoring graduates of the Distinguished Student Scholarship of His Highness the President of the UAE, December 21, 2015

that you will win, and eventually you will win. The message is simply: do not surrender.

The Healing Power of Faith

Willpower was an important weapon in my battle with cancer but was preceded by another God-given gift: my faith in God Almighty, which I believe is a strong and genuine faith. In some aspects, faith is a certitude in the soul that there is a higher power guiding your steps, a power that is present everywhere whether perceptible or imperceptible by the human mind. Faith is also a power that tells you in the innermost depth of your soul that there is a guardian who surrounds you with care and chooses for you paths and ways you cannot envision depending on your personal faculties. Human inner power, when based on faith in God, multiplies and builds up to a point where every difficulty is eased. At certain moments, it is enough

With H.H. Sheikh Mohamed bin Zayed Al Nahyan, Crown Prince of Abu Dhabi and Deputy Supreme Commander of the UAE Armed Forces (may God protect him), during the International Defence Exhibition and Conference (IDEX), February 14, 1993, as I was Head of Media Committee for IDEX, in its first edition

to read the verse of the Holy Quran [… and never give up hope of Allah's Mercy. Certainly, no one despairs of Allah's Mercy, except the people who disbelieve] to make you feel something similar to nuclear fission happening inside you that eventually produces boundless positive energy. I understand faith as a constantly renewed relationship between the human soul and its Creator. With this understanding, I recited the Holy Quran and listened to it. Every time I did so, every word, verse and letter would carry a new meaning that I had not noticed before.

Thus, I pondered on the holy words of God, […and We are nearer to him than his jugular vein], when my veins were burdened with medical devices and dozens of needles piercing them every hour, and I felt as if I read it for the first time. I felt that the holy verse that I had read and listened to thousands of times before had a subtle meaning that I only grasped at this moment. A light of certitude shone in my heart telling me that God Almighty was guarding me. I realized that hundreds of millions of people may have listened to this verse and every time they would understand it in a way consistent with their conditions, what they are going through and the pain they feel. Each one of them would feel that this holy verse speaks to no one on Earth other than them.

Unforgettable Visits

Along with the previously-mentioned two factors, there was a third one that also helped me conquer the disease. The visit made by His Highness Sheikh Mohamed bin Zayed Al Nahyan (may God protect him) to me during my medical treatment in Houston, USA, was a major milestone on the road to recovery.

With H.H. Sheikh Mohamed bin Zayed Al Nahyan, Crown Prince of Abu Dhabi and Deputy Supreme Commander of the UAE Armed Forces (may God protect him) during a visit in the UAE, 1999

His two honorable sons, Their Highnesses Sheikh Khalid bin Mohamed bin Zayed Al Nahyan and Sheikh Diab bin Mohamed bin Zayed Al Nahyan, visited me separately as well. The visit by His Highness Sheikh Mohamed bin Zayed Al Nahyan in particular was meaningful and inspiring, as I used to gain a valuable lesson from every meeting with him, every word heard from him, and every decision taken by His Highness.

Back then, I may not have had the chance to express what was on my mind when His Highness Sheikh Mohamed bin Zayed Al Nahyan visited me. I was too overwhelmed by his presence to express my feelings in words. However, when I reflect on my healing experience, I find that, after God the Almighty, I owe His Highness (may God protect him) my recovery. His

With His Royal Highness Prince Turki Al-Faisal Al Saud, Chairman of the Board of King Faisal Center for Islamic Research and Studies, and H.E. Sheikh Fahim Al-Qasimi, former Secretary-General of the GCC, during the ECSSR's 14th Annual Conference titled "Human Resources and Development in the Arabian Gulf," February 2, 2009

Highness's visit gave me endless hope and strengthened my will to resist the disease at a time when I needed it most. Also, I cannot forget that His Highness Sheikh Mohamed bin Zayed Al Nahyan (may God protect him) generously paid for my medical treatment, in a noble gesture not limited to my humble person, but an embodiment of a deep-rooted common culture characterizing the relationship between our wise leadership and the citizens of the United Arab Emirates.

When His Highness Sheikh Mohamed bin Zayed Al Nahyan (may God protect him) extended his hand to shake mine, I felt as if it delivered to me all messages of kindness and encouragement. His towering figure has such glory that anybody who comes close to him would see an innate modesty that would make you feel he is the closest person to your heart, and an aura of personal grandeur that does not evoke fear in you but admiration and

With H.H. Sheikh Abdullah bin Zayed Al Nahyan, Minister of Foreign Affairs and International Cooperation (Minister of Information and Culture at the time), on the sidelines of the ECSSR's 5th Annual Conference titled "2000: The Making of the Future," October 9, 1999

With H.E. Dr. Anwar Gargash, UAE Minister of State for Foreign Affairs, and Dr. Hassan Al-Ansari on the sidelines of a conference titled "Gulf Security: A National Perspective II," UK, April 29, 1998

With H.H. Sheikh Abdullah bin Zayed Al Nahyan, Minister of Foreign Affairs and International Cooperation, during his visit to the ECSSR, January 15, 2014

With H.E. Dr. Anwar Gargash, UAE Minister of State for Foreign Affairs, during the ECSSR's 14th Annual Energy Conference titled "Nuclear Energy in the Arabian Gulf," November 24, 2008

reverence for him. It is the grandeur of great men who inherited nobility, generation after generation, and who were raised in an unparalleled school of humanism, the school of the late Sheikh Zayed bin Sultan Al Nahyan (may God rest his soul in peace).

The message of the visit was that His Highness Sheikh Mohamed bin Zayed Al Nahyan (may God protect him) found time in his busy schedule and enormous responsibilities to visit one of his people, although he could have sufficed himself with a phone call to ask about my health condition, with his generous payment of all medical expenses or with conveying his greetings and wishes for recovery through friends.

Visits by honorable UAE sheikhs continued, in familiar gestures of support. Such gestures

H.H. Sheikh Saud bin Saqr Al Qasimi, Member of the UAE Supreme Council, Ruler of Ras Al Khaimah with my son Dr. Khaled, during my son's wedding ceremony, March 29, 2013

are well known to the sons and daughters of the UAE from all segments and positions, and the benevolence and goodness of these gestures cover them in all situations they pass through. During my stay at the hospital, His Highness Sheikh Abdullah bin Zayed Al Nahyan, Minister of Foreign Affairs and International Cooperation, visited me, accompanied by His Excellency Dr. Anwar Gargash, Minister of State for Foreign Affairs.

Throughout the years of my battle with cancer, my wife stood by me, supporting me with her heart and mind, and following every detail of my situation. With unmatched patience and composure, she endured painful moments of unbearable anger and fear, trying to comfort me and always make me feel safe and close to healing until we overcame this difficult period together. Our long life journey acquired a new meaning hardly found between couples, a meaning that might not be expressible in ordinary words.

Key Turning Points in My Life

When I reflect on the most impactful events in my life, chronologically, I find my marriage and the birth of my firstborn Khaled to be the first ones. My life gained a new source of hope and strength with the presence of a life partner who possesses all the necessary qualities on which the success of the family depends, and who provides its members with happiness and stability. With the birth of my son Khaled, I experienced the sense of fatherhood and the joy it brought me, a joy that any other event could hardly produce—the joy of the first look at a being that belongs to me more than anything else. The joy of the first smile and the first sounds forming on his lips, and the first steps which I observed with a mixed feeling of happiness and concern. That joy continued throughout all his childhood and youth, and his wedding ceremony was one the most joyful and memorable occasions in my life.

During a conference titled "Gulf Security: A National Perspective I," Abu Dhabi, April 5, 1997

The second event was receiving my PhD. It was a culmination of a long journey in which I contentedly endured hardships and difficulties mixed with hope of reaching the end of that journey, and then starting another path of success and build a new bridge to the future, equipped with this degree. My goal was not just an academic title with which to adorn my name. Rather, my pure belief in science and knowledge was my prime motive.

The third event was when I was introduced to His Highness Sheikh Mohamed bin Zayed Al Nahyan (may God protect him). That event represented a major turning point in my life, giving me the chance to use the experiences and scientific knowledge I gained to serve my country and community. His Highness provided me with considerable help and support at both professional and personal levels. I always find myself short of words to describe His Highness's generosity and to express my gratitude to him.

A wonderful shot with my late mother (may God rest her soul in peace) that will stay in my memory forever; with my children Khaled, Nora, Dana and Farah, in 2002. Her hearty prayers paved for me the road of success and excellence

The fourth event was my diagnosis with cancer. As a result of suffering from the disease, I rediscovered life. I started to see things from a different perspective. The sea and its waves, for example, which constantly produce new wonders. It is a great sea able to impose its laws and rules on everything within its boundaries, and on its surroundings as well. I was greatly fascinated by the terrific philosophy of sea waves. I had repeatedly tried to find a connection between the sea and myself, in terms of having a strong will that never gives up the love of life. Even though my view on many things in life changed, my faith in God and the way He protected me remained unshakable. The love I felt from people overwhelmed my heart with hope and optimism, and helped me triumph over the ordeal. This love taught me that life is a blessing from God that should not be wasted in futile activities, so I devoted all my energy to work after God had blessed me with recovery.

The fifth event was the death of my mother (may God rest her soul in peace). With her passing, I lost a piece of myself and my soul. I still feel the

At the launching ceremony of my book *The Mirage* in Cairo, December 14, 2014

grace of her sincere prayers surrounding me with protection and tranquility in the most difficult moments. The love and compassion she overwhelmed me with still fill me with positive energy for hope and love, making life more colorful and pleasant.

The final (sixth) event was my decision to give up smoking on November 15, 2011, after more than 40 years as a heavy smoker. I consider my success in quitting smoking as liberation from shackles to which I had abandoned myself for a long time until the habit had become so deeply rooted in me. Stopping it had become a fierce battle that took a lot of effort and suffering to win, but I did not surrender, and it was another triumph of my will.

My books, studies and articles always focus on the objective rather than the subjective aspects

A Book of a Different Nature

Since the start of my writing endeavor, all my publications have fallen under the category of academic research, including my articles and interviews in newspapers. This indeed requires a very high degree of objectivity, with no room for subjectivity. Although my field of research is humanities and social sciences – which involve some sort of subjectivity – they are still subject to rigorous and calculated factors and methods that any researcher should take into consideration when approaching them. Researchers exam-

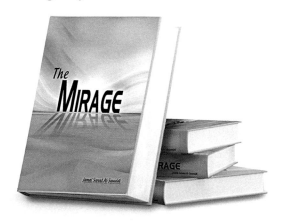

Delivering a lecture about my book *The Mirage*, at the ECSSR, March 3, 2016

ining the same topic are supposed to reach similar findings if they use the same research tools.

To achieve that level of objectivity, I rely on facts and figures in all my writings because they provide an indisputable underpinning and prevent wordiness. This is what I trained my students in, and what I ask researchers working with me to abide by. I explained this in the introduction of my book titled *Prospects for the American Age: Sovereignty and Influence in the New World Order* where I said: "In this book I have sought to present an informed view that is comprehensive, objective and analytical – one that is based on statistics, data and information, rather than casual personal impressions, biases or opinions." This life-long commitment to objectivity has marked all aspects of my life so strongly that it has become difficult to shake off. Hence, embarking on a new genre of writing that is based on subjectivity would require of me some degree of readjustment in order to

With H.E. Sheikh Nahyan bin Mubarak Al Nahyan, UAE Minister of Culture and Knowledge Development, during the charity marathon organized by Cancer Patient Care Society (RAHMA) in Yas Island, Abu Dhabi, November 7, 2015

give rein to personal views and impressions which the strict methods and rules of academic research have dictated me to exclude from my writings.

The topics of my books and studies have centered on security issues and developments; globalization and its related concepts; transformations; global and regional balances of power; conflicts of ideas and principles and influential powers; obstacles and challenges to the development process in the UAE and the Arab world; the future and its variables and realistic workable programs to deal with them. This has been the main realm of my interest and writings. However, this book is my life story, memories and experiences. Since the tasks I have undertaken, and still do, are political in nature, writing about my life

With H.E. Hashim Al-Qaysiyah, special adviser to H.H. Sheikh Tahnoon bin Zayed Al Nahyan; Nora Al-Suwaidi, Director General of Rahma Society; and the Filipino boxer Manny Pacquiao during the charity marathon organized by RAHMA Society in Yas Island, Abu Dhabi, November 7, 2015

would run the risk of mixing what is personal and what is political. I had to readjust my way of thinking to embark on such a project. Nonetheless, I still find it difficult to set aside being an academic researcher and all what that entails.

Target Audience of the Book

This book is directed to every person who seeks to achieve a noble national goal to serve themselves and their community. The lessons of my experiences contained in this autobiography may be helpful in achieving that goal. It is also directed to the people of the UAE, the Arabian Gulf, the Arab world and all of humanity. Our countries need to channel all the effort of their loyal citizens in the right way. They need a practical guide to enhance their performance capacity and avoid ways and practices that hinder their progress or waste their effort and energies in misdirected endeavors. My experience has already proved to me that it is not necessary to be born with a silver spoon in your mouth in order to be able to serve your country. All citizens can serve their country, irrespective of their status or attributes.

With my children, Khaled, Nora and Dana, in France, summer of 1993, on a trip in which we visited the Louvre Museum in Paris

Every human experience has its uniqueness, distinctiveness and imperfections. Circumstances surrounding a person may make some advice useful and some useless to them. In all cases, there are general rules for success that can be learned, which require the necessary flexibility and awareness to choose the proper alternatives, and creative thinking in the face of problems and innovative solutions. This book contains some of what could be considered foundational factors of success, the foremost of which are determination, perseverance, willpower and never yielding to challenges. These factors are best summarized in the saying: "Victory is but one more hour of patient perseverance."

The book is also directed to those who face difficulties in their education, or a serious health challenge like cancer. With glimpses of personal experience, the book explains to cancer patients a factor of healing and gives them the feeling that there is an attainable hope for beating the disease. It is directed to their relatives so as to be supportive of them in the face of pain and fear. The role of relatives is critically important because they can energize the will of the patient and set them on the path to recovery. This book is one of the two parts of my humanitarian mission; the other part is the voluntary work provided by the Cancer Patient Care Society (RAHMA).

This book is also directed to my children and my brothers and sisters, with whom I was not able to spend enough time at every point of their lives as mush as I wanted to due to other responsibilities. I have always wished to be with my children every day when they woke up in the morning, and to take them to school, enjoying their lovely smiles and cute frowns. I wish I had been with them at every school party where they would sing their little songs, and with them to answer the innocent questions they would ask me in their quest to understand the world. Perhaps, my children might give me an excuse when they know that I had been frequently away from them only to perform a humanitarian and national duty before I was diagnosed with cancer, which also prevented me from being with them the way I hoped. Perhaps, they may be delighted to know that they were one of my healing factors and sources of hope that gave me more strength and desire to live.

This book is also directed to my grandchildren. I would like them to know that they are descendants of a man who had dedicated his life to the service of his country, people and family, and to explain to them the importance of success. A man whose eyes have always been focused on the future and thoughtful preparation for it. This future, on which I have my eyes set, is embodied by them and their peers who would live on this earth and reap the fruits of what we have managed to sow during the course of our journey in this life.

Chapter 1

Early Life

Chapter 1

Early Life

I was born prematurely at seven months, on Thursday, July 30, 1959, at 12 noon and was put in an incubator.

At the age of 1, in 1960

Pre-term birth was anything but easy. It was filled with worries and anxieties because I came to this life before completing the normal pregnancy period. My mother was not expecting such a premature delivery. Like all mothers, she was haunted by fears for the health and life of her baby. The incubator in which I was placed did not calm her fears. Dozens of cases of premature babies who did not survive rushed to her mind. With the passage of days, however, her worries gradually subsided.

Even if I survived this stage, the long days of waiting would leave lasting scars in my mother's heart. Since a mother's love for her child is part of her God-given nature, long days of fear of losing it fuel this love, giving it more depth and warmth mixed with apprehension and turning it into a feeling that manifests itself at every moment. This is what happened then. My mother showered me with boundless affection, weaving the first threads of a special relationship that would bond me with her forever. Friends and loved ones often tell me that my words, my sentiments, my voice tone and even my body language are all different when I talk about my mother.

At the age of 3, in 1962

My maternal grandfather died long before I was born and my paternal grandmother, Atheeja bint Kalban, who was from the Emirate of Ras Al Khaimah, died when she was giving birth to my father in the 1930s. My maternal grandmother died when I was about 6 years old. She helped in my upbringing at that delicate stage of my life, and I still remember her words, advice and love in which she always immersed me.

By the time I was 6 years old, death had visited our family a number of times. When I was only 4 years old in 1963, my brother Muhammad died at the age of 3 after a brief sickness, which I do not exactly remember. Muhammad was taken to the hospital, which was a few kilometers away and its medical services were very poor, as was the case back then in general. I hardly remember his features because he died when I was very young. Nonetheless, the incident of his death, and its related episodes, remained vivid in my memory. What I remember about medical services in general in those early years was that there were only two types of injections for medical treatment: one was penicillin and the other was a white fluid whose name I do not recall. All diseases were treated by these two injections. Whether the patient had a cold, headache, stomachache, eye infection, ear infection or any other health issue, they had to be treated by one of those two injections.

My cousin, Muna, the daughter of my maternal uncle Ali, died when she was one. Our relationship with my uncle Ali was not an ordinary one. We used to live in the same house, and Tariq, my maternal cousin, was my closest companion and friend during childhood and in the later stages of my life. Tariq and I grew up together. He is one of those who remember the details of that period we lived together until the end of secondary school. I remember that my uncle Ali bought us our first television set, a Philips TV, as a gift for his sister, my mother, and her children. It was black-and-white, as color TVs came

At the age of 5, with my maternal cousin Tariq, in 1964

later when I was about 14 years old. Although my uncle Ali died in 1967 (may God rest his soul in peace), when I was 8 years old, he has occupied a special place in my heart throughout my life.

When I was 3, my life went through a huge transformation when I completely stopped eating meat, chicken and fish. I have been a vegetarian since then, perhaps even before I myself or others knew the term "vegetarian." That transformation was difficult indeed. In the Arabian Peninsula, meat and fish are the main staple foods. Arabs had many creative ways of cooking the most delicious mutton, goat meat and other delicacies with special flavors and spices brought from overseas by commercial vessels. In addition, the fish-rich coast of the Gulf made fish the main diet for people living around it. They also had special ways of preparing fish dishes, whose savor fascinated travelers who talked about their high quality.

There was another difficulty. At that time, mothers had a lot of strenuous work in caring for children and households. My shift to a vegetarian diet meant an additional burden on my mother who would have had to cook one type of food for family members and a different one for me. My mother, who always feared for me and constantly prayed for me in hard times, was unconditionally prepared to shoulder additional burdens for my sake when my character began to show signs of independence. She never complained about a burden being added to the many burdens that she willingly and readily bore. A new cooking pot was added to the existing kitchenware, in which my patient mother would cook rice, lentils, broad beans and other vegetarian food. Fortunately, the list of forbidden foods did not include eggs and dairy products, and this probably made the task somewhat easier for my loving mother.

At the age of 4, in 1963

My family was expectedly surprised at the beginning, but none of its older members tried to force me to change my diet. There was an understanding from my father, mother and siblings of my special nature. This was perhaps an indication of a family environment that did not exercise repression or coercion as a way of treatment but tended to respect personal choices and convictions of each individual member. To this healthy environment, I can arguably attribute the blossoming of my capabilities and the development of my independence and free thinking. All these characteristics enabled me to succeed and excel in later stages of my life.

Some of my friends often attribute my shift to vegetarianism at this early age to being overly pampered. Personally, I am not sure about this, but maybe, at the beginning, it was a result of being pampered. With my mother's keenness to please me, it turned into a permanent habit, maybe. It may also had something to do with the death of a young child in front of me, at that early stage of my life, after he was hit by a car.

With H.H. Sheikh Mohamed bin Zayed Al Nahyan, Crown Prince of Abu Dhabi and Deputy Supreme Commander of the UAE Armed Forces (may God protect him) on the occasion of my honoring with the French Medal of Merit First Rank, December 17, 2002

I remember many embarrassing situations that I faced because of my dietary choice, as many people could not understand my choice of being a vegetarian. Such situations are bound to happen, in a society that expresses its generosity and respect toward guests by slaughtering a number of animals and that considers not eating from them a wrong behavior that sometimes borders on shame or humiliation. You may find someone who would solemnly swear that you must eat, and another one who would insist on you to taste a piece of this meat, which was especially prepared on their private farm. If you refuse, you would definitely hear the unpleasant comment: "it seems that you do not like our food."

Dr. Abdulla Al-Niyadi, chairman of the Al-Tawasol International Tent, one of the entities that honored me, told me a funny story relating to this diet issue. He coincidentally met me more than once at the dining table of His Highness Sheikh Mohamed bin Zayed Al Nahyan (may God protect him); Dr. Al-Niyadi noted that His Highness smilingly asked me "Is the kit available?" Dr. Al-Niyadi felt curious about the 'kit.' When he asked about this mysterious code word, some of the attendants explained to him that the 'kit' was special vegetarian dishes for me, which His Highness Sheikh Mohamed bin Zayed Al Nahyan (may God protect him) knew was the only food I would eat. Dr. Al-Niyadi remarked jokingly "In fact, I feel jealous (of Dr. Jamal), every time, His Highness Sheikh Mohamed bin Zayed Al Nahyan wants to make sure about your food himself. These are the morals of our sheikhs and leaders, and also an indication of the nature and strength of the relationship that connects both of you. These are the unforgettable memories and meanings in our life."

In addition to my grandmother and my mother, there was another female character, my sister Aisha, whom I consider the closest to my soul. She has always been my closest friend and my role model. My mother and my sister Aisha had the biggest influence on my personality in my formative years. People close to me know that when I say "my sister" without specifying a name, I mean Aisha. However, when I talk about any one of my other sisters, I always mention their respective names.

Aisha, who is 12 years older than I am, was a second mother to me in almost every sense of the word. She has taken special care of me since my first days. She was my first true mentor. Before I enrolled in school, she allocated time to teach me the alphabet, numbers and basic principles of arithmetic. This perhaps enabled me to outperform my peers, or at least eased the burden of my first school days and helped me sail through them. When I talk with my children about memories of my early years, I usually tell them that I may not recall everything about my childhood, but my sister does. She is the only one who has the most important information about my childhood. My sister Aisha was not only a second mother to me, a first teacher, a compassionate sister, a guide and supervisor who closely followed up on my educational progress, as would be shown later, or a loyal friend; she has also become a repository of memories. Memories are certainly the most private thing to a human being. When a person considers another person as their repository of memories, it reflects the highest level of psychological and spiritual closeness. A bond that could never be broken.

The name 'Jamal' was jointly chosen by my father and my maternal uncle. It is understandable to find a child born in the late 1950s carrying the name Jamal. Like millions of Arabs, my father and my maternal uncle, who were close in age, admired the late

With my late father (may God rest his soul in peace) in 1963

Egyptian President Jamal Abdel Nasser as a person and politician. They appreciated his call for unity of the Arabs and consolidation of their positions. They admired his fervent enthusiasm and devotion to pan-Arabism.

Pan-Arabism, or Arab nationalism, had a strong presence and influence among people. I remember when we were young, people did not use to say this person was Syrian, Lebanese, Iraqi or Egyptian, but would instead use 'our Arab brother.' It was an emphasis on the comprehensive meaning of brotherliness between the people of the Emirates and every person from any other Arab country, and that the umbrella of Pan-Arabism would accommodate everyone, even if one knew the country to which the person he was addressing belonged.

My father and my maternal uncle, along with my older brother who was 15 years older than me, would take me to the mosque to instill in me religious values and to learn how to perform prayers since my early years. At the mosque, my first lesson was of engaging in a society intent on preserving its customs and values and teaching of manners of talking and behavior. Accompanying my father, uncle and older brother allowed each one of them to provide me with guidance. My curious eyes would watch and my mind would record and gain lessons from meetings of the adults and their conversations. The daily trips to the mosque were among the methods of educating individuals and preparing them to engage in their larger environment, particularly in a society that used to live as a harmonious, integral whole and its members were connected together with the closest bonds.

In that period, the family, mosque and society, and then school, were educational institutions that played a major role in instilling values, customs and traditions. Mosques at that time were a place where the soul would find serenity and comfort. Back then, the idea of religiosity was associated with tolerance, virtuousness and moral sublimity. The mosques' Imams were good-hearted people and loved by everybody. The society was religious in general and religion played a major, fundamental role in the lives of its members. However, religiosity at that time was associated with good moral behavior, decency, honesty, truthfulness, asceticism, respect for everyone and an array of virtues and values. There were no manifestations of superficial religiosity as we see today such as shortening of clothes or lengthening of beards. If a person began to depart from the familiar and well-known path of moderate religiosity and to overdo its superficial formalities, he would be viewed as insane. If you told someone that there were people who called themselves "Muslim Brotherhood," he would immediately ask you: if these are the Muslims, then who are we? Were we disbelievers, for example? In our hearts, certainly every one of us deeply believed that it was impossible for a Muslim to blow up a mosque or murder worshipers, no matter how ruthless a criminal he was.

In our childhood, we did not see the horrifying sectarian intolerance that is engulfing our life today. I very well remember that in our early life we used to join our Shiite brothers in their religious events and celebration We used to go to their *Hussainiyat* to drink 'Vimto.' None of our fathers mothers or siblings prevented us from that, nor did we see anyone offending our Shiite brothers who shared life with us for hundreds of years. There were no such fearful fatwas, which instill in children's hearts and minds the seeds of hatred, animosity, self-isolation and defamation of others.

Like Abu Dhabi, Sharjah and all the Trucial States at that time, Dubai was a destination for people from different cultures, religions and races. We grew up in an environment that understood this diversity and considered it God's Way with His creation. I think, at that time when a country like the United States of America was plagued by racism, and black people, for example, were looked down on, we viewed all people in our cities as equal human beings with the same rights and duties. Even women were viewed with respect and reverence, and their role in our life was not less than that of men. Perhaps, closeness to innate human nature, with its pristine purity and moderate understanding of life, was the reason for that.

The sea, the Arabian Gulf, was a central part to our life. In fact, we were preoccupied with it. It was the pivot around which the lives of adults and children mostly revolved. Those who were not working in public services, such as education, hospitals and municipalities, were working in the sea and looking to earn a living from it. The Arabian Gulf waters were deep, but I was able to swim skillfully before entering school. As my father and my uncle taught me how to pray, they also taught me how to swim when I was 3 to 4 years old, as if they were building my physique and spirituality in a balanced way that sometimes makes me wonder how our fathers were able to achieve it with such amazing easiness. They were keen on establishing an intimate relationship between me and the sea – which was the most prominent feature of natural environment around me and had the greatest effect on the people of our city and other coastal cities – in a response to ligious calls and societal traditions aimed to instill courage and skill in one's soul. The sea was a convenient place to develop physical abilities and train a child to confront adversities and overcome fear and hesitancy.

At that particular time, an unforgettable accident occurred. Near the place where we used to swim, there was a dry dock and it seemed that some workers placed their tools carelessly or they did not expect children to reach their dangerous working area. When one of our companions was swimming in that area, he received a deadly injury from an iron rod. Blood began to gush out profusely from his wound and changed the color of water around him. That gushing blood was very likely to attract the sharks that infested the Arabian Gulf waters. Although professional divers quickly arrived at the scene and took the child to hospital, they could not save his life because the injury was severe and hospitals were not properly equipped to provide the required life-saving services.

An accident like that could have filled me with fear and scared me away from the sea, but I felt no fear at all. Strangely enough, I went back, after a few days, to the same place where the accident occurred, driven by curiosity and eagerness to explore. But I swam with extreme caution and I focused all my senses to spot any danger before I could get hurt. I think that our upbringing, when we were young, removed fear from our hearts, made us tough and prepared us to confront hardships and difficulties. Life was not easy at that time, and courage and audacity were among its fundamentals.

There was another accident that has stuck in my memory since early childhood. By mere coincidence, when I was about 4 years old, I witnessed a speeding car running over a little child of my neighbors and killing him. The death was quick and happened in front of my eyes. The scene of that accident settled deep into my psyche and showed me another aspect of life that we should comprehend and live with. That accident might well be behind my dislike to eating meat, chicken and fish and my early shift to vegetarianism.

In addition to bloody incidents I witnessed and early encounters with death, what also remained vivid in my memory was the 'circumcision' that I underwent when I was about 5 years old. Male circumcision was not an ordinary event at that time but an important social occasion to which relatives, neighbors and all people of the neighborhood would be invited. Feasts and celebrations would be organized where gifts would be given to the child and his family.

Circumcision was not performed in a hospital, as the case is today. It was customarily performed in the family home at that time. Usually, in line with the prevailing norms, preparations for circumcision process began the day before the surgery where I spent my night in an atmosphere that made me feel that something unusual was about to happen. Among these measures was my sleeping without clothes, and when I woke up in the morning, I found the house crowded with people, cooking tools and animals to be sacrificed. All sides of the house were decorated with festive colorful lights, infusing joy and happiness into the hearts of the crowd. Everybody was engaged in food preparation because the occasion equally belonged to them as it belonged to me and my parents. I had a feeling that I was somehow the focus of everyone's attention and the center around which the events evolved. In addition, the mixed feelings of joy associated with this important ritual among family members and neighbors, and pity for me and fear that some inadvertent surgical error might occur; all increased my feeling that today was not like the rest of the days.

Memories of circumcision bring to mind some characteristics of society at that time in general. I particularly recall the "connectedness" as a noble societal value for which I feel nostalgic. Everyone at that time knew all their neighbors, while some today do not even know their next-door neighbors.

Family ties were closest and strongest, as well as the ties between residents of the neighborhood. When your neighbor or anybody got sick, news would spread very quickly and you had to visit them once or perhaps several times. The presence of general social values was stronger in our life and any contravention of them

The first from right, with some friends in 1965

would be met with harsh social punishment. The simplest form of punishment could be social isolation.

This harmony was a product of public values, culture and traditions, which derived their roots from the genuine Arab heritage and from the necessities of life that required unity and solidarity for their association with generosity, altruism and help for everyone. The society highly promoted these values. With great admiration, successive generations passed on to the next the narratives of people who surpassed others in these virtues in order to embrace them as models. People memorized these virtues and recorded them in their folk poems as a source of wisdom, experience, sentiments and history. They recorded their views on various life issues and conditions of human psyche in fascinating aesthetic forms reflecting the richness of spoken language.

People would gather in mosques and public squares in all events to share happiness and sorrow with each other as well as easy days and difficult days. Everyone would think about their public environment not just their private, narrow ones as we see today. TV was not yet commonplace. Sitting around the radio to hear the news or other programs was an opportunity for discussion, conversation and exchange of ideas; like a school in which young people engaged and learned the community culture and values. Such gatherings were schools of manliness, forums for exchange of life experiences and learning lessons from those who were toughened and matured by such experiences over the years.

In our childhood, it was normal to go to any neighbor's house because they had a telephone and use it as if it were your own. It was normal for people of the neighborhood to gather at the house of anyone who possessed a TV to watch a certain program or a movie without them feeling that you violated their privacy because you had something to offer to them. Houses were open as well as hearts. It was shameful to say you lent money to someone from your neighborhood, as lending was a usual practice, almost one of their rights. Borrowing money from anyone in the neighborhood was not a stigma or disgrace to the borrower. That was an unwritten contract between residents of each neighborhood, and parents were keen to pass it to their children in order to gain respect in a society that attached great weight to moral values. Any violation or disregard of these values would cost the violating person their status and respectability, no matter how wealthy and powerful they were. Disregarding such values was akin to moral suicide. Hence, moral values were the most important source of respect and status in our community.

The community gave individuals their legitimacy and status. Arguably, the quarter or neighborhood was the identity to which we belonged. The loss of this belonging by committing a moral vice would entail a punishment equivalent today to the withdrawal of citizenship. As a result, belonging to the culture, values and traditions of local community was an existential necessity. At that early age, we never knew the concept of the State, as the United Arab Emirates was formed almost a decade later, and the establishment of its identity in the hearts of its citizens took time. Therefore, whoever would dare to diverge from this collective community spirit would be rejected and become an outcast.

There were large numbers of Indians, Iranians and other nationalities living with the people of the Emirates and interacting with them in intertwined relations. In my view, I can say that there was no racism of any form in the community in which I lived at the time. There was no discrimination between local and non-local citizens, between Shiite and Sunni or between Muslim and Christian. It was shameful for any person to commit such a mistake. At that time, when you met a person, the last thing you would ask them about was their religion or nationality. You would greet and chat with them without knowing whether they were Shiites or Sunnis, rich merchants or poor workers. Nobody would ask anybody about such things. There were no social classes and no difference between those who would sleep at night with an empty stomach and those with a full stomach. They both enjoyed the same respect and appreciation as long as they adhered to the established value system. This is the sense of connectedness, the sense of collectiveness, and the sense of community.

Traveling was difficult; a kind of luxury practiced only by well-to-do people. In air travel, there were no direct flights so you had to travel from one country to another to reach your final destination. The destination that nowadays takes only a one-hour flight to reach used to take a whole day. If your destination was a European country, you would need many days to get there. Travel between one city and another within the United Arab Emirates was even more exhausting. It would take hours to travel from Dubai to Ajman. The usual means of transport at that time were beasts of burden or small boats (jalboots) in case of traveling by sea. A person would travel to another emirate only once a year. All this has changed now.

Those who were in our age group in the neighborhood were usually within our circle of friends. Our relations were more dependent on sporting activities, especially swimming and football, which was our most important entertainment. We would play football in public squares. There were no formal clubs or playgrounds. Football matches were social events where a large number of Omanis, with whom we had fraternal ties, shared such events with us. Sometimes, at that young age, we would gather and sit around a black-and-white TV to watch mostly repeated cartoon series. I still remember the episodes of the cartoon 'Popeye the Sailor Man.' To us, and our parents, black-and-white TV and the telephone held fascination and wonder, and they were viewed as marvels in the first half of 1960s.

Circumstances were not free of hardships and difficulties, but they strengthened our character and hardened our physique. I think the strong will and endurance of our generation were, and still are, among its distinctive characteristics. I do believe that difficult circumstances induce creativity and stimulate individuals to find solutions to their problems and sharpen their mental abilities and faculties. I do not mean that our life was all hardships. Eventually, some facilities began to emerge in our life, but we had more endurance and patience to live a life devoid of the luxury and extravagance that the current generation enjoys and takes for granted. I remember a funny incident relating to that period. In one of the Eids – I am not sure whether it was Eid Al-Fitr or Al-Adha – my family had allocated AED100 to celebrate the occasion. Unfortunately, strong winds blew away the money and we could not celebrate it that year. That incident always comes to my mind when I see today some families whose children spend thousands of dirhams just to celebrate Eid.

I think our world at that time was expansive, although if you went just a few kilometers out of your environment you would consider yourself "on a journey." When we went two kilometers out of our neighborhood, we would consider ourselves on a trip. The world's expansiveness, which I mean, was conceptual, as we, the children, did not lack places to play and practice sports. The sea was enough to accommodate our tender energies and open our eyes to contemplate its depths and discover its endless mysteries and hidden creatures; fish, oysters, pearls and other marine creatures that we feared despite our desire to watch them. We enjoyed the sight of the water with its changing colors and the richness of shadows and lights; the environment with its sweltering heat and scorching sun, with its trees and wonderful winter. We merrily watched the uninterrupted inflow of boats and ships carrying goods and people from remote parts of the world. The world was a wider place for knowledge and experience although some people might think it was limited and narrow, with few opportunities for fun, entertainment playing and knowledge at the same time.

Primary School

I enrolled in primary school in 1965 at the age of six. At that period in particular, the Emirates were moving ahead from one stage to another with steady steps – albeit rudimentary – toward what would become lat-

The first from right, 1965, as we used to play football with friends after returning from school

er an experience of development that would make it the focus of the world's attention and a model of success in economic and social management and development. It might be noticeable that the year in which I enrolled in school was the same year in which the Dubai Chamber of Commerce and Industry was founded, as it was opened on July 1, 1965. A British report showed many indicators of thriving trade in 1964; this included 116 ships dealing in gold trade, which made huge returns that year reaching £25 million, leading to a large inflow of Indian merchants to Dubai for business. In 1965, when I started school, the number of male and female students in Dubai schools was 3,572. That figure might seem small, but it was a significant achievement then.

My mother played the biggest role in preparing me for school, and for moving from family care to school care. Educators nowadays set the ideas and theories that facilitate a smooth transition of the child from a family's warm embrace to a new world with different rules; orientation lectures are held and advice is provided to parents about procedures to be taken into account. It seems that my mother, with sound instinct and marvelous awareness, realized the nature of this transition and the conscious, thoughtful way needed to handle it.

In 1965, school was not as it is now. It was very strict and frightening. Corporal and moral punishments were common in all grades. Homework and assignments were burdens straining the students and

With two friends, 1967. The photo shows some features of our simple life in late 1960s

tiring them out. Fortunately, my mother prepared me psychologically and my sister helped her by teaching me the basics of how to write and read. In her conversations with me before I joined school, my mother focused on the importance of learning, religiously and socially, the status of educated people, and the bright future of those who would take their education seriously enough. She was always careful to implant reassurance in my consciousness, encourage me, and praise my abilities. She knew that my mind and heart always needed her words and advice. She would look for all bright sides of the school and focus on them and downplay much of the fears of what we would hear about the harshness of teachers or the restrictions imposed by our commitment to school attendance and our forced deprivation from playing and having fun. I think that without this clever preparation, I would have faced countless difficulties during my primary education. My mother continued to play the role of a mentor, guide and shock absorber until I was able to cope with my new world.

The round-trip journey to school was a daily hardship I had to endure. The distance between home and school was more than eight kilometers and I had to walk it carrying a bag full of books on my back. We had to carry all those books to school, and if anyone forgot to bring any of them, he would be severely punished. On some days in September and October when the school year started, or in May and June when it ended, tem-

The first from left, with my cousin Tariq, in 1969

peratures would exceed 45° Celsius, and we had no choice but to walk. When a student one day found a car to take him the whole way or part of it, they would consider that their luckiest day.

Sometimes, such hardship forced some students to quit school and suffice themselves with the 'Katateeb' (religious schools), which were more prevalent then. It is worth mentioning that education at the time, for some of our society members, was not as important as it is viewed today. Perhaps, the daily round-trip journey to school was the first challenge to which I refused to surrender, and the earliest confrontation I had with difficulties. At the moments of extreme physical fatigue, I would tell myself that retreat was a defeat and it would not befit me to be defeated. I would evoke in my heart all the essential traits of true manliness – patience, fortitude and endurance of hardships – which my parents taught me. I never gave in.

Another burden relating to the daily long-distance walk was that each student had to be neat and presentable, no matter how hot the temperature was. We had to come to school in clean and neat clothing. There was no unified school uniform. Inspection of tidiness and personal hygiene was a constant daily routine in morning line-ups. Daily inspection included nails,

The second from left, standing, at grade three of primary school in 1967/1968

hair and shoes, and other things such as making sure that the children had washed their faces well.

The school's care for its students extended to their homes as well as values and traditions practiced in them, as child nutrition was among the issues of concern to teachers. The school provided its students with wholesome free meals containing all the nutrients a child's body needed to grow. The school's mission at that time included the nourishment of both mind and body of the student. Among the important things in this regard was the significant attention paid to physical education, which was counted like any other school subject. There were three weekly school classes allocated for physical education in which we would practice various exercises and workouts. Every student had to pass the exam of physical education. I think that was one of the best things at school.

Music was also among the subjects we had to study—two classes a week. Teaching music was taken very seriously. All students were required to memorize musical scales and understand musical rules regardless of whether they had the talent or not. Also, art education was given the same level of attention where students were trained to paint and taught other forms of artistic expression. I think some of the students who had physical, artistic or musical talent discovered it during this period because of the school's attention to it. It is strange that the attention to these subjects – which I consider fundamental – declined over time and they no longer enjoy the status they had then. These subjects were part of the refining process of the soul and spirit, and the building of character in an integrated manner. School is not only a place

On the way back from school, in 1967

where a child crams his head with information. It should also be a place to nurture and develop the talents and skills that may remain hidden or wither away and disappear completely if educators do not nurture and enhance them.

During that period, I had an inclination toward, and interest in music, as well as acting. However, this interest did not continue, perhaps because of the changes a person would undergo at that stage. I am not exactly sure why these two skills declined and my interest in them faded away in terms of practice, although I still appreciate and enjoy good music and drama performances. Music and acting, whether in cinema, theater or TV, are still among my interests, and I see them as a way to discover beauty and expand one's knowledge horizons at the same time.

The school had a canteen that provided nutritious food to students. Fast food had not yet found its way to us. Classrooms were well-constructed and equipped with fans that helped mitigate the scorching indoor temperatures that sometimes reached 50° Celsius. Of course, there were no air-conditioning devices. In fact, we did not even know such devices existed in the first place. The school day started at 7:30 am or 8:00 am and ended at 2:00 pm or 2:30 pm. Our daily round-trip journey to school and back home was eventful and full of experiences. Sometimes we would stop by grocery stores to buy

The first from right, standing, at grade 3 of primary school, 1967/1968

some small items. I think the school environment provided an opportunity for both education and physical health.

When I think back about that period, I become more certain that the choice of the name 'upbringing and education' adopted by the Ministry of Education was perfectly fitting. It indeed embodies what was practiced in schools. Back then, the school was equivalent to the family in importance and the comprehensive care it provided to students—mentally, psychologically and physically. The formation and refinement of personal character were among the schools' objectives, and the various educational curricula were designed to achieve that objective. There was keenness on directly instilling values and morals and emphasizing them. In addition, moral values were indirectly included in the various school subjects. In the subject of Arabic language, for example, the moral dimension was included in every lesson and every selected text. In the subject of history, moral contents were drawn from every incident, event and life story of a great personality. In the Islamic education subject, the moral dimension was the most manifest, as a matter of course. Even in neutral subjects like mathematics, the teachers would find a way to transmit some moral values to their students.

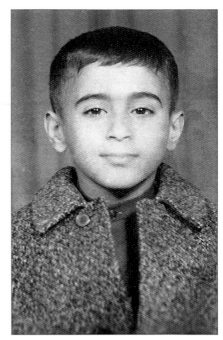

Discipline was a fundamental value emphasized in schools. A teacher would not consider his mission limited to teaching students some school subject so that they could pass a test; rather, their objective was to build a balanced character that would appreciate moral values and adhere to them. Nowadays, I

At the age of 10, in 1969

feel sorry because many of today's schools no longer care about the moral aspects in performing their mission. Their utmost aspiration today is to have teachers who explain lessons to students and then go home. I think that those who joined schools in the mid 1960s – now nearing the age of 60 – represent a distinct generation that learned discipline and civility during their study. Moral adherence, on which they grew up, was one of the foundations on which the federation of the United Arab Emirates was built. I can even go further to say that this generation was influential in all Arab countries due to the moral education received in those years.

Our school was for boys only. Co-education was not socially acceptable at that time and female education was still nascent. The issue of school attendance and absence received great attention from the school administration. In the case of absence, punishment was severe, despite the difficulties of getting to school. Teaching in primary school and beyond was in Arabic. English-language lessons were taught in elementary school, while French was taught in secondary school as a third language. Based on my experience, I do not think there was any benefit from studying French for two or three years. This is because after that the little vocabulary and grammar one thoroughly learned, at the hands of teachers who might not have possessed the sufficient technique of teaching French, would quickly evaporate due to lack of use. This would eventually render all the effort exerted in learning it futile and a waste of time.

At the age of 11, in 1970

In primary school, the teaching staff was composed of Emiratis and teachers from other countries, such as Egypt, Jordan, Syria and Palestine. However, the percentage of Emirati teachers was larger than today, and most of them had studied abroad. About 95 percent of the school students were Emiratis, and the rest were mostly from the Sultanate of Oman, in addition to some other Arab students. The standard of teachers was very good but their most distinguishing characteristic was that they felt they were carrying out a mission, not just doing a job for a living. They felt that they were shouldering a heavy responsibility for our upbringing and character development. The teacher's mission was not limited to teaching at school but extended to the street when he met his students – which often happened – where the provision of guidance and advice would continue as well as the role of overseeing and counseling. A student might be punished for a mistake he committed outside school if the teacher saw him or was told about him.

The nature of that period necessitated the study of some subjects in a certain way. The subject of history, for example, dealt with the history of the world and the region because the United Arab Emirates, as a country, had not yet come into existence. There was nothing related to our national identity because it was not yet established. Curricula were not standardized and unified across schools. Students studying in the same stage in Sharjah or Ajman, or even in some schools in Dubai, studied a curriculum different from ours because there was no

Playing football with friends, in 1970

Ministry of Education at that time and the institutions responsible for supervising education were in their developing stage. Curricula in the various schools, which were built by self-help and donations from merchants and philanthropists, were still subject sometimes to individual discretion and personal views of teachers and principals that reflected their interests and orientations.

There were many positive aspects to the education we received. Nonetheless, there were also negative aspects, which I think had their impact, notably the absence of critical thinking. Students had no chance to express themselves or put forth their own opinions. They were required to be receivers only and remain listeners who would not dare to discuss or differ with their teachers. Who were you to have your own opinion? Who were you to differ or argue? The relationship between students and their teachers was akin to that of soldiers and their commander in a military unit. There was one side who issued orders and the other side had only to listen and execute them without any objection or discussion.

Any student who put forth a different opinion was seen as odd and out of the norm. Even if the teacher gave an erroneous piece of information, the student had no right to comment or correct it because that was considered unacceptable and a violation of the rules of respect and the required obedience to teachers and the school. The teacher was a supra-authority who imposed discipline but also exercised repression, and sheltered itself with the

At the age of 10, in 1969

prestige, status, rules and societal norms. It was difficult to talk to your teacher fearlessly without feeling worried. Contrary to that, today – which I also see as a negative development – there is a decline in the status and image of teachers and a diminishment of their prestige, in the positive sense of the word. I think the ideal situation lies midway between these two extremes. Teachers should have prestige but without turning it into a tool for suppressing independent thinking or abolition of students' personality. The world at that time relied on the large numbers of disciplined workers who were trained in a conventional way, whereas development today relies on creative, innovative energies that create wealth out of knowledge and invest in the human mind's capabilities to develop the society.

The other negative aspect during my primary education – also related to the idea of authority – was corporal punishment. Flogging of students by their teachers was common and acceptable. It was often harsh and painful. Teachers used canes, which some of them would always carry to classrooms to flog students on their palms and sometimes on the back of their hands, causing enormous pain. In some cases, flogging was done on the soles of the feet, which was a much harsher punishment. It was also common for teachers to slap students on their faces, causing both physical and moral harm. This treatment was practiced on children as young as 6 or 7 years old. Fear would settle deep down into the souls of some of these children and negatively affect their psyches. School classes would last about 45 minutes. Children at this age would sometimes need to go to the restroom during the class. Some of them would not ask for permission to go to the restroom for fear of the teacher. As a result, children in some cases would urinate in their clothes. Such incidents would leave a feeling of embarrassment and stigma because it happened before their peers. That was a harsh experience. I think the banning of corporal punishment in schools was a very important step, and should have happened much earlier.

I did not have any special interest in politics at that time. I was too young, and sources of knowledge and information were not easy to find. However, I remember the impact of the 1967 defeat in the Arab-Israel war on people around me. The defeat occurred after a sad personal incident, which was the death of my maternal uncle (may God rest his soul in peace) as I mentioned before. The two incidents became connected in my memory because the time gap between them was significantly small. I remember the gloom that struck the people and the signs of sorrow and hopelessness, the details of which I could not understand back then, but I felt the impact of the incident on them. The explanation given to us as children, and even to some adults, of what had happened was that 'the infidels defeated the Muslims.' The whole issue was explained to us in such a brief description. At that time, Arabs and Muslims were commonly considered identical. However, I reiterate here that this characterization did not involve any kind of hatred or degradation of others within our societies. In the society around me, I never sensed any hatred toward Westerners or Christians who lived among us or who came to our country because of who they were. The anger caused by the 1967 defeat was related to seized Arab rights and occupied Arab land, but not because it was the Jews who did that.

Another thing relating to political events during my primary education was the flood of emotions that poured around me on September 28, 1970. On that day, I saw many people in the neighborhood – men and women, the young and the elderly – literally crying. An overwhelming sense of grief engulfed our house and the houses surrounding us. The grief was so intense that I thought someone from our family or from the families close to us had died. When I asked, I was told that the one who died was Jamal Abdel Nasser. I was 11 years old and I remember the deep grief on that day and the atmosphere of mourning and sorrow. I have never seen such lamentation for anyone, until November 2, 2004 when the late Sheikh Zayed bin Sultan Al Nahyan (may God rest his soul in peace) passed away. Regardless of Jamal Abdel Nasser's politics, and all the criticism that could be leveled against him, he made the Arabs unify their way of thinking and he established a unique emotional relationship with citizens of all Arab countries. Everyone felt they were weeping for one of their own. Most of those weeping for him had never visited Egypt. He died while suffering a crushing defeat, but they did not say it was Egypt's defeat. They considered it a defeat for all Arabs.

The voice of Ahmad Saeed, the broadcaster on the 'Voice of the Arabs' radio, was thundering from Cairo and we were thrilled by it even when we were children. Although I am now certain that what he was doing was just shouting propaganda, his discourse at that time reinforced Arab identity and gave us a great positive feeling. I think the most important achievement of Jamal Abdel Nasser was that he made all the Arabs, from Morocco to Oman, feel as one family. At that time, just turning on the 'Voice of the Arabs' radio from Cairo had many meanings. When I started writing a series of articles in early 2015 about a number of personalities who left their mark on the history of the region and the world at large – which have been compiled into a book titled *Eternal Imprints: Figures that Made History and Others that Changed the Future of their Countries* – Jamal Abdel Nasser was one of those I wrote about. I emphasized his leadership, charisma, belief in Arab unity and his early warning about the dangers of religious extremism and the dangers of the 'Muslim Brotherhood.'

I think the importance of primary school memories is not only about events. When I contemplate these memories in light of experience gained over the years, I particularly contemplate the ideas and ideals that have influenced my mind and personality, or resonated with values already existing in me. What a person's memory stores from early age is not random. The mind would perform a process of selection, retention, removal and arrangement of past events according to the nature and psychological make-up of the person in question. Discipline is one of these values that I regard as an important basis for success of any work, and it contributes to self-development of the person himself. In addition, when people treat their assigned tasks as a mission, not just as an assignment, it raises their value in my eyes, even if their performance is marred with some imperfections. While I was retrieving these events and their protagonists, I discovered the deep respect and reverence I have always had for my teachers. Their positive traits remain more lively and present, despite my rejection of corporal punishment and suppression of different opinions practiced against the students.

By the same token, freedom of opportunities, management of difference and understanding of its reasons, building of an independent and balanced character capable of comparing, assessing and judging things and exploring new areas intellectually and mentally – which are among the characteristics of 'critical thinking' – are goals that should be achieved in education and life in general. In addition, corporal punishment and moral abuse that affect the individual's self-esteem and confidence are unacceptable, especially at the stage of character formation and building.

The sense of *Halal* (lawful) and *Haram* (unlawful), as well as social and moral right and wrong is instilled in the child at this stage. For instance, the child could be convinced that drinking alcohol is a permissible behavior or a forbidden disgraceful behavior, and this will settle in their minds for a long time and affect their entire lives. The evidence is that alcohol is available nearly everywhere, but we do not drink nor even come close to it. I think the value and moral system, which we were taught at the period, was strong and solid. It was a combination of firmly-rooted religious and societal values dictated by the nature of social environment, its intellectual heritage and social norm. In fact, there is no contradiction or difference between these two sources of values. They have become harmoniously compatible centuries ago, intertwined and blended in many aspects. They concurred on the appreciation of sublime human virtues such as honesty, altruism, courage, generosity and goodness and righteousness in their general sense. Despite the development of institutions and the availability of facilities at present, I have a feeling that the future generations of the Arabian Gulf and Arab countries may lack these kinds of values or public morals, which were among the preoccupations of the society and the various educational institutions in the past.

It is the family that teaches you the basic principles, if you could understand and absorb them. My family, particularly my mother, bore the responsibility of my upbringing at this stage. With remarkable educational awareness, my mother attentively and patiently taught me what is *Halal* and what is *Haram*, what is right and what is wrong. She exercised discipline and guidance kindly and without compulsion, engulfing all that with tenderness, making it easy for me to understand and accept what she taught me. The school played a significant role, as I mentioned before, despite its restrictive and authoritarian system. These two institutions – family and school – are the most important in character building. I do not think the role of friends would be significant at this early stage of life. Maybe there is some exaggeration in what people say about the role of friends. If it is possible to express it numerically, I do not think their role exceeds 20 percent at best. Friends' role may be greater during the stage of adolescence.

Elementary School

I finished primary school in 1970 and joined elementary school. I stayed in the same building because the school comprised both primary and elementary stages. This meant the eight or nine kilometers journey continued for the next three years, but the hardship was not as exhausting as it used to be before. During those three years, positive changes gradually lessened the harsh conditions. Economic transformations taking place in the United Arab Emirates allowed us to enjoy some new conveniences. Although development signs and manifestations were still few and modest, it made a big difference for those who lived the difficulties of past days. The number of cars increased. Transportation became easier and convenient. Roads became less rugged than when we started our primary education. The change was slow and in its beginnings, but we felt it.

One of the incidents I still remember was that my family decided that I could use a bicycle in my daily round-trip journey to school instead of walking. They wanted to make the trip easier for me. One day I had an accident while I was driving my bicycle, and I abruptly fell off. There were no cars on the road and nothing visible obstructed my way, but the fall was severe. I sustained two cuts because of this fall and because the bicycle's mirror was shattered into scattered, minute fragments. The cuts were then stitched at a nearby clinic. Using the same bicycle, I participated in a race organized during that period, in which hundreds of contestants participated, but I achieved a low ranking – near the 100th or a bit below – because the bicycle was a normal one, not designed for racing.

Throughout the three years of elementary school, I was responsible for the school radio. I think I trained myself in many skills during that period, which might have benefited me later. At that time, morning line-ups were highly disciplined and organized. They were considered an integral part of the educational process. In addition to sporting exercises, strict inspection of personal cleanliness and clothes (which varied between shirts and trousers, and national dress), the school radio received great attention. At that time, the school radio was indeed a means of education and learning because students might not find the chance to hear any news, for instance, or to know what was going on in the world except through it.

The fixed broadcast schedule of the school radio contained recitation of some verses of the Holy Quran in addition to some songs, which my colleagues, who worked

During the ECSSR's 2nd Annual Conference: "Gulf Security in the 21st Century," January 6, 1996

with me at the school radio, and I would select and arrange their broadcast under the supervision of a teacher in charge. The radio played the role of an in-house media tool where we continuously broadcast advertisements about all events or festivals at the school and instructions issued by the school administration. We also conducted interviews with the school students and teachers in which we would discuss many topics, as one of our tasks was to bridge the distance between the students on the one hand, and their teachers on the other. Many funny and amusing incidents happened during these interviews, which helped establish relationships and created a subject for discussion that was somewhat free from the strictness of the school.

At the school radio, I acquired the basic skills of preparing a broadcasting program and organizing its parts, and the ability to use correct enunciation and classical Arabic. I also gained the ability to attract the audience by choosing items that would gain their interest and conducting discussions, and by selecting sayings, maxims or news to broadcast. The training in all these skills was important and beneficial to me in later stages of my life. Perhaps, facing large audiences at that early age helped me later to become a good lecturer. Of course, facing the audience in itself is a useful skill that some academics and public figures lack, although they are highly educated and have a lot that they could say. So, I owed a lot to the school radio.

Our school contained a library, which I started to use at elementary level, primarily for purposes related to school syllabus. Teachers would choose texts related to school courses and ask us to go to the library to read them, which was a good way to connect us with this fundamental educational facility. Libraries at that time were the major and most important source of knowledge, culture and information. We would be asked to summarize some novels and read certain sections of history, religion or general culture books as part of the school courses in Arabic language, history and Islamic education. We would also borrow books outside the curriculum to which we were attracted by their titles or topics, and the school administration sought to encourage us to do that. Although many of the books I borrowed and read in the library were mainly related to the school syllabus, and the number of books outside the curriculum was not large, a special relationship grew between me and the library and later expanded during my university study and beyond. The library was at the top of my priorities when I took part in establishing the Emirates Center for Strategic Studies and Research (ECSSR) where "The UAE Federation Library" was the main section to which I devoted great effort.

At elementary school, the curricula became somewhat difficult, particularly with the subjects of history, geography, English language, chemistry and physics. We were required to make greater effort in studying, homework and assignments. Nonetheless, the subjects were ultimately not too difficult to understand or absorb.

My school performance was generally good at this stage. I do not deny that I had a desire to excel. However, excellence and distinction required some factors that perhaps were not adequately available to me. My father was busy with earning a livelihood, and my mother's family responsibilities did not allow detailed follow-up of all my affairs, although her care and attention for me remained the same. Excellence also requires teachers who are academically and morally competent in dealing with the subjects they teach and with students. I excelled in the classes that had this kind of good teacher, who explained them in a simple, understandable way. However, when the teachers explained the subjects in a difficult way, I found them unappealing. At that time, I did not have the ability to compensate for the weakness of teachers' capabilities or the difficulty of their explanation by studying on my own, as my age did not allow that. I gained this ability later on.

At this stage, I began to realize my inclination toward studying literary subjects rather than scientific ones. I took an interest in history, geography and the Arabic language, and later in logic, philosophy and psychology, which I chose later as a minor specialization in my university study. I did not feel much inclination toward subjects such as chemistry, physics and mathematics. This was an early sign that I would specialize in one of the theoretical sciences, although I did not envisage at that time which sub-discipline I wanted to study. At elementary school, I was preoccupied with attaining good results and finishing my studies and never thought about what was next. Like many of my fellow students, I was thinking about the present moment only and nothing beyond that.

Elementary school days saw my first attempts at writing. Like many at my age, my writing was overly imaginary. I started to record the daily events I saw – something like a diary – and write down thoughts and sentiments inspired by my daily experiences or the ideas triggered by my readings in the library. Sports activity also continued to attract me and my peers, and football remained the center of our interest. We also played traditional games, one of which was similar to small wars in which we would fight. Friendships were easy to establish, but many of them did not continue because long summer vacations would cut off our contact. In addition, the remoteness of the school and students being from areas other than our neighborhood hindered the continuation of these friendships.

Teachers maintained their imposing position and we were afraid of them because some were harsh on us. In fact, we hoped classes would finish so that we could leave the school quickly. We did not like to meet the teachers outside the school. The teacher was an authority figure while we began our first steps to break free

The historical photo of the foundation of the UAE, on December 2, 1971. The late Sheikh Zayed bin Sultan Al Nahyan (may God rest his soul in peace) appears while he was raising the flag of the Federation for the first time at Qasr al-Diyafah in Jumeirah, Dubai. On that day the real launch of our country started toward progress, prosperity and the future

from authority and control. We were at the threshold of adolescence and our sense of self was growing. I think some teachers were not trained enough to understand and study the psyche of students at this stage and were not enlightened about the serious consequences of corporal punishment.

During elementary school days, we used to make some kind of colorful simple ice cream in the form of cubes and sell it in the neighborhood. Like my peers, I used to feel happy with the small amount of money we earned from sale. It was not a job; it was not driven by a family responsibility or a need

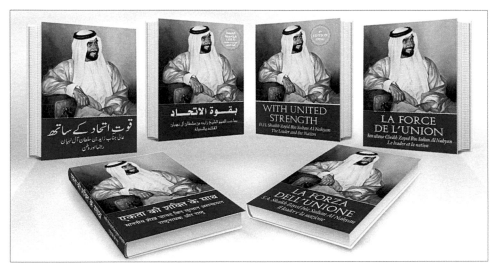

The book *With United Strength: Shaikh Zayed Bin Sultan Al Nahyan: The Leader and the Nation*, published in Arabic, English and other languages, is a scientific study issued by the ECSSR in 2004. It is unique in its kind; documenting the life and achievements of the late Sheikh Zayed bin Sultan Al Nahyan (may God rest his soul in peace). A fifth edition of it including new chapters was issued in 2013

to gain money, and I did not do it regularly, but I felt happy when I did it. I think it was some kind of expression of self-assertion and proof of ability to do something and make money like adults. Maybe it was a manifestation of my entering adolescence and of the feelings of independence and self-pride.

Around the middle of the elementary stage, like all the people of the Trucial States, I witnessed the momentous event that radically changed our life and miraculously took us from one situation to another—the establishment of the United Arab Emirates on December 2, 1971. It was a massive development. We celebrated at our school and felt the sense of joy and pride that overwhelmed everyone around us. For the first time, we began to look at ourselves through a different lens and to understand the meaning of belonging to a big country with a single identity, and that any student who was studying in Abu Dhabi or Fujairah was our brother who shared with us the sense of belonging to one's country.

Nevertheless, I think our level of understanding was not up to the event and could not grasp its enormous, far-reaching dimensions and significance. We knew that a major change had occurred, but we did not predict the effect it would have on our life and the unimaginable results that such a great step would bring about. I think we, the students, were not alone in that state of incomprehension; our teachers were no different from us in this matter. Later on, we began to strongly feel the qualitative developments the 'Union' brought into our life, and to understand the meaning of the travel document 'or the unified passport' through which we first came to know the 'Union,' unified curricula and unified thoughts. We began to reap benefits we never expected and enjoy the services, which were increasing in quality and quantity and changing our lives for the better.

We never knew that the late Sheikh Zayed bin Sultan Al Nahyan (may God rest his soul in peace) would uplift the UAE to an unimaginable level within just a few years and place it at the top of the world's countries in terms of development, prosperity, security, stability and happiness. The unique political insight of the late founding father and his brothers, the founders and rulers of the emirates, enabled them to achieve the great aspirations he had for his people and country. Through his political wisdom; high sense of humanitarianism; in-depth understanding of the geopolitical map of the region and the world; ability to foresee, promptly respond and choose the right alternatives in a fast-changing world, the late great leader managed to achieve a development miracle by all standards, in a very short period of time that was full of serious challenges. His accomplishments deservedly placed him among the great leaders who established strong successful countries and provided the world with lessons in nation building, creating accord and harmony, unifying and harnessing effort toward advancement and progress.

By the end of elementary school, the October 1973 war erupted between Egypt and Syria on the one hand – with huge support from Arab countries – and Israel on the other. People gathered around radio sets, which were the most common media outlets at that time, to follow eagerly the war news.

I was one of those who gathered around the radio to follow the war news and I shared my country people their happiness with its results. As all Arabs do with all pride, I still remember the everlasting saying by the late Sheikh Zayed bin Sultan Al Nahyan (may God rest his soul in peace), "Arab oil is not dearer than Arab blood."

At the age of 15, in 1974

Secondary School

Secondary school was the period in which my thinking matured and the road to the future started to become clear to me. In the middle of secondary school years, I decided on the specialization I would study at the university. I did not need much time to decide that the literary stream was my choice, after my areas of interest and the fields that stirred my curiosity and desire for knowledge became clear.

In one of the early months of the second grade of secondary school my achievement in mathematics was not good and my grades in the monthly mathematics tests were very low. That incident could have gone unnoticed and my performance could have continued to decline further had it not been for my sister's intervention to reverse that possible trend, in her own way. She immediately brought me a private tutor for this subject. She chose the same schoolteacher who taught me mathematics at school to ensure that the tutor was more familiar with me, unlike a new tutor who would have to start with me from scratch. That tutor was excellent indeed. In the following month, my grades in mathematics test increased considerably. I am not sure whether he was just being charitable to me or not, but I kept scoring good results in mathematics until the end of the year. After that, I chose the literary stream and no longer had to study mathematics in a deep way. In the literary stream we studied simple, uncomplicated mathematics.

I remember that I understood the tutor's explanation of the subject at home very well and I did not need him for long. I do not know whether his explanation in the classroom was complicated while simple at home or whether I was too busy to focus in his class and ended up scoring poor grades in mathematics. However, that incident has convinced me beyond any doubt that no school subject is difficult to understand, and if the teacher simplifies and explains it to his students in a proper approach, they would most likely understand and love it.

That incident reflected my sister Aisha's quick action and habit of not leaving issues to worsen, out of an understanding that nipping problems in the bud would end them. I think my sister Aisha was teaching me one of the practical lessons that I comprehended fully during my professional life and helped me to succeed; that is detecting the problems and addressing them quickly. In addition, my sister's wisdom was manifested in choosing the right tutor and making me see my negligence as nothing more than a temporary matter that was not difficult to overcome and restore the right track. I thank God that my sister was there to save me at the right moment.

The relations with teachers improved significantly in secondary school, as we were relatively older. Our sense of becoming older made us want to behave ourselves so as not to harm our self-esteem. Corporal punishment became much less frequent and violent or odd behaviors declined, both on the part of students and teachers. The hardship of the eight- to nine-kilometer round-trip journey to school and back home was over because secondary school was closer to home, cars became more available and life was easier in general. At that time, we developed a strong sense of belonging to the United Arab Emirates, and we saw its positive effects in many ways. However, the big boom had not yet started during the period 1974–1977 in which I finished my secondary school. That boom came later by the late 1970s and early 1980s.

Cheating on exams was an enormous vice that would damage the reputation and honor of the cheater among his colleagues and the entire society. The problem did not only lie in the formal punishment of the cheater despite its severity, but in people's view toward him and the fact that cheating was considered a despicable crime that could not be condoned or tolerated. This was part of the moral framework governing our life. People established their status through unblemished moral commitment. I think this is one of the differences between the society then and what we are today because people today judge each other without giving much weight to moral principles, which were then highly observed and maintained.

During secondary school days, our imaginations were developing, as well as our experiences. During that period, I remember that I came to know a man called Muhammad Khamees, who was working as a chauffeur for a family in the neighborhood. Neither his old age nor the different nature of his life and work inhibited me from becoming friends with him. I used to accompany him on trips to the desert and visit people who were different from those I knew in my life. I was excited to discover the tent life in the desert, which was unknown to me, and seeing a new world that embodied the entire image of the past. In the beautiful evenings we spent sitting around the fire among scattered tents, I enjoyed the same life that our people have lived for hundreds of years and preserved much of its features without any change. It was a fascinating meeting with the past with its customs, traditions, language, proverbs and songs where I discovered the diversity of our life in the United Arab Emirates and its human and social richness. I think that our rich folk heritage needs great effort to document, publicize and study it as part of building and enhancing national identity.

At the beginning of secondary school or maybe a little earlier, I started to smoke. Maybe I started when I was 14 years old. I continued to smoke for nearly 40 years. Many people may be surprised when they know that smoking at that time was not a shameful act at all. On the contrary, smoking was a kind of prestige and a declaration of attaining fully-fledged manhood. We used to say that "a boy becomes a man when he smokes." My father used to smoke, as well as my brother and everyone around me. I used to smoke three packs of cigarettes a day. In 1997, I shifted to cigars, of which I smoked a lot too. At the same time, I used to smoke *shisha* (waterpipe) throughout that period. Even during my cancer treatment, I smoked. When I was in hospital for cancer treatment, my body was covered with various medical devices and syringes. Despite that, I would go out of the room to smoke in the designated smoking area in very chilly weather. Many people believed that I contracted cancer because of my heavy smoking. However, I think my disease was partly due to a genetic predisposition, as my late father (may God rest his soul in peace) died of stomach cancer in 1996. Fate also had something to do with it.

One of the most important days of my life was when I stopped smoking on November 15, 2011. I consider that a life changing event. I thought of taking that step many times before, but I always asked myself: I recovered from cancer while I was still a heavy smoker, why should I stop it now? This was a natural question for anyone like me. Its predefined answer would motivate me to continue enjoying the habit, which I had been practicing for nearly 40 years. Experiences of friends and colleagues were not encouraging because examples of quitting and relapsing were common among them. The sarcastic American writer Mark Twain expressed this when he said: "Giving up smoking is the easiest thing in the world. I have done it thousands of times." I do not want to be one of those who take a decision and then quickly retreat from it because this would be inconsistent with my personality.

Smoking is a real addiction. Scientific studies carried out by prestigious universities and research centers have proved that nicotine is as addictive as heroin and cocaine. It affects receptors of pleasure in the brain and releases dopamine, which evokes temporary feelings of enjoyment and comfort that the smoker would want to sustain. This way, the cycle of needing a nicotine supply from a cigarette or water pipe begins and continues endlessly. Given the continuous and stressful work that had become an inherent characteristic of my life, smoking was an outlet to relieve some of the stress.

Psychologically, there is the power of habit that controls the smoker. In addition, smoking gives smokers a feeling of privilege and superiority over non-smokers. They feel they have much more pleasure than those who are outside the "smoking kingdom" and who never have tasted the thrill of fulfilling the need for a cigarette, sometimes tens of times a day. A friend of mine described the feeling of superiority and privilege derived from smoking in a sarcastically exaggerated way. He said: "The only difference between a human being and an animal is that a human being smokes while an animal does not."

Quitting smoking means relinquishing part of myself that I have known for 40 years. It is a voluntary self-deprivation from stolen moments of happiness and satisfaction, and readiness to resist my body and senses. The fingers that have long been used to the touch of a cigarette; the lips that have been waiting to grab the filter; the calculated ritual of lighting cigarettes using matchsticks or lighters—another subject of fondness; the movement of the respiratory system sucking the smoke of the lit cigarette; the feeling of the smoke seeping through the lungs, influencing the brain, soothing the tension and causing a pleasurable numbness; the distinct smell of each type of cigarette or water pipe you have smoked; even the formations of smoke that would look like abstract paintings rising up toward the sky or the ceiling of the room. That experience in which all senses (touch, sight, hearing, taste, smell) are involved becomes your foe and your senses urge you to commit to the contractual relationship you have willingly established with smoking for a period of 40 years—in my case.

The power and influence of smoking are clearly seen among smokers who know they are exposing their health and possibly their life to an imminent danger. They are clear among those who belittle the medical warnings, awareness campaigns that warn of the disastrous consequences of smoking, and even jeer at horrifying images depicted on cigarette packs showing the effects of smoking. I admit that I was one of those people. So, the decision to quit smoking was one of the decisions that overstrained me before I made it. I postponed it many times until the right moment for confrontation came. I gathered my strength and took the decision to quit. I have to mention here that His Highness Sheikh Mohamed bin Zayed Al Nahyan (may God protect him) played a significant role in making me take that decision. His Highness implicitly drew my attention to the dangers of smoking after I recovered from cancer. I took his words as a timely directive.

So, November 15, 2011 was the day I quit smoking. It was an unforgettable day. I mobilized all my positive energy and strength in order to quit smoking once and for all. Quitting smoking was associated with quitting the sleeping pills that were part of cancer treatment. That was another challenge that added a lot of hardships and difficulties. The difficulty to quit sleeping pills made my need to smoke stronger and the battle more severe. If quitting sleeping pills was necessary due to their tangible side effects and their immediate harm to vital body functions, smoking was something different. This makes it understandable and logical to quit the pills, unlike cigarettes or water pipes, which I had been using most of my life.

I spent two months in the hospital, from November 15, 2011 to January 16, 2012, to rid myself of both sleeping pills and smoking. I experienced the worst moments in which I felt tremendous physical pain, my face became stiff as if it was temporarily paralyzed and I could not feel its muscles. Pain was not new to me. I went through indescribable horrors during cancer treatment and its complications. My insides literally burned when I underwent chemotherapy treatment. However, the difference in the case of chemotherapy was that I did not have any other choice but to endure it. Whereas for smoking, the pain could end simply by stretching my hand to the nearby cigarette pack, grabbing a cigarette and lighting it up. Sometimes I felt that what I was doing was nothing but a kind of self-torture. At times of severe pain and need for smoking with all its rituals, I asked myself: "Is it worth all of this?" Succumbing to the lure of smoking was apparently a comfortable option, but there was internal voice warning me: "Do not surrender."

There were times I felt that going out to the hospital garden and smoking a cigarette in a quiet corner surrounded by flowers and shadows with the autumn breeze of Abu Dhabi blowing gently was the ultimate dream I could think of. Nev-

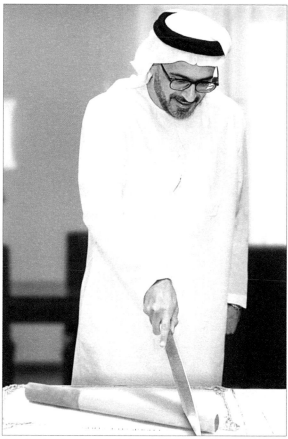

A cake in the form of cigarette brought by my family members on November 15, 2015 to celebrate the fourth anniversary of my quitting smoking

ertheless, I felt that retreating did not befit me and defeat was not a feeling I would like to try. The decision to quit smoking was a pledge I took and I was not the kind of person who would renege on his pledges.

One morning, I woke up to find my burning urge to smoke had simply vanished and I had overpowered it instead of being overpowered by it. I experienced a new joy no less than the joy of smoking. It was the joy of liberation and triumph over weakness. This is a reminder of the Arab proverb: "In the morning, night-walkers feel pride." That means when an individual finds that he has reached his goal in the morning, he feels pride and satisfaction because he has tolerated the hardships of nightly walking with all its fears, dangers, gloomy darkness and hungry beasts searching for preys. Similarly, when my morning has risen, I felt pride and satisfaction because my suffering during the strenuous two months of agony was worth it, my endurance ultimately bore fruit. In November 2015, I celebrated with my family my fourth anniversary of quitting smoking with a cake designed in the shape of a cigarette.

I relied on willpower and a firm decision not to give in to the lure of smoking. I never tried to quit smoking before despite the disease. However, when I decided to quit, I fought with the spirit of a warrior in a battle and I thank God for helping me triumph. Since I succeeded in quitting smoking, I believe anybody can do it—because my need for smoking was overwhelming, and being accustomed to it for decades made me at times think that my life could not function without it.

Once again, talking about secondary school, we studied French language for the first time. I remember that I, and all of the class students, relied solely and entirely on memorization in this subject. A constantly recurring question in the final examination was to summarize an already known story or topic. We would memorize the summary unthinkingly and write it down in the exam as we had memorized it. The teaching of French language was not teaching in a real sense of the term. My colleagues and I soon forgot all that we were taught. Teaching of the English language was not much better either, but studying it for six years made our knowledge of it better than that of French.

My decision to study political science dated back to the second year of my secondary school. I did not tell any of my friends about my decision, but I told my sister Aisha and discussed it with her. She liked the idea and encouraged me. In fact, I did not know the exact motivations behind this choice, as at that time we did not study subjects related to political science, such as economics or national education. In the literary stream, we studied Arabic, English, French, history, geography, philosophy and logic, which all appeared unrelated to political science. My choice of political science might have stemmed from the interest I saw from my father and maternal uncle in following political affairs, which was the reason for naming me Jamal, as I have previously mentioned. It may have stemmed from the changes we saw, which started to manifest themselves strongly in various aspects of our life as a result of the establishment of the UAE 'Union.' For example, at the school level, curricula and examinations became unified, the entity responsible for education became a federal ministry in charge of administering educational affairs in the whole country, and

A booklet issued by the UAE Ministry of Education. On its cover is an image of the cover of the book *With United Strength: Shaikh Zayed Bin Sultan Al Nahyan: The Leader and the Nation* published by the ECSSR. This book is part of the curriculum of Social and National Civic Education for Grade 12, in the academic year 2016/2017

what I studied became the same as what a student in Abu Dhabi and Ras Al Khaimah studied. Media became more influential and widespread after 1974, in which I enrolled in secondary school. Perhaps, I started to realize that all these changes in infrastructure, services and various aspects of life were a result of some political transformation. That might have motivated my decision to study political science.

There was a sense that a new identity started to develop. Speaking of national identity, I remember that I presented a proposal to the Ministry of Education in 1999/2000, at the request of His Highness Sheikh Mohamed bin Zayed Al Nahyan (may God protect him), to regard the founding father, the late Sheikh Zayed bin Sultan Al Nahyan (may God rest his soul in peace), as the symbol of the Emirati national identity. The founding father of the UAE was still alive at that time. Strangely, the ministry's officials then sent a message excluding the late Sheikh Zayed bin Sultan Al Nahyan (may God rest his soul in peace) from the symbols of national identity because symbols, as they thought, had to be deceased personalities. That attitude made me extremely angry because it showed an unawareness of the reality of the UAE history and ignorance about the fact that every country on Earth would look for a hero embodying its values and identity. Although, at that time, His Highness Sheikh Mohamed bin Zayed Al Nahyan (may God protect him) gave the ministry a grant of about AED2.5 million to formulate the syllabus of civics, the final produced syllabus was really poor. That shocked me personally because the produced syllabus reflected ignorance about UAE history and unawareness of the importance of building UAE national identity. The question that kept bugging me was: "If the Ministry of Education is not aware of the importance of national identity building, then who is? And if it really does not know the history of the United Arab Emirates, then who does?"

The Ministry of Education corrected the huge shortfall years ago as part of a comprehensive development plan. The UAE and some Arab countries started focusing on education as a means for transformation. A sincere effort was made, particularly during the last decade, and especially in the UAE, to include some educational subjects that would deepen the sense of identity and belonging among school students. I was honored that some of my studies and books were chosen as part of the curricula of social studies and national education for Grades 9 to 12. These books include *The Mirage* and *Eternal Imprints: Figures that Made History and Others that Changed the Future of Their Countries*, in addition to a number of ECSSR's publications such as *With United Strength* and *The Three Occupied UAE Islands: The Tunbs and Abu Musa*.

Friends in secondary school were more mature and appreciative of the value of friendship. I think that the influence of friends at this stage of schooling would become greater than at previous stages. Our characters already started to take shape. We would often go to each other's homes and spend a long time together, and go to coffee shops, which started to become more prevalent and popular. As friends, we shared the same hobby of playing football, which always ranked first among other hobbies. After school hours, we would gather in our neighborhood or go to other neighborhoods to engage in heated sport competitions. Card games were also among the means of entertainment that entered our life.

At that time, Video Home Systems (VHS) and Betamax appeared and became considerably widespread and popular, and their rental stores increased. During that period, we watched a large number of Arab and foreign movies, which opened a window to a new kind of knowledge in addition to entertainment. We would look eagerly for any new movie because we had already watched almost all the videos in the rental stores. Given our age, we were mainly interested in action movies. I remember that among my favorite Egyptian actors at that time were Mahmood Yaseen, Noor Al-Shareef, Najlaa Fat'hi and Nilly, who were among the big stars in the 1970s. Among the renowned Gulf actors, I liked Abdul Hussain Abdul Ridha, Saad Al-Faraj, Ghanim Al-Salih, Suad Al-Abdullah and Hayat Al-Fahd.

Extracurricular reading was not yet a priority in my list of hobbies and activities during secondary school. Due to our collective interest in sport and the time we spent in school, homework, assignments and friends' gatherings, as well as my rather significant preoccupation with studying, my reading activity was confined to the school syllabus. I continued to write fictional topics and note down my thoughts and sentiments, besides some daily events I witnessed, but I did not see my writing as deserving to be shown or presented to a wider audience. I also could not continue my school radio activity, which I passionately did during elementary school years, because the secondary school in which I enrolled completely disregarded music and radio activities, for reasons unknown to me.

I often used to study my lessons alone, as I did at the previous stages, and sometimes with friends. Some colleagues began to ask me for help in some subjects, which they believed I was good at compared to them. This allowed me to play the role of a teacher at an early stage of my life. I would try to simplify the topics and explain them as clearly and easily as possible, and this developed my teaching skills. Tutoring each other was common practice among students. Any student who had greater ability or talent in a specific subject would explain it to his classmates and friends. This practice was beneficial to both sides and served as a way to strengthen ties among students and deepen their friendships and foster the positive aspects of such friendships.

Secondary school, however, was not free from student violence. Some fights and scuffles would occasionally break out between students. The nature of relationships would force you to side with your classmates if the fight was between them and students from another class, and to fight alongside your schoolmates when the fight was with students from another school. There were "cliques" of sorts and differences or rivalries between them, which would cause problems that sometimes would develop into violent quarrels. At that time – and maybe until now – belonging to a clique or group would compel you to intervene. I think this phenomenon indicates that the need of human beings for group belonging is strong and inherent. This is one dimension of the idea of identity, regardless of how it is soundly used or badly abused by certain bodies.

I remember that one day after school hours were over, I found a classmate of mine engaging in a quarrel and surrounded by a large number of students from another class and they were prepared for that quarrel. They were more than 20 students, while my classmate had only one other classmate with him facing this large number of bullies. Without any hesitation, I joined the two classmates to defend them, and, of course, I got my share of beating from the bullies. I do not think I ever regretted my intervention, but I learned that 'multitude overpowers courage,' which is a good translation of the concept of strategic balance that later became the focus of my attention. Ignoring such a factor may not be harmful in case of a brawl between students, for example, but would prove catastrophic if a country does not take it into consideration when taking its important decisions. Anyway, the school administration recorded the occurrence of fights between students and identified the places and times in which they would usually occur. They would often occur at school bus parking lots after the end of school day at about 2:30 pm. The school administration assigned some teachers to monitor the school entrances and school bus stops. Their early interventions succeeded in reducing this phenomenon considerably.

The practice of private tutoring started to spread widely. It was a sign of the decline of the concept of education as a mission, but of course not the end of it altogether. This might be because education became a government affair, unlike in the 1950s and 1960s where education effort stemmed from social responsibility felt by individuals who took the initiative of establishing schools and donating money to them. When the government stepped in and assumed the responsibility, the idea of employment, rather than mission, became dominant and hence self-interest found a wider space to grow. Some teachers started to lessen the effort they made inside the classrooms in order to get more requests for private tutoring. With the improvement of economic conditions and the emerging importance of education, parents sought to hire private tutors in certain subjects for their children at home. I remember that the tutor who taught me private lessons in mathematics used to work from 3:00 pm until 11:00 pm. As far as I am concerned, I received private lessons only in mathematics for a short period, as I mentioned before.

Secondary school days were associated with the changes of adolescence and rebellion against family authority, and life questions about religion, faith and the meaning of life would begin to hover heavily in one's mind. Perhaps, I saw some colleagues who went through these experiences and were affected by them to various degrees. However, regarding many friends and myself, I think we passed this stage of life without rebellions and our religious and social constants and principles remained intact and unquestioned. This might be attributed to the deep-rooted concept of community, well-established collective values and strong relations between members of the community. As such, anyone who would exceed the proper bounds of the community – especially religious constants or traditions – would face social exclusion or even rejection. Personally, I did not suffer from harsh or tyrannical family authority throughout my upbringing, as my mother and my elder sister provided me with an atmosphere of affection, love, understanding and trust. My maternal uncle, who was involved in my upbringing, died in 1967. In addition, due to some circumstances that left an impact on the

My late brother Abdullah (may God rest his soul in peace) carried the burden of responsibility at an early age to look after us

shape of my life later on, paternal authority disappeared from my life when I was at the beginning of secondary school.

During that period, polygyny was common, which continued until recently. My maternal uncle got married twice. My father too got married again and had his own life, which kept him somewhat away from us but without formal separation. My late elder brother, Abdullah (may God rest his soul in peace) was then old enough to provide for the family and shoulder full responsibility for it financially, while my mother took the responsibility of upbringing, education, household chores and guiding us all. My late paternal aunt (may God rest her soul in peace) also played an unforgettable role in our upbringing during that period, along with my mother, sister and brother. Given the peaceful nature of my mother, I was not subjected to authoritative restrictions that would drive me to evade or rebel against them. The same thing applied to my elder brother who did not represent an authority or a constraint to me. The absence of my father put on me a moral responsibility that I should keep my family away from the consequences of any uncalculated behavior. If my brother bore the full financial responsibility, I should at least contribute by minimizing the moral burdens through commitment and careful thinking about any action before taking it.

Secondary school was the stage of maturity where my sense of responsibility and my desire for a better future increased. The third year of secondary school was an important bridge to that future. Scoring good grades would increase my study options and enable me to join the specialization I wanted. This drove me to intensify my studying effort, as the Ministry of Education's preparations for the unified third year secondary school examinations gave them more significance accompanied by procedures different from all previous school years. I scored a good grade that enabled me to join the specialization I wanted quite easily. In general, my school performance was steadily improving as I advanced in age, knowledge and experience because of my growing sense of responsibility. I was an average or above-average student in primary school; my performance became better in elementary school; and I achieved remarkable progress in secondary school. In undergraduate and postgraduate studies, I would not accept less than absolute distinction and the highest grades despite the difficulty of study and fierce competition.

When I decided to join the Political Science Department, I was in the second year of secondary school. It was my choice for two reasons: first, my sister got married in Kuwait at that time and my mother moved there to live with her; second, Kuwait University enjoyed good reputation and respect among the Arabian Gulf countries, with its excellent education standard, especially in its Political Science Department, which established for itself a prestigious position since its inception in 1970. In fact, the rich political atmosphere of Kuwait did not factor into my calculations at all, but I benefited from it later.

The moment I took the decision to study at Kuwait University, there were no problems to prevent that from happening. It was very common for the people of the UAE to go study at Kuwait University. However, the year 1976 saw an important national event, which was the opening of United Arab Emirates University in Al Ain as a step toward educational renaissance, which was the focus of the country's leadership. The College of Humanities and Social Sciences, which was one of the four colleges that the university started with, had a Political Science Department.

The building of United Arab Emirates University in Al-Ain, opened for the first time in 1977

Of course the nascent UAE University wanted to attract as many Emiratis from those who finished secondary school as it could to join it to continue their university studies. There was no reason for an Emirati student to go to another country, even if to a brotherly one, to study a specialization that was already available at the national university, which was seeking to establish its status and position. I sought to meet the Minister of Education (at that time), His Excellency the late Dr. Abdullah Imran Taryam (may God rest his soul in peace) and I explained to him my motives to attend Kuwait University. His open-mindedness and ability to understand my situation helped me convince him. Perhaps, his personality – known for genuine, deep and comprehensive knowledge – and his wide view of knowledge and education and his ability to go beyond the narrow confines of administrative directives and job restrictions were all behind his generous decision to allow me to study at Kuwait University on a scholarship from the UAE.

By God's grace, circumstances were taking me to where I wanted. As usual, my sister Aisha gave me a special present as a reward for my success—a tourist trip to Iran with all costs paid by her. Iran was a destination for many

During a tourist trip to Shiraz in Iran, 1977

people of the UAE and the Gulf in the 1970s, especially given its geographical proximity, great tourism resources, fascinating nature for most of the year and mild climate of many of its areas in summer compared to the climate of the Arabian Gulf countries, making it an ideal place for summer vacations. That was the first trip in my life outside of the UAE or Kuwait, to which I had traveled regularly. We visited Tehran and Shiraz in the company of some close friends. Iran was in a better situation before the Iranian Revolution of 1979. That trip was a beginning of innumerable trips in which I toured the world, east and west, for work, tourism or gaining more knowledge. Traveling has become an important part of my life and a source of memories and experiences, which will be further described in this autobiography.

Traveling to Kuwait was a major qualitative leap that strongly connected me with it academically and personally. In Kuwait, I set my feet on the road to success and began my first steps toward accomplishments of which I am proud, and which I will recount in the next chapters.

Chapter 2

The Path to the Future

Chapter 2

The Path to the Future

Studying political science was the major change that opened for me a wider path to the future. It showed my personal abilities and talents, and gave me the opportunity to play a leading scientific and national role through various posts and positions of responsibility in the United Arab Emirates (UAE). The university period, with all its richness and vibrancy, was the real beginning of my scientific and professional career that was not quite clear during secondary school.

The study of political science took a longer time than I had thought it would when I first decided to pursue it while I was in the second year of secondary school. It was not just about the four years required to get a bachelor's degree. During my undergraduate study, my aspiration to achieve higher academic degrees started to take shape. So the academic journey continued for 13 consecutive years, from 1977 to 1990, that culminated when I received my PhD. During that journey, I worked for a short period at the UAE Ministry of Foreign Affairs, between 1981 and 1982, which was not an actual discontinuation but a period of planning and preparation for post-graduate studies and a search for possible alternatives until I settled on a final destination.

Those Who Taught Me

Professor Sayid Noor was one of my teachers at Kuwait University, where he taught me Statistics. I believe he was the best in teaching this subject with a very simple way of explanation and robust content. He was a professor with high teaching and academic capabilities. I was delighted to have met him later on when I started teaching political science at United Arab Emirates University. He was then Vice Chancellor for Planning and the most influential personality in the University administration.

Among my unforgettable teachers was the late Professor Izz Al-Din Fouda (may God rest his soul in peace). He taught me the "Introduction to Political Science" course in my early days at the university; it was an entry course to the world of political science. I remember that the lecture theater where this course was taught was huge, but still got crowded with an attendance of nearly 200 students. I used to sit in the front row in order to focus on every word said. In addition to that course, Prof. Fouda taught me "Introduction to International Law" and "Diplomacy." In all these subjects, he was a high-caliber professor.

The late Prof. Fouda was strict and imposing. His authoritative nature might have appeared to some people as arrogance or a display of superiority, but I personally knew the true meaning behind it. I remember he gave a test to students in one of his lectures, and he graded the answers in the same lecture once a student finished the test. We noted that the process of grading the answer papers did not take the usual necessary time to read them. This way of grading the students' answer papers would call the process into question. In fact, some students did object to it. However, his long academic experience might be behind his fast evaluation of their answers, and also his knowledge of his students, their abilities and ways of expression might be a factor behind such quick evaluation of the answers. Even if there was a disagreement on the way he graded test papers or his dealing with his students, there was a consensus on his great scholarship abilities and scientific contribution.

Dr. Shamlan Yousef Al-Issa was one of my most influential teachers. I was not only influenced by his academic competence, but by his character and style of teaching. Our relations developed from that of a student with his teacher to a firm personal and family friendship that has become much stronger over the years. Our cooperation has continued to this day, and we have carried out many joint research projects. In 1991, we published a joint research paper titled "Attitudes of the Students of United Arab Emirates University on the Gulf Crisis" in Kuwait University's Journal of Social Sciences. Dr. Al-Issa also helped me prepare the initial proposal I presented to His Highness Sheikh Mohamed bin Zayed Al Nahyan (may God protect him) to establish the Emirates Center for Strategic Studies and Research (ECSSR).

With Dr. Shamlan Yousef Al-Issa, professor of political science at Kuwait University; and Mr. Nabeel Najm, from Abu Dhabi TV, then, during a visit to the ECSSR on September 24, 2000

The issue of *Journal of Social Sciences* which included a joint research authored by Dr. Shamlan Yousef Al-Issa and I, published by Kuwait University in 1991

Dr. Al-Issa joined the teaching staff of the Political Science Department in 1978 when I was in my second undergraduate year. He had just gained his PhD from the prestigious Fletcher School of Law and Diplomacy in Boston, USA. I learned a lot from him academically. I was also influenced by his modesty and closeness to students, his ability to attract them through his likable personality and graceful jokes and by presenting the most complicated concepts in a way that made them easy to understand and attractive to their minds.

With Dr. Faisal Al-Salim, former professor of political science at Kuwait University, during a visit to the ECSSR on February 3, 2015

The closest teacher to my heart and mind was Dr. Faisal Al-Salim, who had the greatest influence on my personality. There were many factors that made Dr. Al-Salim such a prominent figure to me, including his vital, original academic studies; his approach to the most serious issues in Kuwaiti society, as a vibrant Arab community full of a strong social and political mobility; his ability to understand the nature of political and social change and consciously observe its manifestations and laws; in addition to his remarkably modest personality, his closeness to students and his ability to inspire them.

Dr. Al-Salim was known for appreciating the high-achieving students and providing them with all forms of support. Thankfully, I was one of those high achievers. As a way of supporting me, I remember he made me teach some academic matters and explain them to my colleagues. That was an early preparation to me and at the same time reflected his confidence in my abilities; a confidence that I badly needed then. My friendship with Dr. Al-Salim has continued throughout the past years. I visited him many times in Paris, where he now lives, and I was overjoyed when he visited me with his wife and daughter at the ECSSR in February 2015.

Also among the distinguished teachers was the late Professor Nora Al-Falah (may God rest her soul in peace) who taught me Political Sociology. She was one of seven female students who were the first ever to travel outside their country, Kuwait, to study for a bachelor's degree in 1956, an act that required exceptional courage and resolve at that early time. She then chose to pursue higher education and get a PhD. After that, she returned to Kuwait to play a pioneering academic and social role in confronting militant and extremist movements until her death in 2008. She had her own distinct way of teaching, which makes me consider her among the most prominent of my teachers.

The late Professor Hashim Bahbahani (may God rest his soul in peace) was also one of my influential teachers. The way he treated us was similar to that of Dr. Faisal Al-Salim in his modesty and likable personality. Prof. Bahbahani was left-leaning and fluent in the Chinese language, in addition to English, French and Persian. He lived in China for some time and specialized in its foreign policy, and for that purpose he learned Chinese. His education journey from the United States of America, where he got his bachelor's degree, to Beijing University and Oxford and Cambridge Universities later on to get his PhD spoke of a person who believed in knowledge and who devoted his life to it.

After his return to Kuwait in 1979, Prof. Bahbahani taught us a course on China and Vietnam. He had a profound grasp of everything related to these two countries. Like Dr. Faisal Al-Salim, Prof. Bahbahani was fully aware that students were interested in their exam grades and that fact overshadowed the primary goal of education: gaining knowledge for the sake of it, developing mental capacities, and absorbing the thinking methods and using them in life. To change that mindset, they downplayed the importance of exam grades and attracted the students more to what they received in lectures and to methods of thinking and understanding they were being trained in. They trained their students to put themselves in place of the lecturer rather than in place of passive recipients. This way, the students would build their characters and develop the skills that would help them in their future careers and make them excel.

My wife and I visited Prof. Bahbahani in 2010, a year before his death. I felt painfully sad when I saw he had a serious health condition. In 1985, he suffered a disease that left him paralyzed from the waist down and even affected his ability to talk. With his strong will, determination and his life-loving spirit, he resisted the disease and continued to teach for years while using a wheelchair. He was able to smile and crack sarcastic jokes even in his worst moments of pain.

Professor Sulaiman Al-Shatti was one of those who also left their mark on my life. He taught me "Arabic Language course II." With his distinguished way of teaching it, I believe that it was he who made me love the Arabic language. The way Arabic language was taught was rigid, monotonous and devoid of liveliness. However, Prof. Al-Shatti managed to infuse life in it through his character, his extensive cultural knowledge and ability to surprise us with the lively, innovative subject he delivered. I think Prof. Al-Shatti succeeded in solving the intricate equation by freeing Arabic language from the shackles of the inert, traditional way of teaching, and bringing it to the boundless world of effective, creative and distinguished teaching thus making it attractive to the students.

There was an unforgettable incident related to Arabic Language curriculum during my university education. In my first year, I chose the course "Arabic Language I," which was an Arabic grammar course. I scored C+ in the exam, the lowest grade I ever got throughout my undergraduate and postgraduate studies, and it never happened again in any subject, particularly the specialization subjects in which I always scored either an A or A+. The reality of the matter was that a mistake in prioritization was behind that low score. If I had postponed that course to my second or third year, which was permissible, I could have received a better grade. That incident made me aware of how important it was to choose the suitable timing for any work in order to succeed. I developed a fear of Arabic language, almost distaste, as a result of that experience. Fortunately, Prof. Al Shatti brought my relationship with it back to a right track, and I scored a high grade in "Arabic Language course II" that was consistent with all of my grades at the university.

The list of teachers I revered included men and women. It included old teachers, such as Prof. Izz Al-Din Fouda who was over 60 years old at that time, and young ones in their thirties, such as Dr. Faisal Al-Salim. It also included teachers from various specializations, ranging from political science and sociology to psychology and Arabic language. In addition, it included teachers from different political movements, left and right; graduates from Arab and non-Arab universities; and even different religious sects and nationalities. I think I was able to embrace everyone as long as their contributions were distinguished and their academic and scientific abilities were outstanding. However, big mistakes would remove some teachers from their esteemed status. Among my teachers, there was a distinguished Arab academic, but his unacceptable stand after the invasion of Kuwait in 1990, and the unjustified insults he hurled at the Arab Gulf countries in which he lived and was welcomed to work at their universities, placed him far behind and demoted him to academic decline and eventual fading.

The Political Science Department at Kuwait University was part of the College of Commerce, Economics and Political Science and has now become part of the College of Social Sciences. Like other universities, the Kuwait University system required the students to choose a minor specialization in addition to the major, and I chose Psychology as a minor specialization. Psychology was taught in another college. One of the interesting things was that some Psychology courses were taught in Keefan campus, which was exclusively for female students. I had to get

With a number of Kuwait University professors during a reception organized by Dr. Abdul Ridha Aseeri, former Dean of Social Science College at Kuwait University to which he invited a number of friends and colleagues from university days, on the sidelines of the signing event of my book *Prospects for the American Age: Sovereignty and Influence in the New World Order*, at Kuwait University, March 16, 2014

the permission of the college dean in order to attend the lectures. In some courses, I was the only male among 40 female students. My exam grades were always high in Psychology courses. I was strongly interested in the subject and, fortunately, teachers of Psychology were of excellent personal and academic capabilities. I also scored high grades in the English language courses, which I attended at the College of Arts.

I think the study of Psychology and Sociology helped me a lot during my study at Kuwait University, and later in doing my master's and PhD in the United States of America. This is manifested in my master's and PhD theses, which included a social dimension in addition to the political one. The study of Psychology also helped me handle various life situations, whether during my time teaching at the university or during my directorship of the ECSSR and many research and academic projects. Certainly, the study of various branches of Humanities would deepen the researcher's understanding and vision about any issues they tackle, hence leading to better results. Although strict, narrow specialization is a feature of current academic life, any additional or supporting knowledge would mean more broadening of vision.

At the university, I became a distinguished student. I quickly gained a good reputation among my teachers and colleagues. In every course I took, I got excellent grades. My

With university classmate at the Political Science Department, Mr. Kamil Abdul Jaleel, General Manager of the National Library of Kuwait, on the sidelines of "Storm of Thought" symposium held at the ECSSR, September 1, 2015

performance in lecture theaters was outstanding, whether in discussions, academic assignments or other activities such as teaching some subjects and delivering lectures. My feeling of the status conferred to me by this distinction, in and outside the university, motivated me to exert more effort to retain it. Encouragement from my teachers and support from family and friends helped me to do that. It was clear that I was in the right place that suited my abilities, where every effort I made was out of true inner desire rather than forceful imposition. I loved what I studied and realized its importance. As a result, I managed to make a wide forward leap.

The UAE paid its students studying at Kuwait University on scholarship a monthly allowance of KWD136 (equivalent of AED1,600) and housing allowance. I did not need housing because I lived with my sister. Through its cultural attaché office, the UAE Embassy followed up on our affairs, but not that intensive, continuous academic follow-up which I instituted when I later established the Distinguished Student Scholarships of His Highness the President. It was in fact a light follow up of some 120 UAE students studying at Kuwait University. The cultural attaché office was very proud of the high achievers among the UAE students and I was thankfully one of them. The sense of pride shown by the cultural attaché office motivated me further to achieve more success.

New Interests... Fierce Battles

My personal interests changed during that period. My interest in sporting activities – which were central in my life, especially football – declined and gave way to cultural and intellectual activities. During the last two years of my university study, I frequented a venue called the Art Club, which attracted people with talent in art, music, and the academic

With my friend the late Abdullah bin Rashid Lootah, on a trip to Cairo, in the summer of 1978, I was then a student at the second year in the Political Science Dept. at Kuwait University

field. I actively contributed in the activities held at the club to the extent that the people in charge of it asked me to participate in its management. I accepted their request and benefited a lot from my experience in it, whether by gaining organizational and managerial skills or through deepening my cultural knowledge. During my university study, I attended many art and cultural events, of which the State of Kuwait was famously rich. Those activities further refined my character and added new dimensions to it.

Also, the Political Science Association, established by the students of political science, was an open forum for various activities in many of which I participated. I remember that the Association invited the British actress Vanessa Redgrave who, in 1977, produced and narrated a documentary film titled *The Palestinian* that supported the right of the Palestinians and showed the Israeli crimes against them. The actress faced a Zionist smear campaign harassing her in the USA and other countries. The campaign reached its peak at the Oscar Awards ceremony in 1978 when she received an Oscar for the Best Supporting Actress. We played the film, *The Palestinian*, at a big theater, for two weeks and invited a huge number of students to watch and discuss it in preparation for a symposium attended by Vanessa Redgrave, where she delivered a speech supportive of Palestinian rights.

In 1979, I also participated in a protest against the Egyptian-Israeli peace treaty. The protest included thousands of students who marched from the university to the Egyptian embassy and the riot police fired tear gas at us. The protest was organized by different student unions and associations, including the National Union of Kuwaiti Students. The Democratic Center List, which I will talk about later, played a significant role in it. The organizers of the protest were mostly nationalists and leftists. Religious voices were not that loud then. I do not think I quite understood the consequences and details of the peace process, but I was driven to participate by enthusiasm for collective opinion. Maybe the presence of a large number of Palestinian students in Kuwait played a role in this.

In 1980, the university organized a trip to Tunisia. It included a large number of male and female students. On our way to Tunisia, we stopped over in transit at Beirut International Airport. We could see heavy smoke billowing from the nearby mountaintops indicating ongoing battles between adversaries in the civil war.

Our trip to Tunisia was rich with experiences and important meetings. We met with Al-Shazali Al-Qulaibi, who was the Secretary-General of the Arab League (at that time) after its headquarters was moved from Egypt following the Camp David Treaty. We also met with Muhammad Mazali, then Prime Minister of Tunisia. Discussions during our meetings were strong and frank. The trip also included art shows, exhibitions and plays directed and performed by the students of Kuwait University, showing the diversity of intellectual and artistic movement at the university. We visited the city of Sousse too. I remember, among those who were with us in the trip was Dr. Siham Al-Qabandi, who is now a professor at the College of Social Sciences, Kuwait University; and Ms. Khalida Al-Ahmadi who currently lives in Jeddah, Kingdom of Saudi Arabia.

During a university trip to Tunisia, 1980, where we learned about Tunisian history and civilization

With the Tunisian Prime Minister Muhammad Mazali during a university trip to Tunisia, 1980

University trips enhance relations between professors and students. This photo shows a friendly gathering with professors and colleague students during our university trip to Tunisia, 1980

I joined the Political Science Association, which was widely influential at that time. I always frequented its headquarters and engaged in a lot of activities through it. I wrote a regular series of articles, titled "Memoirs of a Poor Man who Traveled to London" published in the *Free Forum* journal issued by the Association. That journal was popular with a readership base of more than 3,000 readers inside the university. I chose that title because I traveled to the United Kingdom for the first time in 1978, during my university study. I stayed in the Four Seasons hotel and visited many of the known landmarks in the country. The visit to the United Kingdom was personal, not an official

With a number of our respected professors and colleagues during the trip to Tunisia, organized by Kuwait University, 1980

university trip like the one we made to Tunisia. Those articles represented an important step forward in the development of my writing where I moved from fictional and emotional writing to a new style tackling political and social issues. That experience helped me develop and mature my writing skills.

During the university trip to Tunisia, 1980

The Beginning of the Battle

During my course of study at the university, I started to engage in a battle that has continued up to now, i.e. for nearly 40 years, when I decided to confront the ideas of extremist political religious groups. Some people may think that my book *The Mirage*, published in February 2015, was motivated by the rising concern about political religious groups today or a

My first trip to the United Kingdom, 1978

few years ago. In fact, my struggle with them is much older than that. I understood their dangers much earlier and knew their devious methods. I saw them infiltrating our communities under the guise of slogans with which they misled the public and through which they exploited the pure religious sentiments of simple people. The Political Science Association was an early confrontation front. When I first joined the university, I supported the Democratic Center List, which stood up for the coalition of political Islamic groups and movements, the Coalition List. Coincidentally, the Coalition List was formed in 1977, the year I joined Kuwait University. This enabled me to closely see their experience and understand what would be awaiting the Arab and Muslim worlds if political religious group managed to achieve their goal and seize power.

I discovered that violence is inherent in the thought structure of political religious groups and they do not hesitate to use it. This is what the Coalition List did in 1978 in the elections of the National Union of Kuwaiti Students and I saw it firsthand. Its member students attacked the vote counting-committees. They claimed there was voter fraud and propagated this false claim to cover up their violation of laws and their use of force. This behavior was consistent with their usual scheme of covering up their crimes by claiming to be "victimized." That attack caused organizational chaos and concern for the authorities. Such an environment was the fertile soil for opportunistic groups to grow and thrive. It enabled the Coalition List to win the Union's election in 1979 and control it afterward, propped up by active support from the Social Reform Society, the political arm of the Muslim Brotherhood in Kuwait. Unfortunately, they succeeded in controlling students' activities, and it was the Social Reform Society that managed the National Union of Kuwaiti Students. The infiltration expanded to include many trade unions. The same thing was happening in other Arab countries as well.

Political religious movements infiltrated the university starting from below, through students. None of the political science teachers supported or sympathized with those who sought to oppose the spread of knowledge. Those teachers belonged to a different generation with high national, Arab and humanitarian ambitions; a generation known for its conscious, unrestricted openness to the world and human thought. The regressive invasion could not deal with rational, knowledgeable people who would use reason and logic. Hence it started to infiltrate from below whereby it could control the minds of young students when they were still at secondary school or earlier than that, before they could reach mental maturity and gained the ability to compare and evaluate serious matters. So, the invasion concentrated on primary and elementary schools. It was a malicious scheme, as I later discovered after its bitter results started to show. This generation of students and the next one infiltrated the universities and the various institutions like an organized invasion, and drove the Arab societies into a deep, dark tunnel.

I was not allowed to participate in the activities of the National Union of Kuwaiti Students because it was only limited to Kuwaiti students. Nonetheless, membership of the Political Science Association was open to all. Despite the success of political religious movements in controlling the Union, the various Associations at the university remained out of their reach, especially the Political Science Association, and the Democratic Center List remained able to win its elections. Members of the Democratic Center List had very good relations with students from different political movements and affiliations. We were close to their minds and hearts. As a result, the Democratic Center List continued to succeed in elections of the Political Science Association while declining in most other areas. Even this comparative advantage did not last long in the face of the Coalition List. The Democratic Center List started to weaken and gradually lose its appeal among students and its good relationship with them. Its members secluded themselves in an ivory tower, further eroding their influence. This enabled the Coalition List – an affiliate of the Muslim Brotherhood – to gain new ground and to almost extend its claws to the Political Science Association as it did before in many entities that became under its control.

With Prof. Hassan Jawhar, Head of the Political Science Department at Kuwait University; Kuwaiti journalist and writer Dr. Ayid Al-Mannaa; Dr. Abdul Ridha Aseeri, former Dean of the College of Social Sciences at Kuwait University; the university colleague at Political Science Department, Mr. Kamil Abdul Jaleel, General Manager of the National Library of Kuwait; and Dr. Ibrahim Al-Hadban, professor of political science at Kuwait University – during the "Storm of Thought" symposium held at the ECSSR, September 1, 2015

Part of the problem rested in the lack of a strong, convincing leadership in the Democratic Center List, and the dominance of incompetent individuals who did not have the necessary abilities to confront a strong current that swept its rivals using an elusive religious and moral discourse. The problem was not so much about the strength of political religious groups as it was about the weakness of their rivals. I can undoubtedly say that the playing field was almost empty for these groups to dominate. I think this unfortunate situation was literally being replicated in the rest of the Arab countries. The nationalist and leftist movements of the mid–1970s were failing and withering away. They were retreating in the face of a well-planned and thought-out attack by the movements of political Islam. By the beginning of the 1980s, these movements had completely taken over Arab societies.

My awareness of this fact led me to cut my connection with the Democratic Center List, as nothing was worse than siding with a group that you knew had its misdeeds and saw with your own eyes its deviation from what was right. Courage entails maintaining ethical integrity, self-criticism

With Dr. Siham Al-Qabandi (second from right) who was one of those who joined me to confront the political religious movements during my study at Kuwait University, and Dr. Abdul Ridha Aseeri, former Dean of the College of Social Sciences at Kuwait University, and a number of participants in the ECSSR's 21st Annual Conference titled "Youth and Development," March 8, 2016

and honesty with oneself, not obstinacy and denial. In my final year of university study, I, with a like-minded group of students, formed a new list, which I named the New Center List, in order to run for elections against both the Coalition List and the Democratic Center List.

We rejected many leftist ideas that would diverge from reality and distance us from our electoral support base. That meant I was fighting a battle against almost everyone, relying on a small number of students who became certain that they could no longer continue to support a failing list led by incapable persons. The struggle now was not with the regressive groups alone, but also with previous colleagues who went to the extreme in their hostility and did whatever they could to exact vengeance upon us and punish us for our independent opinion and free thinking.

One of the questions we asked ourselves was: would the New Center List not divide the votes of students who refused the dominance of political Islam and thus serve the interest of the Coalition List? This was a reasonable question, but we agreed that the Democratic Center List was no longer fit for representing the more illuminated and receptive students who needed someone who could establish for them an entity capable of competition and presenting an alternative. It was important to reject the student leaders who were not up to the challenge and were not aware of its seriousness. We sounded an alarm that there was a rift in the illumination movement and it had to be fixed with the utmost courage and ability for self-accountability and admission of failure.

The New Center List included a number of female and male colleagues. The behavior of the Democratic Center List leaders toward us proved the reality of our moral and political assessment of them. They resorted to violence, and some members of the Democratic Center List damaged some of our female colleagues' cars in what looked like a warning to us. They went so far as to even fabricate accusations against me and report them to the police. I was summoned by the police for investigation. In the end, I was not found guilty of any of the accusations laid against me. It was obvious that mysterious assaults targeted only the members of the New Center List, especially those who had been members of the Democratic Center List. We very well knew the people who were behind those acts. Despite the explicit and implicit threats we received throughout this period, we never gave in, we never surrendered.

Continuous challenges during my university years were a test of my ability to refuse to surrender to pressure. Standing up to a religious movement – which was getting stronger and throwing accusations of *Kufr* (disbelief in God) and blasphemy in the face of its opponents – in a way that endangered myself, was not an easy task, nor was my entering into hostility with the Democratic Center List and leading a movement against it. However, I pursued what I deemed right and was ready to face any consequences. My final year at the university saw the peak of confrontations. Different forms of animosity emerged and I dealt with each one according to its circumstances and nature. Despite the brotherly feelings I sensed throughout my stay in Kuwait, some people were not happy to see an Emirati student excel in his study, become one of the most distinguished students in his batch, enjoy friendship and care from

Kuwaiti and other professors because of his excellence, engage in political rivalries with no fear, write and publish, and participate in various activities and events. One of the available options was to seclude myself and focus only on my study, satisfied with good grades in the exams. However, my sense of duty would not allow me to embrace appeasing positions or weakness when confrontation was necessary.

Abundant Years

The period in which I was at the university, 1977–1981, was full of momentous events, from the visit of the former Egyptian President Muhammad Anwar Al-Sadat to Jerusalem, to the Camp David Treaty, the Iranian Revolution, the Iraq-Iran War, the seizure of the Grand Mosque of Mecca (Al-Masjid Al-Haram) by Juhaiman Al-Utaibi and his group, and the assassination of President Anwar Al-Sadat. All those events interacted with what I was studying at the Political Science Department. As a result, my awareness gradually became mature and I began to see regional and global events with the new perspective of a reader who thoroughly examined their backgrounds, details and repercussions. The scope of my vision was widening as a result of my studies, experiences and intellectual and political confrontation that I found myself in the middle of all this increased my ability to understand, analyze, and evaluate what was happening around me.

In late 1978, the Iranian Revolution erupted and overthrew the Shah in early 1979. I was at the beginning of my political science studies at that time. Like many others, I viewed that event through a romantic prism, as public sentiments were supportive of the revolution in which many saw a beginning of change. Sectarian tension was not existent as it is today, and Kuwait in particular reflected the true peaceful coexistence of Sunni and Shiite citizens without any doctrinal prejudices. The arrival of Ayatollah Khomeini from Paris was an event that attracted our attention and sympathy. Unfortunately, the Iranian Revolution took different turns toward sectarian and ethnic intolerance, the dimensions of which I could not understand at that time.

However, in September 1981, I was able to use the analytical tools in which I was trained, and now I was no longer that student who blindly followed collective sentiments as happened in the 1979 protests. In September 1981, two months after receiving my bachelor's degree in political science, I was with some colleagues and I read the news that the Egyptian President Muhammad Anwar Al-Sadat arrested more than 1,500 persons from all political parties—right, left and center. I said to my colleagues that the President would not complete one more month in power. On October 6 of that year, President Al-Sadat was assassinated by militant religious groups.

I think the difference between my view about the Iranian Revolution when it took place and my view on the 1981 arrests, and what they would cause in Egypt, embodied the distance I traveled from a beginner student to a graduate with a good qualification in political science that enabled me to foresee the future based on careful reading of the reality on the ground. This is the credit I owe Kuwait University and its professors, and the political atmosphere in which I experienced and engaged in during the years of my university education.

Compared to the UAE, which was always characterized by quietness and controlled political discussion, Kuwait was witnessing a remarkable political richness, political movements, associations and blocs engaging in endless confrontations and battles among themselves, an active student and workers movement as well as media activity led by a large number of newspapers, magazines and academic periodicals. The same could be said about musical and theatrical activity – in terms of composing, acting and directing – TV activity, symposiums, lectures and meetings occupying the halls and gathering venues in the vibrant country. Kuwait was like a huge freedom forum from which I learned a lot about every aspect of life and it motivated me to continue my pursuit of knowledge.

I think that the distinguished group of professors who taught me at Kuwait University had the most influence on my decision to pursue my

With Dr. Shamlan Yousef Al-Issa, professor of political science at Kuwait University, and Prof. Augustus Richard Norton, professor of international relations and anthropology at Boston University, during a conference titled "The Challenges of Nation-Building in Arab Countries that have Recently Witnessed Change," held at the ECSSR, October 6, 2015

postgraduate study and receive a master's degree and PhD. Some of these professors passed away and some are still alive. Dr. Faisal Al-Salim, Dr. Shamlan Yousef Al-Issa, Professor Hashim Bahbahani and others were role models whom I looked up to. I wanted to follow their footsteps and pursue the same path they had pursued before me.

This brilliant constellation of professors was behind my academic excellence. I always scored the highest grades, despite my engagement in political, social and art activities. I ranked first among political science graduates in 1981. I still keep a commemorative book titled "Graduates Book," issued by the Alumni Association office at Kuwait University, with my picture and name at the top of graduates in that year. The university administration honored me along with colleagues who achieved the top ranks. That honoring was a source of pride for me.

Dr. Abdul Ridha Aseeri brought us back to the unforgettable university days when he organized a gracious reception in 2014 on the sidelines of an academic visit I made to Kuwait. Dr. Abdul Ridha Aseeri invited many ex-colleagues with whom I studied at the university. We recalled our memories, which remained unchanged by the passage of days and years. We exchanged reassuring news about those who were absent from the reception and prayed for those who passed away and asked God to bestow His mercy upon them. I still have some lasting friendships from the university days, despite geographical distance and pressure of responsibilities, which many of us have been carrying.

Along with my continuous progress in scientific and academic aspects during that period, my artistic and musical taste formed and remained unchanged until now. Um Kulthoom, Muhammad Abdu, Abdul Kareem Abdul Qadir, Abdul Haleem Hafiz, Warda Al-Jazairiya and Fairooz have been my most favorite singers and I still listen to them whenever I seek comfort and some relaxation after long working

Receiving from Dr. Abdul Ridha Aseeri, former Dean of the College of Social Sciences at Kuwait University, a commemorative autographed board bearing the signatures of colleagues and friends and their words, on the sidelines of the signing event of my book *Prospects for the American Age: Sovereignty and Influence in the New World Order*, at Kuwait university, March 16, 2014

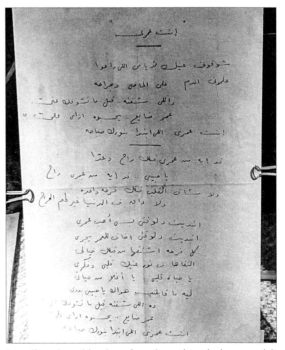

I meditated on this piece for a long time during my visit to Um Kulthoom Museum in Cairo on June 13, 2014. It is the lyrics of the song "Inta Umri" in the handwriting of its composer the poet Ahmad Shafeeq Kamil. Um Kulthoom first sang it in 1964

hours. At that time, I tried to listen to Western classical music and I kept a number of records from its great composers, but it did not touch my inner chords. I liked the genius and excellence it exuded, but I did not feel it belonged to me or I belonged to it, nor did it speak to my soul as Arab music does.

"The Secret Cell" and Editor-in-Chief Position

After graduation, I returned to my country full of ambition and hope. Like any distinguished student, my first dream was to

An autographed photograph from the famous Kuwaiti singer Abdul Kareem Abdul Qadir, July 9, 2015

be appointed at UAE University, especially given my strong admiration for my teachers at Kuwait University and my wish to be like them; a teacher who would lead his students to advanced knowledge and make science and its methodologies close to their hearts. I also wanted to serve my country with the education I received and I believed that having achieved the highest grades in the Political Science Department at Kuwait University, and the honor and attention I received, would open wider doors for me to achieve my dream in my home country. However, that turned out to be difficult in reality, and the appointment of lecturers was governed by biased calculations that did not give much weight to excellence, qualification, merit or citizenship, but favored other considerations.

The late Dr. Izz Al-Din Ibrahim, the chancellor of United Arab Emirates University at that time, was a leading figure in the Muslim Brotherhood group.

He had left Egypt following a showdown between the group and the Nassirite regime. He settled in the UAE, got its citizenship and occupied important positions in it, the last of which was the position of cultural adviser to His Highness the President of the UAE. The presence of Dr. Izz Al-Din Ibrahim in such an important position was part of the Muslim Brotherhood's active pursuit in all Arab countries to control education in order to control the minds and instill in them the group's ideas. I discovered that obstacles were placed in the path of anyone who did not belong to the group or sympathize with it, in order to secure employment opportunities exclusively for its members. There seemed to be close relations between branches of the Muslim Brotherhood group in the Arab Gulf countries—the Kuwaiti Social Reform Society and the UAE Reform Movement were considered the arms of the Muslim Brotherhood group in the two countries. The exchange of information between them was so vigorous that my name became known to those Muslim Brotherhood leaders who were in control of education affairs in the UAE. That meant I would not be allowed to become a faculty member at its universities.

During my attempt to get appointed at the university, the officials I met, including the chancellor of UAE university, secretary and other officials, used strange excuses, claiming, for example, that the university was self-sufficient and had enough Emirati faculty members in 1982, which was completely false. When I returned after getting my PhD and was appointed at the university in 1990, I found that there were only 150 Emirati teachers there, and many specializations were badly understaffed, refuting the claim of self-sufficiency. The real reason was that the political Islamic movements kept the teaching positions vacant for their members, who they managed to send abroad for study, so as to occupy them upon their return. Also, among these dishonest maneuvers, one of the officials I met said to me: "In this drawer, I have applications which were backed by the university chancellor. In the other drawer, applications which were backed by other influential personalities; where shall I put your application?" Strangely enough, that official – now retired – was not a member of the Muslim Brotherhood group, but the dominance and influence of the group were so pervasive that such an official and others would work in its service and carry out its instruction even when they were not part of its ranks. I think the Muslim Brotherhood group sent a large number of its members to study abroad, funded by UAE money, in a calculated plan of control. At a certain time, the plan succeeded in achieving its goals where followers of political Islam spread in Arab universities and controlled the decision-making process in most of them and made them launching pads in their attempt to control the whole society. Arab societies are still paying the price for those acts and behaviors to this day.

However, every cloud has a silver lining, as the saying goes, provided that your spirit remains strong and you do not give in. When I lost hope in joining UAE University teaching staff, I applied for a job at the Ministry of Foreign Affairs, which was a suitable place for political science graduates and was not among the institutions targeted or infiltrated by political Islam. My application was immediately accepted and I was appointed in 1981 at the Ministry as a third secretary; the first step on the diplomatic career ladder. Although 10 years had passed since its creation, the Ministry of Foreign Affairs at that time was still in its early stages. It was created after the formation of the Union at the end of 1971 and had to start from scratch. It has continued to build itself to become an edifice of national work. In 1981, however, it was still at the stage of laying the foundations, and its main focus, and the focus of its former minister His Excellency Rashid Abdullah Al-Nuaimi, was to expand the representation of the country abroad and to build as many embassies and consulates as possible. That was not an easy task, given the lack of qualified national professionals.

I worked at the Ministry of Foreign Affairs for about one year, from late 1981 to August 1982. I learned a lot about diplomatic work and had the chance to be in direct contact with diplomats and closely follow what they were doing. Diplomacy, as a science, was not alien to me. I studied its theoretical

With H.E. Rashid Abdullah Al-Nuaimi, former UAE Minister of Foreign Affairs, during an honoring ceremony to present him with the "Federal Personality Award" in its third edition. This Award was granted under the patronage of H.H. Sheikh Mohamed bin Zayed Al Nahyan, Crown Prince of Abu Dhabi and Deputy Supreme Commander of the UAE Armed Forces (may God protect him), December 11, 2014

principles at the university; saw its practice first-hand and my experience in it deepened at the Ministry of Foreign Affairs. During that year, I worked directly with the Undersecretary of the Ministry of Foreign Affairs (at that time) His Excellency Abdul Rahman Ali Al-Jarwan, who was a member of the first generation that persistently worked day and night to build the Ministry. It was His Excellency who received me and oversaw my training. I owe him a lot of credit for what he provided to me during that period and his confidence in my abilities. As evidence of that confidence, he assigned me to the post of Editor-in-Chief of *The Diplomat* journal issued by the Ministry.

Being an editor-in-chief of a specialized journal was a new challenge. Although I practiced writing in the *Free Forum* journal issued by the Political Science Association at Kuwait University, I had never been in charge of a publication targeting a highly-educated and experienced audience consisting of the Ministry staff and people interested in the diplomatic field. Given the small number of the Ministry employees, there were not enough staff to publish the issue. To overcome the shortage, I had to make additional effort to publish it the way I wanted. In fact, His Excellency Abdul Rahman Ali Al-Jarwan knew that he might have taken a great risk by assigning the editor-in-chief position to a young man who had graduated just a few months ago and had no previous journalistic experience. However, I think His Excellency carefully examined my CV, read some of my writings

The April/May 1982 issue of *The Diplomat* journal, published by the UAE Ministry of Foreign Affairs, when I was its Editor-in-Chief

and checked my academic performance and the high grades I scored during my studies. I remember that the proficient UAE journalist Khalid Muhammad Ahmad, the editor-in-chief (at that time) of *Al-Ittihad* newspaper, played a major role in publishing that issue in which I sought to include some additions in terms of form and content. I think that the vast space of freedom and great support provided to me by His Excellency Abdul Rahman Ali Al-Jarwan were among the factors of my success in that task.

During my work at the Ministry of Foreign Affairs, I came to know many of its young employees who later occupied important positions through which they served the UAE and contributed to achieving its current world status. Many of them have retired and some are still continuing their mission. Among these diplomats was His Excellency Ambassador Muhammad Imran Al-Shamsi who joined the Ministry after receiving his master's degree and became the UAE Ambassador to Lebanon. There were also His Excellency Abdul Rahman Hadi who has retired recently; His Excellency

Ambassador Hassan Muhammad Ubaid Al-Suwaidi who was the country's ambassador to a number of countries including Canada and the Philippines; His Excellency Ambassador Abdul Aziz Al-Shamsi, who has retired recently after serving at the UAE

With H.E. Al-Asri Al-Dhahiri during my visit to the International Defence Exhibition (IDEX 2017), February 21, 2017

embassies in Switzerland, Brazil, France and Italy; and His Excellency Al-Asri Al-Dhahiri whose diplomatic experience has spanned more than 30 years until now, in which he served as the country's ambassador to the United States of America, Saudi Arabia, Bahrain and Morocco. I believe that His Excellency Al-Asri Al-Dhahiri is one of the most highly skilled and competent diplomats who gave a lot to their country.

These young diplomats did their work fully equipped with the excellent education made available to them by the government, which generously invested in its human resources while doing another equally important task: building of citizenship. In those early days of the Union, there were still some remnants of localist tendencies where people were identified as being from Abu Dhabi, Dubai, Sharjah, etc. Loyalty and belonging to the United Arab Emirates and the sense of citizenship were not yet as fully developed as was desired. There was a common awareness among the people at the Ministry of Foreign Affairs of the need to end this localism and entrench the concept of citizenship as a value necessary for the achievement of desired development. They worked hard to accomplish that goal. They made a marvelous success of it, which is now reflected in the deep-rooted concept of citizenship and superiority of loyalty to the UAE over any other entity. As I see the manifestations of this sense of citizenship now, I applaud and speak highly of those who tirelessly devoted their lives to make it a reality.

Work at the Ministry of Foreign Affairs was promising. Local teams received high appreciation and respect. That was enough for me to continue, but my dream to complete my graduate studies never stopped. My feeling that there was much more to learn by doing master's and PhD degrees drove me to look for an opportunity for a scholarship to study abroad. At that time, the Ministry of Foreign Affairs did not give its employees a chance to study because it was in a dire need of their work. The only two entities authorized in the country to give scholarships were UAE University and the Ministry of Education. UAE University shut the door on me because it was controlled by political Islamic movements. So I went to the Ministry of Education only to find the same movements controlling it. In fact, even the Minister of Education himself was a member of the Muslim Brotherhood group.

My visit to His Excellency the late Dr. Abdullah Imran Taryam in 1977 seeking approval to study at Kuwait University was a success because his only motive was to serve the public interest. In contrast, my attempts to get a scholarship from the Ministry of Education to pursue my graduate studies in political science abroad were a miserable failure. I met the Minister of Education at that time and explained to him my request, but he rejected it because he was one of the leaders of the Muslim Brotherhood group. He now lives as a fugitive in a European country. I was rejected because my dispute with the ideological forces desiring to monopolize influential positions was pronounced and declared. My high academic performance, excellence and being from the UAE did not matter to those in charge of scholarships. One had to be ideologically affiliated to them in order to receive a scholarship to study abroad, even if the recipient did not have the mental capacity and academic achievement that would qualify them for it. In fact, they worked against outstanding academic achievers in particular and put barriers and obstacles in their way. They favored low achievers with low intelligence and talent who were easy to control and manipulate into loyalty to entities outside the UAE, and who would strictly carry out their orders.

The Ministry of Education's refusal to grant me a scholarship meant I would have to study at my own expense if I insisted on my goal. It also meant I would lose a stable job, a good salary, a promising future of promotions in diplomatic posts and living among my family and friends in the city of Abu Dhabi, where it took me a few minutes to commute from home to work. However, I did not give in to these difficulties. When I reviewed the idea to my family, they thought I was unaware of what I was about to do because I was going to sacrifice tangible privileges and venture into the unknown. Despite all objections, I made my decision and tendered my resignation. His Excellency Abdul Rahman Ali Al-Jarwan accepted it with deep regret saying that he expected the Ministry to benefit more from my work, and he tried to persuade me to stay. Eventually, he wished me luck and success in a brotherly kindness reflecting his noble feelings.

I was pursuing my dream, which would have been unachievable had I not found someone who would stand by me, support me and ease the difficulties I might encounter. I got married on March 29, 1982 to my university colleague who shared with me the four years of education and competed with me for top academic performance in some courses. We were like-minded in political and humanitarian issues, and together we fought tough battles including that of the New Center List. Our intellectual harmony, coupled with a closeness of souls and spirits, led to a blissful marriage which I consider the main factor of my success in life. The period of swaying between the choice of work and that of travel to study abroad was an opportunity to discover the support which I would receive from my wife throughout my life. During that period, she encouraged me to follow my dreams, willing to sacrifice the stable life and secure income and to face with me the unknown of which many trusted loving ones warned me. In the end, they blessed my decision and gave me every support they could. As I was indebted to teachers such as Dr. Shamlan Yousef Al-Issa, Dr. Faisal Al-Salim, and Professor Hashim Bahbahani for instilling in me the seeds of dream, I was equally indebted to my wife for tirelessly nurturing those seeds and taking care of them until they germinated, blossomed and bore fruit.

In a sense, my travel to study abroad was a response to the injustice I suffered and a challenge to the tight control of the movements of political Islam over the UAE educational institutions at that time, as they intended to exclude anyone who would dare to confront them. It was a refusal to give up and a message to those who tried to discourage me, telling them that I would continue my battle as I always did, even if they thought they won by objecting to my appointment at the university and denying me a scholarship. I believe they were putting a nail in their coffin by what they did to me and to other UAE students who suffered unjust exclusion because those students, most of whom were brilliant and promising, mobilized their effort to abort the plot of the regressive groups after they saw themselves how dangerous they became.

The Master's Stage: Hello Wisconsin

On August 12, 1982, I arrived in the United States of America for the first time in my life. My wife and I took a flight from Dubai to Chicago. From there, a car drove us for about an hour and a half to Milwaukee, the biggest city in the State of Wisconsin in which my stay extended for eight years, but my relation with it has continued to this day and I regularly visit it for personal and academic purposes. I arranged for my enrollment at the University of Wisconsin, which was established in 1885. In fact, my decision to study at this university was not a completely voluntary choice. If I had gotten a scholarship from my country, I would have chosen a different university renowned in the field of political science and Middle Eastern studies as my academic record would easily qualify me for that. However, what I experienced during my studies at the University of Wisconsin proved to me that indeed every cloud has a silver lining, as I said before. The University of Wisconsin provided me with great opportunities to learn and excel. Such

During my years of education in the USA, I visited many cities and states. This was taken in San Francisco, 1984

In San Francisco, USA, 1984

opportunities might not have been available to me had I joined one of the other universities whose names appealed to me, especially the ones from which my great teachers graduated.

I chose the University of Wisconsin mainly because my brother-in-law (my wife's brother) was in Milwaukee studying at the same university. That meant many things would be facilitated, such as finding suitable accommodation, buying furniture and a guide to the best ways to live in the city. His presence there would also help reduce living expenses because I would spend from my small savings to cover family necessities, tuition fees, rent and all other personal needs. I remember that in order to save for buying plane tickets, I spent two consecutive years in Wisconsin before I returned to the UAE in 1984 for the first time.

This situation continued for three years in which I suffered a lot of hardship. It only changed when Dr. Khalifa Muhammad Ahmad assumed the position of Cultural Attaché at the UAE Embassy in the United States of America in 1985. He made great effort to help me and other UAE students

With the late Egyptian actor Hassan Mustafa and actress Isaad Younis at Walt Disney World in Los Angeles, USA, 1984

In San Francisco at the Golden Gate Bridge, USA, 1984

improve our situation. As a result, the Ministry of Education paid for my tuition fees and health insurance, and provided me with a monthly allowance and annual flight tickets to the UAE. My situation improved significantly since 1985 but some of the financial challenges still existed. My monthly allowance was $1,285 while my apartment rent was nearly $1,085. That meant I had to continue to spend from my savings, which were about to run out. But that was an easy situation compared to the first three years.

The challenge I faced at the beginning was how to continue to excel in my graduate studies. Academic excellence would give you a feeling that you find hard to relinquish or lose. I faced the challenge of studying the various courses and subjects in English, as well as writing my master's thesis later in English. I was competing with students whose native language was English, and others who had studied in English throughout their schooling years, while I had studied in Arabic. Nonetheless, I was determined to maintain my academic excellence no matter what effort that might take. I refused to give in to the idea that I would not achieve the desired level, or that other students had a comparative advantage which would put them ahead of me even before the race started. I was certain that by exerting greater effort I would overcome this problem.

I began to study English at an institute affiliated to the university. At the same time, I attended political science lectures with undergraduate students in order to get to know political terminologies in English. The teaching staff were highly competent and had a genuine desire to help us. Indeed, this desire to offer any form of help was a characteristic of all the university's employees, teachers and personnel; a thing which was quite contrary to what we saw in our dealings outside the university and in all aspects of our social life. The study of the English language was not only an academic requirement but was also a way to get closer to the culture of the society, understand its values and adapt to them. I always watched newly-released movies and followed local news and intellectual and cultural activities as part of my attempt to understand and adapt.

It appeared to me that differences in education between Arab countries and the United States of America were huge. It was the difference relating to students that first drew my attention. Contrary to Arab students, American students were highly committed and education to them was a matter of life and death. I was surprised to see American students spending all they had on education. They often worked to pay their university tuition fees; there were no parents, or government, who would pay tuition fees while their child enjoyed his time playing. In most cases in American society, the financial responsibility of parents would end when their child reached 18 years of age. Only a few families would continue bearing this responsibility. I greatly appreciated the idea of working in order to continue study.

Although American history was taught in most high schools, the Americans' knowledge of things outside their local community was very limited. White people in Wisconsin were not friendly toward foreigners, whom they called "aliens" – which means strangers or creatures coming down to Earth from space. That aspect was contrary to the welcoming and supporting attitude I felt inside the university.

Although about 25 percent of Wisconsin population were black, I lived in a predominantly white social environment. There were also Mexicans, Iranians and Arabs in the city, who all fell within the "aliens" category. Black Americans lived in specific neighborhoods and gathered in certain places. White Americans did not interact with "colored" people easily. When white Americans knew we were newcomers in the city, they told us about the neighborhoods inhabited by black people and warned us against frequenting them. Ironically, they viewed us as colored and at the same time warned us about black people and against visiting their neighborhoods late at night. That was completely opposite to our way of thinking because we belonged to societies where such kind of racism was nonexistent and where skin color would not count in evaluating human beings.

The American society is largely an immigrant one. The indigenous people are the "Red Indians." In light of this fact, it is paradoxical that the Americans look to foreigners, the "aliens," with such suspicion. Racism in the American society was deep-rooted. This was particularly obvious in the behavior of the police, whether traffic or other police. You could sense this feeling in seemingly ordinary actions, but they would reflect racism, nonetheless. When a traffic police officer stopped a nice car and found that the driver was from the "aliens," they would show some surprise, ostensibly innocent, but its clear message would be: "These aliens can drive cars like us!! There are many strange things one can see in this life."

These implicit racist messages repeatedly occurred in ways that would make them seem not rude or direct, but they would strongly convey the feeling of racism. If you did a good thing, made a good remark or showed a high performance in any aspect of life, you would be asked: "Are you an Arab?" You would reply: "yes" and the question would be repeated again:

"Sure?! Are you sure you are an Arab?" Such question would sometimes be directed to your wife and children, with the implicit message: "It is strange that an Arab has such intellect and ability to succeed and behave in a proper manner." Of course, we could not wear traditional dress, like the *Kandora* or *Ghutra,* so that we would not be an easy target for this racism.

Although the declared laws sought to fight racism, it happened in different ways that would not fall under penalties prescribed by law. Racism was deeply ingrained in the structure of the society, its system, culture and mindsets of its members. There was no stated law or legislation preventing black people from upward social mobility and access to prestigious jobs. However, on the ground, 99 percent of the university students were white, which meant that these white students would find an open path to important and influential jobs due to their better qualifications. That was a kind of modernization of the old racist system and its explicit mechanisms by imposing old values under a new social cover.

The other aspect, a more positive one, was that the State of Wisconsin was an open, culturally rich collection of communities. Its ethnic diversity allowed everyone to show their cultures, customs and traditions. The city would always be crowded with exhibitions and events, with each community showing its particular culture. In these exhibitions, we were exposed to values, history, religions, music, literature and foods of various communities, from Africa to Latin America, Russia and Iran as well as Native Americans, who inhabited the land long before the arrival of the Europeans.

The Arabs participated in these activities in a city famously known as "the City of Festivals." Given the large number of Arab students from Palestine, the Gulf and other Arab countries, there was a society at the university called the Arab Student Association. Unfortunately, disagreements among them were similar to those in the Arab League and Arab countries, although the Association succeeded sometimes in solving

From right: Professor Mark Tessler, professor of political science at Michigan University – Ann Arbor; Dr. John Duke Anthony; and Dr. Michael Andah, an American of Nigerian descent and university colleague at the University of Wisconsin (on the left of the picture) during the ECSSR's 3rd Annual Conference titled "The Impact of the Information and Communication Revolution on Society and State in the Arab World," January 4, 1997

these disagreements. I remember that prominent Palestinian figures visited the university in 1986, including Saeb Erekat, who later became chief Palestinian negotiator, and the Palestinian academic Dr. Khalil Al-Shiqaqi, the older brother of Mr. Fathi Al-Shiqaqi, the founder of the Islamic Jihad Movement in Palestine who was assassinated by Israeli Mossad agents.

Among those who visited the university and delivered lectures there was the late Dr. Hassan Al-Turabi, the Sudanese leading member of the Muslim Brotherhood group. At that time, I was oblivious to the reasons behind inviting personalities like Dr. Hassan Al-Turabi. After many years and the emergence of many facts, I discovered that it was part of a planned activity by the Muslim Brotherhood group to address the circle of decision making and influence in the United States of America and Europe and to establish relations with them. Thirty years ago, the Muslim Brotherhood group was aware of its need to gain influence in the corridors and institutions of American politics.

The time we went to the United States of America coincided with the beginning of the spread of TV and visual media in general. We subscribed to the newly introduced cable TV with the HBO network. There were some

With Professor Mark Tessler, professor of political science at the University of Michigan – Ann Arbor, on the sidelines of a lecture on "The Social and Political Attitudes of Arab Publics: Selected Findings from the Arab Barometer Project" held at the ECSSR, June 25, 2014

activities that I practiced constantly, including football which I was interested in participating in its weekly matches. Video games, which were widespread at that time, were part of my interest. Video games were played in areas designated for them. I also allocated some of my time to watch movies and visit amusement parks, the most famous of which was a chain of amusement parks called Great America found across the United States of America. All of this was part of my effort to engage in the society and understand its culture.

I built friendships with many Arabs and Americans. Some of my teachers were among my closest friends, such as Professor Mark Tessler who became a valued friend of mine and my family during my graduate studies. We regularly exchanged family visits and I knew his children very well. Professor Tessler was the supervisor of my master's and PhD theses, and his academic supervision was a great factor in all the successes I achieved. He currently works at University of Michigan – Ann Arbor. The striking thing about Professor Tessler is that his facial features are not typically American but rather similar to those of Middle Eastern people. These various activities

With Dr. David Garnham, professor of political science at Wisconsin University, and participants in a workshop titled "Deterrence Essentials: Keys to Controlling an Adversary's Behavior," held at the ECSSR, January 28, 1995

and friendships enriched our social life and deepened our knowledge of the environment in which we lived.

I saw hurricanes and tornados for the first time — before that they had been just a phenomenon I read about. In mid 1984, a powerful tornado hit the State of Wisconsin and other neighboring states causing severe damage. A nearby town called Barneveld was almost wiped out of existence; most of its buildings were flattened to the ground and its infrastructure was destroyed. Nine people were killed and hundreds injured out of a total population of only 600 people or so. Although I was familiar with the desert climate and knew very well its harshness and whims, seeing such frightening natural phenomena was something new to me.

At the White House and the US National Security Council

After studying the English language, the master's degree in the United States of America required the study of a number of subjects such as international relations, which Dr. David Garnham taught me, and subjects about Middle Eastern policies.

There were compulsory as well as optional subjects. Some of them could be taught at the department of political science and some at the departments of psychology and history. Such system exposed the students to greater diversity. After passing the exams of these subjects, there would be a more difficult exam that could last six hours sometimes. Then each student would prepare a thesis to be evaluated by his teachers. During the PhD stage, it was the first time for me to experience "open book exams," which was a completely different experience to a student who had been accustomed to a kind of exams in which even a glance on a book would be considered as cheating. The idea of "open book exams" was quite understandable because we were not supposed to simply memorize and recite information as we were used to.

Some of the subjects I studied during my master's degree posed a great challenge, due to the knowledge background and experience they required. Among those subjects was one about urban development. We knew nothing about this subject because it did not deal with any city outside the United States of America. In this subject, we studied issues such as methods of electricity and water development and distribution to residential areas, and city urban planning in general. I scored a high grade in it, and that was a considerable achievement. There was another subject about urban development in Western European countries. We also studied statistics, taught by a very competent teacher with a degree from a prestigious university. Statistics was a difficult subject and required extra effort, but I excelled in it too. These challenges enhanced my studying abilities. They instilled new concepts into my mind and introduced me to new fields of knowledge, which I soon found myself interested in pursuing research about.

The return of Professor Mark Tessler to the University of Wisconsin in 1984 was an important event to me. He asked about postgraduate students and chose to be my master's and PhD supervisor. Since then, academic co-operation between us in many issues and research projects has continued to this day. Professor Mark Tessler has a vast experience in the Middle East. He wrote about it and lived part of his life in some Arab countries. He later played a prominent role in establishing the Arab Barometer, which he co-directs. The Arab Barometer carries out a significant scientific job of measuring Arab public opinion and analyzing its trends regarding key issues, such as democracy, religious and social values.

The length of a master's thesis at the University of Wisconsin was customarily between

After my master's graduation ceremony at the University of Wisconsin, USA, 1985

30 and 40 pages because it was part of an academic program consisting of strenuous courses and subjects. My goal, however, was not just completing the thesis and getting the degree. My goal was to present a real scientific study with which to begin my research career. I wanted to present a robust, elaborate thesis by making use of everything I learned during the stages of my education, whether in terms of scientific content or research methodologies in which I took great interest. Instead of 30 pages, I wrote a 400-page thesis. In addition to the theoretical content of the thesis, field work represented a significant and central part of it. Moreover, a huge statistical effort was made in it, with advice from Professor Mark Tessler.

Field study added an important aspect of completing the picture, which would be incomplete in an exclusively theoretical study. Field study would bring you closer to the pulse of the street and movement of people, and would produce findings about human nature and behavior that abstract theories would not produce. The statistical part of a study would demonstrate the scientific nature which is based on accurate, specific and indisputable figures and would distance the researcher from personal impressions and biases.

During my master's graduation ceremony at the University of Wisconsin, USA 1985

My master's thesis dealt with women and the labor market. A number of people helped me in completing it, particularly my wife who gave me a lot of help as she was also a graduate of political science. The issue of women's role in a labor market of a Arab Gulf community was something new. There were not enough studies about

Presenting a gift to Dr. David Garnham, professor of political science at Wisconsin University, on the sidelines of the workshop titled "Deterrence Essentials: Special Applications to the United Arab Emirates," March 9, 1996

it in Arabic, or even in English. It even preceded the existence of any significant role of women in the American society itself. During the first half of the 1980s, American women did not have the same role they had in 1990s. I think the effort and time I spent on my master's thesis benefited me during my preparation of the PhD thesis in many ways: first, my master's thesis was a huge academic work in which I used English language and strictly committed myself to the highest degree of accuracy and scientific robustness; second, in preparing my PhD thesis, I benefited from the scientific research approaches and methodologies I used in my master's thesis.

I think my effort in preparing the master's thesis led my Professor Mark Tessler and Dr. David Garnham to nominate me to attend an important event organized by the Foreign Student Service Council in collaboration with the US Information Agency. The Council was very active during 1960s, 1970s and 1980s. Ambassador Richard Murphy, who was highly experienced in the Arab world, was one of its chairpersons.

About 20 top foreign students studying in different American states were

With Ambassador Richard Murphy, former Assistant Secretary of State for Near East and South Asian Affairs and Roscoe Suddarth, former President of the Middle East Institute, during a lecture titled "US Perspectives on the Middle East Issues," organized by the ECSSR, March 11, 2000

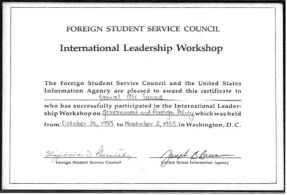

A certificate from the Foreign Student Service Council for participating in the "International Leadership Workshop," held in the USA, November 2, 1985

selected to participate in this event. It was an intensive program of visits and meetings in Washington in order to acquaint these foreign students with the American values and decision making process in the United States of America at an early stage of their life. Since top foreign students studying there were likely to occupy important positions in their home countries or abroad, this event meant that the United States of America would gain new friends who would respect its values and appreciate its policies.

Our trip to Washington continued for about 10 days in which we visited the White House, the National Security Council, the State Department and the Council on Foreign Relations. We met with a large number of officials at the agencies we visit-

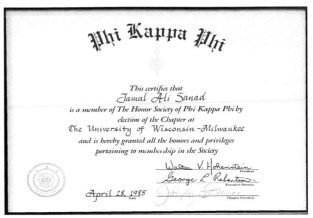

A certificate of membership of the renowned scientific American Phi Kappa Phi Society, April 28, 1985

ed. We met with Ambassador Richard Murphy, who was then Assistant Secretary of State for Near Eastern and South Asian Affairs and a prominent member of the Council on Foreign Relations, and we had a long conversation with him. Throughout the trip, we were given full freedom to ask about anything we wanted and there were no red lines on opinions and positions held and expressed by students.

Selected students included Germans, Dutch, British, Mexicans, Brazilians and other nationalities. I was the only Arab among them. We stayed together at homes of former American ambassadors, which gave us an opportunity to get to know each other much better. I stayed at the home of Michael Sterner, the first American ambassador to the United Arab Emirates. Each of us had the feeling that we did not only represent ourselves but also our countries and cultures. So we were all eager to show the best we had. Each student had useful things to say to benefit the others and add to their information and knowledge. We gained wide friendships and relationships, as well as deep experiences which benefited us educationally and personally and enlightened us about an important aspect of the political process that was not available in lecture rooms and bookshelves. I closely learned about some aspects of the American policy-making regarding the

My daughter Nora, in the USA, 1985

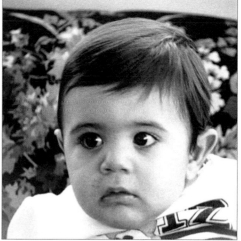

My son Khaled and my daughter Nora were born in the USA while I was pursuing my graduate studies. This photo shows my son Khaled in 1985

Middle East. I think that many of those who shared this experience with me came out of it with more appreciation and respect for the American values and culture, regardless of their positions toward American policies.

Before this useful scientific trip, I received an honor from the Phi Kappa Phi Society, a scientific society established in 1897 that is still active. I was selected for membership of the society by its chapter at the University of Wisconsin. Membership of this society is given by its chapters only based on distinguished academic achievement and high personal and scientific ethics. I am proud to have received that honor.

PhD: Years Full of Work

My effort during the master's stage gave me a good scientific reputation. It helped me get a long-hoped-for chance of being accepted at Stanford University in California, which was and still is one of the most important and the highest-ranking universities in the world. However, my happiness with the acceptance I long dreamed of was short-lived. Joining Stanford Uni-

My son Khaled, in early childhood, wearing a military uniform in the USA, 1984

With my daughter Nora, in the USA, 1986

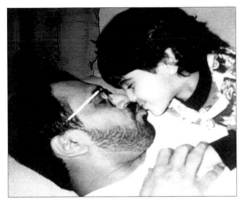

With my daughter Dana, in the United Arab Emirates, 1992

With my daughter Farah, in the United Arab Emirates, 1995

versity was highly expensive and I could not afford its financial cost, no matter how hard I tried. Despite my frustration of losing this chance, I did not let the feelings of frustration drag me back. I did not give up. Instead, I said to myself that individual effort was what would distinguish one student from another despite the higher importance of the quality of education a student received. I continued my study at the University of Wisconsin armed with enthusiasm and hope.

My years of study in the United States of America were generally full of work. However, my PhD years were particularly loaded with addition-

With my son Khaled and my daughter Nora, in the USA, 1988

With my daughter Dana, in the USA, 1989

al burdens, including teaching some courses at the University of Wisconsin and Marquette University – where my teaching journey started and has continued for 25 years – participating in research projects and activities, and publishing articles in scholarly periodicals. All that meant

With my children and the children of my relatives in the USA, 1989

more involvement in work, and more responsibilities borne by my wife. While my wife did not have a formal job, she did spend some time doing voluntary work at Marquette University and the University of Wisconsin. We welcomed our first son Khaled in 1983 and then, 11 months later, our daughter Nora. It was my wife who took our two children to school each day. It was she who reviewed their lessons with them and helped me with some assignments. When we had free time, we would go to entertainment places, of which there were many in Wisconsin. However, free

My son, Khaled (third from left, last row), with the football team of his primary school in the USA, 1988

time was not always available. My focus on my studies kept me away from my children sometimes, but my wife filled in for me.

My daughter Dana, in the USA, 1989

I do not remember being home-sick that much. My presence with my wife and children lessened that feeling significantly, although what the political Islamic group did to me kept triggering bad feelings in me toward political Islam, its groups and organizations. Life in Western society was easy because of the advanced and complete infrastructure. Perhaps, a negative side effect of that period was that my son Khaled and daughter Nora, who spent their first years outside the UAE, have struggled with the Arabic language to this day. Even after our return to the UAE, they enrolled in a foreign school where they continued to use English language in most of their dealings. My daughter Dana, however, was born in 1988 and she was only two years old when we returned to the UAE, while my daughter Farah was born in 1994. As a result, their relationship with Arabic language was stronger, although they both studied at foreign schools too.

The birth of my son Khaled showed me a perfect example of the ease of life when basic services are provided. The caesarean section operation was performed on my wife by Dr. Jasmine De Barcon who was of Asian descent. What I noticed from that experience was that the doctor was not working alone but within an integrated medical system. This might be the difference between health systems in Arab countries and Western countries. In Western countries, it is not about individual competence of doctors but the whole system, while in Arab countries we talk about individual good doctors or nurses. Western countries set the system and every doctor and nurse would work according to its rules and principles. I remember that the medical team performing the caesarean section delivery, which involved epidural anesthesia, included: a doctor to monitor me during my presence there and observe my reactions and health situation, a doctor to perform the operation, a reserve doctor, a nurse to monitor breathing, three or four nurses to assist the doctor who would perform the operation, and an anesthesia specialist.

However, life in the United States of America was not without difficulties. Violence was rife in the city. I remember that there were many Arabs who owned small grocery stores or supermarkets, and their shops became targets of armed robbery. The solution to this problem was not easy. Murder was an ordinary occurrence, with the easy access to guns and the spread of them in the hands of people and the deliberate marginalization of the black and colored populations. Despite the freedoms and human rights in Western societies, I felt that human beings did not have great value in reality. Police did not act properly to stop these crimes. Political or societal institutions did not seek to address the root cause, which was racism because the society did not want to abandon such practice even if laws incriminated it. There were well-established indirect methods of social exclusion to deny the colored people their rights.

The security situation did not pose a serious problem to me and my family because the choice of residence played a role in provision of security. If you chose to live in a sep- arate house, you could be

During a fishing trip in Wisconsin, USA, 1988

a target for robbery; however, if you lived in a multi-apartment building guarded by security personnel, you would be safe. Choosing an apartment like this was important because there was a common stereotype of Arabs suggesting that each Arab possessed an oil well, immersed in a lake of oil and suckled oil instead of milk. This stereotype included all Arabs, not only the Gulf Arabs, making them easy targets for criminals.

The Arabs living in Wisconsin – even those who had American citizenship – remained completely outside the stream of American culture. In contrast, the Jews were a community deeply integrated into broader American society and were part of it. They occupied important, influential positions while the Arabs engaged in lower-level activities. I think that the Jews did not show any hostile or racist feelings toward the Arabs just for being Arabs, but racist tendency was part of the society's racism toward foreigners in general.

Like the master's degree, obtaining the PhD required studying some subjects and then writing a thesis, but the most important things at this stage were research and scientific activities, which the master's degree opened their way for me. I became a member of many American scientific associations including the American Midwest Political Science Association, the American Political Science Association and the Middle East Studies Association of North America.

In April 1986, I participated in a conference held by the American Midwest Political Science Association in the city of Chicago. I presented a paper in English titled "Women's Religious and Civic Values." The same year in November, I participated in the 20th annual meeting of the Middle East Studies Association of North America, which was held in the city of Boston, and I presented a study in English titled "Determinants of Women's Participation in the Labor Force: The Case of the Arabian Gulf Societies." The following year, I participated in the Association's 21st annual meeting, which was held in the city of Baltimore. In 1990, I published a review of a book titled *Oil and Labor in the Middle East: Saudi Arabia and the Oil Boom* in the *International Journal of Middle East Studies*.

Professor Mark Tessler played a significant role in my ventures. Together, we co-authored a number of research papers published in scholarly journals and books. In 1988, we published a joint research in the *International Journal of Middle East Studies* titled "The Economic Orientations of Kuwaiti Women: Their Nature, Determinants, and Consequences." We also published a joint research titled "Women and Religion in a Modern Islamic Society" in a book by Emile Sahliyeh (Editor) titled *Religious Resurgence and Politics in the Contemporary World*, which was released in 1990. This joint research was written in 1988.

Participating in scientific seminars, conferences and research forums, publishing in reputable journals in accordance with high scientific standards, and co-authoring books with prominent professors were all adequate preparation needed by anyone who aspired to be a true researcher. Dealing with the PhD degree, as if it were a goal in itself that had to be quickly achieved in order to get a promotion or the scientific title, would limit the student's ability and potential to produce anything of value in the future. The goal should be to gain knowledge and experience. I remember that the late great intellectual Dr. Edward Said participated in one of the conferences

With H.H. Sheikh Diab bin Zayed Al Nahyan and Dr. David Garnham, professor of political science at the university of Wisconsin, on the sidelines of a workshop titled "Deterrence Essentials: Special Applications to the United Arab Emirates," held at the ECSSR, March 9, 1996

that I attended during that period. He delivered a public lecture attended by more than 500 people in which he talked about the Palestinian issue and the Arab world. His speech was quite distinguished, reflecting a high level of knowledge, genuine vision and ability to defend his views based on real understanding of what was happening in the world.

In addition, teaching was a new experience during that period. Between 1986 and 1990, I worked as a teaching assistant at the University of Wisconsin with a monthly salary of $1,000, which was a good amount of money that I needed to meet my increasing family responsibilities. However, the scientific and moral benefit was more important than the salary. At the University of Wisconsin, I taught "Introduction to Political Science" (1986/1987), "Introduction to International Relations" (1986/1987), "Middle East Policies" (September 1988 and September 1989), and "Developing Countries Policies" (January 1989). I taught two courses in International Relations at the University of Wisconsin about "Religion and Politics: A Global Perspective" (January 1988) and "Research Methods in International Relations and Comparative Politics" (1989). I benefited a lot from the latter course in preparing my PhD thesis. Teaching research methods helped me understand them in depth, and to apply them practically in writing my thesis. The teaching experience was also an early training for me on how to teach professionally and how to face the students.

In the classroom, teaching the subject of "Middle East and North Africa Policy" at the University of Wisconsin, 1988

In 1987, I was a teaching assistant to Dr. David Garnham in the subject of "Introduction to International Relations." One Friday, I had an accident that broke my ankle and my foot was put in a plaster cast. On Monday morning, the first working day of the week, I went to the university in a wheelchair and did my job. I did not allow any difficulty to stop me from

With my students, discussing the subject of "Middle East and North Africa Policy," at the University of Wisconsin, 1988

performing my duty. As always, atmospheres of strict commitment and seriousness perfectly fitted my nature and drove me to become part of the disciplined system of work. That was an early manifestation of "the triumph of the will."

Teaching in English was a challenge. Many of the students were Americans and some studied in English throughout all their school years. Writing in English was not a problem but speaking it with a native accent was a challenge. After four years in Wisconsin, I mastered the language and improved further with time. However, I did not seek to mimic the native accent because I considered that pretentious. A person working in a supermarket could acquire the native accent, but what could not be easily acquired was the academic language, which needed a huge organized effort. I excelled in the academic language which enabled me to achieve great success in my profession.

In the classroom, teaching the subject of "Middle East and North Africa Policy" at the University of Wisconsin, 1988

Social media was not yet existent at that time, nor were many educational technologies. So the heavy reliance was on the teacher's personal skills, good knowledge of their subject and ability to deliver it in the most attractive ways. I relied on the library and required my students to read certain subjects. My top priority after each lesson was to ensure that the students fully absorbed and understood what I explained them. I always sought to make my students love the subject I taught to them.

All teachers, including teaching assistants, assistant professors, associate professors and professors, were annually evaluated by students according to unified standards without any bias or discrimination. I was proud to receive high teaching evaluation scores, mostly ranking among the top five, for five consecutive years although the evaluation included 30 teachers, each of whom had PhD degree and some of them were prominent experts in their fields and some were my teachers. None of us viewed the evaluation as a contest to determine who the best was, but the objective was to improve teaching efficiency. Such evaluation of my work pleased me and motivated me to exert more effort because when you succeeded in a pursuit, you would love it. I think that my success in teaching stemmed from my love for it. I believe that teaching is a gift, a talent or a hobby that some people enjoy. I am one of those who enjoy teaching.

As American students differ from Arab students, so do American professors differ from their Arab counterparts. Professor Mark Tessler, for example, has written dozens of large, important books and published numerous articles in major refereed scholarly journals. What makes an American professor different is not an inborn superior mentality or an inferior mentality of Arab professors relating to ethnicity for example. The difference is a manifestation of a complex set of conditions; it is a product of the opportunities available to the American professors and the availability of teaching experience that enhance their abilities, in addition to the keen interest in publishing and making a research achievement, which is the cornerstone in the academic field. My Professor Mark Tessler, as a specialist in the Arab world, has not limited himself to only reading about it but lived in Tunisia, Morocco and Egypt for long periods, and visited other Arab countries and participated in research projects in most of them. This would deepen his knowledge in his scientific field of specialization and provide him with an understanding which is hardly attainable from books. The outcome is obvious. The Arabs have been declaring for decades that their central issue is Palestine, including hundreds of academics who have written studies about the issue but have failed to present a work comparable to that written by Professor Mark Tessler about the same issue. Professor Mark Tessler's study, which was about 900-pages long, includes a comprehensive scientific view of the conflict based on a high degree of neutrality and scientific vision.

Many American professors were given sabbatical leave in order to study and write. They would usually teach for three or four years and then were given a year off, which they spent focusing only on scientific research. During this sabbatical year, a professor could carry out research or travel to some place that would serve their studies and research activities. So, I think the difference between an Arab professor and an American professor lies in the fact that the latter has wider educational opportunities, and there are institutions that provide financial support to professors. In addition, Arab professors in Arab universities have heavy teaching workloads that negatively affect their ability to conduct scientific research because they would not have adequate time for it.

In terms of libraries, for instance, the library of the University of Wisconsin, one of 4,000 universities in the United States of America, contained five million books, reflecting the high attention paid to everything necessary to the education process. When a professor at an American university supervises three PhD students, he would certainly learn from them as they would learn from him. The supervisor of the thesis plays a great role in it; he understands every idea in the thesis and becomes a member of its discussion committee and defends it with you. All this is done in a positive atmosphere, free from the well-known tension and control at Arab universities. When I was getting myself ready to defend my PhD thesis before the discussion committee, many colleagues – some of whom already obtained their PhDs and some who had not yet – were preparing a joyful celebration for me. Such atmospheres are nonexistent in many Arab universities.

No professor in American universities would think that his footsteps must shake the ground or his posture would suggest that "I am the supreme Lord of you all; so worship me." No one would say "I am a chair Professor and can do whatever I want and my word is a law unto itself." You could hear such snobbish language from some professors in Arab universities, but you could not hear it in an American university. I knew professors at American universities, some of whom gained their PhDs 40 years ago, and none of them used the language used by Arab professors to aggrandize their already bloated selves. There is no subjugated student who would carry their professor's bag or feel the fear and dread with which Arab professors surrounds themselves.

Modesty is one of the beautiful prevailing values in American universities. As a professor becomes more experienced and publishes more scientific research papers in major academic publications, they become more humble with colleagues and students. Professors eat at the university cafeteria the same food that their students eat. Some of them might be in your football team or your rival team in leisure times, and you would find them beside you at all stages. I discovered that many of the professors whom I deeply admired and respected at Kuwait University learned and absorbed these traits during their study at foreign universities and applied them when they returned home. This is what made them the closest to their students, academically and psychologically. Certainly, there are some exceptions, whether in American or Arab universities, because each person has their own traits and characteristics. However, I am talking about the majority which is a natural product of the 'system' that constitutes the professional values and practices, and applies them to all and everyone whereby their only option is to conform with others and join the system.

I chose for my PhD thesis a topic about the relationship between personal religiosity and political and social behavior. Whether in my master's or PhD thesis, I was keen to combine different disciplines. In my master's thesis, there were politics, economics and statistics. In the PhD thesis, I combined sociology and political sociology as well as some analysis of religious and Islamic law, in addition to the comparative method, which required a field work effort to study three populations distributed in two countries. The comparison was between Kuwait, Egypt and the Palestinians. I selected the Palestinian sample from among the Palestinians living in Kuwait, who totaled approximately half a million people at that time.

During the field study, I faced various problems, some of which related to the difficulties of conducting such a study in Arab societies. As a result, the field work took longer time than expected. The reason behind that was obvious—some Arab countries were, and still are, mostly authoritarian. Caution and fear dominating the people make them distrustful when you ask them questions relating to their political positions and opinions about sensitive issues. Also, religion and politics are among the traditional 'taboos' in the Arab culture. To get my work done, I had to make additional effort to reassure the wary people and gain their trust in order to get true

With Prof. Saad Eddin Ibrahim, Chairman of the Ibn Khaldun Center for Development Studies, Egypt, on the sidelines of his lecture "From Edward Said and Orientalism to the Arab Spring," at ECSSR, September 30, 2015

answers from them. Needless to say, strong and useful findings can only be reached when respondents reveal their opinions frankly and honestly, and become convinced that what they say will remain confidential and will only be used for scientific purposes.

I was seeking answers for the following questions: does personal religiosity make a person conservative or non-conservative? And to what extent? To answer these questions in the field study, I designed a scale for personal religiosity and a statistical measure for political and social behavior and then tried to find the correlation between them. Personal religiosity was measured through questions about worshipping, while measurement of political and social behavior was based on whether a person was conservative or non-conservative, done through specific questions as well.

That was in the late 1980s when political religious movements dominated the Arab societies. The question "Where are we heading?" bothered me for a long time—it still does. For that reason, I wanted to jump to the future in my thesis and try to predict what awaited us. I remember that I went to Egypt during that period and visited Prof. Saad Eddin Ibrahim, professor of political sociology, at the old campus of the American University in Cairo, near Tahrir

Square. He had already written an important study in 1983 about the religious activities of students in Egyptian universities. In that early study, he found that many students in scientific disciplines, such as medicine, engineering, mathematics, physics and chemistry, belonged to political religious groups. That was indicative of the future path and an early warning against what later happened after 2011: the rise of Islamic movements to power in Tunisia and Egypt. My visit to Prof. Ibrahim benefited me a lot. Our friendship has continued to this day, as well as our discussion about political Islamic groups. We agreed on some issues and differed on others. We specifically differed on the evaluation of the danger posed by the movements and activities of the Muslim Brotherhood group and its affiliates. Prof. Ibrahim explained some aspects of our difference in opinion in an article he published in *Al-Masry Al-Youm* newspaper on December 19, 2014 titled "The United Arab Emirates: 43 Years in Love of Egypt," in which he wrote:

"A highly-equipped scholarly center no less distinguished than a university, it is the Emirates Center for Strategic Studies and Research (ECSSR), established by the luminous academic figure and the devoted son of the United Arab Emirates (UAE), Dr. Jamal Sanad Al-Suwaidi. Dr. Jamal Sanad Al-Suwaidi is the most prominent member of the first Emirati generation who received their higher education in the United States of America and returned to participate in building the institutions of the nascent federation state of the UAE. He established the ECSSR, and because of his keenness on excellence in line with international quality standards, his studies and publications are refereed and peer-reviewed by scientific committees consisting of scholars and experts from the most prestigious universities in the world."

Prof. Saad Eddin Ibrahim continues his article: "Dr. Jamal Sanad Al-Suwaidi was one of the first Arab intellectuals who cautioned against the Muslim Brotherhood and the danger of their rise and even their participation in power. This is the point on which I (Prof. Ibrahim) differed with him. My viewpoint was extremely idealistic as I thought in the 1980s that their mere participation in power in their countries, especially in Egypt, would be enough to make them more moderate in their interpretation of the religion and less radical in worldly matters. However, Dr. Al-Suwaidi's viewpoint was contrary to mine, especially regarding the Muslim Brotherhood's position toward worldly matters. He believed that if the Muslim Brotherhood gained power, they would monopolize it and would never allow anyone to share it with them,

With my children, Khaled, Nora, and Dana, in the USA on the day my PhD thesis was discussed, May 12, 1990

particularly those whom they consider secular. Dr. Al-Suwaidi stated this in an interview published in the UAE *Al-Ittihad* newspaper on March 21, 2007—more than seven years ago."

The discussion of my PhD thesis was scheduled to take place on May 12, 1990. The university allows the students to choose the thesis discussion committee and no department or faculty would impose it on them. This did not mean that a student could select the professors whom they know. Even if there are personal relationships between the student and the committee members, that would not lead to leniency from the committee because everyone is governed by strict academic rules. Since my thesis was on political Islam, the discussion panel included a specialist in history alongside professors from the Political Science Department. I defended my thesis for about an hour and a half. I stayed up late the night before preparing for the defense, worrying about what awaited me in the discussion session, despite the huge effort I made in writing the thesis.

After the thesis discussion ended, I left the hall to let the committee reach an agreement on the final evaluation. A group of colleagues gathered around me. They congratulated me in advance while I was preoccupied with what the committee might decide inside the hall. A little while later, Professor Mark Tessler came out of the hall to congratulate me on my success. Friends prepared a celebration for me in one of the faculty halls. Professors, students and colleagues shared with me this unforgettable occasion. My wife, of course, was the happiest among them all, for she was an integral part of this long academic journey and endured a lot for the sake of this moment of successful culmination.

Human emotions move in incomprehensible ways. Sometimes they get confused and lose direction, where joy is mixed with sadness, and smile shines in the flow of tears. Sometimes the flicker of hope dies under the weight of frustration and despair, and sometimes the feeling of anxiety fades in the face of a promising new start. I experienced some fluctuation of emotions that day. Instead of being overwhelmed with happiness, I started to get worried about the evaluation result, and even after the announcement of the result and my supervisor congratulated me, what I felt was not an overwhelming joy. More specifically, it was a feeling of freedom and liberation from a long suffering. I endured difficult financial pressures although I was from a rich country that spent on other students. The students, however, were chosen because they belonged to a certain political group, not according to the criteria of competence, excellence, patriotism and ability to achieve real educational success. Thank God this biased, unjust situation is completely over now. I played a role in this regard by establishing the Distinguished Student Scholarships of His Highness the President, which was the main step in my struggle against regressive groups. In Chapter Three of this book, I will talk about this scholarship institution through which more than 450 UAE male and female nationals studied abroad and received the highest levels of education in the world.

One of the interesting and frightening incidents during my stay in Wisconsin was the case of a serial killer and sex offender named Jeffrey Dahmer, who cannibalized his victims after murdering them. He lived near Marquette University in which I taught some courses. This criminal's story occupied the headlines and became the talk of the town. He was arrested one year after we left, but he committed most of his monstrous crimes during the final years of our stay there. It was believed that he killed about 17 people. His crimes had a racist aspect, as many of his victims were black. He was killed in prison by a black inmate who bludgeoned his head with a metal bar. The inmate might have been revolted by the racist nature of Dahmer's crimes. The strange thing about the Dahmer story was that he was turned into a legend before his death in 1994. He received letters of admiration and love from male and female fans from many countries, and even marriage proposals from some women.

My journey, which lasted eight years, had finally come to an end. I prepared myself to return to my country to start a new stage of my life. However, a momentous event was awaiting me, making my return completely different from what I expected.

The Escape from Kuwait

By the end of July 1990, a month since my return from the United States of America to the United Arab Emirates, I got an approval of my appointment as a lecturer of political science at UAE University, and the official appointment decision was about to be issued. In mid-July, my wife and children traveled to Kuwait to spend some time with the family there. I decided to travel to Kuwait as well to see my mother and sister, and then return to the United Arab Emirates with my wife and children. On July 29, I traveled from Dubai to Kuwait. Only three days after my arrival, the Iraqi invasion of Kuwait took place on August 2, 1990, and my family and I found ourselves trapped for about 20 days in which we could have simply lost our lives.

Nobody expected Saddam Hussein to invade the State of Kuwait. We followed the Jeddah talks between the late Sheikh Saad Al-Abdullah Al-Sabah and His Highness Sheikh Sabah Al-Ahmad on the one hand and the Iraqi delegation, led by Izzat Ibrahim, on the other hand. The Jeddah talks failed to reach a solution for the Iraq-Kuwait dispute, but still nobody expected the Iraqi regime to make such a move. During the 20 days I spent trapped in Kuwait, I saw people living in a state of shock and fear wondering why an army of an Arab country would invade and occupy another Arab country. I would be lying if I said I expected the invasion. Despite my specialization in political science and my reading of every published material at that time about the Iraq-Kuwait crisis and the expected scenarios, I did not find anyone who predicted such a course of action.

On the night of the invasion, Thursday, August 2, 1990, I was passing in my car through the Al-Wafra area in southern Kuwait. It was about three o'clock in the morning. I saw a huge number of black cars, belonging to the Kuwaiti royal family, heading out of Kuwait, and I could not figure out why. I spent the night as usual. On Friday morning, I stood on the roof of the house to see what was going on. I saw a column of Iraqi tanks moving in the area after they pushed more than 200 kilometers into Kuwait. I said to myself, "the stability of the region is gone." My brother-in-law (my sister's husband) was standing next to me. He looked at me with astonishment and said, "stability?! What stability?! The whole country is gone."

The invasion began at about 2:00 am in the morning of Thursday, August 2, 1990 when Iraqi forces stormed the border area and entered the State of Kuwait after a few clashes. At that time, many of the Kuwaiti officers and soldiers were on summer leave. Even if the Kuwaiti armed forces were in full force, it would not have made a significant difference. The Iraqi army consisted of nearly 70 divisions with each division consisting of three brigades and the number of soldiers in each division was nearly ten thousand. These enormous divisions were battle-hardened and had experience in fierce fighting over eight years—they knew war very well. On the second and third days of the invasion, I saw many dead bodies of Kuwaiti soldiers who were martyred resisting the invasion. The Iraqi soldiers received orders to open fire heavily in the air to intimidate civilians and spread panic among them. So the Iraqi soldiers cruised the streets in small pickup trucks and fired their weapons. Once, I was driving my car behind one of these trucks at night. I noticed that the Iraqi soldiers did not target anyone with heavy firing of their small and medium-sized guns. They wanted to scare people because when residents of nearby areas heard the sound of gunshots in the middle of the night, they would think that battles were taking place and people were being killed and death may be upon them at any moment.

The following day, I went to the UAE embassy which was close to the Egyptian and Iraqi embassies. The three embassies were besieged by Iraqi forces. We were allowed to enter the UAE embassy and we met the Chargé d'Affaires (at that time) Muhammad Rashid Al-Boot in order to arrange for our return to our home country. In the following days, the UAE embassy operated through the embassy of Bahrain because it was far from the Iraqi embassy. The Bahraini ambassador, the late Eisa Jamie (may God rest his soul in peace) played a significant role in sheltering the Emiratis and other nationals, and issued them Bahraini or diplomatic passports to leave Kuwait. Many Emiratis resorted to the Bahraini embassy and received valuable help and assistance.

It was the professional Iraqi soldiers who entered Kuwait first and many of them thought that the occupation would last a month or two at most. Those soldiers occupied vital areas in Kuwait and executed the mission assigned to them by their military command. They did not get involved in looting and pillaging activities. However, the situation worsened terribly when the paramilitary, Iraqi Popular Army (also known as the People's

Army or People's Militia), entered approximately two weeks later. It was not a regular army. Its members were barbaric and savage, relying entirely on robbery, plundering and looting. They robbed even petty articles such as beds, blankets, electric appliances and even clothes. After the spread of their immoral activities, the Iraqi authorities decided to bring in police forces to maintain order and security. However, that did not change the situation much; if you deploy large groups of untrained poor people who have guns but nothing to eat and sustain themselves with, they would certainly loot and kill. Kuwait was rich and sparsely populated with its citizens enjoying a life of luxury and wealth, while members of the Popular Army were poor and uneducated who looked for anything to loot and steal.

The most horrible thing that happened during our final days in Kuwait was the Popular Army's invasion of hospitals, where there were UAE patients too. Patients were subjected to cruel conditions and some of them died as a result. Those hardly educated savages were not aware of what they did. Some of them disconnected patients on life support and dumped premature newborns from incubators. The condition of hospitals worsened. There was a severe shortage of medicines and medical equipment. The lives of patients with heart diseases and diabetes became in real danger after their life-saving medicines disappeared from hospitals and pharmacies that were still operating, and it was no longer possible to perform surgical operations on patients who needed them. Also, many physicians fled the hospitals. Even food and drink were hard to get, let alone medicines.

The distress I suffered in these 20 days in Kuwait during the invasion was further multiplied; I had to shuttle regularly between two areas for 50 minutes by car because my wife and children were living in one area while my mother and my sister and her children in another. I had to do all of this in an environment that had lost its security and stability. There was no law, police, ministry of interior or any agency that could ensure the security and safety of people living in Kuwait. In this lawlessness and chaos, anybody could simply do whatever they want with impunity. Anybody could break into your home and kill you and your family members and no one would care about you or even ask the killers why they did so.

Due to my academic specialization, I read numerous studies about wars and the suffering of people. However, reading about the loss of food, water and security is one thing, and going personally through such an experience is another completely different thing. One week after the invasion, grocery stores, cooperative shops and markets almost ran out of food and water stocks. Due to absence of security, many shops closed their doors and their terrified owners fled for their lives. Food and water scarcity became more severe and the threat of hunger endangered the trapped people. I think that those who stayed in Kuwait after we had left must have faced even more difficult circumstances. Finding drinking water was really difficult and talking about bathing water was of course an inconceivable luxury. Fortunately, the electricity supply continued uninterrupted during those scorching days. Perhaps, what happened in Kuwait drew attention to the danger of the Gulf countries' dependence on food imports (about 80 percent) and the serious threat of water shortage in case of emergency.

Some of the Arab public, and even Arab officials, frequently talked about an international conspiracy that fooled Saddam Hussein into invading Kuwait. In my view, such conspiracy exists only in the minds of those who talk about it. In the end, it was Saddam Hussein's forces that entered Kuwait. Whether there was a conspiracy or not, the invasion occurred, and Saddam Hussein gave orders to troops commanded by none but him. He entered another country and occupied it. If there was a conspiracy whereby the Americans and Europeans tricked Saddam Hussein into invading Kuwait, as some people claim, why did not the Iraqi president listen to former Egyptian president Hosni Mubarak and many other Arab presidents and leaders who warned him of what was bound to happen? Anyone who studies the behavior of Saddam Hussein during the Arab Summit, which was held in Baghdad

صفحـــات مـــن تـــاريـــخ أمـــة

A copy of my article titled "Pages from the History of A Nation," published in *Al-Khaleej* Arabic newspaper, January 12, 1991

from May 28–30, 1990 will realize that there were strong indications of an intention to invade, but those indications were not quite understood until after two months, with the occupation of Kuwait.

Neither economic motives nor the problem relating to the exploitation of oil fields were the reasons Saddam Hussein invaded Kuwait, as alleged. Rather, miscalculations, arrogance and delusions of grandeur motivated him. Saddam Hussein thought he could march forward, unaware that he was bringing about his own demise. Iraq bore the consequences of the actions of one self-conceited, violent individual. Saddam Hussein was no stranger to miscalculations. I remember that during the Iraq-Iran War, the Iranians occupied a remote mountainous area and Saddam Hussein wanted to regain it. So he sent three paratrooper units to that location, but all the units were completely annihilated.

The Iraqi invasion of Kuwait brought inter-Arab cooperation to an end. Irrespective of who was behind it and whether it was a conspiracy or not, I believe that Saddam Hussein dealt a death blow to inter-Arab cooperation. I said then, in an article titled "Pages from the History of a Nation," that we laid joint Arab work into a coffin and blocked any opportunity for it. The generation concurrent with the invasion of 1990 was fully responsible for what happened. It is true that some countries advised Saddam Hussein to withdraw from Kuwait, but their effort failed miserably. If the establishment of the League of Arab States (the Arab League) marked an era of Arab history, the Iraqi invasion of Kuwait marked another era. The effect of the invasion on the Arabs was similar to that of World War II on the world, which shook the economy and redrew the world order. Similarly, the Iraqi invasion of Kuwait produced profound outcomes and changes, including the end of inter-Arab cooperation.

The day of escape from Kuwait was unusually difficult. We drove along the route linking Kuwait and Saudi Arabia. We were in a convoy of about five cars carrying my family, the family of my brother-in-law, my sister-in-law, my sister and my late mother (may God rest her soul in peace). In normal circumstances, the route would take two hours, but it took us about 12 hours, from 5:00 am to 5:00 pm. We were stopped at many checkpoints and suddenly met with lines of trenches dug by Iraqi soldiers and we had to drive around them by taking routes unknown to us. The vehicles shook violently and their occupants collided with each other because of the rugged terrain.

In front of the trenches and other checkpoints, the Iraqi soldiers stopped us asking for only two things in order to let us pass: bananas and cigarettes. At one point, we did not know where we were exactly. An Iraqi soldier stopped us for two hours, during which he was eating the bananas we gave him and smoking. After he had finished eating and smoking, he allowed us to pass. After we moved ahead, another Iraqi soldier stopped us and pointed a machine gun at us yelling that passing was not allowed. He fired some shots at us while we were moving, but we were far away. Shortly after this, we saw a police station ahead of us, which I thought belonged to the Iraqi forces, but fortunately it was not and we had actually reached the border with Saudi Arabia.

The hospitality of the Saudis was overwhelming. Everyone who crossed the borders, irrespective of their nationality, was given *abayas* (black gowns) for the women and 100 Saudi Riyals to meet their necessary needs. That was part of the kindness of the late King Fahd bin Abdul Aziz and his generosity. The cooperation from the Saudi authorities was great. We should know that the number of people fleeing Kuwait was huge since it was a home for more than four million workers from different nationalities who could only flee through Jordan or Saudi Arabia. All of those workers lost their jobs and businesses and escaped for their lives. Many of them had nothing for sustenance after the country fell prey to the invasion.

On my way back home to the UAE, many things changed in my view of events around me. I was preparing to start a new critical stage of my life as a lecturer at UAE University, the doors of which the Muslim Brotherhood slammed in my face eight years ago, and then to the establishment and directorship of the ECSSR. That period witnessed different forms of challenges and difficulties, as well as achievements in which I take immense pride. This will be explained in the following chapters.

Chapter 3

Professional Life

Chapter 3

Professional Life

Facing the Invasion

On August 18, 1990, the moment I had waited for so long finally arrived. While I was making arrangements to flee Kuwait after the Iraqi invasion, a decree was issued by the UAE educational authorities and I was appointed a faculty member at the Department of Political Science at United Arab Emirates University in Al-Ain. It is worth mentioning that Al-Ain is the garden city that boasts plenty of lush trees and gardens scattered everywhere, like a green carpet over the sands of the desert. It manifests the value of pride and challenging nature for the Emirati people, as they made lovely oases in the middle of deserts. You can see water flowing all around the city, as if it echoes the words of the founding father, the late Sheikh Zayed bin Sultan Al Nahyan (may God rest his soul in peace), about the strong will of the Emirati people, who will transform the desert into a green garden.

My appointment at UAE University was my springboard for a career that now exceeds three decades full of challenges and hardships. Achieving success is not easy; it is only attainable through a bumpy road that is jam-packed with ceaseless sacrifices and effort. My painful journey with disease, to be addressed in Chapter 4, might be a result of physical and psychological stress and work pressure that have never eased. Nevertheless, I did not surrender at any stage.

No sooner had I arrived in my country after coming back from Kuwait, than I carried out a humanitarian and national task during the difficult months that the Arab nation had gone through following the invasion—amidst the distorted images and the disrupted standards that dominated the Arab awareness. On the first day of my arrival in the United Arab Emirates on August 21, 1990, I gave an interview to the Arabic daily newspaper *Al-Khaleej* regarding the invasion. In the interview, I recounted my observations from within Kuwait and talked about the hard times awaiting Kuwait and the Arab world. However, I was confident that the invasion would be defeated. A few days later, I was busy using the years I spent in Wisconsin in explaining the dimensions of the plea of the Iraqi invasion of Kuwait to the American public. On August 27, 1990, I gave an interview to the *Milwaukee Sentinel* newspaper, for an article titled "Crisis in the Gulf." My experience in Wisconsin made me aware that American citizens needed someone to explain to them the nature of the crisis. I drew on my deep knowledge and understanding of the mindset of the American society and the means to influence it.

Attending the 24th Annual Conference of the Middle East Studies Association of North America (MESA) in the period November 10–13, 1990, in San Antonio, Texas, was a suitable occasion for highlighting the case. There, I presented a scholarly paper titled the "Arabian Gulf: Present and Future," in a session titled "Current Events: Prospects of the Gulf Crisis." Being one of the most knowledgeable academics of what was happening in the region, and being the best to express the views of the citizens of the Gulf, in my paper, I presented my perspective to the audience – including an elite group of specialists in the region. My weapon was my mastery of academic methodology and full knowledge of the issue and its dimensions, in addition to my ability to express my own ideas in a language understood by a knowing academic audience. In an interview I gave to the San Antonio's *Express News* newspaper on November 13, 1990, I talked about expected permanent impacts of the invasion. In a

With Dr. Abdulreda Assiri, former Dean of the College of Social Sciences, Kuwait University, on the sidelines of the signing of my book *Prospects for the American Age: Sovereignty and Influence in the New World Order*, at Kuwait University, March 16, 2014

press interview with *University of Wisconsin Report*, I also spoke about the possible repercussions of the invasion. The interview was published in Vol. 11, Issue 6, released in December, 1990. On November 16, there was a lecture at the Kuwait Embassy in Washington, D.C., about the psychological and humanitarian consequences of the invasion. The lecture was attended by the Kuwaiti Ambassador to the United States of America (at that time), the late Sheikh Saud Nasser Al-Sabah. Myself, Dr. Abdulreda Assiri and Dr. Shamlan Al-Issa were the participants. In Washington, D.C., too, there were many events aimed at raising awareness; Arab ambassadors and citizens wanted to know what really was happening in the Arab region, and we tried to explain this reality to them, as we had done in Texas.

Within the United Arab Emirates, such activities had never stopped, even for a day. On September 23, 1990, in front of thousands of female students, I talked about the dimensions of the crisis. The following day, I talked about the same subject to the male students (as male and female students are taught in separate buildings). At the "Political Society", founded by students of the Department of Political Science at UAE University, I gave a lecture on October 22. A few days later, I gave a lecture on the political implications of the Gulf crisis at the Youth Sports and Cultural Club in Dubai; then I talked about its political, economic and cultural effects in a public forum at UAE University. Later, I gave a lecture at Zayed Military College in Al-Ain on the "Origin and Development of the GCC," in line with

With H.E. Sheikh Nahyan bin Mubarak Al Nahyan, Minister of Culture and Knowledge Development (Minister of Higher Education and Research at that time), at Abu Dhabi International Book Fair (6th edition), April 1, 1996

the 11th Summit of the GCC leaders in Doha (December 22–25, 1990), where I highlighted to these future military officers the importance of the GCC and its pivotal role in protecting the security of its member states. On January 18, 1991, with the start of the Kuwait liberation war, my lectures extended to the research domain that continued to be among the topics I used to focus on throughout the following years, when I presented to the audience in the Emirate of Sharjah my perceptions of "Security in the Gulf."

In addition to lectures and symposia, press, radio and television interviews were among my other means of addressing the public in the Gulf and beyond. On September 9, 1990, I talked about the crisis on Abu Dhabi TV. A few days later, I was talking on Dubai TV about the implications of the crisis on the Muslim world, then on Sharjah TV about the "Media and the War," followed by *Al-Khaleej* newspaper about the 11th GCC Summit. Moreover, interviews with foreign media followed. I spoke in mid-November on Voice of America Radio in Washington during my stay there, about the interactions of the Gulf crisis. I also spoke on World Net TV network via satellite, more than once, about the American policy in the Gulf region and the expected results of the crisis. This role that I played had extended to post-Kuwait liberation, where I spoke on Dubai TV on March

With H.E. Sheikh Nahyan bin Mubarak Al Nahyan, Minister of Culture and Knowledge Development, (Minister of Higher Education and Research at that time), at the ECSSR 7th Annual Conference titled "Human Resources Development in a Knowledge-Based Economy," February 9, 2002

10, 1991, about the "Inter-GCC relations after the Gulf War." Also, on April 3, 1991, in a symposium held by the Cultural Committee of the Sociologist Association in the Emirate of Sharjah, I talked on "Prospects for social, economic and political developments of the Gulf states after the war."

In many of these meetings, seminars and lectures, I was joined by colleagues and academic friends from the United Arab Emirates, the State of Kuwait and other Gulf states, including His Excellency Dr. Anwar Gargash, Dr. Abdul Khaleq Abdullah, Dr. Abdullah Jumah Al-Hajj, Dr. Shamlan Al-Issa, Dr. Abdulreda Assiri, Dr. Fahad Al-Thaqeb and Mr. Khalil Ali Haidar. During the period between August 1990 and January 1991, these academics had fought fierce battles, no less serious or important than the war that was actively being prepared for.

His Excellency Sheikh Nahyan bin Mubarak Al Nahyan, then Minister of Higher Education and President of UAE University, played a great role in my appointment at UAE University. Dr. Syed Noor, one of the teachers whom I admired at Kuwait University for their academic capabilities, in his post as Deputy Vice Chancellor for Community Service, played a role in my appointment as well. He used to recall my diligence at statistics, which I loved thanks to him. He deemed that my presence at the University would be a positive addition. Following the decision to employ me, however, many people wondered where I was and why I have not come to take over his position. Some people volunteered to search for me because the faculty members were supposed to begin preparing for the start of the academic year—they had no idea I was still in Kuwait.

This board was gifted to me, bearing the signatures and handwritten words of appreciation from colleagues and friends from the College of Social Sciences, Kuwait University, on the sidelines of signing my book *Prospects for the American Age: Sovereignty and Influence in the New World Order*, at Kuwait University, March 16, 2014

Upon returning to the UAE, there was a role we had to play. The invasion was supported by some Arab countries in spite of the clarity of the issue. Some Arab organizations supported Saddam Hussein's position. The thing that amazed and angered me was that certain Arab forces, present in Kuwait at that time, created their own checkpoints, and its armed members were asking people to show their IDs in order to be allowed to pass through. That force is well-known and I do not want to open that bitter page again. Moreover, some Arab intellectuals also aligned themselves with the invasion; one of them wrote a press article claiming that "the white bull has been eaten and it is now high time for the black bull." He meant that as Kuwait had been occupied, the United Arab Emirates, in turn, would follow. The countries and entities that adopted this stance tried to promote themselves through misleading propaganda campaigns that created chaos and confusion among the Arab public. It was a necessity to counter such campaigns at the intellectual level, and to expose their falsity and absurdity.

As educated elite in Arab countries, we had to reach out to people through symposia, lectures, press, radio and television interviews and articles. In the GCC countries, this was much more urgent. We were on the verge of a fateful war that could not tolerate the existence of reluctant or indifferent people. Nor could we tolerate others influenced by the pro-invasion misleading propagan-

Studying political science at Kuwait University was my springboard. In this photo, I am with Dr. Abdullah Al-Shayji, Head of Political Science Department, Kuwait University, during the signing ceremony of my book *Prospects for the American Age: Sovereignty and Influence in the New World Order*, at Kuwait University, March 16, 2014

da, whether from those who supported the invasion explicitly or those who were injecting poison into the sweet talk of unrealistic and illogical solutions that would have given Saddam Hussein a chance to force his scheme or impose a de facto situation. Many people did not realize the reality of what was going on, its motives, dimensions, or the consequent disastrous results if the Arabian Gulf states had bowed to Saddam Hussein's practices of extortion and intimidation. Had the Gulf states weakened in front of such extortion, they would have paid dearly for their security, stability and economic capabilities—not for one, two or several years, but rather for decades to come.

Those months represented an opportunity for me to address the GCC and UAE public, and to deepen their understanding at a critical period—this benefited me later. I think I was lucky because I experienced the invasion in a way unavailable to many. I had lived its details inside Kuwait itself. Moreover, my understanding of the Kuwaiti society was immense because of my studying at Kuwait University; my mother and sister living there; being married to a Kuwaiti; and my extensive family connections and personal friendships. Moreover, I had just returned from the United States of America to look at the issue from a broader perspective, bearing in mind the major powers' calculations and the shifts in the international system, which were formed again in the wake of the collapse of the former Soviet Union. I was surprised to see that a lot of Arab academics and intellectuals were unable to see the event outside its narrow local or Arab scope. Consequently, they were not able to see the inevitable results or the dangers of the lack of understanding.

No less important is the fact that over the past eight years I had been studying political science in an academic system that I thought was highly sophisticated. This system triggered analytical capabilities to the fullest possible extent and defined the future through a real and profound understanding of the reality, away from wishful thinking, ideological biases and all the obstacles that prevented a proper understanding of what was happening and what was expected to result from the invasion. I was armed, as I thought, with the proper tools needed to understand and judge, and this was what gave me a greater opportunity to address people, convince them and clarify their confusion.

Of course, there was a personal side in my approach to the crisis of the Iraqi invasion of Kuwait; a side related to the previously mentioned family ties and connections. However, I was always interested to see the issue from a researcher's perspective, which necessitates impartiality and objectivity. Anger did not rob me of sober-mindedness, thus my insight could not be confused nor diverted from the scholarly path. On January 12, 1991, I wrote an article that showed some of this anger—this did not prevent, however, the emergence of the idea I sought to convey to readers. The article, titled "Pages of the History of a Nation," an obituary of the joint Arab action, diagnosed the incurable diseases of the nation, and bitterly criticized the confused and shameful positions of Arab countries, groups, thinkers and intellectuals who were enthusiastic to support the crime, justified it, downplayed it, or distracted others from its reality.

In my article, I wrote: "It is really a story of downfall. Even the intellectuals of this nation promote the language of destruction. Poor you, my nation. Do whatever you want, but you will never be able to deceive a crumbling nation; as

H.E. Abdullatif bin Rashid Al Zayani, Secretary-General of the Cooperation Council for the Arab States of the Gulf (GCC), during his lecture: "Cooperation Council for the Arab States of the Gulf: Achievements and Aspirations," at ECSSR, January 20, 2016

there is nothing left that could be deceived in this nation. We are used to slogans and the logic of speech. We evolved and started to get used to the destruction of mankind. We are used to building palaces and making profits over the bodies and pains of the victims. Woe, O nation, these are thy children! They are in a coma." I concluded the article saying: "Oh my little girl who was awakened by the sounds of guns and tanks instead of the school bells: Do not grieve! You are part of a dying nation... a nation that has lost [the act of] giving and has become a captive of the coffin made by its own children."

The late Sheikh Zayed bin Sultan Al Nahyan, the late King Fahd bin Abdul Aziz Al Saud, the late Sheikh Jaber Al-Ahmad Al-Sabah and the group of leaders in the GCC and some Arab states played a significant role in ending the brutal invasion of Kuwait. The Gulf states formulated an epic of unity and cooperation during that difficult period. Kuwait and its people are lucky to belong to a Gulf state. Between August 1990 and February 1991, the GCC states managed to provide Kuwaitis with jobs, salaries, housing, healthcare and all of life's basic needs. Many of those who headed to the United Arab Emirates were living in houses where the UAE government paid their rents. Moreover, schools and universities in the UAE, Saudi Arabia, Qatar and Bahrain opened their doors for Kuwaiti students. Kuwaiti university professors also joined Gulf universities immediately, as part of the faculty. Its is not only the way governments took responsibility, but also the way in which Kuwaitis were received by the nations of the Arab Gulf states that was a model for togetherness and unity. Kuwait's National Assembly and government convened their meetings in Saudi Arabia, and from there they fought the diplomatic, political and economic battles that led to defeating the aggression and the return of Kuwaitis to their country. Moreover, the Gulf states were the starting point of the international military buildup, and their armed forces had participated actively in the battle of liberation. This was a strong and living proof of the importance of the GCC.

Had what had happened to Kuwait taken place in another country, for example, its population would not have had people providing them with food, shelter or work. Consequently, the population would have become refugees, and the case might have ended with the invasion and occupation being endorsed. This event underlines the role of the GCC in times of distress and crises, regardless to what is being said of problems in GCC's work and activities, or slowness and faltering in the development and elevation of joint action. If we agree that the GCC work mechanisms need to be developed, and that aspirations and expectations are greater than what is achieved so far, we must not forget that the GCC was the umbrella that shaded the nations of the Gulf in the toughest crisis they encountered, and it proved its strength and effectiveness in overcoming the most serious threats suffered since its inception in 1981.

The military buildup took about five months, during which time the world united against the invasion as it had never before—the United States of America sent hundreds of thousands of soldiers, backed by large forces from European countries, and armed forces from the GCC countries, led by Saudi Arabia. Even Russia and China, the traditional antagonists of the United States of America, took a different stance following blatant aggression on international legitimacy and the notion of nation-state that had been established in the Peace of Westphalia in 1648. Most Arab countries joined the international coalition, including Egypt, Syria and Morocco, in confirmation of the legitimacy of the war to liberate Kuwait, at the Arab level.

The balance of power in this war was not equal at all, as just two days after the start of the air strikes, coalition forces were able to dominate the skies. Coalition ground forces could carry out operations on the ground in Kuwait and Iraq the way they wanted, without facing serious resistance. All of Saddam Hussein's military calculations proved wrong. He thought that the 70 military divisions he had would be able to defeat the international coalition, but the fact was that coalition forces were facing a weak army that had been devastated by air strikes alone. The international coalition forces could have marched into Baghdad and occupied it within few days if they wished to do so.

The war was absurd. It was full of tragedies. When the Iraqi soldiers were withdrawing from Kuwait, in panic under the air strikes, the US military forces landing behind their lines were fighting inside the Iraqi borders, and the rapid return of the retreating Iraqi soldiers meant they would clash directly with the international and Arab forces fighting inside the Iraqi territory. The US air forces were left with no other option except to bomb the retreating Iraqi soldiers – not out of a desire to kill, but to prevent a confrontation between them and the forces that landed behind them. Thus, a terrible massacre in the area between Kuwait's Jahra and Farwaniya governorates happened, the victims were the retreating Iraqi soldiers. Even the trips returning to Kuwait, after liberation, were not free of tragedies; we lost a friend of ours – engineering professor, Dr. Jafar Assiri, Dr. Abdulreda Assiri's brother – in a car accident during his return to Kuwait after liberation. Eventually, Arab and non-Arab countries sacrificed many of their sons to stop the ambitions of tyrants.

Moreover, Arab lives and fortunes, which could have been used to support growth and development rather than sabotage and aggression, were wasted. Iraq was the biggest loser. It is still paying a hefty price 25 years later.

During a visit to the ECSSR by a delegation from the College of Humanities and Social Sciences at UAE University, headed by Dr. Abdul-Wahab Ahmad, Dean of the College at the time, December 6, 1998

A Bitter Experience

Working at UAE University (1990–1994) was a sequel to a fight that was put on hold since I left Kuwait University—that was my battle with the extremist political religious groups. During my work at the Ministry of Foreign Affairs, I had not encountered elements of the group. Also, I had not experienced this problem during my post-graduate studies abroad. At UAE University, however, I found myself in a working environment almost fully dominated by the Muslim Brotherhood group and its supporters. The battle began early, and one of the seminars I attended in 1990 was the scene of a confrontation that greatly affected me.

The colleges of female students at UAE University used to host ceaseless cultural, political and intellectual seminars. Female students were enthusiastic to attend and participate in these seminars. The guest of one of these seminars was Jalaluddin Haqqani, who was introduced then as one of the "Afghan mujahedeen," who became a known terrorist later. Jalaluddin Haqqani had committed heinous crimes against his own people and against Islam, which he claimed to be speaking in its name.

Our colleague, Dr. Nesreen Murad, was in charge of moderating Haqqani's lecture, but she insistently requested me to moderate it on her behalf, due to pressing circumstances. I responded to her request. The moment Haqqani began talking, I was appalled by the volume of lies, exaggeration and irrationality in his talk—he was exploiting the religious sentiments of the young female students. I remember how he was talking in artificial emotion about personal "miracles" that he made during his *jihad*, and how the mujahedeen used to emerge unharmed after the mines they walked on exploded. He claimed that he himself walked on a mine that exploded, but he was unharmed! Haqqani supplemented his illogical story with a dramatic movement in which he raised his footwear in front of the students, saying: "The mine exploded, but my footwear was not harmed." While I was watching in disbelief, cheers of glorification were hailed by the supporters of the group in the hall, talking of faith, victory from Allah and fighting the infidels and blasphemy. The female students were in full admiration of this *mujahed*—they were taught by their professors to accept erroneous logic and to believe in it. Moreover, their strong religious passion disabled their ability to think logically.

For me, the theatrical performance of Haqqani was poor and his lying was obvious. He was covering his pretension with heavy use of verses from the Holy Quran, quotes from the sayings *(Hadiths)* of the Prophet and stories of his Companions—he used to twist their meaning and manipulate them to serve his own objective. But the false aura of holiness cast on him by political religious groups and the qualities bestowed on him by these groups made anything he said believable, even when he knowingly twisted the meaning of the texts and misinterpreted them to serve his own purposes and interpreted them in accordance with his whims and his deviant understanding of Islam. I wish I could have asked him to step on a mine in front of us to demonstrate the miracles he claimed, and to examine in reality what would have happened to his footwear, which he proudly raised before our eyes. What Haqqani did was a literal application of the expression I quoted in *The Mirage* book, from the Arab philosopher Ibn Rushd (Averroes), "If you want to control an ignorant, cloak every falsehood in a religious shroud."

In a moment of intensified emotions bedazzled by false heroism and alleged redemption, emotions proud of mujahedeen, Haqqani spoke about the *jihad's* need for money. Soon, a bearded Emirati man – he was standing next to Haqqani on the podium – came down to the hall, opened some bags and gave them to the female students to be passed among themselves after they put in them their donations for the holy *jihad*. The female students began removing their gold bracelets. Thus the first bag was filled, then the second, the third and the fourth followed. Some of those female students were from poor backgrounds; among them there were probably daughters of fathers who worked long to buy them such gold items, and here was an impostor using religion as a commodity to simply rob them of their jewelry, taking advantage of their kind-heartedness and religiosity. This reminded me of insects that sting and drug their victims to be able to suck their blood without the victims realizing what is going on. This was a cheap commercialization of religion. It is a pity that these jewelry pieces would be used, at most, to finance the purchase of arms, recruit the misguided people and supply the violence machine with more fuel.

We should not ignore that this incident took place inside a university that comprises faculty members, students and staff—all of whom were of good educational and intellectual level. What about other social institutions that had been unfortunate to attain a good level of education and knowledge? All these questions haunted me and made me restless during the events of that bizarre evening. I saw that it was my moral, professional and religious duty not to let the incident go unnoticed. Therefore, I went to the university administration and explained to some of its officials the seriousness of what had happened and the possible consequent problems. But it seemed that Haqqani was more persuasive to the university administration than I was, and that the Muslim Brotherhood supporters who lurked in the corridors of the university administration were so powerful that they did not leave a chance for my voice to reach where it should have been heard. It took many years for the university officials to realize that the concerns of this "humble man" [me] were not illusions, and that the open, accessible and paved road for Haqqani and his kind would eventually lead to the destabilization of the United Arab Emirates and the Gulf states and spread chaos there. This was a vicious plan, with

With Dr. Ali Al-Sharhan, former Minister of Education, during the ECSSR celebration of its 4th Anniversary, March 15, 1998

tightly linked rings, which would have grown bigger, and then facing it would require greater effort than we imagined.

Those who used to come to the university as guests and speakers were mostly among the likes of Jalaluddin Haqqani. They were treated like celebrities during their stays, in terms of attention paid to them and the glorification and admiration they greatly enjoyed from the administration, students and faculty. This, however, was not out of the blue, but rather the result of an enormous propaganda campaign carried out by the promoters of their ideas and persona through the Muslim Brotherhood propaganda machine from within the country. The Emirati Students' Union, an organization that was controlled by the Muslim Brotherhood, was spreading its propaganda considerably among students, and inducing large numbers of them over time, with the help of faculty members belonging to the group. In an educational lecture for female students colleges, a colleague of mine clashed with me because he insisted that all female students attending the lecture should be veiled and he prevented non-veiled ones from attending. I considered that a stark interference in personal liberty which should not have happened at the university.

Only one week before Haqqani's lecture, I witnessed an incident never seen in UAE University before, neither after—thank God. That was the attack of the university female students on the University General Requirements Unit (UGRU) and the destruction of some of the equipment and their attempt to destroy files. It went to the extent that they attacked and beat a member of the basic education faculty. The University General Requirements Unit, created during the academic year 1990/1991, was a step on the road to reforming university education and addressing the weakness that public high school graduates suffer from. The unit was headed by Dr. Ali Al-Sharhan, who later became Minister of Education.

The female students' revolution was the result of constant provocation by the Muslim Brotherhood inside and outside the university. The introduction of the University General Requirements Unit at the university meant that pre-university education could not fulfill students' preparation for the requirements of the university. Considering that education was dominated by the Muslim Brotherhood at that time, the establishment of the University General Requirements Unit was a sign of their utter failure and that this failure required an additional year of receiving classes. This meant hardship on the students and extra costs and expenses incurred to the education budget. That was also an indication that the UAE intends to take genuine reform steps in regard to education, based on identifying and treating deficiencies. This threatens the traditional stronghold of the forces of extremism, and that is why the Muslim Brotherhood incited the female students—the group used a plan repeatedly used by its followers, based on fabricating lies, agitating passions and creating chaos by using Islamic slogans that weep crocodile tears on religion and the assault it faces, as they claim.

Some English language teachers at the UGRU were foreigners, something that is normal and often educationally required as qualified native English speakers are the most capable of teaching the language. Some of the foreigners were also teaching computer skills and mathematics. Malicious rumblings had begun to spread that female and male "infidels" were teaching our daughters, and that they performed acts that contradict our customs and traditions. Baseless inci-

With H.E. Mohammed Ahmed Al-Murr, former Speaker of the Federal National Council (FNC), during the ECSSR celebration of its 20th Anniversary, December 11, 2014

dents were fabricated to support these allegations. There was a story written by the Emirati author Mohammed Al-Murr, former Speaker of the Federal National Council, titled *Saleh*, which was taught as part of the Arabic language curriculum. The extremists falsely claimed that the story offended the Prophet of God Saleh (pbuh). To ensure the spread of this falsehood, they depended on the idea that there would be no one to read and judge it. Some preachers in the mosques of Al-Ain, who were affiliated with the Muslim Brotherhood, started talking about the disasters of the University General Requirements Unit, the insult to the prophets and the Christianization of the university—just to stir emotions. Exploiting their young age, the female students were mobilized to the degree that hundreds of them attacked the faculty members and smashed up the premises.

This incident revealed to me the seriousness of incitement—anyone familiar with the calmness, goodness and respectfulness shown to teachers by Emirati female students realizes that their violent behavior was a serious indicator of the dangers of incitement. It also highlighted the dangers of allotting mosques to extremists. Among the other significant indicators in this regard was that the person who gave the sermon at Friday prayers against the UGRU was one of the members of the secret organization that planned to overthrow the UAE government. He was sentenced to 10 years in prison.

With H.E. Dr. Anwar Gargash, Minister of State for Foreign Affairs, on the sidelines of a conference titled "Gulf Security: A National Perspective II," United Kingdom, April 29, 1998

I was trying with a group of the faculty, who were appalled by the threat of extremism, to face misconceptions. It was not an easy battle. I remember a lecture His Excellency Dr. Anwar Gargash and myself gave in which we talked and presented our beliefs that opposed the ideas that the followers of political religious groups

With H.E. Dr. Anwar Gargash, Minister of State for Foreign Affairs, during the visit of an Arab delegation to ECSSR, October 5, 2003

were trying to instill. This caused a rise of tension and heated debate, to the point that a student attempted an attack on us. The group was inciting its followers against those who it believed had threatened its control in one of its strongholds, and falsely charging us with infidelity, blasphemy, Westernization and secularism—their aim was to tarnish our names and ruin our image. This tactic is ongoing to the present day.

As I have previously said, these groups do not hesitate to use violence because it is part of their eliminative nature. The violent verbal attack by students, which almost turned into a physical attack, was one of their attempts to intimidate us and enforce a morale siege on us. His Excellency Dr. Anwar Gargash and myself remained calm and kept on using persuasion and dialogue, raising the voice of reason above the demagogic voice. I told that particular stu-

Giving my lecture titled "The UAE's Demographic Imbalance: Current Situation and Solutions," at the UAE Armed Forces Officers Club, October 23, 2000

dent that it was a shame to even attempt an attack on his teachers.

Nearly three years after that incident, I met the same student at one of the old shopping centers in Dubai, in a music shop where he was buying some tapes. We exchanged a short talk and he revealed to me the truth about what was happening. I asked him why he did what he did in the lecture. He answered: "This was in university days, it is over now. I was a student adjusting to my surroundings and influenced by the ideas I received." The ideas he meant in his brief words were provocative, and the adjusting to the surrounding required him to take part in attacking those deemed a threat by the groups that commercialize religion.

In 1991, the university was an attractive target for political religious groups. There were 8,000 female students and 2,000 male students – about 10,000 students in total, all at a vulnerable young age. They received an intellectual preparation at elementary and secondary schools in accordance with the plan of those groups. These students would graduate and spread to various locations and sectors, taking with them their ideas. Some or many of them would join the lines of radical political religious groups and find themselves a majority in any given moment. The spread of ridiculous ideas reached the extent that one Arab professor had gone to the accommodation of female students to "expel demons" residing there through reading Holy

Quranic verses. I could not understand how the expulsion of demons or witches can be the prevailing idea in an academic institution, how the major interests of a student of economics, engineering or computer studies revolve around such ideas, or how students spend most of their

At a symposium titled "Future of the Press in the Age of Multimedia," January 19, 2003

time following issues such as the torments of the grave or the proper ways of defecating in the "open" at a time when there were no longer any "open" [lavatories]; rather, the restrooms nowadays compete with living rooms in term of luxury.

I supposed that their minds should be preoccupied with knowledge, as this is the essence of the religion that mandated us to seek knowledge in the farthest reaches of the globe. Students should have been busy dealing with the latest engineering achievements, scientific inventions, technological developments and economic theories, and respecting scientific methodologies. I considered preoccupation with these trivial issues as a deviation that had to be addressed. In fact, this was not only the atmosphere in UAE University, there was a similar infiltration, slightly different in degree but not in type, happening in almost all Arab societies and universities in the early 1990s.

My career in university teaching lasted for seven years. In the first four years, I was teaching at UAE University and in Guided Learning Centers, and in the last three years, I taught only at Guided Learning Centers because my workload and the establishment of the Emirates Center for Strategic Studies and Research in Abu Dhabi, in addition to other tasks that steadily

With H.H. Sheikh Abdullah bin Zayed Al Nahyan, UAE Minister of Foreign Affairs and International Cooperation, (His Highness was a student at the Political Science Department then) with some of his colleague students, and some faculty members of that department, UAE University, in 1991

increased during that period, did not give me a chance to teach university students in Al-Ain on a regular basis.

I taught varied classes during those seven years at UAE University, including: Scientific Research Methodology (1990/1991); Arab Political Systems (1991/1992); the Muslim World (1991/1992 and 1992/1993); a seminar on Latin America (1991/1992); a seminar on the Middle East Policies (1991/1992); a seminar on the United States of America and Europe (1992/1993); and a course on Contemporary International Issues (1995/1996 and 1996/1997). Among the distinguished students whom I remember teaching are His Highness Sheikh Diab bin Zayed Al Nahyan, His Highness Sheikh Abdullah bin Zayed Al Nahyan, H.E. Ahmad Mohamed Al-Humairi and Mr. Abdulla Al-Rostamani.

As a member in the committee in charge of developing study courses in UAE University, I created two new courses I believed that the Department needed. First, a course on Theories of Political Change, which I taught in the academic year 1993/1994, and the second was a course on research methodologies in political science, which I taught continuously for four academic years in the same college, starting from the academic year 1991/1992. I received a letter of appreciation from His Excellency Sheikh Nahyan bin Mubarak Al Nahyan, the Minister of Higher Education and President of the University (at that time), for introducing those two classes, and for the development I added to the course of the Muslim World.

Contemporary Islamic Issues, book cover. This book was taught to the students of UAE University

What I remember of the Muslim World course, one of the general education courses, is that I was teaching at the women's campus, and that the lecture hall seated more than 200 female students; a large number in the scale of UAE University. I was teaching the same class at the men's campus, a drive of almost 15 minutes away. Therefore, I had to move quickly to reach the building and enter the lecture halls of the male students on time. The lectures of the majority of the faculty were divided between male and female students, and rapid movement between the two campuses was indispensable. Teaching is not without funny incidents, of course. In one of my lectures, when I was reading the names of the female students, I found a student named *Tamatem* [tomatoes]. It was the first time I came across such a name, and I thought I read it wrong, but I discovered that it was correct and it was a common name among the girls of a certain tribe in the UAE. I conducted a research later on names as a social phenomenon, and attained results worthy of consideration.

However, not all incidents were funny, as some needed confrontation and challenge. This was the case in the "Muslim World Problems" compulsory course, which I taught for six consecutive years, from the time I joined the university in 1990 until the year in before I stopped teaching. This course caused a fierce battle I had to fight with the movements of political Islam at the University. The students were studying a book titled *Contemporary Islamic Issues* prepared by a group of colleagues. The book included direct propaganda about the ideas of political Islam, glorified its groups and parties, and instigated against rational and moderate trends, add to that its low academic value and abandonment of all the rules that should govern the process of university teaching. The book stirred anger in me to the point that it made me say to my students: "Throw this book in the trash can." I developed an alternative curriculum based on the lectures that I gave them and from reading chapters and parts of specific books I chose from the university's library.

To tell your students to "throw a book in the trash can" seems like an exaggerated reaction for those who are not familiar with the case and have not read the book. However, reading a few paragraphs into it justified my anger. The first pages of the book contain a provocative perception of the relations between countries; Chapter One, titled "Conflict between Islam and Colonialism," includes the following paragraph: "Although the majority of Muslim countries gained independence, the issue of the conflict between Islam and colonialism has not necessarily ended as the collapse of the traditional colonialism has paved the way for new types of modern colonialism, political, economic and cultural. Thus, the main idea of this chapter is based on the premise that conflict between Islam and the colonial powers is still present, based on the Quranic verse [Never will the Jews nor the Christians be pleased with you (O Muhammad) till you follow their religion]" (Hassan Al-Alkim et al., Contemporary Islamic Issues, 1990, p. 7).

Such erroneous perception of the idea of relations between the countries means that there is a continuous sacred religious war that must not stop, and that all states in the world are targeting our religion, Islam, and they want to force us to abandon it. Therefore, we are enemies of all and all are our enemies. One can imagine that a student of political science, who could become a diplomat, academic, media professional or minister, holds such a thought about the world.

In Chapter Two, which deals with the Ottoman Empire, the author, a citizen of another Arab country, goes against all the rules of logic and science when he describes the empire by writing "We should say that it [Ottoman Empire] is a *mujahed* country because its goals are noble and linked to the holy *jihad*. The title of *ghazi* [conqueror] was bestowed on Ottoman rulers and Sultans—it is one of the highest titles in content and meaning, as it means the *mujahed* and fighter serve the cause of God. It is a linguistic usage taken from the first phase of the era of Islam, when the battles of the Prophet Muhammad (pbuh), against the enemies of Islam, the infidels, were known as Islamic *ghazwat* [incursions]," (Hassan Al-Alkim et al., p. 47). The strange thing is that the author of this chapter was not affiliated with political Islamic groups or close to them, but out of an opportunistic sense, he was writing what he deemed as catering to the desire of the dominant movements at the university, and what helps him achieve his objectives and serves his approaches and ideas.

While the above-mentioned professor was intellectually far from political Islam, another female professor, from an Arab-African country, was involved with a political Islamic organization and presented extremist thoughts. She believes that scholarships abroad promote colonial ideas, as she wrote in her chapter: "Colonialism affected Muslim students who were sent to study in Western countries. This was achieved through spreading the secular teachings that they carried with them after they returned to their home country," (Hassan Al-Alkim et al., p. 73).

The dangerous aspect in this book also was that it revealed the admiration the political Islamic movements had of the Iranian Revolution, although the revolution had disclosed hostility to Arabs, sectarian extremism and national arrogance. The chapter "Islamic Awakening in the 20th Century" allocated a section on the Iranian Revolution, portraying it as a positive development and a great success. The vast financial resources of the Shiite political Islam were among the reasons for that admiration, as the book notes: "Shiism frees clerics from political power, thus making them financially independent, as they rely on their financial resources on al-Khums [literally one fifth of gain] and the support of private institutions, especially the bazaar. The men of the bazaar prefer the clergy to secular leaders because the Islamic system respects trade and encourages it, as the holy verse says [Allah has permitted trading and forbidden Riba (usury),] and it [the Islamic system] respects the ownership of the individual within the limits of the Islamic law, (Hassan Al-Alkim et al., pp. 133–135).

Perhaps that book represents an important document on the schemes of political religious groups aimed at brainwashing college students, manipulating their awareness, wrecking scientific foundations and preventing any chance for objectivity or methodological analysis based on sound principles. The ideas presented in that book were just an extension of what was present at primary, elementary and secondary schools—the domination of the ideas of the regressive movements and the vast spread of their elements.

Another phenomenon that bothered me at the university was academic plagiarism. Some faculty members used to plagiarize research papers and publish them in an incredibly daring way. The plagiarists kept silent about the extremists because they could expose them easily. For example, one faculty member published a book that I had read and found to be a literal copy of Samuel Huntington's book *Political Order in Changing Societies*, published in 1968, without including any references or notes referring to the source. Certain parties within the university's administration have tried to categorize us as either extremists or plagiarists, but they failed. I understood the game as well as other faculty members who undertook the mission to counter negative phenomena.

With Dr. Mohammed Al-Mahmoud, professor of political science at UAE University in a visit by the University's Political Science Association delegation to the ECSSR, May 1, 1995

Emiratization* of the teaching positions at the university was one of the battles that we had fought in that period. Out of our intense enthusiasm, we called it "liberating the university from the non-national colonialism." I, with a large group of Emirati faculty, were strongly pushing in that direction. Today, I cannot judge whether what we were doing was wrong or right, or whether our actions were sound or not. I do not want to judge, but that was our main preoccupation. The university administration did not differ with us about the importance of Emiratization, but it had the hope that Emiratization would happen gradually, whereas my colleagues and I – in the dash of youth – wanted it promptly.

Our desire to Emiratize teaching positions was not driven by any hatred for the non-Emirati faculty members. We had a lot of respect for many of them and we appreciated their effort. Moreover, our objective was not to hire incompetent Emiratis, or fill positions with Emiratis just because they were nationals; competency was rather our primary prerequisite. We tried to promote the outstanding Emiratis and push their names to the forefront. At that time, there were about 150 Emiratis with doctorates whose talents we wished to use at the university, and many lectures, seminars and activities that we used to hold were designed to prove to the university administration that Emiratis

---

* Emiratization, an initiative launched by the UAE government to employ Emiratis in the public and private sectors to increase the contribution Emiratis make to the economy.

have exceptional capabilities. So, we used to invite the excellent Emiratis and give them opportunities to show that. I believe that our effort was successful, and that the seeds of Emiratizing the teaching positions were sown during that period and that they yielded results very quickly, as most of the faculty members in many disciplines are now Emiratis.

Presenting a gift to Dr. Mohammed Al-Mahmoud, professor of political science at UAE University in a visit by a delegation from the University's Political Science Association to the ECSSR, May 1, 1995

One thing that preoccupied me and much of the faculty was the issue of teaching quota hours. Our quota hours were about 15 hours a week, maybe up to 18 hours, divided between separate buildings for male and female students. This meant traveling for between three to three and a half hours a day, in addition to office hours, and tasks associated with membership of committees and administrative works, preparation of exams, etc. The university was based on teaching, not scholarly research, which I think should be its most important function. While foreign universities offer full-time jobs, as I explained earlier, and provide their faculty with suitable environment for academic achievement, we had been swamped with the exhausting teaching and administrative load. For my part, there were many voluntary cultural activities that I was doing, which meant even greater burdens.

The irony was that promotions were often dependent on publishing academic research in English, in academic refereed journals, while the language of instruction at the university was Arabic—it was a puzzling contradiction. Nonetheless, publishing in English was not a problem for me, as I was used to writing and publishing in that language since I received my master's degree, and I fully realized its role in developing researchers' capabilities.

But it was a problem for other Emirati faculty members who graduated from Arab universities. So among their demands was reducing the teaching quota so they would have time to do research and consequently get promoted, in addition to expanding the opportunities for research published in Arabic to be accepted for promotions.

Publishing in Arabic faced another problem—the number of refereed journals in Arabic was very low, barely reaching 20 in total. In contrast, the number of refereed journals in

At the ECSSR 3rd Annual Conference titled "The Impact of the Information and Communication Revolution on Society and State in the Arab World," January 4, 1997

English extended up to 20,000 journals. Expatriate faculty members were spending a short period of time at UAE University, as they would return to universities that provided them with research opportunities. Thus, the heavy teaching load they were exposed to at UAE University would be temporary. Emirati faculty members, on the other hand, continued to be subject to these pressures throughout their university teaching span, which narrowed down their promotion options and opportunities. Interestingly, at the ECSSR 6th Annual Education Conference in October 2015, I listened to a former UAE University faculty member who considered heavy teaching load an impediment to current academic research—this was 25 years after the time we first raised this problem. She added that after she left the university, she produced many books and research papers.

I believe I maintained the successful relationship I formed with my students through teaching at the University of Wisconsin—this was evident in their evaluation of my teaching, as I explained in the previous chapter. Teaching in Arabic was easier and simpler, of course. I think one important element for my success was my passion for teaching. I considered it neither an obligation nor a job to earn a living. Rather, I enjoyed it. Moreover, at UAE University, I believed more in the concept of the mission and role of education in building one's personality—this is normal considering that I believe that everything I do has an impact on students who will become future leaders in my country. This increased my enthusiasm and desire to leave a positive impact on the minds of students.

Teaching technologies were not as sophisticated as today; traditional means were mostly used. However, instead of using textbooks included in the curriculum, I chose good chapters and studies by leading Arab and foreign professors that students could find at the library. I used to introduce them to the views of various schools and trends in each issue, rather than just one closed opinion, the way political religious movements were teaching. My objective was to entrench the idea that there were diverse, and sometimes conflicting, views and approaches toward a same topic, and that it is necessary for us to be open to such diverse approaches and to examine and compare them. This helps us find the best approach or even lead us to create a new one. University education does not solely comprise of specific points that we hear, memorize and reproduce onto exam sheets at the end of the semester. Either way, I made sure to deliver information in the most convenient way and to use many examples that were neither ambiguous nor complex, ensuring that all my students absorbed what I said.

My evaluation of students' exams was precise; those who deserved to, passed the exam. I was also very strict about cheating—I had zero tolerance for it. In an exam I was supervising once, I caught a student cheating, and I threw him out. Moreover, I did not allow any student to enter the class after me. I also used to start the lecture exactly on time. In case a student entered after that, I used to stop the lecture and ask them to quietly leave.

Every student always got the exact grade he deserved, without the slightest appeasement and regardless of their social status. To my students, that was an indication that there was no room for appeasement or carelessness, and that if other colleagues appease a student for a specific reason, I was not one of them. I think this helped them understand the need to respect university ethics, laws and equality for all—this is part of building a disciplined character capable of achieving success.

Besides teaching, there was the important experience I gained through the "Political Society" created by students of the Department of Political Science at UAE University, which was headed by some colleagues. I had the honor to head it in 1992. The Society gave me direct contact with its student members, many of whom were very aware and aspired for knowledge. The distinctive aspect about the "Political Society" was the several events and activities it carried out, including numerous lectures in which many colleagues from the Department of Political Science and the College of Humanities and Social Sciences from UAE University and elsewhere, had lectured. Those lectures provided opportunities for open and fruitful discussions and dialogue. Female students were always attending these events in large numbers.

My years of teaching at UAE University were rich in activities, both in terms of academic research and engagement in ideological and political education effort, which were important at a time that was witnessing changes, both in the world and the Arab region and in the wake of the Kuwait liberation war. In regard to the academic activity, I traveled in the summer of 1992 (from June 22 to August 2, 1992) as a visiting faculty, to the University of Wisconsin, where I taught a course titled "Political Systems in the Middle East and North Africa." This meant that I taught continuously for almost 11 months, as there was no way to stop. In the previous academic year (1990/1991), I spent the summer teaching what is known as "summer training" at UAE University, and I oversaw the Department of Political Science as well. At the same time, I supervised the training of male and female students at the UAE Ministry of Foreign Affairs and the Ruler's Court in Al-Ain.

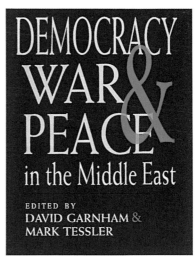

The book cover:*Democracy, War and Peace in the Middle East*, 1995

During those years, I published a number of research papers, including a joint research with Dr. Shamlan Youssef Al-Issa, titled "Approaches of UAE University Students toward the Gulf Crisis," published in 1991 in the refereed *Journal of Social Sciences* published by Kuwait University. I also published a research in English titled "Iraqi Invasion of Kuwait and the UAE's Policy Trends" in the *Journal of South Asian and Middle Eastern Studies* in the Winter of 1994. Moreover, with Prof. Mark Tessler, I co-authored a chapter in a book published in English in 1994, titled *Israel at a Crossroads*. This chapter included a scholarly reading about the results of a survey on "Will the Arab Public Accept Peace with Israel?" I also prepared a study to participate in a scholarly conference titled "Democracy, War and Peace in the Middle East," held jointly by the University of Wisconsin/Marquette University and the Center for International Studies in 1992. The research was published in a book in English titled *Democracy, War and Peace in the Middle East* in 1995.

Furthermore, I participated in conferences in the United States of America held by the Council on Foreign Relations (January 1992); the American Political Science Association (September 1992) and the Fletcher School of Law and Diplomacy, in conjunction with the US Naval Operations Command and the US Institute for Foreign Policy (November 1992). These conferences addressed topics on the foreign policy of the GCC states, peace in the Middle East, and the strategic role of naval forces in the present and future. I also participated in a conference held in Paris on the history of the Arabian Gulf. These research participations put me in the heart of the global policymaking process, allowed me to understand the dimensions of the transformations happening in the world, and to follow up on the positions of the stakeholders. Therefore, I sought to make the ECSSR's scholarly conferences varied and abundant, consisting of participants that were the most prominent politicians, opinion leaders, researchers and experts from all around the globe. This allowed all concerned segments of society to avail of such communication with the ideas and opinions raised in the world in a timely manner, and made them open up to broader prospects of thinking and understanding.

My activities inside the UAE were not lesser than the ones abroad, evidently. I participated in dozens of educational seminars in various UAE emirates. They revolved around the Arab-Israeli peace process; inter-GCC relations; GCC relations with the Arab world and with world powers in post-Kuwait liberation period; the new world order that was forming; and security and social challenges. I also participated in conferences and wrote articles in local newspapers. I remember an article I had written titled "A Thesis on the Issue of Democracy," published on November 10, 1991. It consisted of a prediction I had anticipated regarding the future of the Arab world; 20 years later, my prediction had materialized in an event that is now known as the "Arab Spring." In that article, I wrote that "the process of transition to democracy is linked to political stability. Any transition under the prevailing political and social climate may in some cases lead to the collapse of the entire political system, especially if it was not carried out through a comprehensive and gradual change in the prevailing cultural, economic and social values." This later happened in Iraq, as well as in other Arab countries.

Community service was part of the faculty members' work of at UAE University—a positive task there. That period involved participation in the

With H.H. Sheikh Mohamed bin Zayed Al Nahyan, Crown Prince of Abu Dhabi and Deputy Supreme Commander of the UAE Armed Forces (may God protect him), during a visit to Albania, May 22, 1997

support of public institutions that were in need of academic and research support. I prepared a study, in 1991, for the Federal National Council on the notion of democracy and mechanisms of transition. I also participated in a project to develop a government education policy for the UAE Ministry of Education, as part of an ad hoc committee in charge of national identity, and another one in charge of the UAE foreign relations. Moreover, I participated with a team from the UAE Ministry of Foreign Affairs for the formal negotiations between the United Arab Emirates and Iran on the latter's occupation of the three UAE Islands – Abu Musa and the Greater and Lesser Tunbs – since November 29, 1971. All of those issues had become part of my personal interest in the research areas as well as the interests of the ECSSR, which covered them in depth through many events and publications.

Among the important activities that later left an impact on me was heading the Higher Media Committee at the First International Defence Exhibition and Conference (IDEX), in February 1993. I was honored then to work with a group of qualified officers from the UAE Armed Forces, including Major General Ateeq Jumaa Al-Hameli, who later became Commander of the UAE Air Force and Defense; Major General Suhail Shaheen Al-Marar,

With H.H. Sheikh Mohammed bin Rashid Al Maktoum, Vice President and Prime Minister of the UAE and Ruler of Dubai (may God protect him); H.H. Sheikh Mohamed bin Zayed Al Nahyan, Crown Prince of Abu Dhabi and Deputy Supreme Commander of the UAE Armed Forces (may God protect him), and H.H. Sheikh Abdullah bin Zayed Al Nahyan, Minister of Foreign Affairs and International Cooperation, at IDEX, March 19, 1995

who became Commander of the UAE Naval Forces; Major General Obaid Al-Hiri Al-Ketbi, current UAE Ambassador to Australia and former Deputy Commander-in-Chief of Abu Dhabi Police. His Highness Sheikh Mohamed bin Zayed Al Nahyan (may God protect him) granted us the opportunity to work in the Media Committee of the first edition of the exhibition because His Highness fully and clearly realized early on the importance of holding IDEX on UAE soil, the importance of media and the political, economic, military and strategic benefits the success of the exhibition would imply.

We worked continuously day and night for about a month to make the exhibition appear to the world at its best. On the sidelines of the exhibition, the "First Military Communications Conference" was held under the auspices of His Highness Sheikh Mohamed bin Zayed Al Nahyan. Mikhail Kalashnikov, the inventor of the rifle named after him, also participated. Moreover, the Russian S-300 missile defense system was displayed for the first time—it is still considered an important weapon. The UAE Armed Forces also struck a number of important deals. IDEX needed great effort to reach the world appropriately, through the Media Committee, despite no known work rules to follow. Since this was the first edition of IDEX, our mission was to start everything from scratch—a difficult process.

This villa was the headquarters of the ECSSR, at its inception in March 1994

We used to hold a daily press conference in both English and Arabic, prepare press briefings about the activities of the exhibition, and answer questions from journalists and local, Arab and international media, around the clock. When I look at IDEX now, after 23 years during which it entrenched its prestigious name, success and global reputation, I feel proud to be part of the team of the first edition. It was my colleagues and I – some of whom have retired while others are still working – who shouldered magnificent national tasks and did our utmost during those early days.

There were some positions I filled while teaching at the University, such as Deputy Dean for Postgraduate Studies, Deputy Vice Chancellor for Academic and Educational Affairs (in charge of Academic Research) and Head of Research and Administrative, Financial and Economic Consultations Division. In reality, however, those positions were neither real nor functional; rather, they aimed at keeping me silent and distracting me from the battles I was relentlessly fighting with the political religious movements. Despite the sparkly title of these positions, and their link to academic research that appeals to my interest, they were nothing more than "desk and chair."

The ECSSR premises

Emirates Center for Strategic Studies and Research: An Icon of Success

At the beginning of the academic year 1993/1994, I was seconded from the University to work in the Armed Forces. I was tasked with a national mission that is still going—the establishment of the ECSSR. This scholarly research institution has become one of the most successful and influential institutions in the world. The ECSSR made its way toward a high regional and global position, and was the catalyst for the accomplishment of important national tasks.

The ECSSR started work in 1994. It is hard to constrain the ECSSR's achievements and influence in a short chapter in a book—in order for its achievements to be highlighted, more space is needed. I believe what has been accomplished during 23 years has been enormous quantitatively and of the highest possible standards, qualitatively.

In the beehive-like, eight-floor building and its annexes, several sections and departments are working simultaneously. Handpicked researchers work on the preparation of policy studies and papers on political, economic and social topics, which are then submitted to the decision makers. They are also involved in research projects, some of which are presented to the public. Moreover, editors, who have experience in research and media, prepare newsletters and publications, including important political and economic analyses that are either dedicated to the public or to decision makers. Newspapers and news agencies quote the editorials of ECSSR's newsletters targeting the public. There is also a team of news monitors with high research experience. They monitor all international satellite channels and news agencies in a room equipped with modern equipment and technologies, to inform a group of decision makers and senior officials in the UAE of all the important news of the moment, via an SMS system designed specifically for this purpose. Work in the monitoring room is 24/7, on a shift basis.

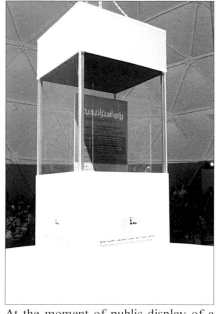

At the moment of public display of a mockup of the scholarly refereed periodical *Strategic Visions* during its launching ceremony, December 12, 2012

With Dr. Suha Taji-Farouki from the Center for Middle Eastern Studies, UK, during her visit to the ECSSR, December 27, 1998

Alongside the monitoring team is the team of *Aafaq Al-Mustaqbal*, an Arabic quarterly journal that consists of topics, analyses and visions combining in-depth political, economic and social content that is easily understood and which addresses a wide audience interested in knowledge. Meanwhile, the audience of Arab researchers and academics enjoys the Arabic quarterly

Former President of the French Republic, Nicolas Sarkozy, during his lecture "The World Today: A Conversation with Nicolas Sarkozy," at ECSSR, January 13, 2016

journal, *Strategic Visions*. Launched in December 2012, it is considered the most important refereed Arab periodical of its kind. The Publications Department, where this scholarly periodical is issued, includes a team of editors specialized in editing academic studies, as well as translators and proofreaders, who work to supplement the Arabic library with a set of scholarly Arabic and English books and series characterized by adherence to the highest-known standards in the world in the field of scholarly publishing, both in terms of form and content. Along their side, the distribution team ensures that these important publications reach their targeted audiences all over the world, and that they get showcased at significant local, regional and international book fairs and events, to ensure maximum benefits.

On another quiet floor in the ECSSR building, a number of staff with research capabilities, race ceaselessly to prepare events, including conferences, symposia, workshops, lectures, seminars and discussion panels held by the ECSSR, and to host activities of other entities seeking to benefit from

At the graduation ceremony of the 3ʳᵈ Batch of the Scientific Research Diploma students, at ECSSR, August 13, 2002

the sizable capabilities of the Center in preparing and organizing research meetings. The Public Relations team, among other tasks, is in charge of contacting the participants in these events, including senior politicians, officials, experts, academics and military officers from all over the world. The team also takes care of all travel details of those participants, to and from the UAE, including finalizing all relevant procedures, receiving guests, arranging their accommodation and accompanying them in their every move, meticulously and in full alertness most of the day.

Another team with research background conducts polls and field studies. Some support studies of other research departments in the ECSSR; some for the benefit of ministries, institutions and entities in the government aspiring to improve their performance; and others are carried out for decision makers. The team, also, includes fieldwork groups, trained to complete these continuous activities. While this

With US diplomat Mark Brzezinski during the visit of a delegation from the US College of National Defense to ECSSR, October 25, 2003

team monitors the public opinion, other colleagues may be attending training halls, joining one of the continuous courses organized by the ECSSR. To raise the staff efficiency, and to develop their skills and performance, diploma programs are offered with carefully devised curricula that have been set in

With H.H. Sheikh Hamed bin Zayed Al Nahyan, Chairman of the Crown Prince Court of Abu Dhabi, during his visit to the UAE Federation Library, at the ECSSR, November 24, 2015

accordance with the highest practical and scientific standards. An ECSSR employee may be a trainee today and a trainer tomorrow—each employee has something to offer, and each employee has something to learn as well.

The "UAE Federation Library," laid over three elegant floors, is one of the most important and specialized libraries in both the UAE and the region, in the fields of politics, economics, strategy, management, history,

UAE Federation Library, at ECSSR, March 24, 2016

With a member of the British Parliament delegation during a visit to the ECSSR, April 27, 1999

At the 28th Cairo International Book Fair, February 24, 1995

information science and military science. It contains more than half a million titles in Arabic and English, in addition to sets of private documents, official reports, rare books and electronic databases. It is very rare for a book to be released in the world, within the Center's field of interest, without the UAE Federation Library acquiring a copy of it within days from its release. In a peaceful atmosphere that parallels the calmness of places of worship, visitors to the Library receive services unavailable at any other similar place, in terms of supporting their research projects.

This effort is supported, and greatly facilitated, by a team of information technology professionals. They provide advanced technology services and manage internal and external e-networks aimed at keeping the flow and exchange of material between relevant parties. They work within a

Presenting a gift to the researcher Matthias Sailer, of the German Institute for International and Security Affairs, on the sidelines of his visit to the Center, November 3, 2015

With His Royal Highness Prince Turki Al-Faisal bin Abdulaziz Al Saud, Chairman of the Board of King Faisal Center for Islamic Research and Studies in KSA, during the ECSSR 12th Annual Conference titled "Arabian Gulf Security: Internal and External Challenges," March 5, 2007

strict framework of privacy due to the secrecy and sensitivity of much of the information, recommendations and ideas involved.

The recruitment process for all the departments and sections at the ECSSR is carried out by a qualified recruitment team that selects the best talent and experts from among thousands of applicants who apply to work at the Center from all over the world. Moreover, all units and departments in the Center are served by a developed and effective administrative system, which facilitates providing these units and departments with their requirements.

Transmitting the image of the Center's effort to the world is done through the ECSSR's website. It is managed by a small, yet highly efficient, editorial and technical team who updates the Center's information and data, both in Arabic and English and around the clock. It also follows up on the relentless activities of all the ECSSR's departments and sections, and publishes political and economic analyses of current events written by the team's editors as well as a number of Emirati, Arab and foreign writers and analysts.

During the meeting of the Scientific Advisory Council of the Publications Department, ECSSR, March 15, 2015

The vast majority of the Center's employees have a research background. Even if their job title does not refer to research explicitly, due to the nature of the work, knowledge of research is required. For example, employees of the Conferences Department, even those whose job is organizational, must have this insight. Editors of the media bulletins also write from a research perspective; and editors of ECSSR books and series have the ability to evaluate and revise scholarly studies. Moreover, the Library staff, who often deal with researchers, must have a background in research knowledge as it makes it easier for them to help the Library visitors.

Talking about high standards may seem easy, yet applying them is not. I can give an example of the procedures of publishing a study or a book by the ECSSR, which lies within the jurisdiction of the Publications Department. The first step begins with the department's specialized editors, who possess a research background, receiving a study or research, either in Arabic or English, by a writer in a digital format. The editors then give the material a preliminary reading to make sure it meets the required scholarly standards. They have the authority to reject the work at the first stage, if they deem it not up to the required level. If the work is approved, it goes to the next stage, to be refereed.

With the Pakistani diplomat Akram Zaki during the workshop titled "United Arab Emirates-Pakistan Relations," organized by ECSSR, March 30, 1996

The Publications Department has a network of scholarly referees comprising of the most prominent professors and experts in the Arab world, whose fields of specialties are in line with that of the ECSSR, in addition to a number of hand-picked foreign professors for cases that require their effort. After passing the initial evaluation, the work is sent to three professors who have lengthy experience in research and academic achievement in the same field. Referees have three choices: approving the work, rejecting it, or approving it conditionally (pending for changes to be carried out). Each referee writes a report on the research detailing a scholarly opinion about it, noting its

With Dr. Giacomo Luciani, Prof. at the Graduate Institute of International and Development Studies, Geneva, during a press conference on a symposium titled "The Future Relations Between the GCC and the EU" held at ECSSR, May 22, 2002

methodology, language and strengths and weaknesses. This evaluation grants the researcher a helpful and profound reading of the work, as it helps them to develop their skills. In most of the research that get approved, the referees suggest certain changes the researcher is required to make in order to pass the second step on the road to approval. After the required changes are made and approved by the referee, the book or research enters another process; it gets edited by the editors of the Publications Department, at the ECSSR.

With the Iraqi academic Professor Adel Al Kayyar, visiting the ECSSR with a French delegation, February 22, 1997

Presenting a gift to Professor Giacomo Luciani, Prof. at the Graduate Institute of International and Development Studies, Geneva, on the sidelines of a symposium titled "The Future Relations Between the GCC and the EU," organized by ECSSR, May 22, 2002

After editing, the book/ research is handed over to the Proofreading section, where proofreaders make sure the language is fully intact, in Arabic and in English, in terms of grammar, syntax, structure etc. The proofreaders consult the editors to clarify any ambiguity of sentences, structures or information they deem necessary to revise, in order to ensure "zero mistakes," which is everyone's slogan. Then, the book is sent to the Desktop Publishing section for cover design and page layout in accordance with the highest meticulous standards. At all stages, there are people tasked with reviewing the work in terms of editing, proofreading and layout, to be

During a conference titled "Gulf Security: A National Perspective I," Abu Dhabi, April 5, 1997

eventually handed over to a special committee tasked with reviewing all of its aspects and submitting their feedback, if necessary, to ensure the material comes out at its best. Such methodology had established what could be considered an editorial and linguistic school in the ECSSR

With H.H. Sheikh Abdullah bin Zayed Al Nayhan, Minister of Foreign Affairs and International Cooperation (Minister of Information and Culture then); the late Staff Major General Hayai Juma Al-Hamili; and part of the audience at the ECSSR 5th Annual Conference titled "2000: The Making of the Future," October 9, 1999

publications, characterized with accuracy, correctness, clarity and smooth flow, along with cohesion. Finally, the author finds that his work became publicized with an added value resulting from such process. Moreover, the author's knowledge of the evaluation of their work by the referees is absolutely another added value.

Furthermore, the research papers presented at various conferences and many symposia, organized by the ECSSR, are published in dedicated books. Some of these research papers are in Arabic and some in English.

Thus, translation is carried out between both languages to create a version in Arabic and another in English, thereby documenting the proceedings of the conferences and symposia. This enriches the Arabic library and provides – through the English version – international readers with a picture of the scholarly and research activities the Arab world is witnessing. This also acquaints them with views that serve Arab interests.

Signing a research cooperation agreement with the Bahrain Center for Strategic, International and Energy Studies (DERASAT) during my visit to the Kingdom of Bahrain, March 26, 2015

This process has some other aspects that complement the features of success. From the moment the Publications Department starts its work, it becomes clear that there is no room for lessening or abandoning such standards, regardless of the pressures. It is not part of the ECSSR cul-

During the lecture "The World Today: A Conversation with Nicolas Sarkozy," delivered by Nicolas Sarkozy, former President of the French Republic, at the ECSSR, January 13, 2016

ture for somebody to call me and request publishing their research. Even if someone did that, they know that my immediate action would be to refer the work to the concerned department to subject it to the applicable procedures. Moreover, unless the work is worth publishing, it will not be published, even if I was the one who sent it. It became known that there is no mediation or compromise regarding the established standards.

German Chancellor Angela Merkel, giving a lecture titled "Challenges for European Foreign Policy," at the ECSSR, February 5, 2007

Hence, those who tried to use such methods have stopped. Had mediation or appeasement been used in our work, the lifespan of our publications would have been too short.

The generous financial reward, for authors and referees alike, is also part of this system. It is necessary to support scholarly research and to provide those in charge, referees and authors, with an incentive to continue their work as much as possible, and to make them realize that quality work, dedication and effort they exert is not wasted. If we want to motivate these researchers and not lose their thoughts and effort, we should offer them, as much as possible, a reward that matches their effort. I want to push them away from taking the easy way out, and to tell them that there are people who respect and appreciate your output, financially as well as morally.

His Majesty King Abdullah II bin Al-Hussein of Jordan, delivering the keynote address at the 6th Annual Conference titled "Leadership and Administration in the Age of Information Technology," organized by the ECSSR, November 5, 2000

I believe the ECSSR's success is primarily due to the quality of its employees. I am proud that anyone who witnessed the first stages of our work recalls how I used to follow every detail and every small step, directing, discussing, comparing and encouraging the employees to mobilize their energics. Remarkably, behind what seems easy today, lie difficult experiences in the early years. Each experience added something new in terms of approving the steps and procedures that proved successful to make them an adopted tradition, and equally learning from mistakes or forms of failure discovered due to a rigorous assessment system, and then avoiding them. A few days ago, a former employee from the Conferences Department reminded me of the early conferences that we had organized. We had stayed up past 2:00 am and I was instructing them how to arrange tissue paper boxes on the tables, neatly and appropriately. This was to ensure that the conference that was convening the morning of would be arranged in the best way possible.

With Kuwaiti academic Dr. Mohammad Al Rumaihi; the late Hisham Nazer, former Saudi Arabia's Oil Minister and ambassador Hussain Abdullatif, former Ambassador of the Sultanate of Oman to the United Kingdom, on the sidelines of a conference titled "Gulf Security: A National Perspective II" held in the UK, April 29, 1998

During the proceedings of a conference titled "Gulf Security: A National Perspective II" held in the United Kingdom, April 29, 1998

Such a system ensured work traditions to stabilize after years of experience, thus enabling anyone tasked with a mission to execute it easily. This is exactly what I sought to achieve ever since I got acquainted with the nature of work in the United States of America, as I had previously explained in my talk about the health system there, which impressed me when I attended the birth of my son, Khaled. It is a system in which everyone engages easily and does not leave a thing to chance, randomness or variation of the levels or abilities of the individuals.

In every department, there is an integrated system now. Any person joining this system, regardless of their position, will find that they are playing their role easily. For instance, on the same day I was writing these lines, a conference was taking place at the Center, and the Deputy Director concerned was

With Philip Ruddock, the former Australian Minister for Immigration and Multicultural Affairs during the lecture "Australia's Experience in Managing its Immigration Program and its Linkages to the Labor Market" at ECSSR, October 1, 1996

absent, along with another Deputy Director, and the Head of the Conferences Department had just started this new position a few days earlier. However, everything went as planned. Why? Because there is a precise and rigorous system established since the 1990s. Systems are the strongest—they are able to accommodate everyone, and they do not eliminate individual skills or efficiencies. They do not, however, make success dependent or based on a particular person. Systems are what I tried to build in the ECSSR to make success sustainable.

I was working at all the departments of the ECSSR at the same time. I could be discussing with the Media Department employees, who were very few at that time, all the details, identify priorities, review carefully all the material in terms of form and content, the pattern they should take, the most appropriate size, and the nature of the audience they are targeting. Then, I commit myself to what had been approved until the basics of the system are set in place. A similar process was happening in developing mechanisms for the purchase of books for the UAE Federation Library, furnishing it and choosing its appropriate technologies. Moreover, the same occurred for every conference, symposium and workshop—to the extent of taking care of lighting in a hall, the spaces between the lines of a newsletter and the colors and designs of the covers of our publications.

The Yemeni War of 1994: Causes and Consequences in English and Arabic, which I participated in its compiling and editing in 1995

After years of hard work, the system stabilized in all of the Center's departments and sections. The ECSSR's "DNA" was implanted in every employee—you can see it in the work of the receptionist; in the way name-cards are issued for our conferences' guests; and in the way ECSSR operators answer telephone calls. You will find that same "DNA" in a study submitted to decision makers, or recommendations concluded at a panel session on an issue of concern to the world and the Arabian Gulf region.

In early May, 1994, two months following the ECSSR's inauguration, the Yemeni War broke out. It was an assessment in which the Center proved that it could deal with events from a wider perspective, through a new approach. On July 26 and 27, 1994, the Center held a symposium on the Yemeni War, which hosted a number of world leading experts on the issue. These experts included an Arab studies professor at Georgetown University (he had earned his PhD from Yale University); an anthropology professor at University of Oxford, specializing in Yemeni tribes; the ambassador of the United States of America to Yemen (at the time); a political science professor at the American University of Beirut (he has earned his PhD from

Princeton University); and another with a PhD in political science from the Massachusetts Institute of Technology.

If you take into consideration the difficulties of communication in that period, and the difficulty of gathering those experts under one roof, in a short period of time, it becomes evident the extent of the effort exerted to convene this symposium at such early time. Evidently, the determination was in selecting those with the best competencies, rather than holding a symposium merely based on those who are present, or taking the easy way and retreating due to the pressures of the difficulty of communication, coordination and the usually crowded agendas of these experts who combine great scholarly reputation and experience in the region. The symposium's conclusions were delivered to the decision makers in the UAE, and its lectures were translated and collected under my direct supervision. I also edited them myself in the first few months, thus laying down the traditions that are still applied in the process of preparations for conferences and symposia, the selection of participants and the organization of the panels and discussions. During the phase to issue the proceedings of the symposium in a book, I provided the team concerned with practical guidelines regarding the level required for translation, editing and proofreading, in order for these mechanisms to evolve with experience and become established, the way we see now The book titled *The Yemeni War of 1994: Causes and Consequences* concluded with a prediction that I wrote myself—the fate of the Yemeni unity. I made it the conclusion of the symposium and the book.

In the first few years of the Center's establishment, there were no official working hours; you could find the premises of the ECSSR – which consisted of two opposing apartments at first, then a few villas later – as busy as a beehive at 2:00 am, or find the employees going back to their homes after midnight to begin their work at 7:00 am the next morning. I used to be the last one to leave the ECSSR and often the first to arrive. From the start, this type of work excluded those who were unable to engage in it. However, those who accepted the challenge and sought success found in this type of work satisfaction in their desire to excel and to be part of a unique experience. Thus, the process of excluding the unfit – or rather themselves backing out of their

With Mikhail Gorbachev, former President of the Soviet Union and Nobel Peace Prize laureate on the sidelines of his lecture "The Role of the Superpowers in Gulf Security," organized by ECSSR, December 4, 1994

own will– and the process of hiring those who can meet the requirements of this type of performance, were constantly going on. Moreover, a few employees were performing tasks supposed to be carried out by at least twice as many people. Although the number of employees increased, and the pace of pressures and workloads somewhat eased, this spirit remained part of the work culture at the ECSSR.

Since its inception, the ECSSR's activities have been distinguished by their ability to grasp the core. Reviewing the titles of the activities of the first two years, I believe that we reach a clear conclusion—the issues and topics that the ECSSR had focused on are still at the top of the list of priorities in the UAE and the region. An issue, such as the Yemeni War, was the title of the Center's second symposium; the Center's First Annual Conference was titled "Iran and the Gulf: A Search for Stability;" the Second Annual Conference was titled "Gulf Security in the Twenty-First Century;" and the first lecture given was by former Soviet President, Mikhail Gorbachev, on December 4, 1994, on "The Role of the Superpowers in Gulf Security."

Likewise, the list of lectures in the first two months of 1995 included lectures tackling issues such as "Theoretical Sources of Iranian Foreign Policy," "The Revolution in Military Affairs (RMA)," "The Issues of

With H.H. Sheikh Mohammed bin Rashid Al Maktoum, Vice President and Prime Minister of the UAE and Ruler of Dubai (may God protect him), when handing me the Arab Social Media Influencers Award 2015, March 17, 2015

'Al-Shura': the Written Law and the Nation's Historical Experience" and "Civil Society in the Middle East." Probably, whoever follows up on what the political and intellectual Arab arena is witnessing, after 20 years of holding such events and others, will realize that they are still the most influential and important issues, and that putting them forward at that early time had stemmed from the realization of their gravity and significance for the future.

The ability to evaluate the significance of phenomena and developments was evident in a step taken early on by the ECSSR, which indicates a recognition and proper assessment of what work environments would be in the future. In a statement I made to the UAE's *Al-Ittihad* newspaper, published on March 22, 1995, I

With Caspar Weinberger, former US Secretary of Defense, during his visit to the ECSSR, April 16, 1994

With Dick Cheney, former US Vice President and H.E. Ahmed Al-Humairi, Secretary-General of the Ministry of Presidential Affairs, during Mr. Cheney's visit to the ECSSR, March 19, 1996

With Mrs. Margaret Thatcher, the late former British Prime Minister, writing in the ECSSR's guest book, during her visit to the ECSSR, June 20, 1994

With former President of the French Republic, Nicolas Sarkozy, on the sidelines of his lecture "The World Today: A Conversation with Nicolas Sarkozy" delivered at the ECSSR, January 13, 2016

Presenting a gift to the late Dr. Kurt Waldheim, former UN Secretary-General and former President of Austria, during his visit to the ECSSR, December 1, 1997

said, "The ECSSR is proud to be the first agency to adopt the Internet, which included 30 million computers worldwide at that time, and which encompassed numerous groups of data banks and centers." This step was taken just a few months after the ECSSR started its work. The number of employees then did not exceed a few dozen. While there were large prestigious and well-funded institutions in the UAE, they did not introduce the Internet to their work until a later stage.

H.H. Sheikh Mohammed bin Rashid Al Maktoum, Vice President and Prime Minister of the UAE and Ruler of Dubai (may God protect him), delivering the keynote address at the ECSSR 10th Annual Conference titled "Arab Media in the Information Age" on January 9, 2005

Moreover, the ECSSR later organized various events on information technology and its applications. I received several awards in this field, including the Arab Social Media Influencers Award from His Highness Sheikh Mohammed bin Rashid Al Maktoum, Vice President and Prime Minister of the UAE and Ruler of Dubai (may God protect him). I believe that this step had alerted other institutions in the country to the importance of the Internet, which was new at that time. They then took the same step. This helped the UAE to occupy a leading position in this field early on.

The dignitaries who visited the ECSSR in its first two years may give an idea about the status the Center occupied, which was strongly entrenched within a short period of time. In April, 1994, it was visited by Casper Weinberger (US Secre-

H.H. Sheikh Abdullah bin Zayed Al Nahyan, Minister of Foreign Affairs and International Cooperation (Undersecretary of Information and Culture then) during the inauguration of the United Arab Emirates Database established by the ECSSR, May 31, 1996

With H.H. Sheikh Mohamed bin Zayed Al Nahyan, Crown Prince of Abu Dhabi and Deputy Supreme Commander of the UAE Armed Forces (may God protect him); and Michele Alliot-Marie, Head of EU Parliament Commission for the Relations with the Arabian Peninsula, French Minister of Defense then, December 17, 2002

tary of Defense from 1981 to 1987); followed by Margaret Thatcher; Mikhail Gorbachev; a delegation of US congressmen; Hasan Muratović (former Prime Minister of Bosnia and Herzegovina); Lord David Owen (former British Foreign Secretary) and Dick Cheney (former US Vice President).

In this context, the visits of prominent international figures such as, former US President, George W. Bush, and among others, Angela Merkel, the German Chancellor and former Malaysian Prime Minister Mahathir Mohamad, and their addresses and lectures at the ECSSR, were just a continuation of such tradition that accompanied the Center since its inception. The ECSSR's guest book is rich with entries by dozens of visitors, including heads of state, prime ministers from major countries of the re-

With H.H. Sheikh Abdullah bin Zayed Al Nahyan, Minister of Foreign Affairs and International Cooperation (Minister of Information and Culture then) talking to Ms. Jody Williams, 1997 Nobel Peace Prize Laureate, on the sidelines of the ECSSR 5th Annual Conference, "2000: The Making of the Future," October 9, 1999

On the sidelines of a workshop titled "Negotiation Skills," by Dr. Alsayyid Eleiwa, professor of political science at Halwan University, Egypt, organized by ECSSR, May 4, 1996

With H.H. Sheikh Abdullah bin Zayed Al Nayhan, Minister of Foreign Affairs and International Cooperation (Minister of Information and Culture then), during the proceedings of the ECSSR 4th Annual Conference titled "Challenges of the Next Millennium: Education and Development of Human Resources," May 24, 1998

During the visit of the Zayed University delegation to the ECSSR, January 6, 2002

With H.H. Sheikh Abdullah bin Zayed Al Nahyan, Minister of Foreign Affairs and International Cooperation (Minister of Information and Culture then) during the ECSSR 5th Annual Conference titled "2000: The Making of the Future," October 9, 1999

gion and the world, in addition to Nobel laureates. This reflects a regional and global recognition of the importance of the ECSSR as a think tank and a decision makers' supporter, and underscores the outstanding level that characterized its activities throughout the years.

Above all, visits by the leaders of the UAE, such as His Highness Sheikh Mohammed bin Rashid Al Maktoum, Vice President and Prime

During a visit to the ECSSR by the late ambassador of the Kingdom of Bahrain and the former ambassador of the State of Kuwait to the UAE, October 19, 1994

Minister of the UAE and Ruler of Dubai (may God protect him), who has visited the Center more than once, reflect the confidence the Center enjoys. Moreover, the visits of His Highness Sheikh Mohamed bin Zayed Al Nahyan (may God protect him) were inspiring for me and the ECSSR's staff. The Center also proudly received visits by His Highness Sheikh Hazza bin Zayed Al Nahyan, Lieutenant General His Highness Sheikh Saif bin Zayed Al Nahyan, His Highness Sheikh Mansour bin Zayed Al Nahyan, His Highness Sheikh Hamed bin Zayed Al Nahyan, His Highness Sheikh Diab bin Zayed Al Nahyan, His Highness Sheikh Abdullah bin Zayed Al Nahyan and many other UAE officials whose visits and participation in the Center's activities provided a lot of backing and morale support.

The ECSSR began its work with almost the same departments it comprises today, with a general structure similar to the present status at the moment; although departments evolve and expand over time in response to circumstances and emerging issues. While the name of The ECSSR suggests that it would only be dedicated to the preparation of studies and research, the construction phase that the UAE was passing through at that time, alongside the country's need for pioneering effort in a variety of areas related to scholarly research, prompted me to diversify the interests and activities of the Center. There was effort in the field of media, publications,

With H.H. Sheikh Mohamed bin Zayed Al Nahyan, Crown Prince of Abu Dhabi and Deputy Supreme Commander of the UAE Armed Forces (may God protect him), during his visit to the ECSSR on April 6, 1994

conferences, symposia, lectures, workshops, training, specialized libraries and measuring public opinion. The aim was to pave the way for the establishment of independent institutions, each of which is concerned with one of those areas to excel in, and to present a work model to be adopted by anyone interested in it, or anyone who wants to advance on the road to excellence and development.

The Center's various activities played an important role in the early years—we can call these years "tuning the public domain." The ideas and topics put forward by the ECSSR had rearranged the intellectual scene, which was clearly experiencing confusion and disorder. The legions of political Islam were presenting to the intellectual and cultural façade false manipulated issues that increased the distortion of consciousness; this included intellectual and cultural invasion, conspiracy theories and Christianization associations – only by their imagination. They were also offering misconceptions while addressing issues, such as Bosnia and Herzegovina or Afghanistan, to fuel hatred among Muslims and prevent their integration in a world heading quickly toward integration and balance of interests. These groups, moreover, were promoting a model of

With H.H. Sheikh Mohamed bin Zayed Al Nahyan, Crown Prince of Abu Dhabi and Deputy Supreme Commander of the UAE Armed Forces (may God protect him), amid military talks in Taiwan, September 25, 1994

governance and values that diverged from the requirements of the ambitious development plan of the UAE. They were also trying to mobilize society for the benefit of myths and ideas in contradiction with the society's interests and the necessary moves that the geostrategic reality dictates.

Falsified and deviously prepared topics – aimed at serving political religious groups, especially the Muslim Brotherhood – occupied a space on the intellectual arena due to the absence of an alternative. They did so by imposing their prominent figures on people and their kept-by-heart sayings that had gained a false power due to frequency of use and insistence on them, rather than being realistic or irrefutable via discussion or analysis. The ECSSR's activities and events, and its way of reading and evaluating events, came to displace outdated ideas the way sunlight dissipates the darkness of the night. In accordance with the success and popularity the ECSSR's activities achieved, the intellectual and educated elite, being able to discern good from bad, started to forge their old thinking and adopt a realist perspective, looking for the same level it found in the ECSSR's activities. It was like tasting good food that revealed how distasteful the one consumed before it was. Thus returning to the bad one was impossible. It was hard to reveal the futility of the issues raised without offering a better alternative, and this is what the ECSSR did.

The idea of creating a center for studies was on my mind since my time in the United States of America, as reading the studies and research produced by such centers, in addition to attending their various events, helped me realize the importance of their role in making recommendations to decision makers. However, I felt that this goal would be difficult to achieve and that I would eventually go back to an Arab country in which the intellectual arena is dominated by elites not willing to

With H.H. Sheikh Abdullah bin Zayed Al Nayhan, Minister of Foreign Affairs and International Cooperation (Minister of Information and Culture then), during the proceedings of the ECSSR 7th Annual Conference titled "Human Resource Development in a Knowledge-Based Economy," February 9, 2002.

With H.H. Sheikh Abdullah bin Zayed Al Nayhan, Minister of Foreign Affairs and International Cooperation (Minister of Information and Culture then), at the meetings of the UAE-French Strategic Dialogue, March 4, 2003

evolve. Nonetheless, it turned out that my calculations were incorrect as I forgot an important element—that our country's leadership possesses a clear vision for the future, has a plan for development based on science and knowledge, and that the leadership is looking for competent and qualified nationals to transform ideas into reality on the ground. Once I presented the idea to His Highness Sheikh Mohamed bin Zayed Al Nahyan (may God protect him), I was surprised by the amount of the support he provided me with, the momentum he added to

With H.H. Sheikh Mohamed bin Zayed Al Nahyan, Crown Prince of Abu Dhabi and Deputy Supreme Commander of the UAE Armed Forces (may God protect him); during the 1st edition of IDEX, on February 16, 1993, as I was head of Media Committee at IDEX

the idea of the ECSSR and the extent of his willingness to overcome all obstacles and to provide financial and human resources that will allow it to start off well.

His Highness Sheikh Mohamed bin Zayed Al Nahyan (may God protect him) was Chief-of-Staff of the UAE Armed Forces at that time. He was imple-

A copy of one of my statements published in *Al-Qabas* newspaper, in Kuwait, on February 15, 1993, while I was head of Media Committee at the 1st edition of IDEX

menting a plan to modernize the Armed Forces, including support of education, training and high-end knowledge. It was known then that the military was – for circumstances related to the establishment period – accepting holders of basic school degrees. However, His Highness Sheikh Mohamed bin

Zayed Al Nahyan was initiating a new phase in which the UAE Armed Forces were being armed essentially with education and knowledge. Therefore, establishing the ECSSR as a unit affiliated to the Armed Forces was part of this sophisticated vision. Now, you find a lot of Armed Forces officers and affiliates holding the highest levels of education and qualifications, many having studied at the most prestigious universities in the world. His Highness also realized that the ECSSR would fulfill a real need of the United Arab Emirates and the GCC

A copy of the cover of the Executive Regulations of the ECSSR

states—it could skillfully shoulder responsibilities that will leave a positive impact. Hence, His Highness enthusiastically supported establishing the Center. Moreover, we are honored that His Highness has been President of the ECSSR since its inception; it is a clear expression of his support. As much as I felt honored that His Highness Sheikh Mohamed bin Zayed Al Nahyan was the President of the ECSSR, it also meant a great responsibility that I have to shoulder—I wasted no time to always be up to his trust.

My first meeting with His Highness Sheikh Mohamed bin Zayed Al Nahyan (may God protect him) was in late 1990 or early 1991. His Highness Sheikh Abdullah bin Zayed Al Nahyan, Minister of Foreign Affairs and International Cooperation, was then a student at UAE University's Department of Political Science. His Highness Sheikh Abdullah organized a lecture given at Al-Maqam Palace in Al-Ain. His Highness Sheikh Mohamed bin Zayed Al Nahyan was present there. I participated in the lecture along with a number of Kuwaiti and Emirati faculty members. The theme of the lecture was on the Iraqi invasion of Kuwait, where lecturers discussed the various aspects of the topic. I cannot say for sure whether this meeting attracted the attention of His Highness Sheikh Mohamed bin Zayed Al Nahyan or not, or whether it was the basis of the task he honored me with three years after that event.

With an American media delegation during their visit to the ECSSR, March 17, 2002

The other experience that I think left an impact in this regard was heading the Media Committee of the first edition of IDEX in February, 1993. My work there continued for nearly a month, alongside a professional team with unique capabilities from the UAE Armed Forces – as I have already mentioned. In that period, His Highness Sheikh

With Prof. Giacomo Luciani, Christian-Peter Hanelt and Felix Neugart, on the sidelines of a symposium titled "The Future Relations between the GCC and the EU," May 21, 2002

Mohamed was closely monitoring our performance and evaluating it, especially in an international event that His Highness knows well that its success would yield great results. I believe our effort were successful, in spite of the difficulties related to the establishment phase and the development of the first foundations.

I was greatly motivated by His Highness Sheikh Mohamed bin Zayed Al Nahyan's keenness on progressing toward the future with a fully-integrated vision, politically, economically, militarily, socially, educationally and culturally. This vision was based on full confidence in the capabilities of UAE nationals, with science and knowledge being the cornerstones. My doubts about the difficulty of establishing a sophisticated studies center in an Arab country soon disappeared. Hence, I decided to prepare a proposal for the establishment of a modern center for strategic studies and research, whose core mission would be supporting the decision makers in the United Arab Emirates, on sound scholarly bases, in addition to serving the community in various ways and entrenching a culture of scholarly research.

In writing the proposal, I was helped by my professor, Dr. Shamlan Yousef Al-Essa. I submitted it to His Highness Sheikh Mohamed bin Zayed Al Nahyan in a few papers in mid–1993, in a meeting with

With H.E. Dr. Salman Rashid Al-Zayani, a member of the Advisory Board of the GCC Supreme Council, during his visit to the ECSSR, October 13, 1997

With Dr. Abdul Aziz Abdullah Al-Issa from the Department of International Cooperation at Naif Arab Academy for Security Sciences, with its headquarter in Riyadh, KSA. during a visit to ECSSR, March 9, 1998

With the delegation of the Diplomacy Studies Institute in Saudi Arabia, headed by Dr. Saleh Abdullah Al Rajehi, Professor of International Relations and Organizations, during their visit to the ECSSR, September 14, 2003

A Group photo with H.E. Dr. Ali bin Tamim, Director General of Abu Dhabi Media Company and Secretary-General of Sheikh Zayed Book Award and Editor-in-Chief of the news portal 24 (www.24.ae), and the team of "24.ae" news website during my visit to their offices, February 17, 2016

His Highness in the Gulf Hotel. His Highness was convinced of the idea and directed for it to be implemented. He honored us with being the President of the Center and with his strong support since the first moment. He also honored me when he entrusted me with directing the Center and working directly under his leadership, despite the fact that my age at that time was barely 34. Many people in the Armed Forces expressed their enthusiasm for the idea, and supported it, including, as I recall, Retired Staff Major General Juma Ali Khalaf Al-Humairi.

There was a simple bureaucratic obstacle: there was no regulation for civilians working in the Armed Forces—any civilian transferred to the Armed Forces was assigned a military rank. My salary at the university at that time was equivalent to the salary of a colonel in the Armed Forces. Thus, a decision was issued assigning me the rank of colonel, then I was promoted to brigadier major general followed by major general later.

The Center began its work as a unit of the Armed Forces. It was affiliated with the Armed Forces until 2003, after which the Center became an independent body with its own regulations. It was an important development in the history of the ECSSR. There is no doubt that being affiliated with the Armed Forces at the initial stage of the Center provided us with greater

On the sidelines of a ceremony when I was selected President of the "Green Hands" program, which was launched by Al-Tawasol International Tent, at a press conference hosted by the ECSSR, February 24, 2016

opportunities and benefits. Separation from the Armed Forces came after frameworks and rules of work had been completed. This in turn allowed for other opportunities to come, in response to changes that made such step an important leap forward.

We started working in a room on the podium of the military parade on Al-Khaleej Al-Arabi Street in Abu Dhabi. We carried out job interviews to select staff; with us was His Excellency Mr. Ahmed Al-Humairi, currently Secretary-General of the Ministry of Presidential Affairs. We interviewed more than 100 people, selected from a massive number of applicants. We chose a group of nationals and another of expatriates in accordance with criteria that guaranteed their ability to successfully assume the tough responsibility. Moreover, full willingness to withstand pressure and adapt to the size of an immense, fast and accurate workload was among the criteria that could not be compromised. When the number of applicants selected became enough to allow us to begin working, we moved to an apartment that became our first headquarters. Later, we moved to a villa close to Al Nahyan Camp.* With the expansion of the Center's work, a group of neighboring villas were added later.

---

* Al Nahyan Camp, an area in Abu Dhabi that extends east from 20th to 24th Street, between 19th and 11th Streets. Originally, it was a military camp that was redeveloped for residential and commercial use over 10 years ago.

I cannot say that I knew precisely and in detail what the task entailed. In theory, the idea was clear, and methods of its application were present in my mind, but I did not know whether putting ideas into practice would be easy or if I was going to face unforeseeable obstacles. I had no other choice

With Marc Perrin de Brichambaut, former Secretary-General of the Organization for Security and Co-operation in Europe, on the sidelines of the meetings of the UAE-French Strategic Dialogue, March 4, 2003

but to do my best because beginnings identify many features of the future. Thus, I was following every step of the work myself, reading every [typed] character, examining the equipment and supplies, testing the ability of the staff to act and fully achieve the desired goals. I still remember the tensions of the first symposium, the first lecture, the first book, the first newsletter, the first press statement and the first annual conference, as well as the tough assessments I used to do for any work and my meticulous follow-up of the views and notes on the activities and events of the first few months. At an unexpected speed, I found that the Center became a force to be reckoned with on the intellectual and political scene, locally, regionally and globally. A positive worldwide reputation began to spread with the first conference, to increase strongly in subsequent years. Thus, regional and international interest and anticipation, follow up and extensive coverage of the Center's activities became the norm and tradition. Focusing on vital issues such as the Gulf and GCC security made us a think tank for the Gulf region and an "expertise house" on its issues—this was one of the goals we had achieved.

There were things, however, that I did not give enough attention to and discovered after a while that I made a mistake in estimating their weight and value—perhaps including public relations. My idea was that success markets itself and that my true voice will necessarily reach large audiences; but the reality was contrary to what I believed.

With Ambassador Abdulaziz Nasser Rahma Al Shamsi and then Staff Lieutenant-Colonel Ahmed Mohammed Rahma Al Shamsi, on the sidelines of the visit by General Jean-Pierre Kelch, former French Army Chief of Staff, to ECSSR, December 13, 1998

The concept of a research center in a developing country was a mystery for many people; sometimes it caused serious and misunderstanding, and frequent talks to the press and appearances in the media were not among my priorities. First, because I did not have time for this considering my continuous work, day and night; and second, because my idea was to express myself through work alone. The nature of the Center, and being a unit of the Armed Forces serving the decision makers in the country, required shrouding its activities in confidentiality and privacy. This made some people go to great length in fabricating fictional stories about the Center. Among the funny incidents that happened was when a lady visited the Center in 1996 and upon entering she asked me, "Where is the prison?" I replied that we are not a security nor a police institution that has a prison. She answered that they say there is a prison here. I suggested that we tour the Center and search every corner to find the alleged prison. I actually let her go through every corner of the Center to get rid of her illusions that appeared to have been widely spread among many people.

There were many things that made me feel that the Arab cultural circle generally needs a long time to mature and to act according to what is expected of it, in order to keep pace with global changes. I remember that a major reputable Gulf cultural institution, affiliated with an important Ministry in a brotherly country, announced in 1995 that it is going to publish, as part of its series, Lester C. Thurow's book, *Head to Head*, which the Center had obtained the rights to translate and publish in Arabic—it had already published the translation almost a year before. In order to preserve the rights, I sent a friendly letter to that institution asking them not to publish the book. I pointed out to them that such action represents an infringement on the intellectual property rights. I received a strange reply from the institution saying, "Similar to almost all the Arab countries, we are not committed to any international conventions for the rights of authors and publishers, and the series... issued regularly since 1987, published a big number of translated books without prior copyrights from foreign authors." That institution resorted to a strange ploy to avoid the Center claiming its rights; they changed the serial number of the book in their series, and published it under a title different from the one they announced at the beginning—it was a type of fraud I could not accept, so I resorted to legal means.

Early on, I was trying to instill in the Arab world the values of dealing with the global changes. This was based on a perception that rapid globalization will impose rules and regulations on the entire world, which we must be prepared to meet their prerequisites, and that recognizing such changes earlier will save a lot of our time and effort. Many bodies, however, rejected such kind of movement toward the future. They imagined in vain that they can stop the wheel of history and prevent it from spinning. Among such values is the intellectual property rights, which were not common at that time—the United Arab Emirates will be remembered for always being a leader in recognizing such changes and being prepared to deal with them. This has contributed to laying down a solid foundation upon which the UAE's outstanding achievements were based. I am proud that the Center was part of this culture, or rather was among the pioneers in many cases. Nevertheless, taking the case to court was not out of desire to disrupt a cultural work or in search of a gain, but rather an effort from my part to integrate such new concepts into the current discourse and to draw attention to their importance in the Arab world.

In another incident, a lawsuit case against an announcer on Qatar's Al-Jazeera satellite channel was filed in 2015, under the social media law. Unfor-

In a press interview I gave to *Durrat Al-Emarat* magazine, published in September, 2001. I called for establishing a Higher Education Council in the UAE

tunately, the United Arab Emirates and Qatar had not signed an extradition agreement, despite the fact that both countries are members of the GCC.

Many practices had evolved through experience as well, including the nature of the topics submitted to decision makers. In the beginning, and stemming from our university experience, I used to submit somewhat large studies, up to 60–70 pages, containing theoretical ideas, ample information and historical backgrounds. We soon realized that the chances of benefiting from such topics would increase if the number of pages decreased. Consequently, we reduced the number of pages to about 20 or less. Afterward, we decided to make them less than 10 pages. Now, they are only three highly condensed pages that cut straight to the core of the topic addressed, explore the future and make specific recommendations. Moreover, large-volume research and studies were made the specialty of certain departments in the Center, and were targeting another audience.

Naming ceremony of Martyr's Hall at one of ECSSR's halls, during the commemoration of Martyr's Day, November 30, 2015

A decision maker who is completely busy with tasks and frequently receives analyses from other bodies does need to receive condensed new ideas. Our tools and approaches have evolved through experience and the feedback and comments we receive on the papers we submit—writing concise, focused and in-depth papers is a skill that needs training, and the shift from research and studies to policy papers was among what we have developed through experience. Even matters related to the type of paper used and the cover design and style chosen were among the things we took into consideration. In this aspect, which is unnoticeable to the public due to its nature, lies an important part of the Center's accomplishment and success. The numbers of material prepared by the Center to the present day exceeds 400,000 on various issues of interest to the United Arab Emirates. In addition, the proceedings of every conference, lecture and symposium are documented in writing and on DVDs and submitted to the decision makers, along with recommendations based on the conclusions of the content of such activities. Many of the recommendations contained in these papers had crystallized—many political, security and economic institutions were created upon our recommendation; many policies contained in the Center's papers were implemented; and many political, economic, social and security decisions, which we believe we had somehow contributed to, were taken.

In this regard, I can cite an example on a great educational leap achieved in the UAE—an example not subject to the confidentiality requirements that characterize many of the recommendations and subjects the ECSSR works on: The Center called, in many of its papers, for creating a Higher Council for Education in the UAE. The recommendation appeared in early press interviews. For example, I called for the establishment of this Council in an interview I gave to *Durrat Al-Emarat* magazine. Moreover, in another interview I gave to *Akhbar Al-Arab* newspaper, published on April 23, 2001, I said, "We pointed out earlier the need for the establishment of a Higher Council for Education to oversee the steps of development and perform an ongoing evaluation of the education process, to make sure that it keeps pace with the requirements of the time. The Council should include experts in education, academics, intellectuals, businesspersons and representatives from the planning and labor ministries." Indeed, Abu Dhabi Education Council (ADEC) was eventually established in 2005, to take over the tasks that we recommended, a long time before that interview, through several studies submitted to decision makers, albeit some aspects of our recommendations have not yet been fulfilled the way we aspired to.

To clarify part of the way we work in the Center, I give an example concerning the 2015 war in Yemen. There are a lot of people talking about the Houthis, Ali Abdullah Saleh and the participation of certain countries in the conflict, etc. But when I approach the subject, I start with various questions, such as: Is it in the interest of the United States of America for the

Meeting with the members of the Advisory Council of the UAE Federation Library, at ECSSR, September 13, 2015

war to stop, or to continue? There would be those who will say its interest is in the war continuing while others will say in stopping. This leads to the most important point that I will need an answer for – whatever the opinion is – Why? The Center's job is to answer the question Why? Moreover, if the Center managed to reduce 100 pages to one page, the one page to a paragraph, the paragraph to a sentence and the sentence to a word, it means that it had succeeded.

The success of the Center is built on two main pillars: First, the unrivaled financial and moral support from His Highness Sheikh Mohamed bin Zayed Al Nahyan. In a recent meeting with the staff of the Center, aimed at exchanging ideas on the best ways of development, one of my Deputy Directors addressed the staff saying something that I deem very important. He said, "Always remember that you are working in a Center presided by His Highness Sheikh Mohamed bin Zayed Al Nahyan." Without the financial support, certainly the work level at the Center will be affected. Nevertheless, the provision of this support does not guarantee the success of the Center unless it is backed up by the second pillar—innovation since inception. Innovation has been one of the Center's main characteristics, be it in the field of publications, conferences or any other events held, or libraries, or other areas of its activity. The innovation indicator moves up and down in any institution, of course, and I think that in the first seven years of the Center's life it was at the top. It might have dropped to some extent at certain periods due to some developments – such as assuring success considering that the first few years were full of challenges – but I work on sustaining that innovation and keeping it at high levels.

During the lecture titled "Europe and the Gulf: Common Challenges and Perspectives" given by Dr. Hans-Gert Pöttering, former President of the European Parliament and Chairman of Konrad-Adenauer-Stiftung, at the ECSSR, September 20, 2010

We, at the ECSSR, always look for new ideas, encourage employees to submit them to the management, and we immediately apply what is ap-

Presenting a gift to H.E. Dr. Rashid Ahmad Mohammed bin Fahad, former UAE Minister of Environment and Water, on the sidelines of a conference titled "Climate Change and the Future of Water" organized by ECSSR, October 14, 2014

plicable among them. In order to develop the library, for example, we established an Advisory Council constituted of a number of renowned intellectual figures from the United Arab Emirates, the Arab world and foreign countries, to receive their suggestions and ideas for the development of work, to ensure the highest level standards. We received a suggestion to create a coffee shop next to the ECSSR Bookshop, which has a separate entrance in the Center's premises, and we are working on implementing it. This is to expand the use of our library by those visitors who prefer to read while sipping their coffee in a comfortable place. They will choose the books they want to read from the library index through an electronic system in the café, and the books will be delivered to them within 10 minutes by the concerned staff. According to the library's rules, food is not permitted on its premises, out of due respect; laptops and mobile phones are also not allowed in, due to privacy and security considerations. At the same time, we want to facilitate the library use for readers who might refrain from frequenting the library because of those rules.

With Dr. Waleed Al-Saadi, Editor-in-Chief of Al-Manara Magazine, presenting me with a copy of his book titled *Khalifa bin Zayed: Knight of the New Millennium*, during his visit to the ECSSR, April 30, 2014

With Dr. Abdul-Hamid Al-Ansari, former Dean of the College of Islamic Law at Qatar University, on the sidelines of his lecture titled "Do Political Religious Groups Possess Applicable Development Plans? Muslim Brotherhood... a Case Study," delivered at the ECSSR, December 30, 2015

The library itself is an example of the Center's ability to excel. It contains half a million titles and more than one million online titles. It provides services not available elsewhere; it is the largest specialized library in the region, and only comparable, in the Arab world, to the Library of Alexandria in Egypt. However, this did not hold us from progressing toward a farther horizon of excellence, as preparations are going on now to construct a new two-floor building for the library.

The concept of the new building will not comprise of solely putting books on shelves, as is the case with conventional libraries – a method I see on the way to extinction – but it will rather be "smart," in line with this era. The library will be electronic, relying on the latest technologies, and its subjects will be available for the new generation, who are used to using the Internet and smart phones, since an early age. I am certain that this generation, who have lived their entire life with the Internet, and to whom

With Navy Staff Lt. General Pilot Sheikh Saeed bin Hamdan Al Nahyan, Deputy Commander of the UAE Navy Forces, and some visitors during the ECSSR's participation in the 6th edition of IDEX, March 16, 2003

With H.E. Nasser Al Sharhan, former Director General of the Ministry of Energy; and Majid al-Munif, Adviser to the Minister of Oil and Mineral Resources in KSA, during the ECSSR's 16th Annual Energy Conference titled "The Oil Era: Emerging Challenges," November 8, 2010

we will extend our services soon, is a generation different from ours. They would have special requirements in dealing with the library material, and this is what we should prepare ourselves for—10 years from now, this generation will strongly enter the work force and its members will become a majority. They will not deal with the library, or any other facility, in the conventional way, but rather their dealings will be fully electronic and "smart." We, at The ECSSR, prepare ourselves for that moment from now; such preparation represents one aspect of the innovation that underpins the success of the Center.

Receiving a delegation from the German Parliament (Bundestag) during their visit to the ECSSR, January 8, 1997

Objectivity, impartiality and presentation of all views were among the things we adopted since the Center began its work— we had never censored any view. The Center's conferences, symposia and lectures witness free and frank discussions in which we do not try to interfere. The

With two former staff of ECSSR, Ms. Salwa Al-Housani, and Ms. Al-Sa'ad Al-Menhali, editor-in-chief of the Arabic version of *National Geographic*, during my visit to the ECSSR's pavilion at the Abu Dhabi International Book Fair, May 10, 2015

audience raises questions and they get answers from the lecturers in an open and open-minded manner. Whether we agreed or disagreed with the view raised by the lecturer or the audience, we still give it a chance to be heard, and I believe that this is one of the factors behind the success of our events. Moreover, the lists of participants in the Center's activities include the entire political and ideological spectrum, from the Arab world or other countries

With a number of the participants in the "Storm of Thought" symposium, in its first round, held at the ECSSR, September 1, 2015

in the world. This is also true of all the Center's publications. Additionally, this is true, to a great extent, of our media newsletters, which report political and economic analyses from international sources. They include views and ideas that we often do not agree with, but we believe that presenting them to our audiences helps to perceive the world as it is, and supports the ability to understand and evaluate it properly.

The audience of the ECSSR essentially consists of research and intellectual elites. Crowding, in the sense of maximizing the number of the attendants of the Center's events is not one of my interests. I care for the quality of the audience rather than its quantity, since those targeted by my activities are not ordinary people. The publications of the Center are generally specialized. They are not read for fun or leisure. They necessitate a background in the subjects they tackle, as well as the lectures, symposia and conferences. Unless a person has sufficient interest, knowledge and specialization, the Center will not be the appropriate destination for them. I am aware that if I ask many of those who live in the vicinity of the Center about the nature of the Center's work, I will receive no answer. This does not worry me. The people I want to reach out to are of special caliber in

With H.E. Hamad Abdul Rahman Al-Midfa, Secretary-General for the UAE Federal Supreme Council Affairs at the Ministry of Presidential Affairs, during the ECSSR 10th Annual Energy Conference titled "The Gulf Oil and Gas Sector: Potential and Constraints," September 26, 2004

the United Arab Emirates, the Gulf region, the Arab world and the world as a whole; those are the ones targeted by my public relations activities and effort.

The number of publications by the ECSSR's Publications Department is approximately 1,200. All publications are subject to strict publishing procedures. This stems from our keen interest in maintaining the uncompromising high level of our publications. We have also held 22 annual conferences, 21 energy conferences, 7 annual education conferences, 20 specialized conferences and more than 44 symposia. In each of these events, dozens of researchers participated. The panels of some of these activities spanned over three days sometimes. We have also organized 54 workshops and about 550 lectures. Moreover, *Akhbar Al-Saah* newsletter, which offers daily analyses, now numbers more than 6,350 issues. Moreover, as I always stress, the highest standards are what we strive for; we accept nothing lower. All this is part of the Center's job, and this is what has given it the high status it enjoys today.

The Center is distinguished by performing a set of activities without any precedent in the UAE. I can give an example of our media monitoring section. Our current Media Department began its work by monitoring the print and audio-visual media, then its activities evolved and expanded to encompass other sections and activities. Getting information then was not as easy as it is now. There was no entity in the UAE practicing such vital activity when we started it; the Center was the first to alert of its importance, and to develop a structure and action plans for it. In many cases, we

Presenting a gift to Staff Brigadier Ahmed Mohammed Al-Amyan from the Jordanian Royal Military Academy (at the time) during his visit to the ECSSR, April 14, 2002

H.E. Ambassador Obaid Al-Hiri Al-Ketbi, ambassador of the UAE to Australia (Deputy Commander of Abu Dhabi Police and member of Abu Dhabi Executive Council at the time), during the lecture titled "Current Socio-Political Developments in the Middle East," given at the ECSSR by John Howard, former Prime Minister of Australia, October 21, 2014

were the first to deliver information to the decision maker on major local, regional or international events. Moreover, we were the first to monitor local, regional and global media trends toward the UAE, or about certain issues, and proceed to analyze them.

The ECSSR constantly organizes focused and intensified training courses for the staff of the Media Monitoring Room in various areas, in order to improve their skills and abilities. A monitoring staff member should necessarily be a researcher be-cause their work requires the ability to analyze the news, determine their importance and rewrite them concisely. If the monitoring staff is not a researcher, big mistakes will occur—we learned this fact from experience.

During a visit to the ECSSR by a delegation from the UAE Command and Staff College, March 25, 1996

As is the case with any type of work, the media mon-itoring section in the ECSSR sometimes suffers from peri-ods of decline or weakness; this is what the assessment and revision mechanisms in the Center rectify and devel-op solutions for. Since cer-tain sections in the Center depend on what the Moni-toring Room offers, it has to

During the visit of a delegation from the German Ministry of Defense to the ECSSR, March 21, 2001

always be at its best. We discovered recently one reason for the deficien-cy that occurs sometimes during a shift. The around-the-clock monitoring shifts are divided into three shifts, each lasting eight hours; a long time if we take into account the degree of concentration and vigilance required, and the large number of media outlets to be monitored at all times. We found that the deficiency that happens sometimes is concentrated in the shift's last two hours; hence, we have divided the day into four shifts, to make each shift only six hours.

When we started the monitoring process, there was no example to follow or somebody to learn from. Today, you will find the methods

During the Flag Day event at the ECSSR, November 3, 2015

developed by the Center applied in numerous institutions. Many times I have been told by the people in charge of those institutions that they were inspired by the ECSSR. During the ceaseless visits to the Center by delegations from institutions inside the UAE and abroad, we used to explain to them the work methodology in the various departments of the Center, including the Monitoring Room. Anyone requesting more clarification or details would get them. We were certain that any institution contributing to such activity is thus benefiting our country, and that its success is an added asset to the UAE. Moreover, many of the ECSSR former employees, working now at other institutions, had transferred with them some of the training they received at the Center. We considered this as an achievement of one of the Center's objectives that is, training national and non-national professionals who would play a role at the Center or other institutions. Training was achieved through work, or through a number of diplomas at the ECSSR's Department of Training, in which several bodies in the UAE would send their employees for training. What applies to monitoring applies also to

With US diplomat William Rugh, and French diplomat and journalist Eric Rouleau, during a symposium titled "Future of the Press in the Age of Multimedia", January 19, 2003

other departments, such as the opinion polls section, as some institutions seek to establish sections drawing on the experience of the Center or of some former ECSSR employees.

Numerous other research centers have been established in the United Arab Emirates. Some of these centers' officials and employees were among those who had worked at the ECSSR and tried to transfer the Center's experience. There is not one center among the emerging ones in the UAE that does not include former ECSSR employees; they are usually considered among the pillars of work in their new locations. In some of these centers' activities, I often saw similarity in the way the ECSSR organized its activities, only to discover later that a former ECSSR employee, or more, was behind that. Without belittling anybody, I think that keeping pace with the ECSSR is difficult, both qualitatively and quantitatively.

Human resources is the challenge I have been facing throughout the years of the Center's work. I am always looking for the creative and simultaneously disciplined kind of employee. I have no place for the employee who wants to perform non-evolving, routine work, because the nature of the tasks require facing continuous problems and finding solutions, noting that the volume of the tasks assigned to the Center is always bigger than the normal capacity of its human resources. Thus, employees have to double their input quantitatively and to be innovative and creative

With Andreas Kassler, former Manager of Groundwater Assessment Project– Emirate of Abu Dhabi, July 19, 1999

qualitatively. Above all, there is no time at all for gossip, long phone calls, visiting other colleagues' offices to tell jokes, following female celebrities news on the Internet or making up excuses to get a leave, the way it happens elsewhere as there is always a list of tasks to be finished—there is no time to waste. We are hiring minds not laborers, and in the recruitment process, we try our best to meet these requirements, and that is what makes it difficult for other centers to compete with us. In fact, it is not easy to get the right people in Arab work environments that are used to taking the easy way. Nevertheless, we are increasing our effort to get and retain them.

No one gets a job at the ECSSR out of charity, and no one remains employed if they prove unable to perform their job properly. There had been a leniency in the application of this rule for a short period of time, but the Center soon corrected its course and eliminated the gap. I read some time ago an inspiring story in the autobiography of the late Dr. Ghazi Algosaibi's *A Life in Administration*, in which he talked about the institution he headed: "In the organization, there was an old driver. He has been working on the railway since its establishment; before that, he worked in the government. The Human Resources Department drew my attention to dismiss him from work given his old age and poor eyesight, but in light of his long service, I refused to fire him" (p. 116, 2nd edition [Arabic], Arab Institution for Studies and

Publishing, 1999). Dr. Algosaibi recalled that eventually his own wife was almost killed in an accident caused by this driver. He concluded saying: "The esteemed reader may infer from the story whatever human connotations they want. As for me, I have

During a visit by Mudhaffar Al-Haj Mudhaffar, former Adviser to the Chairman of the Board of Directors of the General Pension and Social Security Authority, May 28, 1995

learned a lesson in administration that I will never forget: no matter what human emotions I have toward a colleague, I may not keep them in their position if this jeopardizes others' safety," (p. 117). I can expand on the lesson presented by Dr. Algosaibi to say that the safety of others includes their vocational safety and the safety of their performance from possible deterioration if somebody among them was spreading negative values. Thank God, I was not destined to learn a hard lesson, such as an accident involving one of my family members, to reach such a conclusion.

In the same context of protecting the employees, I found – in light of the circumstances surrounding the region – that I need to take security measures that ensure the safety of the Center's employees as well as visitors. This prompted us, almost four years ago, to apply measures that include meticulous inspection of the people entering the ECSSR, along with other measures in the same context. Doing so, I was motivated by a responsibility to protect at least 300 lives inside the Center's buildings. This had raised objections sometimes. Some people saw an exaggeration in it, and some visitors refused to undergo such measures and returned to where they came from. However, many institutions in the United Arab Emirates began to apply similar measures today—the difference might lie in the fact that the intuitive nature of my job makes me sense some phenomena earlier, and I move sometimes before others.

Broken Windows Theory

What I am most careful about in administration can be summed up in three concepts: work performance, work ethics and maintaining accuracy in financial matters. To understand the methodology I adopted in the management of the ECSSR, we may refer

With Dr. Stephen Mangum and Dr. Randy Smith, from the Fisher College of Business Management, Ohio University, USA, during their visit to the ECSSR, July 13, 2003

to a socio-criminological theory that is applied to administration, politics and even the industry. This theory is known as the Broken Windows Theory. It was introduced by social scientists George L. Kelling and James Q. Wilson in an article published in the American journal *The Atlantic* in March 1982, then in a book titled *Fixing Broken Windows: Restoring Order and Reducing Crime in Our Communities*, co-authored by Kelling and Catherine M. Coles, published in 1997 by Simon & Schuster.

The theory is based on a simple idea that the prevalence of crime is the result of tolerance for minor irregularities in the beginning—inaction toward such irregularities worsens their dangers. The two authors gave an example in their article in *The Atlantic*, from which they derived the title of the theory, that if there was a broken window in a building, and it was left as it is for a long time, others will be encouraged to break adjacent windows, which will necessarily be followed with breaking another one. Delinquents will be attracted to this building, and will employ its garden for their drug use. Thieves will also gather there. This makes addressing the phenomenon eventually difficult. Hence, filling the smallest gaps from the beginning helps the society avoid paying a hefty price if it did not initiate the confrontation earlier.

Many of those who wrote about the Broken Windows Theory point out to one of its most prominent applications in New York city, by Rudolph Giuliani, the city's mayor from 1994–2001. Giuliani began applying the law strictly against the perpetrators of minor and petty crimes, such as littering or crossing the road from non-pedestrian zones. Subway trains attracted particular interest, as they

Joy and pride of the country during the ECSSR celebrations to mark the UAE 42nd National Day, November 28, 2013

were dens of crime and insecurity. Hence, wrongdoings as simple as evading paying for tickets or painting graffiti, were assertively punished. The result in the end was stunning, as the number of small and serious crimes alike decreased, and the quality of life in New York increased. Some studies indicate that theft and murders in the city dropped by 85 percent between 1990 and 2013, and that the total number of crimes fell by almost 79 percent.

We can see this theory applied in the world of industry and technology, too. Apple is well-known in that it leaves no space for any security vulnerability, no matter how slim. It quickly and robustly addresses any threat of this kind. This made Apple computers much safer from the viruses that infect other companies' computers easily. This feature is part of Apple's excellence and reputation.

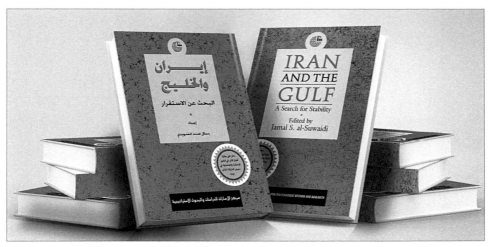

Iran and the Gulf: A Search for Stability a book I have edited and it was published by ECSSR in English and Arabic in 1996

Managing the ECSSR, I adopted the Broken Windows Theory out of my instinctive awareness of its importance, before this theory and its applications became popular. The Center has zero tolerance for occurrences such as lack of commitment to working hours—it is not a matter of the employee coming a few minutes late to work, but rather about the impression it leaves, and necessarily extends to all aspects of the work. Coming to work a minute late, then two minutes and then five minutes late allows eventually for aggravating the situation to exceed hours. Thus the message from the first moment of starting work is that the law will be applied, and that there will be no tolerance for this simple irregularity, or for invoking excuses repeatedly.

Furthermore, the formal dress code that the employees of the ECSSR abide by, since its inception, and the clear and strict rules in this regard, are another manifestation of the system that nobody is allowed to break. The idea behind committing to wearing suits and ties, for example, is not just to maintain the outward appearance; it also embodies a form of preparation, at the appearance level, to shift psychologically and in terms of morale, from the state of exercising monotonous daily activities to a different state, that is working at a place keen on keeping the utmost degree of precision, discipline and commitment. Appearance here goes hand in hand with essence, the first stresses the second and reflects some of its values and traditions.

Some people may think that the mobile phone is indispensable, but it is much simpler at the ECSSR; the employees do not bring their mobile phone into the office, but rather keep it out in their car or in designated lockers in the outside reception area. Often the employees at the Center find themselves free from the enslavement of their mobile phone – unlike many others – because they are away from it for eight hours a day.

The outcome of the traditions I established are evident in everything the Center does. I myself meticulously follow the details of every work and oversee the implementation of every step. Any visitor, reader of the ECSSR's publications, or any official from other entities working on mutual projects with the Center, can clearly realize that they are dealing with an institution different from most institutions they ever saw. Visitors and guests, even lecturers and researchers from different countries, often expressed their fascination with the high level of work at the Center, its excellence and professionalism, and the fact that everyone there knows their role and performs their tasks perfectly.

The challenges of establishing the ECSSR during the years 1994–2003 left me no opportunity to achieve what I aspire to as a researcher, the way I wanted. I was working day and night at the ECSSR and in other places. Nevertheless, I finished writing a number of books while I was at the same time developing rules of work at the Center. I prepared and edited *The Yemeni War of 1994*, oversaw its translation into Arabic, and wrote its introduction and visionary conclusion. I also published a research paper titled "Gulf Security and the Iranian Challenge" in the September 1996 issue of the British scholarly journal *Security Dialogue*. In 1996, I worked on the *Iran and the Gulf: A Search for Stability*, which was issued in English and Arabic; I oversaw its translation, edited the Arabic version and wrote its introduction and the 13th chapter titled "The Gulf Security Dilemma: The Arab Gulf

With H.H. Sheikh Mansour bin Zayed Al Nahyan, UAE Deputy Prime Minister and Minister of Presidential Affairs; and Dr. Abdullah Maghrabi, Director of Studies and Research at the Ministry of Presidential Affairs, during a ceremony held to honor graduates of the Distinguished Student Scholarship of His Highness President of the UAE, January 22, 2014

states, the United States, and Iran." The book was the winner of the first prize for Humanities and Social Sciences at the 1997 Sharjah Book Fair. This indicates that the Center has proved its merit since its first events because the book included the research papers of the first ECSSR Annual Conference.

The collection of my works also included: the *Abu Dhabi Summit and Regional Changes* (1998), which I edited and wrote its first chapter; *The Future of The Cooperation Council for the Arab States of the Gulf* (1999), together with a group of intellectuals; *Air/Missile Defense, Counter-proliferation and Security Policy Planning* (2000), co-authored with Jacquelyn K. Davis and Charles M. Perry; and the Introduction of the *Leadership and Management in the Information Age*, for which I supervised its publishing. Moreover, I wrote a chapter on GCC regional security challenges in a book published in English titled *Oil and Water: Security Cooperation in the Arabian Gulf.* In 2003, I published *The United Arab*

Emirates Society: A Future Perspective, within the lectures of the Emirates Lectures Series, issued by the ECSSR.

With Major General Khaled Fouda, Governor of Egypt's South Sinai, during his visit to the Center, September 30, 2015

The scholarly effort of the Center also included a large number of conferences in which I participated with my research and studies papers, commented on research papers or chaired panels. The locations of these conferences ranged from Sweden, Italy, the United States of America, Australia, the United Kingdom and Germany to Saudi Arabia, Qatar, Kuwait, Bahrain, Oman and other countries. In

Presenting a copy of my book *The Mirage* to H.E. Dr. Lee Yang, member of China's National People's Congress, on the sidelines of the lecture he gave at the ECSSR titled "The Strategic Dimensions of Emirati–Chinese Relations" on February 24, 2016

the scholarly conferences held in Western countries, I expressed the UAE and GCC view on the important issues of the region—they mostly dealt with issues of security in the Arabian Gulf, and the relations of the GCC states with Western countries. Moreover, I lectured in about 50 symposia and lectures in the UAE and abroad; in countries, along with the aforementioned, such as India, Japan, France, Egypt, Belgium, Serbia and Montenegro.

With the prominence of my role in public life, it was natural to find myself busy heading many committees within my interests, and being member of many intellectual and cultural institutions, and to be entrusted with important research projects in the period 1994–2003, which will be covered in this chapter. In addition to my position as Political Adviser to His Highness Sheikh Mohamed bin Zayed Al Nahyan (may God protect him), from 1994 to the present, with all the constant effort it requires, I have become a member of the Advisory Board of the Centre of Excellence for Applied Research & Training (CERT) in the Higher Colleges of Technology (HCT) in Abu Dhabi; Rapporteur of the Higher Population Committee; member of The Sheikh Zayed Private Academy for Girls; Member of the Board of the Emirates Diplomatic Institute (currently Emirates Diplomatic Academy); and Chairman of the Board of The Distinguished Student Scholarship of His Highness President of the UAE, Ministry of Presidential Affairs. I was also a former Member of the Board of Zayed University and Chairman of the Board of Emirates National Schools. In each of these positions, I was keen on performing my duty with all diligence and commitment, which meant additional effort exerted.

During that period, I wrote about 35 analytical articles in Arabic newspapers and magazines. I also gave 60 press interviews in which I tackled the most important issues of the United Arab Emirates, the region and the world, particularly the Arab Gulf security. These interviews left significant impacts, given their boldness and frankness. I also made about 500 press statements on the activities of the Center and gave about 20 radio and TV interviews on various topics.

These responsibilities and actions deprived me of the chance of taking care of my family members the way I wanted. If I was working in the government or an entity with working hours that end at 2:00 pm, and I then go back home, I could have certainly cared more for my children and family. I could have then asked them to tell me in detail their progress at school and their grades, I could have monitored any change in their level or helped them with their homework. But my job did not allow me to do so. I could be in the Monitoring Room at 3:00 am, explaining to its staff what they must do. Moreover, the flow of research requests to the Center prevented me from leaving its premises sometimes. In addition, my frequent traveling kept me away from the UAE for long or short periods. Such a situation could have caused problems for me with my children, but this did not happen, due to my great wife who was more than willing to happily shoulder the added burdens with love and high sense of responsibility.

Celebrating the graduation of my son, Khaled, from high school, 2000

Ever since we were in Wisconsin, my kind wife used to leave me to my studies and research works – and help me sometimes due to her specialization in political science – and shoulder the burden of raising our children and following up with the tiniest details of their lives and their character development—she carried out the mission perfectly. Thank God, my children excelled at all stages of education. In Wisconsin, we both thought that her burden would be temporary, and that when I got back to the United Arab Emirates, I would find the time to help her. However, what happened is that I became busier, and she continued to take responsibility of our children.

Despite my busy activities, I did not miss a single chance to be with my children and family. I made sure to attend, whenever possible, their school parties, activities and the events they were taking part in. I delivered a speech at the graduation of my son, Khaled, from high school. However, this was not always possible in many cases. I have had a big goal well worthy of my sacrifice and a noble task with which I serve my country without delay. I knew that I was not dedicating enough time to my family, but I had no choice. One cannot believe those who say that they can reconcile their responsibilities toward their families to their responsibilities toward their job, if it is the kind of job I found myself responsible for.

Although success made me happy, it also worried me at the same time. The status the Center carved out and the awards it won in its first years made me wonder: What am I going to achieve next? The ECSSR won the 1995 Cultural Personality of the Year Award from the Sultan Al-Owais Foundation, just one year after it was founded. What is next? Keeping the same level is not success, it must always be on the rise and this was a challenge that made my feeling of success flavored with concern and desire to boost and entrench this success.

The certificate of ECSSR winning "1995 Cultural Personality of the Year Award" issued by Al-Owais Foundation

The pride my mother, sister and wife felt in what I have accomplished made me happier with the success I have achieved. Nothing makes me happier than feeling that I made my siblings, parents and children proud. My mother, sister and wife provided me with the perfect conditions to achieve success, and their pride in my achievements took a positive direction, as they asked me to give more and make more progress. There is something important in

The brochure issued by Al-Owais Foundation on the occasion of the ECSSR winning "1995 Cultural Personality of the Year Award"

this regard—while our family's beginnings were not very poor, they were modest. When I was in primary, elementary and secondary school, I did not know that I would achieve this success in the future. The encouragement and support I received from my mother, sister, family – and my wife, later – was among the main reasons for what I have accomplished. Then came the encouragement from His Highness Sheikh Mohamed bin Zayed Al Nahyan (may God protect him), and the great moral and financial support he provided to the Center, to make the achievement of big dreams possible. I am sure that there are many people who are talented, innovative and have good and creative ideas, but they do not find somebody to encourage them, nourish their ideas and provide them with the necessary financial support, thus their ideas remain dormant inside their heads, not finding their way to realization on the ground.

At that stage also, I had to endure the sorrows of losing my father (may God rest his soul in peace) who passed away almost three years after the ECSSR was established. In March 1996, we discovered that my father was suffering from stomach cancer. He died in mid-August 1996. I was by his side at every moment during that tough time. He amazed me with his patience, endurance of pain and acceptance of his fate. I believe that anyone, no matter how wise they are, will feel upon their father's death a feeling as if they have lost some sense of security, or one of the poles of the tent supporting their life had collapsed.

Academic and National Effort

My effort during my career is twofold—the first is the academic effort, the second is the national effort. To the latter, I add a new aspect; the humanitarian side, through the Cancer Patient Care Society (RAHMA). RAHMA made a shift in community effort in regard to the fight against cancer in the United Arab Emirates.

1. The Academic Effort

My academic effort had started before I became a faculty member at UAE University in 1990. I realized the need for fundamental changes in the various aspects of the teaching process, in terms of the curricula and courses, the teaching methods and the quality of the teachers selected for qualifying students, who in a few years will become leaders in the most important positions of the

At the signing ceremony of my book *Prospects for the American Age: Sovereignty and Influence in the New World Order*, at the University of Oxford, April 7, 2014

national duty, or in terms of the way in which the educational process at the University in general is managed. In my view, the objective was to make UAE University one of the most important universities in the world, and I saw that this required an awareness of the change and its importance, and the faith that everything applied in the world's major universities can be applied in UAE University, provided that there is a will and resources. The leadership saved no effort in providing all the resources needed for this desired development.

I tended to face the problems clearly and forcefully. I did not go along with the prevailing thought regarding acceptance of what is already available or give in to the idea that any Arab university suffers weaknesses that cannot be corrected. The university's submissiveness to the Muslim Brotherhood ideology was one of its vulnerabilities. The faculty members who embraced this ideology were attracted to a past of which they created illusions. They wanted to force others to believe this illusion, they refused to see the world in its reality, and they opposed reason, which is the basis of any development. Moreover, they opposed knowledge and science because they look at those who possess knowledge in a suspicious and hostile manner.

A study on my book *The Mirage*, by Dr. Mohsen Tlili, published in the scholarly refereed periodical *Strategic Visions*, in June, 2016

A page from the booklet issued by the UAE Ministry of Education, that includes a summary of my book *The Mirage*, taught for Grade 12 students, within the Social Studies and National Education curriculum, that was approved in the academic year 2016

The low level of the faculty was a threat no less dangerous than the polluted Muslim Brotherhood ideology. I believe that this low level was due to their low qualification. However, this is not an incurable disease, as qualifying is achievable through ongoing training at the best and most prestigious universities, and through supporting those who prove their ability to meet high international standards, and excluding those who resort to slackness and laziness and stop developing themselves.

My interest stemmed from the academic traditions I directly acquired throughout my 12 years of studying in the United States of America, and indirectly through my studying at Kuwait University, learning at the hands of my distinguished teachers who themselves graduated from major world universities. This, I realized, was the reason I admired them, both academically and personally. I believed that applying the same to UAE University was not difficult. Moreover, the rise that the UAE was witnessing in all areas required a well-qualified and educated human cadre, especially at university and beyond, which makes them capable of leading the development process, being armed with initiative, innovation, creativity and understanding of the world, thereby being able to adapt to rapid developments—all of which good education creates.

I put this into practice in all the classes I taught before I had to quit teaching at the university due to other obligations. However, my choice of the classes I taught stemmed from my sense of their importance to building the mind—teaching the "Scientific Research Methodology" class, at the beginning of my career at UAE University, was because I believed that "methodology" is the essence that gives life to all the aspects, manifestations and procedures of knowledge. This applies to everything I taught at UAE University and Continuing Education Centers.

The method (how) was not less important than the content (what) in all the courses and subjects I taught. The approach that was open to all views and that connected students to various sources of information, trained them to examine, compare and evaluate views based on clear criteria, and then being convinced with any of them, or looking for their own vision, was no less important than the content taught. This new approach introduced the students to a method different from the one they were used to, and some of them might have found it a bit difficult. However, but the joy of knowledge and the result of the "learning" process, through which students are trained to acquire knowledge by themselves, had made up for what sometimes seemed to them difficult in the beginning.

The idea and practice went hand-in-hand in my experience at UAE University. As were my lectures, meetings, relationship with students, the approaches I adopted in evaluation, my contributions to the development of curricula and courses, my introduction of new courses, all of which reflected what I called for in theory, which granted me and my ideas great credibility.

This, in turn, has caused the students to hope for those who would replicate the same experience with them. I created a kind of demand for the "new commodity" whose good quality the students discovered, and sought to get later. This led other lecturers to follow the same example and adopt the same approach.

With Dr. Farhan Nizami, Director of the Oxford Centre for Islamic Studies, University of Oxford, UK, while I was planting a tree at that center, October 12, 2015

My academic effort did not end with quitting teaching because I was constantly busy fulfilling my new duties as adviser to His Highness Sheikh Mohamed bin Zayed Al Nahyan (may God protect him) and as Director General of the ECSSR. My academic effort had rather taken another route that was probably more profound and effective. It could be argued that the ideas I called for have been implemented through support from the wise leadership that had been encouraging all the nationals wishing to present ideas appropriate for the advancement of the country. These ideas should be based on sound planning, exact scientific rules, understanding of the nature of the changes taking place in the world, and the ability to interact with and to invest in them to achieve success.

Furthermore, I continued my academic effort through my membership of: the Zayed University Council; the Advisory Committee of UAE University's Department of Translation Studies; through founding of the "Distinguished Student Scholarship of His Highness President of the UAE," with the support of His Highness Sheikh Mansour bin Zayed Al Nahyan, UAE Deputy Prime Minister and Minister of Presidential Affairs; my membership of the Advisory Board of the Center of Excellence for Applied Research and Training (CERT) of the Higher Colleges of Technology; and of many educational bodies and institutions with which the ECSSR is associated through cooperation projects. More-over, my books are taught at various colleges, schools and universities inside and outside the UAE.

Delivering my lecture titled "National Security Challenges for the UAE: Population," June 26, 2000

Based on my long experience, and through being Director General of the ECSSR, I played an important role in evaluating all the initiatives that involve the development of university education in the UAE, in addition to all the trends, plans, laws and regulations that ensure I achieve my objectives; as the ECSSR was the place where most of the relevant projects are produced, matured and evaluated. The Center also enriched the academic life with its many academic-related conferences, studies, and Arabic and translated books. In 23 years, the Center hosted some of the most prominent specialists in academic affairs, who presented their proposals to the concerned officials in the government. This effort had resulted in cooperation projects with local public and private universities, as well as establishing important bodies that played their role in the process of the wide scale development witnessed by the UAE, toward building more effective institutions.

In addition to my consistent follow-up on the developments in the academic field, I kept myself up-to-date with the global practices in this field through my membership of the boards of a number of international universities, such as the Advisory Board of the School of Policy & International Affairs at the University of Maine, USA, and through the cooperation protocols and Memoranda of Understanding with a number of major universities around the world, such as the University of Oxford. All this provides the Center's studies and academic-related activities with a greater ability to comprehensively formulate scientific foresights.

2. The National Effort

Over more than 26 years since my return from the United States of America, I have dedicated much of my time and effort to major national issues. As noted above, I partici-

With H.H. Sheikh Mansour bin Zayed Al Nahyan, UAE Deputy Prime Minister and Minister of Presidential Affairs, H.H. Sheikh Zayed bin Hamdan bin Zayed Al Nahyan, during the graduation ceremony of the 2nd batch of students of the Emirates National Schools, May 13, 2009

pated in 1992 in the official negotiations between the United Arab Emirates and Iran on the three occupied islands: Abu Musa and the Greater and Lesser Tunbs. This participation allowed me to closely examine the details of this national sovereignty case, thereby dedicating a lot of my time and effort to it. The ECSSR issued in 2005, under my direct scholarly supervision, a book titled *The Three Occupied UAE Islands: The Tunbs and Abu Musa*, considered

With H.H. Sheikh Mansour bin Zayed Al Nahyan, UAE Deputy Prime Minister and Minister of Presidential Affairs, and H.E. Ahmed Al-Humairi, Secretary-General of the Ministry of Presidential Affairs and a number of officials, during the graduation ceremony of the 9th batch of students of the Emirates National Schools at the Emirates Palace, May 29, 2016

With H.H. Sheikh Mansour bin Zayed Al Nahyan, UAE Deputy Prime Minister and Minister of Presidential Affairs; H.H. Sheikh Zayed bin Hamdan bin Zayed Al Nahyan, and H.E. Ahmed Al-Humairi, Secretary-General of the Ministry of Presidential Affairs during the graduation ceremony of the 2nd batch of students of the Emirates National Schools, May 13, 2009

the most comprehensive, important and irrefutable book ever written on the case. This enormous and unparalleled work was not my only achievement, as I gave lectures on the case on many occasions, and I organized numerous scholarly and research activities at the ECSSR to highlight all its aspects.

The same applies to other major national issues, such as demographics. My effort in this issue

Receiving a gift from Dr. Ahmed Al Bastaki, Director of the Campus of the Emirates National Schools at Mohamed bin Zayed City, Abu Dhabi, during his visit to the ECSSR, May 22, 2016

dates back to 1994, when I became the Rapporteur of the Higher Population Committee; a ministerial committee for planning population growth and the labor force. I gave many lectures and held numerous events to discuss the subject of demographics and sent courageous early warning calls in the

With H.H. Sheikh Hamed bin Zayed Al Nahyan, Chairman of the Crown Prince Court of Abu Dhabi, on the sidelines of the 21st Annual Energy Conference titled "GCC Oil in World Energy Markets: Continuity and Change," held at ECSSR on November 24, 2015

face of those who downplayed its negative effects and risks on the UAE national security. While this problematic issue did not receive the desired volume of solutions it needs, in regard to the issue of the ratio of nationals to the

population in the UAE, due to factors related to the need of development for foreign labor, there were structural transformations that took place within the country's demographics, concerning certain balances of communities. Changes in structure of the labor force, in terms of their educational level and social characteristics; or the Emiratization of certain strategically important sectors, which I describe as rational, informed and

Delivering a speech at the workshop titled "Future of the National Economy: Economic Diversification Strategies for the Next Century," November 21, 1999

A collection of books selected by the UAE Ministry of Education to be taught at the schools of the UAE. This collection includes a number of my books as well as books and studies issued by the ECSSR for the academic year 2016/2017

forward-looking management of the problem, since it is impossible to fully resolve at present, and being considered one of the manifestations associated with rapid development and the large size of the economy.

The study I wrote and was issued by the UAE National Defense College, titled *The Restoration of Legitimacy in Yemen and its Role in Strengthening Arab National Security*, issued in May, 2016

Cover of the proposal (1999) that included a recommendation to create a Council for UAE National Security, and a detailed concept of its nature and functions (the Council had actually been created)

The national projects I took part in or carried out are numerous. One of the examples is the Emirates National Schools, which began work in 2002, preceded by a period of preparation and incorporation. There are many campuses of the schools in Abu Dhabi, Mohamed bin Zayed City

On the sidelines of a workshop, titled "The Oil Industry.... Concepts and Issues" presented by Dr. Paul Stevens, Professor of Economics and Oil Policies at the Center of Legal and Political Studies for Mineral and Oil Policies formerly affiliated with the University of Dundee, Scotland. The workshop was organized by ECSSR on November 11, 1995

and Al Ain, in addition to the emirates of Sharjah and Ras Al Khaimah, more recently. The number of students enrolled in these schools totals 8,000 male and female students. I took over the establishment of these schools with the support of His Highness Sheikh Mansour bin Zayed Al Nahyan. The vision I developed for the schools was "preparing future leaders through innovation in education and taking pride in the cultural heritage." This is evident in the choice of the word "National" in naming the school as it takes into account the consolidation of the Emirati identity and the promotion of feelings of pride in the country and belonging. In addition, it provides quality education that is of global standards, qualifying students to be admitted to the best universities in the world.

I have already referred to the ECSSR's call for establishing a higher council for education, which was implemented later. Here, we can cite important steps such as the establishment of the Supreme Council for National Security; amendment of the method of selecting members of the Federal National Council (FNC); the UAE National Service Law, which revealed a great amount of belonging to the country and readiness of UAE nationals to sacrifice their souls for the country; and the establishment of the UAE National Defense College, in which I have been a member of its Supreme Council since its inception in 2012. Considering the diversity of the decision-making bodies the ECSSR serves, I contributed to many of the decisions that gave the United Arab Emirates its modern face, through the Center or the committees and bodies formed to achieve particular objectives, whether I was their head or a member.

My strategic planning capabilities put me in charge of a wide range of tasks far beyond security, politics, economics and even education issues, for which I cared greatly. For example, in 2009, I was appointed Chairman of the Higher Committee for the preparation of the National Strategy for Childhood and Motherhood in the United Arab Emirates, by a decree issued by Her Highness Sheikha Fatima bint Mubarak (Mother of the Nation), President of the Supreme Council for Motherhood and Childhood. The Committee included representatives of UNICEF, the General Women's Union, Community Development Authority, Ministry of Education, Ministry of Health, Ministry of Interior, Ministry of Presidential Affairs and the National Bureau of Statistics.

The research and scholarly side, being the basis for decision-making, is part of my national effort. For the last 27 years, there was no national issue concerning the United Arab Emirates that escaped my scholarly vision through lectures I personally gave or presented at conferences, symposia, workshops or lectures that hosted some of the most prominent

Mr. William Mandel and Dr. Allen Chiao during the workshop titled "Future of the National Economy: Economic Diversification Strategies for the Next Century," organized by ECSSR, November 21, 1999

Delivering my speech at the workshop titled "Future of the National Economy: Economic Diversification Strategies for the Next Century," at the ECSSR, November 21, 1999

researchers and officials in the world, for the benefit of the public opinion and decision makers alike. Some of these activities were closed by their very nature, others were open to the public. In many cases, the resulting conclusions and recommendations were actually transformed into action on the ground.

In the last stage, I added another achievement to my national effort—humanitarian work, with the launch of the Cancer Patient Care Society (RAHMA), on September 15, 2015. RAHMA Society was not my first contribution to the acts of charity, as the personal contributions and assistance I provided to organizations such as the UAE Red Crescent Authority, which earned me the Gold Medal from His Highness Sheikh Hamdan bin Zayed Al Nahyan. RAHMA, however, represented the institutional humanitarian work undertaken by a civil society that has its own administrative structure, action plans and major goals it aspires to achieve. The result of all this was a wide range of awards and honors from within the UAE and abroad. All will be detailed in Chapter Five of this book.

Selected Projects

It is hard to count the projects I had participated in up to the end of 2003, the year that was the dividing line between a stage and another in my life, when I was diagnosed with cancer. However, I would choose three projects only as they represent an example that indicates the tasks I was entrusted with. The first was in the field of economy; the second, in the field of education; and the third, in the field of media. The

With Dr. Lawrence R. Klein, Nobel Prize laureate in Economics, on the sidelines of the lecture titled "Implications of WTO Membership and the Role of the UAE in the Global Economy," organized by ECSSR, May 4, 1997

first project was a group of studies on "diversifying the economic base." The second is the "Distinguished Student Scholarship of His Highness President of the UAE." The third was founding the opinion page in *Al-Ittihad* newspaper, for which I chose the title *Wujhat Nazar* (Perspectives).

With a number of lecturers at the workshop titled "Future of the National Economy: Economic Diversification Strategies for the Next Century," November 21, 1999

1. "Diversifying the Economic Base" Project:

Diversifying the Economic Base project is one of the most important research projects carried out by the ECSSR. Work on this project began in 1997. The interest in the project at this early time was proof of the insightful vision of His Highness Sheikh Mohamed bin Zayed Al Nahyan (may God protect him). The choice of the project,

Receiving a gift from H.E. Sheikh Nahyan bin Mubarak Al Nahyan, UAE Minister of Culture and Knowledge Development (Minister of Higher Education and Scientific Research at the time), on the sidelines of the Conference "Electronic Transactions (E-commerce & E-governance)" held at the ECSSR, May 19, 2009

its work mechanism and results, represent an example of the seriousness and accomplishment that characterized the work of the ECSSR.

Diversifying the economic base project was already started by another institution, since diversification is one of the conventional recommendations presented in any economic study. The problem with the recommendations that become "conventional" is that they may lose their meaning over time, and the competent officials see that they are nothing more than an inapplicable verbal formula. I think that many of the real solutions to the problems were done an injustice by being transformed into mere fixed recommendations circulated by researchers and officials without having the ability to turn them into reality through a scientifically real, profound and workable study. It is easy to talk about the need to diversify the economic base, but the difficult part is to answer questions such as: How? In what way? What sectors should be taken care of? Which bodies should be involved? What decisions should be taken?

With Ms. Linda Katehi, Dean of School of Engineering, Purdue University; Dennis Depew, Dean of the School of Technology, Purdue University, USA; and Dr. Philip Smith, President of Midwest Universities Consortium for International Activities, during their visit to the ECSSR, July 16, 2003

The entity that was assigned to the project was not up to the responsibility or challenge. I had the opportunity to read some of the papers it had issued, which I deemed incompetent—the problem with this type of imperfect work is that it consumes time, effort and money wasted in vain. But the most dangerous thing is that it prevents other capable and qualified entities from doing the work properly. It accumulates a legacy of failure that makes those assigned to do the tasks later think that they are facing an unsolvable problem, or they might rely on the previous effort that is weak and untenable. Thus, the new entity's efforts would be of a level similar to its predecessor's. Consequently, government entities might give up after repeated failures and the important project will find its way to the drawers of the archives for dust to accumulate on.

I looked through the names of those who worked on the project. To my surprise, I found that the entity tasked with it had assigned it to people in their twenties. They had no academic qualification in the economic domain, without the necessary expertise to work on studies of such importance and magnitude, and they all were of the same nationality. Moreover, there was part of the project requiring field work. I was shocked when I found out that they were choosing the respondents from one nationality, that being the nationality of the researchers. This un-

With an official from the students delegation of Thunderbird University, USA, during their visit to the ECSSR, January 6, 1998

dermined the foundations of scientific interviews and scholarly surveys. They had not chosen any UAE national or Arab citizen! Worse still, the surveys were carried out on inadequate people. All these catastrophic methodological mistakes were another factor that moved the eagerness of the researcher inside me and drove me to carry out the project at the ECSSR.

The project was carried out in a joint effort between the economic researchers at the ECSSR and economic researchers from a prestigious international institution specializing in economic research. They were carefully selected based on the history of their academic achievement and participation in similar projects in Arab and foreign countries. Those who worked on the project were headed by Dr. Abdullah Mohammed Maghrabi, currently Director of the Studies and Research Department at the Ministry of Presidential Affairs, then an ECSSR staff member.

The project was divided into three consecutive stages. The first stage included a comprehensive survey (field study) of the macro-economy of the United Arab Emirates and an assessment of its performance in comparison with other similar economies, to identify its strengths and weaknesses, and to analyze the ability of national industry products to compete in the export field. This stage also included a comprehensive survey of the information structure in the government, to collect economic data and statistics available in the country, to identify weaknesses in their methods of collection, dissemination and distribution; and to make the recommendations necessary to develop methods of collecting data and information in the country to match their counterparts in developed countries. Information and databases were among the issues that attracted the ECSSR's attention at an early stage.

The second stage included the development of a strategy designed to diversify the production base and the construction of industrial parks, through in-depth studies of the country's leading economic sectors, such as the oil, gas and petrochemicals sector, the financial sector and some other sectors, to know which of them is the most capable to play a role in diversifying the economic base in the UAE.

Finally, the third stage aimed at developing recommendations on the policies and procedures necessary to diversify the economic base, through a comprehensive and integrated diversification strategy and detailed plans to implement the required policies and procedures.

It is not an easy task to cite all the findings of the project, contained in a series of studies, each of which was built on the preceding one. However, the idea was to provide a model for the execution of big projects, the nature of the experts who must work on them, and the need to subject them to the supervision of a national body capable of evaluating the work and participating in it through its national professionals, and able to modify its tracks when deemed necessary. When I look today at the giant steps taken by the country on the road to economic development, or review the studies prepared in this project almost 18 years ago, I feel satisfied for what we had presented at that time because time had proved the effectiveness of the strategies and policies the project adopted and recommended to be followed.

Objectivity and courage in identifying the gaps and weaknesses in the national economy were among the characteristics of the project. In surveying the macro-economy, contained in the first stage, strengths and weaknesses were identified. The weaknesses identified were much more than the strengths and we did not hesitate to clarify this; although the results of the project were available to the public, and not classified, as is the case with many other projects; they were also published in the media. We did not try to avoid facing the problems, and His Highness Sheikh Mohamed bin Zayed Al Nahyan (may God protect him) was keen on everything being transparent, without trying to beautify the situation or show an unreal image.

The project gives a clear image of the vision of the ECSSR regarding its role—our studies are fact-based and workable. We believe that our most important duty is to provide decision makers and the community with applicable recommendations and policies, which if implemented, would lead to a better life.

The second part of the topic concerned the United Arab Emirates and the way it handles good ideas—it does not leave them to fade or die out, but rather consciously chooses what is applicable, and turns it into a reality on the ground. I have always said that the role of the Center is to put the available alternatives in the hands of the decision makers based on a scholarly foresight of the future. However, the implementation of our recommendations depends on the view of the officials and decision makers, who sometimes factor considerations we are unaware of. Fortunately, there is no gap between think tanks in the UAE and senior officials, as is the case in some Arab countries—consider this as part of the excellence and success of our country.

On November 21, 1999, the ECSSR organized a workshop titled "Future of the National Economy: Economic Diversification Strategies for the Next Century." It gathered experts and researchers from the Center and a number of experts and professionals from various bodies in the UAE and abroad. Participants had the opportunity to hold lengthy scholarly discussions about the project, which allowed its ideas and findings to

With H.H. Sheikh Mansour bin Zayed Al Nahyan, UAE Deputy Prime Minister and Minister of Presidential Affairs, and H.E. Ahmad Juma al-Zaabi Deputy Minister of Presidential Affairs, while attending a ceremony held to honor graduates of the Distinguished Student Scholarship of His Highness President of the UAE, April 19, 2017

reach a large number of stakeholders in the economic affairs in the UAE. The positive feedback was an indicator that the effort of three years of continuous hard work had paid off.

I think that the project, which lasted three years, proved itself able to define the future. The UAE government was encouraging the agricultural sector, as it desired to see the desert covered in green. The project, however, drew attention to the fact that agriculture is not among the sectors reliable in diversifying the economic base, due to water scarcity and soil quality. Moreover, among the project's recommendations were: "Encouraging capital-intensive manufacturing activities, which have high added value, and the adopted policies that promote saving and foreign investment, alongside an emphasis on the need to intensify the government's role in guiding the future career of the national human resources in accordance with the requirements of the economic development." I worked on moving the last part of this recommendation from the idea stage to the implementation stage, through the Distinguished Student Scholarship of His Highness

When I was honored by H.H. Sheikh Mansour bin Zayed Al Nahyan, UAE Deputy Prime Minister and Minister of Presidential Affairs, during a ceremony held to honor graduates of the Distinguished Student Scholarship of His Highness President of the UAE, on January 22, 2014. Also in the picture H.E. Ahmed Al-Humairi, Secretary-General of the Ministry of Presidential Affairs; H.E. Abdullah Al-Raisi, Director General of the UAE National Archives; H.E. Dr. Ali Al-Arri, in charge of Scholarships in SCO Office at the Ministry of Presidential Affairs; and H.E. Dr. Abdullah Maghrabi, Director of Studies and Research Sector at the Ministry of Presidential Affairs

President of the UAE, which is the second project that I am going to talk about next.

2. Distinguished Student Scholarship of His Highness President of the UAE:

The Distinguished Student Scholarship of His Highness the President of UAE was established in 1999. I was assigned to found it by His Highness Sheikh Mansour bin Zayed Al Nahyan, Deputy Prime Minister and Minister of Presidential Affairs, who was then Chairman of the Presidential Office of the late Sheikh Zayed bin Sultan Al Nahyan (may his soul rest in peace). His Highness Sheikh Mohamed bin Zayed Al Nahyan (may God protect him) and His Highness Sheikh Mansour bin Zayed Al Nahyan were keen on that the promising UAE youth attain the highest degrees of qualification, and that outstanding students enroll at distinguished universities, because this ensures the highest return on the investment in national human resources.

With H.H. Sheikh Mansour bin Zayed Al Nahyan, UAE Deputy Prime Minister and Minister of Presidential Affairs; H.E. Sheikh Nahyan bin Mubarak Al Nahyan, UAE Minister of Culture and Knowledge Development (Minister of Culture, Youth and Community Development then); H.E. Sheikh Hamdan bin Mubarak Al Nahyan (UAE Minister of Higher Education and Scientific Research at the time); Her Excellency Sheikha Lubna Al-Qasimi, UAE Minister of State for Tolerance; H.E. Ahmed Juma Al-Zaabi, Deputy Minister of Presidential Affairs; H.E. Ahmed Al-Humairi, Secretary-General of the Ministry of Presidential Affairs, during a ceremony held to honor graduates of the Distinguished Student Scholarship of His Highness President of the UAE, at Emirates Palace, December 21, 2015

For my part, I consider this project among the best investments in human resources.

Due to the circumstances I explained earlier, this assignment was of special importance, as I was aware of the need to organize scholarships in accordance with rules that ensure choosing the most qualified and most worthy students, and provide them with all the factors to succeed. Therefore, no sooner had I been assigned that I started meetings with some people to lay the necessary foundations. This was done in a very small office in the Diwan (court) of His Highness Sheikh Zayed bin Sultan Al Nahyan (may his soul rest in peace). As a former scholarship holder and a student who suffered an injustice due to the dominance of the political religious groups on the scholarship decision, I was fully aware of the students' needs and suffering. I also had my experience in university teaching and my work at the ECSSR, which allowed me constant contact with the education issues, policies and

With H.H. Sheikh Mansour bin Zayed Al Nahyan, Deputy Prime Minister and Minister of Presidential Affairs; H.E. Sheikh Nahyan bin Mubarak Al Nahyan, UAE Minister of Culture and Knowledge Development (Minister of Culture, Youth and Community Development then); H.E. Sheikh Hamdan bin Mubarak Al Nahyan (UAE Minister of Higher Education and Scientific Research at the time); Her Excellency Sheikha Lubna Al-Qasimi, UAE Minister of State for Tolerance; H.E. Ahmed Juma Al-Zaabi, Deputy Minister of Presidential Affairs; H.E. Ahmed Al-Humairi, Secretary-General of the Ministry of Presidential Affairs, during a ceremony held to honor graduates of the Distinguished Student Scholarship of His Highness President of the UAE, at Emirates Palace, December 21, 2015

problems and challenges to be overcome, as well my connections to major foreign universities. Furthermore, there was the administrative experience I gained from working at the ECSSR, and my understanding of the challenges entailed in building a new institution. I have been the Chairman of the Board of Directors of this project since its inception in 1999 to present.

The first rule was selecting the outstanding students. Excellence is based, in principle, on an unquestionable numerical standard; i.e. the academic score average in high school, which must not be less than 90 percent in any case; the cumulative grade point average at the university if the student wanted to enroll in post-graduate studies; a high score in the assessment tests which determine the level of the candidate at English, Arabic and computing. This is followed by interviews with the candidates for the scholarship, conducted by the Distinguished Student Scholarship Committee. This committee consists of a group of prominent academic figures capable of assessment and works in accordance with strict rules for selection, which leaves no space for personal impressions or unjustifiable choices. Among the members of the Committee were His Excellency Mr. Ahmed Al-Humairi, Secretary-General of the Ministry of Presidential Affairs; His Excellency Dr. Abdullah Al-Raisi, Director General of the UAE National Archives; Dr. Abdullah Maghrabi, Director of Studies and Research Department at the Ministry of Presidential Affairs; His Excellency Mohammed Salem Al-Dhaheri, Executive Director of school operations at the Abu Dhabi Education Council and Board Member of Scholarships Office; and Dr. Ali Al-Arri, in charge of

With H.H. Sheikh Mansour bin Zayed Al Nahyan, UAE Deputy Prime Minister and Minister of Presidential Affairs and H.E. Sheikh Hamdan bin Mubarak Al Nahyan (Minister of Higher Education and Scientific Research, then), during a ceremony held to honor graduates of the Distinguished Student Scholarship of His Highness President of the UAE, January 22, 2014

With Dr. Ali Al-Arri, in charge of Scholarships in SCO Office at the Ministry of Presidential Affairs, a former ECSSR staff, November 28, 2013

Scholarships in SCO Office at the Ministry of Presidential Affairs. In the beginning, when the project was not popular, the Committee used to contact the distinguished students. Later, however, the number of applications we received became very high due to the success achieved.

The important aspect in the work of the scholarships is that it primarily sends students to the best universities in the United States of America and the United Kingdom to study the promising disciplines that support the knowledge-based economy. Students of the Distinguished Student Scholarship of His Highness President of the UAE are enrolled now in universities such as Harvard, Massachusetts Institute of Technology, Cornell, Stanford, California-Berkeley, Brown, and other top-ranking global universities. There is a calculated degree of interference in the selection of the university, as well as in guiding students to the discipline required for the development plans, to avoid an error that may happen if students swarmed certain disciplines and neglected others that the country needs. This was reported by many studies on educational outcomes in the UAE, which experience unemployment in some disciplines as a result of the large number of graduate nationals, while there is a significant shortage in others. Thus, we orient the students, not through compulsion or coercion, but rather through a thoughtful and conscious guidance, to select disciplines needed for the development projects and those of which we are suffering a shortage. These disciplines included bioengineering, civil engineering, electrical engineering, medicine, information science and computer engineering, in addition to management, social sciences and humanities, etc.

The Distinguished Student Scholarship of His Highness President of the UAE covers a very important side for the students at the initial stage, as it provides them with guidance and an orientation program through which they become familiar with the nature of life in the country they are going to study in, its cultural values, the nature of the university and the problems they may face. Moreover, students will find the scholarship staff on their side when they arrive in the country they are going to study in, facilitating their accommodation and transportation from and to the university, as well as helping them to cope with their new life. Evidently, the scholarship pays the students' tuition, medical treatment, accommodation, textbooks and annual airplane tickets. Furthermore, it provides them with a generous monthly allowance.

We feel that it is our duty to provide all the conditions that make students innovate and bring better achievements. In return, they must be fully responsible and achieve what is required of them. This is the principle I always commit myself to. Therefore, we developed a rigid follow-up system to make sure that the students are fulfilling their duty well, including weekly mandatory telephone calls with the scholarship holders to follow up on their affairs. If a student did not answer a call, their family will be contacted, and consequently they may be penalized. There is also a thorough follow-up on the students' grades and averages in all the exams performed, and they are required to maintain an uncompromising high score. If their academic performance declines, there is a progressive system of warnings and penalties that can reach to compelling the student to reimburse the education expenses if they failed to earn the degree they were sent for. These terms and conditions are made clear to the student and his parents from the beginning, and they sign an agreement to abide by them. I may say that the commitment and accomplishment rate was close to 100 percent.

I believe that setting these conditions was significant to the students themselves—they were not intended to penalize a student or recover a sum of money from them, but rather to motivate them to perform at their highest level. The follow-up system ensures that the students themselves would not move away from their goal nor forget it. Close monitoring of the students' academic progress, alerting them when they lag behind and contacting them on a regular basis are all procedures that serve their interest eventually. Moreover, they fuel the spirit of excellence and competition and mobilize their potentials that could otherwise be neglected or hindered.

The Scholarship was exclusive to UAE nationals. However, in the first years, in 1999 and 2000, we received students who were holders of non-UAE passports. Since they were really distinguished, we did our best to help them acquire the UAE nationality although we did not know them personally at all. In this regard, I would like to thank His Highness Sheikh Mansour bin Zayed Al Nahyan for his help. These students had in fact traveled and studied at the expense of the government in major universities, lived up to our expectations, as they completed their university education with distinction, and came back to join the country's institutions and contribute to the development experience, relying on the high qualification they acquired through the scholarship. I believe that the Distinguished Student Scholarship of His Highness President of the UAE is among the best projects carried out in the United Arab Emirates, due to the significantly positive results achieved. Moreover, as is the case with all the tasks I was assigned, I was keen on following up on all the details at the initial stage because the process of laying the foundations is the most important stage in any work, then it becomes self-propelled. This project is now 18 years old, and is still carrying on its mission successfully, thanks to the great support and encouragement of His Highness Sheikh Mansour bin Zayed Al Nahyan.

Female students enrollment was large as well. Dr. Hawwaa Al-Mansouri, who was among the first batch of the Scholarship holders, probably represents a model of this success. She received her Bachelor of Science in Neurobiology from the University of Maryland, then obtained a degree in general medicine from the School of Medicine, George Washington University; thus becoming the first non-American postgraduate woman from George Washington University. After an extensive study and work journey full of challenges, she attained a George Washington University fellowship in endocrinology after two-years of studying, and the American Board of Internal Medicine. Dr. Al-Mansouri culminated her scientific journey by improving on an ultrasound-compatible peripheral access catheter. This is what we aspire to: that the Scholarship students reach up to the stage of innovation. I believe we made every effort to meticulously select the best for the scholarships, and we were successful in our selections, considering the results achieved; there are dozens of cases in which the scholarship holders accomplished achievements that we are proud of.

Now, there are more than 450 male and female graduates who have ben-efited from the scholarship and have earned prestigious higher degrees. This number of graduates is not a small one, given the size of the work-force in the UAE. These graduates are employed at pivotal institutions in the country. At work sites that require special skills and capabilities, such as Mubadala, you

With Mr. Mohammed Al-Hammadi, Editor-in-Chief of *Al-Ittihad* newspaper, during his visit to the ECSSR, November 8, 2015

find in these graduates the qualifications you are looking for. A significant number of our graduates is working at Mubadala. Not one of these graduates is unemployed, and this is proof that talent is always appreciated. Moreover, it shows that the unemployment that exists among nationals is due to mistakes and flaws in the choice of the academic discipline or due to lack of the educational courses and disciplines actually needed by the labor market.

Among the most important indicators of the success of the Distinguished Student Scholarship of His Highness President of the UAE is that other bodies in the UAE followed our experience and found in it what they were looking for. Therefore, they requested us to help them send their own scholarship holders and subject them to the same system we apply on our own. These bodies included, for example, the Abu Dhabi National Oil Company (ADNOC) and Abu Dhabi Investment Authority (ADIA). Other entities also sought to apply the same standards we apply, especially the elements of the care and follow-up for which we developed strong foundations. I believe that one of the success factors in the UAE is the interest of each entity to take advantage of the successful experiences of other entities, as I have already explained, and try to apply the same or even develop them.

I have thoroughly explained the philosophy of some aspects of the Distinguished Student Scholarship of His Highness President of the UAE in an interview I gave in 2005, saying: "At the initial stage, we had to boost our students' confidence in their capabilities, and assure them that their potential enable them to fulfill the criteria required for joining the scholarship. These criteria were among the things that required a strenuous effort to be adopted; they seemed a bit too strict, for those who were accustomed to a life of relaxation, free from competition. They also seemed selective, to a large degree, as they excluded good, and very good students sometimes, for the sake of excellent students. Then came the move of enhancing certainty in the integrity and objectivity of the process of approving nominated students—this was achieved through adopting strict selection standards and foundations. Finally, it was necessary to carry out an assisting

Supporting national media institutions has always been one of our priorities. This photo was taken honoring the late Taryam Omran, Founder of *Al-Khaleej* newspaper, with the Federal Personality Award, issued by H.H. Sheikh Mohamed bin Zayed Al Nahyan Crown Prince of Abu Dhabi and Deputy Supreme Commander of the UAE Armed Forces (may God protect him). The award was received by his nephew, Khalid Abullah Omran, December 11, 2014

With Mr. Hamad Al-Kaabi, Head of the journalistic Investigations Section, *Al-Ittihad* newspaper, during his visit to the ECSSR, May 12, 2015

and motivating role to support the nominees and raise the level of some of the students with whom the scholarship management distinguishes ability to fulfill its criteria, with some effort and organization. Thus, the scholarship was transformed from an entity that embraces the outstanding students, develops their capabilities and qualifies them into an incentive to raise the level of the most promising students and attracting them into an indirect factor in improving the outputs of education and spreading the culture of excellence and competition among the UAE nationals."

I believe this vision accurately reflects the ideas that governed the founding of the Distinguished Student Scholarship of His Highness President of

Presenting a gift to H.E. Ahmad Ali al-Bloushi, Director of GCC Affairs at the UAE Ministry of Foreign Affairs and International Cooperation, (and Director General of Emirates Media Foundation, which issued *Al-Ittihad* newspaper at that time), July 19, 2000

the UAE, which the scholarship maintained since its inception 18 years ago—and is still carrying out its mission successfully.

3. Creating the Opinion Page *Wujhat Nazar* in *Al-Ittihad* Newspaper

In 2001, I had an appointment with a new mission that was all about creating something from scratch. This mission was the creation of the opinion page in *Al-Ittihad* newspaper, titled *Wujhat Nazar* (Perspectives), the Arabic title I chose for the page. I completed this task with full and constant support from His Highness Sheikh Abdullah bin Zayed Al Nahyan, Minister of Foreign Affairs and International Cooperation, to all the steps I took then. My interest in developing the *Wujhat Nazar* page in *Al-Ittihad* newspaper was older though. Since 1998, I received offers to handle this matter. However, from my experience I knew that these offers lacked the possibility for success for various reasons, including that the assignment was neither unconditional nor decisive; it was limited to just repairing the problems and addressing mistakes. Add to that the fact that the development at the level I desired to accomplish requires sufficient funds, the thing that was not available in the first two offers I received to implement such a project.

This had changed after the attacks of September 11, 2001. The competent authorities identified a huge deviation in *Al-Ittihad's* Perspectives page from the supposed course at that critical stage before I was put in charge of it. The page was dominated by conspiracy theories, irrational and unreasonable discourse in the clarification of the nature of the supposed relationship between the West and the Arab and Islamic countries. Moreover, there was an absence of critical and in-depth analysis of the nature of the fateful challenge the Arab and Islamic world is

"Perspectives" page in *Al-Ittihad* newspaper, UAE, on January 12, 2002. It was the first issue in which *Wujhat Nazar* appeared under my supervision

facing; something not realized by the people who were then in charge of the Perspective page. This page was full of flaws: some ideas were provocative, supporting violence and terrorism, while others were erroneous and overly superficial; to the extent that the newspaper and its writers may be accountable by the law.

The type of the newspaper's Perspectives writers played a role in this; many of them were of a mediocre educational level and held outdated ideas. They were detached from the world's ideas, movements and notions. They lacked the assumed knowledge of those who make and orient the public opinion. Moreover, the page was almost disconnected from the UAE; it was not depicting the events taking place on the intellectual, cultural and political arena in the country, nor portraying the country's regional and international relations and its engagement in the contemporary world in accordance with thoughtful development plans. Replacing those writers, from whom we found a lot of mistakes, was a real battle we had to fight at that time.

Entrusting me with the task of developing the Perspectives page, by His Highness Sheikh Abdullah bin Zayed Al Nahyan, the Minister of Information and Culture (at that time), came with all the factors for success. Moreover, the great support from His Highness was crucial in all the results achieved. It was not just a superficial restoration process, but rather a new beginning in every sense of the word, with the full authority that allowed me to take all necessary decisions, and with sufficient funding to achieve the objectives I desired. It culminated with great support and cooperation from Mr. Ahmed Ali Al-Baloushi, then General Manager of Emirates Media, which publishes *Al-Ittihad* newspaper; he provided me with all the facilities necessary for the success of the project.

Since its inception, the ECSSR has been monitoring the aspects of the media scene in the UAE. It had already prepared a lot of papers and studies on the problems facing it, including the *Wujhat Nazar* (Perspectives) page in *Al-Ittihad* newspaper, being the official newspaper in a way or another. In mid-October 2001, I formed a specialized team from the Center, gathering competent media specialists. The team worked day and night in order to get the job done. I was following the team's work, moment by moment, and I relayed to them the concepts that must be implemented regarding all aspects, to receive from them the plans, details and suggestions, which I used to discuss with them carefully, until they fully formed and developed. This was usually done only after I receive several suggestions that I scrutinize, and compare between various alternatives, ideas and views.

Work sessions included everything, from the editorial policy to choosing the title and design of the page and selecting the writers and royalties. Even the cartoon placed on the page, its content and approach, had all been subjected to long discussions. A lot of ideas about the objectives of the Perspectives page and its role in creating awareness, and the various schools at the most

With H.E. Dr. Ali Rashid Al-Nuaimi, Member of the Executive Council of Abu Dhabi, Director General of Abu Dhabi Education Council (ADEC) and Chancellor of UAE University; and Mr. Rashid Al-Araimi, former Editor-in-Chief of *Al-Ittihad* newspaper, during the events of the ECSSR Ramadan Strategic Dialogue, July 16, 2013

prestigious media institutions on this subject, were presented, in what took sometimes the form of debates to discover the strengths and weaknesses of each approach. I was keen on having all opinions presented in these debates and to hold lengthy dialogues to create, through debating, awareness for the team regarding all the dimensions of its task, and to make everything very clear for them when we start the actual work. These debates often continued until late at night, something uncommon to the staff of *Al-Ittihad* newspaper at that time. Those debates were similar to a training course that benefited all participants and made us work on a solid ground of understanding the task in hand and the means to implement it.

We conducted a thorough and meticulous survey of all Arab writers, academics and intellectuals who could contribute to the page. The best of them were chosen, while a small number of those who were already writing in the page were kept—carefully drafted letters were sent to all of them as to ensure their participation. The royalties were commensurate with the status of the prominent figures writing in the page. These royalties, however, were not the only thing that was important, but rather the quality of those who were going to write was attractive and encouraging to those who were a little bit reluctant. It is usual when you request a writer to contribute to a perspectives page that they would ask you: Who will be writing that page?

I was interested in completing the mission quickly. Nevertheless, I did not let the considerations of speed affect the precision and quality. Therefore, I did not rush finishing any stage before I felt satisfied with the level it reached.

With Mr. Rashid Al-Araimi, former Editor-in-Chief of *Al-Ittihad* newspaper during the celebration of the 16th Anniversary of the establishment of the ECSSR, March 14, 2010

Almost three months of hard work had elapsed before I felt that the moment of start-up had come. Early in January 2002, the *Wujhat Nazar* (Perspectives) page had emerged with a new look. It included the most important and renowned opinion writers, intellectuals and academics from all over the Arab world, with special interest in giving prominence to the UAE and GCC writers, who were previously almost absent from this page. Later on, *Wujhat Nazar* was often described as being the most important of opinion pages in the Arab press. Its reemergence was an important event monitored by the media professionals inside and outside the UAE—many described it as a leap forward on the road to the development of the UAE media.

Human resources were very important for the success of the *Wujhat Nazar* page. I chose Mr. Rashid Al-Araimi to be in charge of it. He had previously received his training at the ECSSR, through the Scientific Research Diploma Program at the Department of Training—many institutions in the UAE used to send their employees to get this diploma. Through my close monitoring, I noticed the vast potential of Mr. Al-Araimi, and the efficiency he proved during the time he was a trainee at the Center. Interestingly, when I proposed Mr. Al-Araimi's name to the officials at Emirates Media, I was surprised they did not know him, and that he was working in a margin-

al place that contradict-
ed the efficiency that was
evident to me.

I discovered that na-
tional talents are already
great, but that the im-
portant aspect is to look
out for them. The prob-
lem is that they can be
neglected and not tapped
into due to various forms
of shortcomings, and the

With Mr. Mohammed Al Hammadi, Editor-in-Chief of *Al-Ittihad* newspaper, during "Al-Ittihad 9th Forum" October 22, 2014

experience of the *Wujhat Nazar* (Perspectives) page was a clear example of this. I am proud that throughout my career, I nominated national talents in the diplomatic, educational, political and media fields; the overwhelming majority of those I nominated proved that I was right. However, there were exceptions because of which I felt that even with my indisputable ability to sort and evaluate, there are people skilled in deception and pretense to such a degree that they may fool even the most experienced people. Thank God these cases were very few.

Among the incidents which I will never forget is an employee working in the ECSSR's Media Monitoring Room who was proficient in such type of deception. This particular person sent in January 2015, a link that included images from indecent websites to thousands of subscribers to the ECSSR's SMS service, which sends the most important news to subscribers instantly, including the most prominent officials in the UAE. I received this SMS during a journey to Houston, Texas, to complete the last stages of my treatment for cancer. At that moment, I had just received the good news of the disappearance of the cancerous cells in my body. Receiving those images, however, spoiled the joy of my full recovery. Although I immediately took legal action against that person, I still feel it was less than the offense he had committed. I consider the moment I received that indecent link among the worst moments that I have ever gone through during my career managing the ECSSR.

Once Mr. Al-Araimi began working, his administrative and research capabilities became clearly evident. He was promoted quickly to the position of Editor-in-Chief of *Al-Ittihad* newspaper, a position he held efficiently for long years full of accomplishments, including his role in the founding of the Sheikh Zayed Book Award, which became the most important Arab award in its field. He served as the Secretary-General of the Award during its important early years and he exerted great effort until he made it occupy its prominent position on both the Arab and international levels.

I believe that the effort invested in founding the *Wujhat Nazar* (Perspectives) page paid off as it is still at the forefront of Arab opinion pages. Following Mr. Al-Araimi, the page was headed by qualified nationals who continued the success story, such as Dr. Abdullah Al-Awadhi, who is currently in charge of it. Moreover, Mr. Mohammed Al-Hammadi, now Editor-in-Chief of *Al-Ittihad*, formerly wrote in the *Wujhat Nazar* page. He is an excellent writer who has become one of the most prominent in his field in the UAE, GCC and Arab world.

In late November 2003, the fierce battle with cancer started. I confronted the disease armed with unshaken faith and confidence in God Almighty, and with a relentless determination that did not break in front of all the challenges I encountered. Moreover, I enjoyed tremendous support from His Highness Sheikh Mohamed bin Zayed Al Nahyan (may God protect him), my wife and children, and thousands of my friends, students and colleagues, as well as those who dealt with me. Their sincere prayers for me to recover found their way to heavens and did succeed in the decisive moments between life and death, to let me eventually win the toughest battle of my life. The following chapter will deal with some features of that experience.

Chapter 4

The Battle with Cancer

Chapter 4

The Battle with Cancer

Each year, toward the end of November, Abu Dhabi enjoys its nicest weather. The shining autumn sun spreads vigor and warmth, alongside a whiff of lively spring. The refreshing air at night never amounts to biting cold, except very rarely. November 2003 was not an exception to the rule. It was even more beautiful as most of it coincided with the Holy Month of Ramadan, with all its spiritualities permeating in the fresh air, filling the hearts with peace, satisfaction, and reconciliation with oneself and life. As for me, the days of Ramadan were an opportunity to take a breath somehow, at the end of a year in which work pressures doubled and increased with the events broiling in the region at that time. The huge burdens were not new to me—I had coped with them until they became part of my days and life. However, this year was harsher than usual.

At an Iftar banquet for the ECSSR staff and guests, October 17, 2006

Since the beginning of 2003, the imminent possibility of war in Iraq engulfed the whole region and seemed to be an inescapable fate. I knew for sure that a wild storm would hit the region along with this war and we had to be prepared. Thus, preparations should be underway to face the ramifications of the

With a member of a US Air Force Academy delegation during his visit to the ECSSR, March 9, 2002

war through close follow-up, swift and deep analysis and presenting decision makers in the UAE with possible options and alternatives.

When the Iraq War broke out in March 2003, the ECSSR was engaging in its own battle, maximizing employee productivity to the extent that the staff had become unbearably pressured, where any extra load would have meant a full breakdown. My share of these pressures was the greatest of all due to my position as a leader of this hard work, my inner feeling of responsibility, the inevitability of producing the work to the best possible quality and my acknowledgment of the dire consequences

Delivering my speech at a symposium titled "War Against Iraq: Implications for the Arab Gulf States," February 2, 2003

of any flaw or shortcoming in this critical and fearful period.

I Discovered My Disease by Myself

It was customary to organize football tournaments during Ramadan. The ECSSR employees participated in them and they would be divided into teams

Attending a conference held by the ECSSR in 2003

Receiving the Ramadan football tournament cup, held by the ECSSR on December 12, 2001

to compete with each other. Since the establishment of the Center, I was keen – as a football fan, in particular, and a sports fan in general – to be one of the players who engaged in the competitions with the most enthusiasm, encouraged by colleagues from the spectator benches with similar enthusiasm. The Ramadan games contributed to the strengthening of relations between the staff, helping them get closer to each other in situations different from the seriousness and discipline imposed by the work environment.

The games were video recorded and hundreds of photographs of the players were taken. The final match of the Ramadan tournament in November 2003 was videotaped as usual. On the evening of November 29, 2003, a few days after the end of the Holy month of Ramadan, and while watching the final match in the Ramadan tournament, which was held in a sports hall close to the Language Institute of the Armed Forces in Al Nahyan Camp, I noticed something abnormal on the side of my neck, and I discovered it elsewhere as well. There was a kind of swelling that caught my eye when the camera zoomed in close to my face. I played back the shots time after time, and paused the video at more than one shot. I looked at the photos from different angles to make sure that there was no optical illusion while I was touching the swelling with my hand. Each time, I was more convinced that it was abnormal.

With Florentino Perez, President of Real Madrid, March 22, 2014

During Ramadan football tournament held by the Center on December 19, 2000

Only by noticing this issue, I went to the Zayed Military Hospital in Abu Dhabi. I was received by Dr. Majdi Lutfi, a physician at the hospital, and Dr. Ahmed Ibrahim, the on-duty surgeon that night. Both doctors examined me attentively and carefully, including all my glands, and it turned out that there was also an armpit lump. I learned that these nodes or glands that are located in different places of the body are called lymph nodes. Both doctors agreed that these symptoms were either caused by a viral infection that led to swollen lymph nodes, or they could be cancerous tumors. I arranged an appointment with both doctors to come to the hospital at 9:00 am the next morning, on November 30, 2003, for blood tests and a CT scan.

A biopsy of the tumor was taken by a simple surgical procedure that entailed anesthesia. Then, the biopsy was sent to Germany to be tested. At first, I felt a kind of denial that is usually felt by patients suffering from a potentially fatal disease. Such patients naturally try not to believe that they developed such a disease. However, after a little while, I reconciled myself to the idea that the worst was yet to come—I might have developed cancer, just like my father (may God rest his soul), who died of gastric cancer in 1996.

I did not have hope that it would be a viral infection, or that it would be a relatively simple condition, so I prepared myself for a hard confrontation. The test result, received on December 3, showed a malignant tumor, which was not quite a surprise for me, despite the difficulty of the matter. The three or four days before the test result appeared were a chance to prepare me to accept the outcome, and to enter a world unknown. It was my first time to hear the expression that sounded almost mysterious: T-cell lymphoblastic lymphoma. This was the enemy lurking in my body for which I had to prepare to fight and conquer through *the triumph of the will*.

Premonitions of Loss

My life was not my primary concern in the face of imminent death; the soul is from God and must go back to its Creator eventually. However, in these moments I thought about the people who would be most grieved by my death, primarily my mother (may God rest her soul in peace), my sister, my wife, and my children. I could not stop thinking about the image of my mother receiving the news of my death. Whenever I tried to get rid of this thought, it came back and controlled me. It would cause a crack in the wall of my resistance and resolved, as I knew that her loving heart could not endure the idea of my death, and her body, being frail by old age, would fail knowing that I had died before my 44th birthday. I was trembling while picturing her crying alone in the dead of night, or holding her tears back in front of others, as not to seem weak. However, God was merciful by sparing us both this painful ordeal.

I knew that my mother would have lived the rest of her life as a prisoner to the moment she lost me, and every corner of my house and those of my brothers and relatives would renew her wounds. I was sure that every family photo would be a source of endless grief, and every mention of my name as well as every phone call would remind her of me. Every street, every occasion and everyone she met, every morning and every night—all these memories would move her to tears and wrench her heart, which engulfed me with love and affection as wide as the universe. When she died a few years later, I recalled the moments of my fear for her, and I found some solace in the fact that the premonitions that haunted me on that distressful day in 2003 did not materialize.

I had the same premonitions about my wife. We did not think or live life as two individuals, but as one. Naturally we became one mind and one soul so united that none of us could imagine life without the other. Also, I thought about my children who might have to deal with life all by themselves at a young age. I thought about the possibility that I might not be beside them when they needed the most tenderness, care, guidance and advice from their father. Back then, my son Khaled had not yet completed his university studies, my daughter Nora was just joining university, and my little daughters, Dana and Farah, were in elementary and primary schools respectively.

Like any father, I recalled that I had always dreamed of the moment they would graduate, and that I would see them building their personalities, making their success stories and forming happy and close-knit families. I would be beside them at all these times to boost, encourage and help them to overcome the difficulties they face in life, which are too common. I knew that my death would leave permanent scars in the tender hearts of my daughters, and restless fear from the changes of time. I felt compassion for them to bear such sadness at a time they should be embracing life and the future with all the power and energies of hope and optimism.

When I returned home that evening, I stopped in front of my house in amazement, as if I was seeing it for the first time. Almost 10 years had elapsed since we moved into this small villa, which I rented in 1993, at the same time the ECSSR was being established. I discovered that I never once had the time to pay attention to the details I saw that night: an old tree clinging to the ground although a strong wind rocked it once so hard that it tilted to the left a bit. The adjacent tree could not resist the wind and fell to the ground, leaving only part of the root that remained as a gravestone after the saws had removed the rest of the broken trunk. The black, short iron columns above the gate, whose highest point took the shape of a curve—the left side of which was higher than the right one. The decorative

The villa where I lived for a long time in Abu Dhabi, and where I was living when I received the news of my cancer diagnosis

small palm tree, with its fresh green fronds resting on the wall as if neutralizing, with its succulent and lively greenery, the death of the adjacent tree blown down by the storm. The grass lawn, which used to be, more often than not, left without proper mowing. The bulging brickwork, which was laid in organized lines above the glass window bulging forward and throwing its shadow on the entrance. I paused this time at dozens of fine details and I found that I was seeing everything from a new perspective.

Getting cancer is certainly an earth-shattering event in anyone's life. Surely, it is by far the most influential and the most persisting event in my memory at every moment, and I have no doubt that it has had the greatest impact on me. I believe that I would not have thought about writing my autobiography and career if I had not experienced cancer, faced its horrors, and eventually recovered my health. A disease, no matter what it is, is an experience that deeply shakes the human consciousness violently, and helps a person see clearer than in the past.

I remember, in particular, the pain associated with my body losing its privacy and sanctity while doctors, nurses and other professionals in the medical field, during my treatment, had easy access to it; something that imparts a feeling of weakness that left a bitter impact on me. In the Arab culture, we are among the nations who are most keen on veiling the body and treasuring its sanctity. There are many tales about fathers who, throughout their lives, appeared only fully clothed in front of their children. This concept of covering oneself is instilled in us since early childhood. I think that many of us find it embarrassing to show up in a swimming suit in front of a group of friends. It is a feeling that is deeper and far beyond the religious sentiment that most probably hits those who have audacious thoughts and views, and are dismissive of the constants of society.

A body covered by nothing and dealt with by hospital staff as something normal was not the case for me. The sense of overwhelming shame never diminished every time I felt that I could not cover my body among people. I always felt, even if they were doctors and nurses, the exposure of my body in front of them was not something that could be forgotten or overlooked. Even in the most painful moments, I felt ashamed and that made me feel that the disease was even harsher than I thought.

Siddhartha Mukherjee, at the beginning of his unique book, *The Emperor of All Maladies: A Biography of Cancer*, published in Arabic with an excellent translation by Arabic Magazine in 2013, quoted the well-known American writer, Susan Sontag, "Illness is the night-side of life, a more onerous citizenship. Everyone who is born holds dual citizenship, in the kingdom of the well and in the kingdom of the sick. Although we all prefer to use the good passport, sooner or later each of us is obliged, at least for a spell, to identify ourselves as citizens of that other place."

The disease that remains only for a few days prompts new ideas and perceptions in the mind of man. However, if that illness is cancer, what happens in the consciousness, self and soul of the sufferer, becomes similar to the "Big Bang," in its extent and impact on the individual level; the first explosion, with all that it brings forth of amazing cosmic wonders.

This disease that forces you for years not to know anything else, not to feel a single thing except its omnipotent power, and to only be overwhelmed by its toll on every organ in your body, is an unbearable pain that makes you slowly lose parts of your body and soul. This disease makes you feel that it controls you, feeds on your cells, blood and bones; sending flames of fire in them. It is a disease that you cannot really describe how you feel about until you befriend it and talk to it as if it were a travel companion you knew for a long time, and struggle with it and fight it as if it were a bitter enemy. This disease makes you see everything with a fresh perspective: the morning; the evening; money; success; childhood; old age; happiness; sadness; victory; defeat; hope; pain; the blue sky; the twilight of dusk; pride; music; plateaus; and valleys; the scorching heat of the desert; salinity of the sea water; memories of departed friends; the paths taken; love; hate. Everything is changing and you then discover that the world, in which you have lived for 44 years and that you had a grasp on, comes to life again in a completely new shape. The disease becomes a reality that encompasses the universe.

Only one thing remains superior to disease: faith. Only faith can beat the disease. Just as everything changes in your life, so too does your perspective of faith in the Almighty Creator. Your relation to Him becomes made up of thousands of feelings that no dictionaries can possibly and eloquently express in words or phrases. The presence of illness in your life cannot be rivaled except by the presence of God and His solemn manifestation in everything around you. I do not think a man gets closer to God in any situation than he does in the peak of pain, where the soul becomes astonishingly purified and approaches the essence of light, mercy and the perpetuity in God the Almighty. These moments do not linger because their continuity is bigger than what one can handle. However, they settle in one's being and nothing before them resembles anything after.

MD Anderson Cancer Center, Houston, Texas, where I fought my major battle against cancer

Your prayer is no longer the one you used to perform. Your fast, if you are still capable of fasting, is no longer anything like your fasting in the past. The mosque, the verses of the Holy Quran, supplications to God, confiding your worries and hopes in Him and His presence in your life all become different than anything you knew before. I think I was lucky, as the disease, despite its cruelty, opened these doors for me to know myself and know the world, and above all to know the Creator in a way that I had never experienced before in my previous life.

His Highness Sheikh Mohamed bin Zayed Al Nahyan (may God protect him) gave his orders for me to travel and receive treatment at MD Anderson Cancer Center in Houston, Texas. The hospital was recognized by prestigious scientific authorities through annual assessment as the best cancer center in the United States of America and the world for many consecutive years. Established in 1941, this University of Texas-affiliated center specializes in treating cancer and is mainly a major research and treatment institution, with a medical research budget that is almost equal to the entire budget of some countries. Every year, thousands of patients get cancer treatment there.

The Royal Marsden Hospital, at Surrey University, UK, specializes in cancer treatment; its foundation dates back to 1851

A Doctor Who Played God

On December 7, 2003, I flew to the United States of America, after making a transit stop in the United Kingdom, a country with an excellent international reputation for cancer treatment. I believed it was logical to consult an oncologist there about my condition. Following the advice of some of my friends, I chose the Royal Marsden Hospital, which specializes in cancer treatment. It is based in Surrey, a 45-minute drive from London. Established in 1851, the Royal Marsden Hospital holds a good reputation worldwide. When I visited it, the hospital had spent more than 150 years treating cancer patients. This meant that any medical opinion I got from there had its own weight, credibility and influence.

After completing the usual routine procedures, I met one of the prominent chief oncologists in the hospital, who headed one of its departments. While studying my case and thoroughly reading my medical reports that I had brought along with me, I watched every expression on his face, all his reactions and every word he uttered. He took a lot of time before he simply said "you will die in two weeks."

It was terrifying—almost like a ruling by a higher court confirming a death sentence. It is similar to an initial death sentence for a person to know that he has gotten cancer, based on the bitter experiences that make cancer itself a synonym for inevitable death, which makes some people tremble at the very thought of the disease. When you sober up from the shock of hearing the death sentence for the first time, a fading hope of treatment grows inside you to find a therapy, looking forward to a great physician, as if he were an appeal or cessation judge in whose hand your destiny lies. The doctor who works for a world-renowned medical institution almost crushed all my hopes, confirming that I would die within just days. Certainly, his words alone could be the cause of death for some patients. He made a terrible mistake against me, and against his profession, without caring about the ramifications. All the circumstances were pushing me to give in to his words. However, an internal and hidden voice kept urging me to resist giving in to his talk and taking it for granted.

I think that the main reason behind this resistance was due to the depth of my religious feeling. Life and death are destined by God the Almighty beyond human limits of perception. This was one of the fundamental principles established in my mind since childhood as a result of my religious upbringing. I am fully appreciative of science and believe in it. I consider it to be the basis of human evolution. However, from a scientific perspective, I know that there are a lot of cases where science cannot have the final say, including the barrier of secrets surrounding life and death issues. I think that my faith and confidence in God were at their peak at that moment. They stimulated my will and injected me with a considerable power to overcome what I consider the most difficult moment of my life, and triumph over despair that was standing nearby anticipating a collapse in my morale. If it had happened, I would not have been able to resist and conquer my disease (thank God). Thus, I consider faith as a source of strength and the main factor that enabled me to survive the clutches of the fatal disease.

When I left the doctor's room, I called His Highness Sheikh Mohamed bin Zayed Al Nahyan (may God protect him), and told him that I had only two weeks to live. My tone might have been strange at that moment. I was overwhelmed with surprise, or still engaged in my internal battles, which required first to ward off despair and surrender, to the extent that His Highness thought that there was something wrong with me. His Highness told me, "Do not pay attention to what was said and go to the United States of America to begin treatment." After finishing my call with His Highness Sheikh Mohamed bin Zayed Al Nahyan (may God protect him), I called my wife. She asked me to forget what I had heard as well, and to continue my journey to Houston as planned to receive treatment.

The strange thing that the British doctor did was that he gave me a letter explaining my condition and to deliver it to the hospital where I would receive my treatment. I still have this letter until today. There were empty cells to write the name of the patient and the hospital to which the letter was addressed. Both were marked with "Unknown," despite the fact that MD Anderson is among the world's most renowned hospitals in the treatment of cancer, if not the best of them all. The language of this letter might explain the unprofessional and inadequate behavior of that doctor toward me. It seems that he was angry when he found out that I was going to MD Anderson for treatment. His anger was reflected in his description of the hospital as "unknown." I know that professional jealousy may lead some people to commit errors. However, the doctor seemed to go beyond "professional jealousy" into apparent hatred. Thus, what the British doctor did was not merely a mistake, it was as serious as a crime.

I might have given the British doctor the benefit of the doubt despite what he did, attributing his behavior to bad temper, or certain pressures in his work or in his personal life. These could have been the main causes of his nervousness and harshness. However, a second meeting with him in 2007 ended all such justifications. In our second meeting, I talked to him softly, reminding him that more than 200 weeks had elapsed since he has told me four years ago of my inevitable death. He looked at me saying in his usual harsh manner, "This is your luck. You're lucky that you did not die."

The arrogant physician did not have the courage to admit his mistake, although it was now obvious beyond any doubt. He did not even say that it was the will of the Creator that kept me alive, or even think about saying thank God for being safe, as a normal person would say. I found that his behavior was consistently bad since the first moment I met him, leaving no room for goodwill. First, he made himself a God, determining destinies and deciding life and death as per his whims. Second, he was vindictive and hateful toward the success of others. He was being racist against Arabs and clearly hated them. The competition blinded him to the extent that he made mistakes that could kill patients. Did he not know that the psychological and morale factors are very important to resist cancer, and if you undermine them, the patient could die? Third, he lacked self-reflection and inability to admit his own shortcomings because his ego prevented him from knowing his true self. It is no exaggeration for me to expect that he wished that I had died just to prove that he was right.

I spent two days in London, where I stayed in Park Tower Hotel in Knightsbridge, one of my favorite hotels that I usually stay in during my visits to the UK. At the hotel, a number of UAE figures visited me, including the cultural attaché and the military attaché, who was accompanied by some UAE Armed Forces officers. These visits reflected a fact of which I would later discover many aspects. Throughout the period of my treatment, I was flooded by visits from my close friends, colleagues and loved ones. It is a tradition that shows one of the aspects of connectivity we enjoy in the UAE in particular, and in the Arab culture in general. It constitutes a significant social advantage and reveals the existence of social sources of potential inner power in the state that are sometimes overlooked by analysts.

During this period, I came to understand the importance attached to visiting the sick in the teachings of true Islam, and its rich contents of noble human values, which extremists prevent from emerging by committing atrocities in the name of Islam and by distorting its tolerant appearance.

Faint Candlelight in the Dark

The journey from the United Kingdom to the United States of America was one of the most unforgettable trips of my life. We took off from Gatwick airport, located in the county of West Sussex. The flight took nearly nine hours, during which I experienced a variety of conflicting ideas, especially since I was traveling to the unknown. My mind started to recall scenes from my early childhood, my youth, adolescence, years of university in Kuwait and in the United States of America, and business trips.

Death became a usual thought that ran simply through my head, as if it belonged to someone else. A week before I found out about my disease, I was on an official visit with His Highness Sheikh Mohamed bin Zayed Al Nahyan (may God protect him) in Moscow. When I recalled my engagements and concerns during this trip and the things I was hoping to accomplish in later years, I realized that I was learning new lessons about life that might change all of a sudden. This showed me a new perspective that I had only heard of. However, as they say, one eyewitness is better than ten hearsays.

When the British Airways flight landed at Houston's George Bush Intercontinental Airport, I was destined to come across other hardships to complement the ones I had already faced in the previous days. The American airports were still under the shock of the 9/11 attacks. Thus, Arabs or Muslims aroused suspicions at European and American airports. Once I arrived, I was directly escorted into an interrogation room. All those whose full name included "Muhammad" or "Ali" were subjected to interrogation. "Ali" is my father's name (may God rest his soul in peace). I had to undergo two hours of psychologically and physically exhausting investigations, at a time when death seemed to loom over me. The words of the British doctor kept ringing in

With H.E. Hashim Al-Qaysiyah (special adviser to H.H. Sheikh Tahnoon bin Zayed Al Nahyan, UAE); H.E. Ibrahim Al Abed (adviser to the Chairman of UAE National Media Council); Ali Khalifa Al Rumaithi, Executive Director for Radio and Television in Dubai Media Incorporated; Ms. Nora Al Suwaidi, Director General of Cancer Patient Care Society (RAHMA), and Mr. Jassim Al Hosni, Member of the Board of RAHMA, at the launching ceremony of the Society (RAHMA), September 15, 2015

my mind from time to time, barely penetrating the defenses I had built around myself to fend off weakness and surrender.

The security officials at Houston's airport completely disregarded the circumstances that could have rendered this interrogation unjustifiable. For instance I came to Houston to seek treatment for cancer, and I had all the official documents to prove this. In addition, I did not come from an Arab country's airport; I had stopped for two days in London and took a British Airways flight to the United States of America. Thus, if I had any intention to carry out a terrorist act, why not choose London as a viable target? But such questions did not mean anything to the American security officials. The rationale was to take maximum security measures and to assume the worst case scenarios. As long as the arriving individual was an Arab or a Muslim, regardless of his nationality, condition, reason for his visit, or any other circumstance, all measures had to be fully applied. I cannot blame the Americans for the actions they were taking, as they had suffered much. If an Arab country had faced a lesser event, similar measures would have been taken in order to protect their security.

During my journey, three people – an elderly biologist, a physician and my office manager accompanied me. They were there to help me properly start my treatment and to find the correct destination at the MD Anderson Cancer Center, with its various departments, specializations and the mysterious world that I knew nothing about. However, instead of going to a T-cell specialist, since I was diagnosed with T-cell lymphoblastic lymphoma, we went to a B-cell specialist. The difference between the two kinds is significant for several reasons, as I came to know later on. The chances

At the launching ceremony of the UAE Cancer Patient Care Society (RAHMA), September 15, 2015

of recovery for patients with T-cell lymphoma amount to 70 percent, with 30 percent of the cases terminal. On the other hand, the survival rate for the patients with B-cell lymphoma is around 30 percent, with 70 percent incurable. Unfortunately, the biologist and the physician accompanying me were neither familiar with my condition nor knew where to begin my treatment. The person we talked to by mistake told us to go to a leukemia doctor.

What the doctor told me left a negative impact on me because I had not yet learned any information that helped me to understand the nature of my disease. While I knew that according to the diagnosis, I had T-cell lymphoblastic lymphoma; here, the specialist guided me to visit a leukemia doctor. Was I suffering from leukemia too? Maybe the British doctor was right in saying I was going to die in two weeks. When I thought of establishing the Cancer Patient Care Society (RAHMA) later, I recalled my distorted thoughts, state of bewilderment and confusion that took over me when I knew about my illness for the first time. This confusion lasted for quite some time and it could have had a negative impact on me psychologically. Despite my significant academic qualifications and knowledge, as I thought I had due to the nature of my research work, I was lost in names and terminology, and subject to anxieties and obsessions that fed on a lack of knowledge and an unfamiliarity with the disease. Therefore, providing full information to patients was one of the things that I aimed to implement at RAHMA, as I will explain later.

When I walked into the office of Dr. Deborah Thomas, whom I regard as an angel of mercy, I was not in my best condition. She was responsible for my treatment throughout these years until she retired in May 2015. When I met her for the first time, I had been through the worst 10 days of my life, during which I received consecutive earthshaking news. However, when I walked out of her office, I was a different person, as I heard for the first time something that I could consider encouraging. There was really very little hope, but after all the bad news I considered what I heard as a lifebuoy thrown to me, even if I was amid crashing, tumultuous waves and a seemingly endless violent storm in an ocean beleaguered by powerful hurricanes.

Dr. Deborah Thomas received me in a calmingly reassuring manner. When I told her what the British doctor had said, she told me in a calm voice that his opinion was worthless and that any physician with the least shred of understanding would not tell a patient that he will die in two weeks. She proceeded with her calm demeanor after examining the papers I brought along with me and said "My dear, I have been treating cancer for 20 years, and if I was destined, God forbid, to develop cancer and was given the liberty to choose which kind of cancer, I would choose the kind of cancer you have because the chances of recovery are pretty high." I always believe that words have their magical effect and influence. Nothing was ever more soothing than the words carefully chosen by Dr. Deborah Thomas to give my internal resistance the first line of defense. For the first time ever, I saw a faint light at the end of the pitch-black tunnel.

In addition to intelligence, professionalism and wisdom, these words also reflected a humane attitude. They were a kind of quick Godly justice that granted me, after only two days, a counterweight to make up for the imbalance caused by the British physician's opinion. My peace of mind was restored. After a long time of despair, a soft rain from a blessed cloud drizzled upon the seeds of hope inside me and their roots started to deepen into the ground, and their sprouts found their way to the light and warmth of the sun.

The physician went on saying "The weekend is coming up and we'll start medication right after it. Can you read English?" I replied "yes." She then told me that she would give me certain materials to read that would explain in a simple way the nature of my disease and the treatment methods to be carried out. She told me that chemotherapy would start the following week and that I should be prepared for head and beard hair loss.

Over the next three days, I occupied myself with reading about my disease in the papers and articles that were carefully and professionally written for this purpose. I knew more about my relentless enemy, and I realized that it was not impossible to beat it. Thus, I took the initiative myself and shaved the hair off my whole body before starting the therapy, in preparation for the battle and to not be surprised when my hair fell out. On Monday morning, I was all set for the first round of the battle, armed with the knowledge I had already gained and the optimism that was growing in me.

A Killer Friend

In the papers that Dr. Deborah Thomas gave me, I got to know my enemy and realized how ferocious it was. Simply put, cancer is an abnormal pathological growth of the cells. It may hit any part of the human body, including its organs, which makes for its various types. The growth and division of the cells take place every second inside the human body, which is necessary for its continuity. This happens according to a system preserved by the human

DNA that controls the growth and division of cells, as well as the suspension of their growth and division at the appropriate time. The abnormality that is caused by cancer triggers the growth of an unlimited and uncontrollable number of infected cells that acquire an aggressive behavior and an ability to invade adjacent healthy cells, destroying them and promptly transferring the abnormality to other organs and parts of the body. This translates into a kind of brutality of infected cells, which devours the intact cells and disrupts their function and performance.

Many factors are thought to cause cancer or pave the way to developing it. However, none of them seem plausible or sufficient to explain why someone might get it and another might survive it. I have read about the 160 causes of cancer. However, I believe the real cause is related to genetics, especially since getting this disease comes down to a dysfunction in genes, even if the mechanisms of such a dysfunction and how it really happens are an enigma so far. Psychological stress, addiction to work and smoking may play a role in developing cancer. However, nothing extremely decisive was announced by any of the specialists in the cancer research field to confirm this. The link still holds true between developing cancer and certain viruses, exposure to certain types of pesticides, dyes or contaminants in general. Of course, exposure to radiation cannot be ignored as another possible cause.

In my case, according to my own explanation, genes might be the most probable cause. As I had earlier said, my father (may God rest his soul in peace) had stomach cancer. There may be another reason. There is no established equation that proves that A leads to B. The most likely explanations given by the World Health Organization (WHO) in a 2013 report, dealt with the changes that convert a normal cell into a malignant one. These changes result from an interaction between the individual's genetic factors and groups of external factors. As to the nature of such interactions, how it works and its catalysts, these still remain unknown.

The lymphocytes were the spot chosen by the cancer to attack my body. The lymphocytes are among the types of white blood cells and part of the defense system, which helps the body resist various kinds of diseases and infections. They usually become swollen by certain diseases, or when exposed to a viral infection, as they turn from a cell one cannot see with the naked eye to a mass that one can feel and touch. The lymphocytes have different types as well, each with its own responsibilities. The B-cells type's function is secretion of antibodies that resist any invasion of the body by bacteria and viruses. The T-cells are tasked with identifying particles and materials alien to the body. In my case, the cancer hit the latter type of lymphocytes, as shown by its name: T-cell lymphoblastic lymphoma.

There are different ways of treating cancer, depending on its type, degree and nature. Among these are surgical intervention, radiation therapy, and chemotherapy. The last one was the treatment Dr. Deborah Thomas recommended for me. It is strange that the discovery of chemotherapy was one of the results of the First World War, following the brutal behavior of using chemical weapons. The opposing factions used poisonous mustard gas, killing tens of thousands and injuring many others. Specialists noted that those who were exposed to the poisonous gas experienced a significant decline in the numbers of their white blood cells. Since lymphomas, as well as other types of leukemia, occur as a result of an excessive and uncontrolled proliferation of white blood cells, the idea is to use of certain chemical compounds to stop this excessive reproduction.

As I came to know from the reading material that Dr. Deborah Thomas had given me, chemotherapy involves a mixture of toxins directed to kill the uncontrolled cells looking to invade other intact cells. However, these cells interfere with healthy cells needed by the body to perform its functions normally. Moreover, other organs in the overstrained body of the person plagued with cancer are affected by a high dose of poison injected in the veins, leaving behind serious side effects that could be life-threatening. Still, you cannot help but deal with this killer running into tissues of your body, and try to befriend it. I got ready for a forced relationship with this friend that kills hostile cells but also destroys other cells greatly needed by the body to resist and survive. Since chemotherapy is almost fatal, its sessions are always followed by transfusing blood or platelets into the patient's body.

Knowledge is power. Within a few days, I became completely informed of what hit me and my enemy was no longer unknown to me. Now, I knew what it looked like and the way it moved. A lot of what I came across while reading was scary. However, it also had some reassuring parts, based on purely scientific evidence and reliable statistics and studies. Also, I had this confidence that I had gained since my first meeting with Dr. Deborah Thomas who took over my treatment. The confident physician took her first steps by successfully attacking hostile cells of anxiety and negative feelings implanted inside me by the Royal Marsden Hospital doctor and completely destroyed them. Likewise, reading, along with thinking, reasoning, observation and inference, brought me back to my real self that I used to know and boosted my will to the level required to line up for the life and death battle.

Eight Sessions

While Houston was starting its first day of the week with full energy, neglecting the severe cold weather, I was heading on Monday morning, December 15, 2003, to MD Anderson Hospital, to finally meet in person my "killer friend."

On that day, I was scheduled to receive my first chemotherapy session. Although I have been through many hardships and problems during my long journey of treatment from various diseases, chemotherapy sessions were the times during which I felt most vulnerable. Plastic bags of different colors surrounded my bed. Medical fluids inside the bags were administered to my body through a surgical opening in my shoulder, where a tube is inserted to administer solutions and medicine. Some bags' content were taken before the chemotherapy dose, while others were to be taken afterward to make the body adapt to the toxins in the dose.

Over time, I became aware of the moments when the pain would increase, and so I would prepare myself accordingly. If green symbolizes safety and fertility for people, for me, the green medicine in the tiny bottle in chemotherapy sessions meant a languishing pain all throughout my body. I could see the smoke coming out of my mouth, in the literal sense, when the green medication went through my blood. Certainly, something inside of me was burning. Consequently, the body becomes fragile and extremely vulnerable to any infection.

In such a case, any common cold or flu can be fatal, as the body that lost its immunity as a side effect of chemotherapy will not be able to resist it. Thus, physicians will attempt to prevent infections from occurring. With chemotherapy, you will have to deal with painful side effects, least of all hair loss. The list of afflictions includes fatigue, reduced immunity, nausea and digestive problems and osteoporosis. Many other organs and their vital functions are affected as well. In my case, on top of all these problems, I had two additional ones: smoking and diabetes.

While I had developed diabetes few years earlier, I got used to it and it did not prevent me from working, sometimes even 24 hours a day, and under immense pressures as well. But with the cancer therapy, diabetes had become a serious matter that had to be considered. What made it even more difficult for me was the fact that I did not quit smoking when I found out that I developed cancer, despite being warned by physicians and friends, and despite what I had read about the seriousness of my habit. I often left my bed in the hospital for a smoke in the designated area outside. If there are people who deny the idea that smoking is a direct cause of cancer, it is at least certain that smoking worsens cancer. Unfortunately, knowing this did not stop me from smoking at all.

Now, I am sure that when I used to smoke while receiving my chemotherapy, I was not doing myself any favors. If I could travel back in time, I would not do it again. Looking back at everything that happened during this period, I consider myself lucky and I thank God the Almighty very much for blessing me with recovery. The combination of cancer, diabetes and smoking was enough to kill me, but the will of God and His providence had the upper hand at the end of the day.

I received tough chemotherapy once every 21 days. I underwent eight rounds from mid-December 2003 to the beginning of June 2004. This period was filled with complications. Right before the eighth session, I suffered a setback. My kidney weakened and a sort of poisoning affected my body's functions. This is one of the results of chemotherapy that should be taken into account. This setback necessitated stopping chemotherapy and placing me under intensive care for three weeks, during which the unforeseen complications were dealt with and controlled until my health was restored, only to start another treatment phase.

One of the important decisions I made during this period, which I think played a role in my healing, was my consent to take experimental drugs. They were banned in Europe but permissible in the United States of America. One of the experimental drugs with which I was treated is commonly used now to cure cancer. It consisted of two types of pills taken alongside the chemotherapy doses. As far as I can remember about this drug, when it first came into existence, one type almost cost $600 while the other cost $70. By 2015, the two pills cost no more than a few dollars, and the treatment of cancer with this drug requires three sessions of chemotherapy rather than eight. The lower cost and the fewer number of sessions are attributed to scientific development and non-stop research. The MD Anderson Cancer Center was one of the beacons of scientific research in cancer-related issues, with a research budget that was as large as those of some countries. This made MD

Anderson, along with a few other hospitals, the best choice of treatment for cancer patients around the world.

The decision to accept the experimental drugs was a serious risk, but God the Almighty guided me to the path of righteousness by giving my consent and helped me through this decision just as He helped me make other decisions all through my life during hard times. God guided me through the many alternatives I had, each with its own issues and concerns, and helped me choose between them, based on my inner intuition and a calculated logical thinking, of course.

It is not always safe to take experimental medications. Evidently, there are many regulations and charters that regulate the phases of drug experimentation until drugs are tried on human beings. However, even after fulfilling many conditions and procedures to ensure their safety, there is still a marginal risk entailed in the process.

I felt an obligation toward humanity when they experimented the drugs on me. Before me, there were people who already volunteered for years to make sure that I could safely take a drug that had not been available before and that would increase my recovery chances. I judged that it was time I return the favor for all those people, whom I did not know, by helping out with the current experiments for the sake of those who might develop the same disease in the future. I was thinking that experimenting with the drug would actually open the door for recovery for other people with the same disease.

The improvement I felt, in spite of many negative indicators, motivated the hospital physicians and researchers to study my case and run some tests on me. My medical record and the improvement I made were part of the scientific research machine in this huge beacon of medicine. I said to myself sarcastically: "Here, I became a human guinea pig!"

The desire to live was one of the factors of my recovery; I never caved in to the idea of life becoming completely meaningless. Such ideas haunt many patients and lead them to psychologically sentence themselves to death by thinking that their death is inevitably imminent. They believe that it is futile to enjoy a music track, read about a new theory in international relations or cheer for the football team they love. Reading a proverb like "work for your worldly life as if you are living forever," motivated me to fight for my life. It is the desire to live and not to surrender.

I remember that at the peak of my chemotherapy – at a time when my white blood cells were lower than 1,000/mcL, which is too low by all measures* – I went with my son Khaled to watch a basketball game between the Los Angeles Lakers and Houston Rockets. The court where the match was to be held was close to our hotel in Houston. Khaled was wearing a Los Angeles Lakers' shirt while we were in Houston, the stronghold of the opposing team's fans. When we arrived at the basketball court, I said to Khaled seriously, but with a touch of humor "If you pick a fight with a fan because of this shirt, count me out, since any slight bleeding could be fatal to me." The will to live, a sense of humor and the passion for the things I love were important factors of my resistance to cancer, with all its force.

I also remember that a Chinese medical intern told me sometime after the treatment started that I was going to die, echoing the prophecy of the Royal Marsden physician. His opinion was based on the claim that if I were to recover, I should have already after two and a half months of treatment and I could have had a chance to live. Now, two months and seventeen days had gone by and I had not recovered yet, which meant that I was dying. Once again, I had to muster all the courage to fight, mobilize the resistance I had inside me and never yield to the idea that I had only two weeks to live, as predicted by the British physician. I had to remind myself that his words were pure nonsense even though he was more experienced and renowned. So why would the Chinese intern's opinion not be sheer nonsense as well?!

---

* Normal range of white blood cells is 3,500 to 10,500 cells/mcL, according to the Mayoclinic website, https:// goo.gl/2ivdcU

During the treatment, we were asked by the hospital management to practice certain activities that had a positive psychological impact on patients. Thus, citizens of the "Republic of Cancer" developed a common identity, due to a strong connection that keeps them bonded. Among these activities are the mutual visits among patients. One of those visits, which I will never forget, was a visit to an Emirati child, who was about 11 years old. Before the visit, I knew that the cancer had spread to many places in his body, including his stomach, pancreas and colon, and that his chances of recovery were nearly zero. As his illness was discovered at a late stage, it resulted in malignant cells infiltration into different parts of his body. The visit was painful because the child passed away shortly afterward and only memories of that visit, with all the sad feelings it brought about, remained.

These activities also involved visiting the Pediatrics Section at the hospital. I spent some time there watching children's faces, whose innocence and beauty still shone despite the disease. The children's toys were scattered everywhere around us and some of the kids tried to dunk the ball in the basket at the corner of the room, imitating the basketball stars they adored. The children were from different countries and nationalities, with different colors, races and languages, but their enemy was the same (cancer). They were males and females of different ages, but alike in the suffering and pain they had to deal with due to their sickness, and they felt that a strong bond linked and united them. At this moment, I realized that cancer does not differentiate between young and old, African and American, one nationality or another, nor different religious sects. Cancer is a danger threatening humanity everywhere. People should realize the things that hold them together and unite them are more than those that keep them apart, and that the humanity of people predates their division into sects, castes and parties. Therefore, humanity should be their highest value.

It is very painful to develop cancer, but in the pediatrics section, I found the situation more severe. It is hard to forget the sight of a girl, who had not

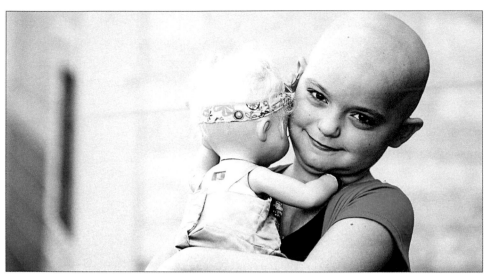

During treatment period, I used to visit the Pediatrics Section at the hospital. I spent some time there watching the children's faces, whose innocence and beauty the disease failed to hide

even turned five yet, that lost all of her hair due to chemotherapy. If you were old, you could understand this. But how could this little girl understand what was going on with her? How could she bear to look at herself in the mirror only to see that she was denied her golden hair that her mother was so keen on brushing every morning? How could she understand why she was different from her peers who play without pain or fatigue, without needles piercing the body and foul tasting drugs day and night? These visits were a chance for me and others to ponder and contemplate our situation in the world from a new perspective. They also helped us to rediscover our humanity in light of pain that fuels the intellect and lights up new corners, which otherwise would not have been able to face the incurable disease.

Strict Administrative System

One of the most important things I realized during my cancer days was how strong the system I had implemented to run the ECSSR was. I considered this the hallmark of success of any business, as I had seen in every successful organization or any sector capable of competition and development. The advantage of a strong system is that it never builds success on the shoulders of a particular person or a particular group, but rather it integrates individuals and groups automatically in its mechanisms so that people joining or leaving the organization would not influence it or render it incapable of functioning properly. I strongly tested the validity of this hypothesis for the first time in 2004, at a time I had to face the ferocity of the disease and the difficulty of treatment, not to mention my involuntary presence out of country.

The strong system has proved itself effective. Work at the ECSSR continued at the usual pace, where the momentum was great, and each person was performing his role at the same level, as the practices had already been established and had become part of the character of the staff and the nature of the Center's work. Since the work's nature seemed deeply rooted, any new employee would find himself facing two choices: adapt to the system and work according to the Center's rules, or leave.

My return to work shortly after helped to maintain the system implemented in the Center, despite my remoteness and the limitations it imposed. I owe this return to the communication and technological revolution, a phenomenon that is among my research interests, whether on the personal level or through the ECSSR activities. In 2004, I had the opportunity to meticulously supervise, guide and closely follow all the Center's events and daily activities. I also carefully assessed its performance and intervened, when necessary, to correct its course.

During that year, the current building of the ECSSR was still under construction. Relocating to the new premises was important since working in a single building equipped with all necessary facilities, and designed from the beginning to accommodate all work requirements differed completely from working in a number of various residential villas distant from each other. The villa with the library, for example, was a bit too far from the ones containing the other departments, and its facilities were not adequate. The Center's conferences and some other activities were held in distant

ECSSR premises, Abu Dhabi, UAE

hotels, which required doubling necessary effort to plan them. This caused logistics problems, considering the confidentiality and sensitivity of such events. On the other hand, the new building contains facilities that guarantee that everything is carried out in the way we desire and at the required level, saving a lot of effort.

The first steps toward constructing the new building of the ECSSR were taken in 1998. By 2003, the building was in its final stages, and all that was left was choosing the furniture, equipment and interior design. The decor was very important to me as it represented the final stage of how the Center would appear. Those who have gone through such an experience know how exhausting it is, as it contains hundreds of details that must be all attended to, including comparisons between different choices, taking into account homogeneity to ensure a unified character of the place and to achieve both aesthetic and practical aspects. I took a look at many designs and graphics and carefully examined them before making up my mind. Sometimes, I consulted specialists and conferred with technicians and engineers, before eventually making a final decision. Even the colors and types of furniture were of concern to me.

At the graduation ceremony of one of the diplomas, at the Department of Training and Continuous Development, at the ECSSR, May 27, 2014

Cancer did not stop me from reading, working and producing. Work was part of fighting cancer and never yielding to it. Work means you are alive and that your role in life continues. Work has always been among the most important values in my life, and I never regarded it as a means to make a living; rather, I saw it as an end in itself. That is why the idea of work-

Presenting a gift to Dr. Mohammed Mukhtar Juma, Egyptian Minister of Awqaf, on the sidelines of a lecture titled "A Culture of Coexistence: Towards a New Vision," at the ECSSR, July 15, 2014"

ing for long hours or the end and start of a work day never meant anything to me all through my life. I consider myself in a state of continuous work. Work might be one of the factors that sharpened my will and contributed to my recovery. Though absolute certainty is unlikely in such cases, the studies on certain types of cancer reported that the percentage of recovery was found to be higher among those who work than those who do not work.

With a group of foreign and Arab clerics, intellectuals and academics, including Egyptian Minister of Religious Endowments; Adviser for Religious and Judicial Affairs at the UAE Ministry of Presidential Affairs; the Mufti of the Lebanese Republic; Chairman of the Emirates Red Crescent Authority; Secretary of the Pontifical Council for Interreligious Dialogue at the Vatican, during the "First Arab Thinkers Forum," held at ECSSR on January 18, 2016

During this year, I kept in touch with all the events going on in the world because of my personal attention and being the ECSSR Director General. An opportunity presented itself for me to read in a way that I never had before. Alongside the reports and studies of the Center, I read a large collection of books in 2004. I had plenty of time; more than was ever available to me during the past years that were burdened with tasks, interviews and business trips and all the time and effort spent on administrative matters. I had to spend one whole week at the hospital every three weeks and there was nothing better to do than read to fill this time. While I was out of the hospital I used to read important books issued in the same year, and other books that I had put off reading until I had a lot of time.

One of the problems I came across was how to keep the whole thing a secret from my late mother (may God rest her soul in peace). Being sick herself, she could not handle such a shock. Fortunately, she got used to me being away because of my eventful work, which entailed many tasks and overseas trips. All through this period, I was very keen on calling her without telling her anything about my illness. Sometimes, she thought I was inside the country and that my engagements were keeping me from visiting her. I did not see her at all, except once during the course of my treatment.

He is Your Soldier, Your Highness

I was once asked by a friend "Were there any disturbing or unwelcome visits during the course of your treatment?" My reply was deci-

Receiving a gift from H.E. Jabr Ghanem Al Suwaidi, Director General of His Highness the Crown Prince's Court, Abu Dhabi, March 5, 2014

sive "No!" There were no disturbing visits. How could there be any such visits when those who called on me were family, loved ones, friends and colleagues, who went through a lot of trouble to come all the way and support me and stand by my side in these critical moments? All those who came from the UAE and other brotherly Arab countries spent a lot of time and effort to be there for me after very long and exhausting flights and checking into the same hotel in which I stayed.

ECSSR staff ceremony to honor me for receiving my honorary PhD from the Swiss University of Lugano, November 26, 2015

They provided me with psychological and moral support, which I believe was one of the reasons why I recovered. I received many calls from people expressing their noble feelings and to make sure that I was well. The callers were keen on telling me that they were going to visit me, expressing their willingness to provide any kind of help I needed. I promised them that I would not hesitate to ask for their help if needed and I tried to convince them not to travel all the way since I already knew how tough the journey was. However, many of them insisted that they would come. One of the calls that I can never forget was the one I received from His Highness the President Sheikh Khalifa bin Zayed Al Nahyan (may God protect him), who deems all UAE citizens as his own sons. His call boosted my morale and helped me to stay strong and resist.

One of the most important visits that contributed to strengthening my morale and relieving a lot of my pain was the visit paid by His Highness Sheikh Mohamed bin Zayed Al Nahyan (may God protect him), at the beginning of April 2004, in the midst of my chemotherapy agony. When I write about His Highness Sheikh Mohamed bin Zayed Al Nahyan (may God protect him), I am always short of words to express what I would like to say; that is how I feel now when writing about him.

I was banned from leaving the hospital, as per strict instructions by my physicians. However, they had to concede after I insisted I receive His Highness myself. They demanded, though, that I sign a personal waiver claiming that I would take full responsibility for any complications that might occur on account of leaving the hospital. They believed this to be a very serious risk as the consequences might be dire from a purely medical point of view. His Highness Sheikh Mohamed's plane was four hours late due to bad weather conditions, as that night, it was raining cats and dogs as we waited until after midnight.

Once His Highness Sheikh Mohamed got off the plane and saw me sitting in my wheelchair, he went down the stairs so quickly that his escorts had to run to keep up with him. He ran to me, held my wheelchair himself, and led me to the car while glancing reproachingly at everyone else who was present and firmly asked "Why did you leave the hospital? You must be there now. Go back right away and I will come to visit you tomorrow." He helped me himself to enter the car that took me back to the hospital. The effects of chemotherapy might have been evident on my

With H.H. Sheikh Mohamed bin Zayed Al Nahyan, Crown Prince of Abu Dhabi and Deputy Supreme Commander of the UAE Armed Forces (may God protect him), on the sidelines of a visit by the late Dr. Atif Obaid former Prime Minister of Egypt, to the ECSSR on November 2, 1997

face, or waiting for hours might have taken its toll on me and made me look exhausted, but it never crossed my mind that I would not receive His Highness upon arrival. The next day, His Highness arrived at the hospital and met with its manager. He scolded the manager saying "How come you discharged a patient in such a condition?" The manager answered: "Your Highness, he is your soldier. You know him."

I had the honor of serving in the UAE Armed Forces, with His Highness Sheikh Mohamed bin Zayed Al Nahyan (may God protect him) as my direct commander. When we shook hands, there was a resolve characteristic of a military commander. I felt as if he was telling me "be strong," and as a soldier I had no choice but to comply. In his handshake, there was compassion, care and kindness of a father, although we are nearly the same age. His fatherly message was to "resist and fight back," and I've survived, resisted and not given up. The message in his handshake is one that is understood by all Emiratis; all your effort is appreciated and your country will never give up on you and is calling for you to rejoin those who are working for its progress and advancement. In addition, you should hold onto life in order to continue performing your role to the fullest extent possible.

After nearly one and a half months of starting chemotherapy, I was visited by His Highness Sheikh Abdullah bin Zayed Al Na-

The Pride of the UAE

hyan, accompanied by His Excellency Dr. Anwar Gargash at the beginning of February 2004. Their visit coincided with the 38th Super Bowl, the final game of the American football championships. It is a great sporting event that seizes the attention of and is eagerly awaited by everyone in the United States of America. The match is held once a year in an American city. Houston was the city of choice that hosted this big event on February 1, 2004.

Playing the match in Houston meant that all of its hotels were fully booked by sports fans who were ready to do anything in order to attend the most exciting event ever. Accordingly, I personally supervised renting a suitable villa and making all the necessary preparations to receive His Highness Sheikh Abdullah bin Zayed and his escorts. I had to take some drugs intravenously, while undertaking the work to complete these preparations because I believed that the least I could do for this kind visit was to leave no stone unturned to welcome His Highness Sheikh Abdullah. The noble words and feelings of His Highness were the best help I could

With H.H. Sheikh Abdullah bin Zayed Al Nayhan, UAE Minister of Foreign Affairs and International Cooperation, on the sidelines of the speech delivered by former US President George W. Bush at the ECSSR Forum, January 13, 2008

ever get at this early that stage of my therapeutic journey. Also, the presence of a friend and colleague, His Excellency Dr. Anwar Gargash, in company with His Highness, reminded me of memories of tough battles we fought together against extremism in UAE University, making me feel that conquering lymphoma was just as possible as conquering and bravely standing up to extremism.

Among those who paid me a visit as well were His Highness Sheikh Khalid bin Mohamed bin Zayed Al Nahyan and His Highness Sheikh Diab bin Mohamed bin Zayed Al Nahyan, each on separate occasions, continuing the heritage of generosity passed on from fathers to sons. Among the meanings suggested by their visits was how the values were passed on to the new generations and instilled into the sons; something the late Sheikh Zayed bin Sultan Al Nahyan (may God rest his soul in peace) was keen on accomplishing.

This whole family is like a school of chivalry and high manners that they encourage each other to preserve, with fathers instilling them into their sons from their early years of childhood. This may be the secret behind the aura of grandeur that surrounds them all, for the ardent youthfulness of the two sons of His Highness Sheikh Mohamed bin Zayed Al Nahyan (may God protect him) that filled my hospital room with life and vitality never overshadowed the grandeur evident on their faces.

The year 2004 did not go without sorrow. We witnessed the passing of the UAE's founding father, the late Sheikh Zayed bin Sultan Al Nahyan (may God rest his soul in peace) on November 2. Back then, I was in Abu Dhabi, as after the completion of chemotherapy sessions doctors allowed me to go back home at various intervals. However, my health condition prevented me from attending the funeral with all the strength and effort needed to go through this ritual. My absence from the funeral was very painful to me because I felt that the disease prevented me from being where I needed to be. However, God the Almighty made it possible for me to bid farewell on the night he died in a different way, which made me feel even closer and eased some of my pains.

On the same night, I accompanied His Highness Sheikh Mohamed bin Zayed Al Nahyan (may God protect him) to Sheikh Zayed's tomb, where we stayed for more than an hour reciting *Al Fatiha* (The Opening) and other verses of the Holy Quran, while a number of other reciters around us kept reciting in reverence. The whole place was surrounded by an aura of awe for the late Sheikh Zayed who engraved his name in the hearts of his countrymen and left behind all the greatest memories and values. He was a true leader who changed the history of his nation.

I think that the way the late Sheikh Zayed bin Sultan Al Nahyan (may God rest his soul in peace) ruled and passed it on to his sons afterward is what helped the UAE to have its present importance among other nations in the world. Justice, equality and sharing the benefits of the wealth endowed by God onto this country were the outcome of the noble principles laid down by the late Sheikh Zayed. His Highness Sheikh

During a visit with the staff of ECSSR to the tomb of the late Sheikh Zayed bin Sultan Al Nahyan (may God rest his soul in peace), where we offered heartfelt prayers for the great late leader, November 2, 2013

Khalifa bin Zayed Al Nahyan, President of the UAE (may God protect him), His Highness Sheikh Mohamed bin Zayed Al Nahyan (may God protect him), and their brothers, sons of the late Sheikh Zayed bin Sultan Al Nahyan (may God rest his soul in peace), have inherited and preserved these ideas and principles in a way that made them an integral part of the country's character and policy.

Chemotherapy Complications

Chemotherapy sessions were not the end; they were merely one stage, albeit the most important in a long-term treatment program that continued almost up until 2013. This treatment program made it mandatory in the past few years to travel to the United States of America just to receive only half an hour of chemotherapy in the most recent years. In 2013, I was told by Dr. Deborah Thomas that my cancer was gone. At the end of 2014 and the beginning of 2015, and after the usual tests, another physician informed me that my recovery from cancer was final, conclusive and beyond any doubt.

As I said earlier, chemotherapy entails killing a killer using a killer. This must take its own tolls. The first toll it had on me was the setback to which I referred before the eighth session. This was followed by other complications. Because my immune system was weakened, a virus known as Cytomegalovirus (CMV) managed to activate itself inside my body, and almost threw me off a cliff. Urgent and tough procedures had to be taken to contain the complications of the virus, which might have been fatal.

In normal conditions, CMV is not harmful and many people develop it during childhood and adolescence as it stays dormant in their bodies without any concerns about causing any great harm. However, this virus might be fatal in some special cases, such as immunodeficiency, or when taking certain medications or undergoing chemotherapy. The last case applied to me, as I had been undergoing chemotherapy for 22 months since my treatment started. In October 14, 2005, when we were in the Holy month of Ramadan, I went into a coma and was admitted to the Zayed Military Hospital in Abu Dhabi. I had a severe fever, and was admitted to the intensive care unit, where I stayed for three days. The physicians discovered a tremendous shortage of white blood cells. After running the necessary tests and sending samples to the United States of America, the CMV virus was detected.

By orders of His Highness Sheikh Mohamed bin Zayed Al Nahyan (may God protect him), a private aircraft was provided to take me from Abu Dhabi to the United States of America, where it was planned for me to be treated at MD Anderson Cancer Center. My wife, her brother Ibrahim Al Mutawa and my son Dr. Khaled accompanied me. One of the funny things that took place was that when we arrived at the airport, my son Khaled discovered that he had forgotten both his and my passports, which kept us for a while in the airport until he went back home to get them. The aircraft was medically equipped with a physician and a nurse on board to provide me with the necessary solutions and nutrients, as well as to monitor my condition while I was lying down in a coma on a fully-equipped medical bed.

The itinerary of the trip, which lasted nearly 18 hours, required we stop in the UK first, where another passenger who came along got off the plane with his own son who had a heart condition to receive treatment. Then we were scheduled to refuel the plane and move on to the United States of America. We landed in one of Maine's airports, a state which is located in the northeast part of the USA. I had been in a coma for a long time, caused by CMV, with intermittent short awakenings. I remember that upon our arrival at the designated airport, a female American customs inspector boarded the plane along with some passport inspectors and policemen to check my condition. When I woke up from my coma, I asked "Where am I?" They responded "You are in Maine." Then I asked: "Where is Maine?" I was not completely conscious during the interrogation scene.

In Maine, we faced another problem. Getting quickly to MD Anderson Cancer Center required flying over US airspace. This in turn required formal arrangements due to restrictions enforced on aviation following the 9/11 terrorist attacks, especially because the plane came from an Arab country and carried Arab Muslims on board. The alternative solution was to fly to Houston through a route that may not infringe US airspace, which meant the trip that usually takes two hours would be extended to six hours at a time where we badly needed to start treatment quickly. Through one of the diplomats of the US Embassy in Abu Dhabi, who was exerting a lot of effort while we were in the air, we received the necessary approval after he spoke to the US State Department, which in turn addressed the competent authorities to facilitate our passage. In Houston, a fully equipped ambulance was waiting for us at the airport.

As soon as I arrived at the hospital, on October 20, 2005, I was admitted to the emergency department. The diagnosis was pretty common; however, the medication necessary to treat the CMV was nowhere to be found in the hospital. The nearest place where it was available was in San Antonio, a two-hour drive by car. Treatment entailed keeping me in complete isolation for more than two weeks. Neither my wife nor any of my visitors were permitted to see me except through a glass window. When nurses entered my room, they were wearing heavy masks and protective clothing, which made them look more like astronauts. I then said to them that I have visited nuclear reactors before, but never worn such heavy masks and insulating clothes. The fact is they were concerned that I would catch a virus and suffer further complications and that my escorts would become infected.

The characteristic that distinguishes MD Anderson Cancer Center and major hospitals for cancer treatment is the integration of the therapeutic process, without which treatment cannot be successful. For example, if a patient suffers from blood pressure, a specialized physician will be available to treat blood pressure that afflicts cancer patients. And if a patient is diabetic, a specialist doctor will be available. Even a psychiatrist who is specialized and expert in cancer patients/family psychology will be by your side should you need one. In case a patient is suffering from CMV, patients receiving treatment for cancer would need a special medical care that is available in the integrated system of MD Anderson Cancer Center. In any case, after being in continuous comas most of the time in the first 10 days, my condition began to show signs of improvement after two weeks, as I somewhat regained consciousness and started to interact with those around me. However, even when I was conscious I could not communicate easily. On November 2, 2005, I left the hospital after the danger disappeared.

The CMV was not the end of the road for the chemotherapy complications. However, before I faced a new health problem, I had to experience something that is no less of a difficulty, related to my mother (may God rest her soul in peace) who first got Alzheimer's, followed by a stroke while she was visiting my sister at the end of 2006. As a result, she fell into a coma until her death. We took her to a hospital in Thailand for follow up, but her condition was severe and almost hopeless, as strokes are different from heart attacks, where the latter can respond to treatment. I traveled nearly five times to Thailand during her illness, and I sat with her most of the time she was in the hospital, although she was unconscious. She passed away in February 2008. With her death, I lost the sincere heart and prudent mind to whom I resorted repeatedly at critical moments of my life to guide me with its clear insight to the righteous path. I was by her side when she died in the hospital, and I returned earlier to the UAE to prepare for the funeral. It seems that the grief over her death ignited in me a general weakness and reduced my ability to resist health issues. I suffered from a severe fever on August 23, 2008, and was taken to Zayed Military Hospital in Abu Dhabi, where physicians suspected a recurrence of the CMV virus. However, tests proved them wrong. I spent almost four weeks in the hospital before I was discharged on September 20, 2008.

The last major health problem occurred when, on July 13, 2009, I fell on the floor at home and suffered multiple hip fractures. Strangely enough, before the fall, I was walking normally and there was nothing blocking my path. However, the fall was due to the osteoporosis resulting from chemotherapy. As usual, His Highness Sheikh Mohamed bin Zayed Al Nahyan (may God protect him) offered me all kinds of help and support. He ordered a specially-equipped medical plane to fly me to Munich, Germany. From there an ambulance transferred me to Murnau; a small town located almost 70 km south of Munich, about one hour drive away.

I had an operation to replace the injured left hip joint, where a titanium joint was implanted. The operation lasted nearly six hours. I found that the tranquil town of Murnau is a gathering place for many people of the United Arab Emirates and other Gulf countries who travel there to seek bone treatment. Large numbers of people are present throughout the year, almost filling its hotels and stimulating its tourism. During my hospital stay, I met the late Juma Al Zaabi, father of Mr. Ahmed Juma Al Zaabi, the Deputy Minister for Presidential Affairs. The late Juma Al Zaabi was being treated for a head complaint, and I paid him a visit during his stay in hospital. I also visited a UAE citizen who had had a serious car accident, leading to multiple fractures in different parts of his body. He underwent a series of mostly successful operations. He eventually remained in the hospital for a long period to complete his recovery.

I spent two weeks at the hospital, and later moved to another one for physiotherapy. There is no doubt that German hospitals are excellent, with excellent doctors as well. However, I noticed a difference in the quality of services compared to hospitals in the United States of America, but only from a non-medical perspective. In American hospitals, you feel as if you are staying in a hotel, offering all means for your comfort, with nurses and

I needed special bone treatment for a long time. The photo shows my foot in plaster, taken at a group Iftar Banquet for ECSSR staff, September 1, 2009

all other employees treating you from such a standpoint. German hospitals and their staff do not care too much about making patients feel at home, or respond to their requirements as found in the American hospitals.

After 2009, my problems were greatly alleviated, and during a visit to MD Anderson Cancer Center in the last days of 2014 and early 2015, I received a final confirmation that my body had become free of cancerous cells. However, a significant medical step had to be taken swiftly as a precaution for the possibility of cancer relapse.

Preventing a relapse of the type of cancer from which I was suffering would require replacing the bone marrow, which is done by transplanting healthy bone marrow taken from a donor. This would require a full match between the donor and the patient, which in many cases would represent a problem. In my case, there were 15 million people in MD Anderson

Cancer Center's blood database, but none of them had the tissues that matched mine. My wife, children and many others carried out tests that confirmed that none of them was a suitable donor in case I needed a bone marrow transplant. One of the stories that I heard was that of a Jordanian major-general who needed such a transplant. All the people of his town, most of them from his tribe or clan, took the tests before he finally found a suitable donor who was not related to him; this donor accompanied him to Houston where he received the transplant.

The full elimination of my cancerous cells in January 2015 solved the problem—I was able to donate from myself and preserve my bone marrow through freezing at a UK hospital, as a precaution for cancer recurrence. This was done by drawing blood from my skull from which hematopoietic stem cells were later extracted. This required a small operation for which I stayed one night at the hospital. Extracted cells can multiply, and their existence can benefit other patients. Through the database, it was discovered that my tissues matched those of patients in need of a bone marrow transplant, and I received a request to donate to them, for which, of course, I happily agreed.

Throughout this journey, my family members were always by my side. Most notably my kind wife, stirring up the power of hope and optimism inside me and boosting my desire to recover and my ability to resist. She was assisted by my son, Khaled, and my daughters Nora, Dana and Farah, who were all keen on providing me with all the support they could offer. My family members fought beside me the whole battle and resisted despair and weakness just like me. Although they went through many tough moments during my treatment years, they always managed to conceal their fears or concerns. They showed me only their conviction that recovery was approaching and that we still had a lot of time to spend together, a lot of joyful moments and achievements, and that we would make up for the time I had to spend working away from them. My family had been beside me at MD Anderson Cancer Center during the difficult phase of chemotherapy sessions. I cannot forget that my daughter Dana volunteered to sell coffee, tea and candy to the hospital visitors as a sort of volunteer work, which made me feel really satisfied, given my complete belief in the need to instill the culture of volunteering in the United Arab Emirates and the whole Arab world.

During the First Arab Pen Forum, held at ECSSR on February 25, 2014

In this difficult journey, my religious sentiments grew much deeper, as I explained before. Despite the fact that religion is part and parcel of the UAE, Gulf and Arab character, and its values and teachings are instilled in us from childhood, the disease and near-death experience gave it another dimension that was never there before. Getting close to death opens a door to spirituality, leading our emotions to spaces we never knew existed. In front of us passes the idea of life being fleeting and brief but, at the same time, a huge blessing that we must preserve. Paradoxically, life takes on a new meaning in case you contract a severe disease that gets you close to death. A near-death experience endears life to you and highlights the value of many other things that you failed to appreciate in the past. The disease reshapes your relationships and makes you more willing to invest your days in everything that is beneficial and useful. When God bestowed recovery unto me, I was keen on continuing what I thought was my mission in life; that is contributing to the dissemination of knowledge and science and serving the community to which I belong through my writing, my mind, and the positions and roles assigned to me.

Cancer Patient Care Society "RAHMA"

A person is the product of his experiences, and through my experience with cancer I realized the need to establish a voluntary organization that fills some of the void by providing all possible support for cancer patients in the United Arab Emirates, for locals and expatriates alike. It all started as an idea that I proposed to His Highness Sheikh Mohamed bin Zayed Al Nahyan (may God protect him) in the summer of 2015. His Highness adopted the idea and entrusted me with overseeing its execution. His Highness instructed the Executive Council to take all necessary measures to assist in making the idea a reality on the ground. A founding committee of the Society was appointed under my leadership and it included individuals related to the health and administrative fields. The committee carried out the necessary steps toward the establishment of the society. RAHMA was launched in a grand ceremony at the Emirates Palace on September 15, 2015. Members of the founding committee have become members of the Board of Directors, which is now working hard to develop plans and carry them out.

Previously, my responsibilities did not give me the chance to do volunteer work, but the time I spent in the United States of America during my therapy showed me what volunteer work can offer to patients. I think that about 60 percent of those working at the hospital were volunteers. As I indicated before, my daughter Dana volunteered to sell tea, coffee and sweets to hospital visitors. Interestingly, the volunteer work at MD Anderson Cancer Center was not confined to young people, as we found participants who were 80 years old participating in voluntary activities. Volunteering has become a deeply-rooted habit in Western culture in general. Despite the fact that Islam encourages volunteering and charitable deeds, strangely enough this kind of activity is nearly nonexistent in the Arab and Muslim worlds.

When I knew that I had cancer and was told it is called "T-cell lymphoblastic lymphoma," I knew nothing about it. The name reminded me of some types of cake. I did not find anyone to answer the dozens of questions

With H.H. Sheikh Mohamed bin Zayed Al Nahyan, Crown Prince of Abu Dhabi and Deputy Supreme Commander of the UAE Armed Forces (may God protect him), while signing a T-shirt carrying the emblem of the UAE Cancer Patient Care Society (RAHMA), to Ms. Nora Al-Suwaidi, Director General of the Society, May 9, 2017

that flooded my mind at that moment. Although I received my education in the West and I have spent my whole life researching and reading in all domains, I found myself wondering, what if the patient was an ordinary uneducated person? This is the main reason why I thought of establishing RAHMA, as it provides via a toll-free telephone number (80090) immediate information to the patient who seriously needs it. It answers all the questions on his mind at critical and impacting moments, as such time can be very decisive.

In addition to information about the disease and its nature, the toll-free number provides information on the most important destinations where a patient can receive treatment for his condition, whether in the United Arab Emirates, the United States of America, the United Kingdom, the Federal Republic of Germany, the French Republic, the Republic of South Korea or the Republic of Singapore. We look forward, with time, to increase the amount of information and services that can be obtained via the toll-free phone. However, this is just the beginning.

During RAHMA Charity Marathon, held at Yas Island November 7, 2015

Spreading awareness and knowledge about the disease is an important task. It is important to determine the disease types, distribution percentages for each type in the UAE, economic costs of the treatment and death ratio caused by each type. Publishing such facts prioritizes the effort in fighting cancer, increases social awareness regarding the disease, and makes people value the work carried out by RAHMA and similar societies active in the same field.

Cancer awareness is not a trivial issue. In October 2015, my father's cousin died in his forties of skin cancer. It was discovered that he was in stage 4, a late stage in this disease. Strangely, he visited some doctors, and the skin cancer was already visible in the interior of his nose. They diagnosed it as an ordinary inflammation, prescribing anti-inflammatory medicines, and thus they wasted very precious time and permitted his condition to become worse. I believe that if there were greater awareness, even among physicians, and medical devices for cancer detection available in all hospitals, it would be possible to detect many cases before they become incurable. Therefore, we intend to purchase equipment that helps in the early detection of cancer with the help of donations and make them available to all hospitals in the country or for hospitals that lack such medical devices.

At the first meeting of the Founding Committee of Cancer Patient Care Society (RAHMA), June 1, 2015

Our planned activities also include providing a specialized introductory library on cancer and related diseases, comprising all the available material in Arabic, in addition to choosing some of the important introductory books in English to be translated into Arabic. While the English materials will be available, tens of millions of Arabic speakers will not be able to make use of them. Therefore, translation seems the most appropriate option.

One of the most important ideas we want people to believe in is that cancer does not necessarily mean death. The truth is that cancer treatment is advancing, and the recovery rate is constantly increasing. Thus, cancer is not a final death sentence, it is just a disease that can be fought and defeated.

For example, drawing from my personal experience, I realized how difficult it is to get the bone marrow, which can save the life of a human being. However, many people in the Arab world are not aware that donating blood from which such cells are extracted is a great benefit for those patients who need it, without any harmful effects on the bodies of the donors. In fact, it is beneficial for cell regeneration. One of the important things that will be undertaken by the Society is the creation of a large database of donors, with their relevant blood details, to help save other peoples' lives. As I said earlier, in the MD Anderson Cancer Center database, there are 15 million donors that did not include a single Arab.

With H.E. Ali Al Hashimi, Religious Adviser at the UAE Ministry of Presidential Affairs; H.E. Hashim Al-Qaysiyah, special adviser to H.H. Sheikh Tahnoon bin Zayed Al Nahyan, UAE; H.E. Ibrahim Al Abed, Adviser to the Chairman of UAE National Media Council; H.E. Dr. Abdullah Al-Raisi, Director General of UAE National Archieves; Mr. Tariq Ali Al Bahr, Procurement Manager at the Emirates National School, and Ms. Nora Al Suwaidi, Director General of the Cancer Patient Care Society (RAHMA), at the launching ceremony of RAHMA, September 15, 2015

My presence at the ECSSR played a major role in the establishing of the society and kicking off its activities. The Center is responsible for RAHMA funding in the first two years, i.e. until 2017, while the budget will depend on donations afterward. We already launched campaigns to raise funds, with the launch of the Society's work. Moreover, we hope to obtain sufficient donations to achieve our desired expansion. I think philanthropists in Abu Dhabi and in the UAE will donate to the Society. I know that many cancer patient care societies from the USA, Arab and foreign countries come to the UAE to receive donations from our citizens. However, these donations go to distant countries and benefit far away nations. I think that cancer patients inside the UAE, whether citizens or expatriates, are entitled to the allocation of such donations. The culture of donating exists in the country, but much work needs to be done in order to consolidate and support such culture.

At the first meeting of the Founding Committee of the Cancer Patient Care Society (RAHMA), June 1, 2015

There are a lot of plans and ideas that will be put into force in accordance with the donations we receive. I think that one of the good ideas is for the Society to offer its services online. We also care for an aspect that does not receive adequate attention in cancer treatment in the Arab countries—"psychological support," not only for the cancer patient, but also for his family. A cancer patient is not the only one who suffers; their family also suffers cases of anxiety, fear and sadness. Consequently, they need knowledgeable and specialized psychological care to contain and prevent aggravation of the negative psychological impacts, and to support and train the family on the ideal way to support and help the cancer patient in achieving recovery.

We also hope that donations will help us to achieve a great leap by providing treatment costs in some cases, in accordance with evaluation procedures for cases that ask for assistance from RAHMA. Such procedures set forth special rules regarding those for whom the Society bears treatment costs; as per its own statute. We also hope that such donations later will allow funding of scientific research on cancer treatment, sending UAE students to advanced nations on scholarships to specialize in this field, holding specialized medical conferences on cancer related issues in the county, or turning the UAE into a hub for relevant research. In general, RAHMA is still in its early days, compared

With the Filipino boxer Manny Pacquiao, during the charity marathon organized by RAHMA Society at Yas Island, Abu Dhabi, November 7, 2015

to other societies in the Arab world and the world at large that have been active for many years. Many things will depend on the Society's success in fundraising. We will put our shoulders to the wheel to achieve this end.

The inauguration ceremony of the Society on September 15, 2015 attracted great interest that made us more optimistic regarding the progress we can achieve. On November 7, 2015, the Society organized a marathon and bicycle race on Yas Island, attended by His Excellency Sheikh Nahyan bin Mubarak Al Nahyan, Minister of Culture and Knowledge Development, with thousands of attendees expressing their interest in the first event organized by RAHMA. The event was also attended by the Filipino boxer Manny Pacquiao, who is known as "the People's Hero."

The Society has made plans for social, sports and other events for fundraising purposes, in addition to online fundraising activities, as well as creating a community of forums and blogs for cancer patients. RAHMA also began to form partnerships with government and private sector institutions, in addition to receiving sponsor support for its activities and events. There

Press conference held by RAHMA Society to launch the cancer awareness campaign under the slogan "Hand in Hand," on January 13, 2016

are also internship programs under preparation to utilize participation of volunteers who wish to serve the community through the Society.

I do not think that the current situation in many Arab countries allows cancer treatment as one hopes for. The issue is not dependent on the skill of a doctor or a small hospital. Cancer treatment requires an integrated system and large funding. In major American hospitals specialized in cancer treatment, there are hundreds of doctors who cover all the aspects that need to be cured. Thousands of patients go to such hospitals that provide doctors, through their treatment, with cumulative expertise and knowledge, increasing their competence to fight this disease. There might be Arab hospitals with some promising potential because they are fully dedicated to cancer treatment, such as King Faisal Specialized Hospital in the Kingdom of Saudi Arabia, Children's Cancer Hospital in Cairo in the Arab Republic of Egypt, or King Hussein Cancer Center in the Hashemite Kingdom of Jordan. However, they still need a lot of effort and work. Support and funding of such hospitals must be provided, as they are indispensable conditions for fulfilling their roles.

With H.E. Hashim Al-Qaysiyah, special adviser to H.H. Sheikh Tahnoon bin Zayed Al Nahyan, UAE; H.E. Ibrahim Al Abed, Adviser to the Chairman of UAE National Media Council; H.E. Ali Khalifa Al Rumaithi, Dubai Media Incorporated CEO for Radio and TV; and Mr. Tariq Ali Al Bahr, Procurement Manager at the Emirates National School, at the launching ceremony of the Cancer Patient Care Society (RAHMA), September 15, 2015

RAHMA has many visions for the future and many goals that it endeavors to achieve, knowing that they need a lot of work and constant effort. However, we have confidence in our community, its positive interaction and support for new ideas when presented properly. Illness might have its pains and complications from which I suffered for years. However, it opened the door for me to serve the community in a new area that has a special place in my heart, hoping that it will have forthcoming results that will benefit cancer patients, their families and the whole community.

Prolific Writing Stage

Despite my illness, I kept an eye on every small detail in the work of the ECSSR, even while receiving chemotherapy in 2004. Anyone who follows the Center's activities after 2003 would notice that it kept the same pace

With retired Lt. Gen. Mohammed Helal Sorour Al Kaabi; H.E. Hashim Al-Qaysiyah, special adviser to H.H. Sheikh Tahnoon bin Zayed Al Nahyan, UAE; H.E. Dr. Abdullah Al Raisi, Director General of the UAE National Archives, during the charity marathon held by RAHMA Society on Yas Island on November 7, 2015

of work. With my return to resume work in the UAE in 2005, things got back on track, and were only interrupted by emergency trips for treatment. However, I was never far from work and its activities.

About nine years of treatment had elapsed, and I had yet to offer the intellectual contributions I wanted to make through writing. After publishing my research titled "United Arab Emirates Society: A Future Perspective," which was taught as part of the courses in UAE University, I did not contribute any book until 2013. For me, that was a hard thing to swallow. I consider myself, above all, a researcher who finds his greatest joy in breaking new scientific ground and contributing knowledge to the Arab library, which needs the great effort of all those who possess the necessary scientific research tools.

Management responsibilities were neither a trivial nor an easy task, especially with the steady expansion of the roles and responsibilities of the ECSSR, and the higher status established by the Center over the years. Consequently, we had to maintain and develop this position. In addition, I found myself obliged to fulfill some other requirements, such as refereeing some academic research and participating in various seminars, conferences and events inside and outside the UAE, as well as mak-

With H.E. Hashim Al-Qaysiyah, special adviser to H.H. Sheikh Tahnoon bin Zayed Al Nahyan, UAE; H.E. Dr. Abdullah Al Raisi, Director General of the UAE National Archives, during the launching ceremony of the Cancer Patient Care Society (RAHMA), September 15, 2015

ing press, radio and television interviews that tackled issues related to our ever-turbulent region. All these endeavors consumed a lot of my time.

I also became responsible for a lot of dossiers. For example, I was appointed Chairman of the Higher Committee for the Preparation of the National Strategy for Childhood and Motherhood in the United Arab Emirates, through a decision by Her Highness Sheikha Fatima bint Mubarak (Mother of the Nation) in September 2009. In 2012, I was appointed as a member of the Supreme Council for the National Defense College, by a decree of His Highness Sheikh Khalifa bin Zayed Al Nahyan, President of the UAE (may God protect him). Such positions needed strenuous work, some of which required leading work teams from multiple entities. By nature, I could not be satisfied with being an honorary or superficial figure in any of my positions. I usually find myself gradually bearing a large part of the research and administrative responsibility, whether as a leader or as a member of a group sharing responsibility with others.

I think I was gaining new positive energy with more evidence of my recovery as my treatment and periodical tests advanced. In 2012, I reached

With Dr. Abdul Rahman Al Shumairi, Director General and Editor-in-Chief of *Al Watan* newspaper, UAE, at a symposium titled "Current Oil Market Developments and their Impacts on the Gulf Cooperation Council (GCC)," held at ECSSR, March 11, 2015

a high degree of optimism, and many scientific ideas were brewing in my mind after long years of observation and pondering. There was a need to translate them into reality, especially the ideas related to issues and challenges playing a major role in shaping the future. Since then, I was keen on dedicating part of my schedule to writing.

The first results of such scientific activities was a book titled *From Tribe to Facebook: The Transformational Role of Social Networks*, which was published in 2013. In 2014, I wrote another book titled *Prospects for the American Age: Sovereignty and Influence in the New World Order*, followed by *The Mirage* in 2015, and *Eternal Imprints: Figures that Made History and Others that Changed the Future of Their Countries* in 2016. Also, I co-edited a book titled *Islamic Political Movements and Authority in the Arab World: The Rise and Fall*, published in 2014.

The main reason behind writing the four books is the importance of their subjects, to understand the present and prepare for the future. The first book dealt with the role of social media. I had already started observing this role a long time ago, looking at how much social media consumes of an individual's time, and the political, social and economic effects it has. In my introduction, I wrote about its contribution to "shaping public

With Her Excellency Dr. Amal Al Qubaisi, the Speaker of Federal National Council, (a member of FNC at the time), and two other lady members of the Higher Committee for the Preparation of the National Strategy for Childhood and Motherhood, during a meeting with the committee, which I headed, February 27, 2011

opinion trends, as well as forming personal beliefs, attitudes and opinions toward various issues and events." I also observed the resemblance between the tribe as a social unit of historical roots in both the Arab and Islamic worlds on the one hand, and the formation of "Virtual Tribalism" on social media on the other. Tribalism, A□abiyya, as a social and political term, was coined by the Arab thinker and forerunner of modern sociology Abdurrahman ibn Khaldoun in his famous book *The Muqaddima* (The Introduction). I have coined the term "Virtual Tribalism" to cope with changes currently witnessed by the world.

Presenting a gift to H.E. Dr. Sultan Ahmad Al Jaber, UAE Minister of State, during his visit to the ECSSR, November 26, 2015

Presenting a gift to Staff Major General Pilot Rashad Mohammed Al Saadi, Commandant of the UAE National Defense College, during his visit to the ECSSR, February 2, 2016

The most significant of my books that I have authored after I recovered from Cancer, with God's blessing and I gained a new energy for work and achievement

One of the questions I usually receive is whether my book *From Tribe to Facebook: The Transformational Role of Social Networks* is related to the so-called Arab Spring. My answer is No. The subjects of the four books were already developed in my mind some years ago, as part of issues such as globalization and the communication revolution. More than 15 years before the book was released, I had devoted a large part of my time and my interest in research and the ECSSR's activities toward this field. It seems that the coincidence between publishing the book and the timing of what was called the "Arab Spring" was the cause of such misconceptions. In general, the subjects that I address always have roots. I believe that none is related to a contemporary event regardless of its importance and effects. Any writing conducted in a hasty fashion often lacks the necessary research depth.

I received an enormous response to the ideas contained in my book *From Tribe to Facebook: The Transformational Role of Social Networks*. In no time, the book was among the bestsellers in the country, confirming that the book market in the Arab world is in want of serious academic

With H.H. Sheikh Abdullah bin Zayed Al Nayhan, UAE Minister of Foreign Affairs and International Cooperation, at the signing ceremony of my book *From Tribe to Facebook: The Transformational Role of Social Networks*, at Abu Dhabi International Book Fair, April 26, 2013

With H.H. Dr. Sheikh Sultan bin Khalifa bin Zayed Al Nahyan, Adviser to His Highness the President of UAE (may God protect him), at the signing ceremony of my book *From Tribe to Facebook: The Transformational Role of Social Networks*, at Abu Dhabi International Book Fair, April 26, 2013

At the signing ceremony of my books *From Tribe to Facebook. The Transformational Role of Social Networks* and *Prospects for the American Age: Sovereignty and Influence in the New World Order*, at the Institute of Applied Technology, Abu Dhabi, October 21, 2014

At the signing ceremony of my book *Prospects for the American Age: Sovereignty and Influence in the New World Order*, at the Sharjah International Book Fair, November 12, 2014

contributions, provided that they fulfill its needs and use the appropriate language to reach a large number of readers, attributes that I am always keen on. I think that readers shun some writers because of their eccentricity and complexity, despite the seriousness and importance of their material. I also believe that mastering an idea leads to its presentation in a smooth manner to enable a wider portion of readers to understand it, without detracting from its seriousness or scientific objectivity. I was pleased that the book combined

At the signing ceremony of my book *Prospects for the American Age: Sovereignty and Influence in the New World Order*, at the UAE's Ministry of Foreign Affairs and International Cooperation, April 23, 2014

At the signing ceremony of my book *Prospects for the American Age: Sovereignty and Influence in the New World Order*, at the Abu Dhabi International Book Fair, May 2, 2014

Presenting a copy of my book *Prospects for the American Age: Sovereignty and Influence in the New World Order*, in English, to Dr. Tod Laursen, President of Khalifa University, Abu Dhabi, October 16, 2014

both quantitative and qualitative impacts. I received a series of comments, views and inquiries from a group of the most important thinkers and writers in the Arab world. Listing the book among the bestsellers made it possible to reach far more readers in its Arabic version. The English version also attracted foreign and Arab readers whom, by their culture, education and living abroad for prolonged periods, prefer to read books in the English language.

I followed all the details related to my books and not only the scientific content that is of interest to many researchers and writers. This was done through talks and discussions in which I received and evaluated others' views, but I would reserve the final say to myself. Page layout, size and typeface are among my many interests because I believe that readers are entitled to get access to books in the best possible shape and content. An excellent publishing style, which is easy on the eyes of the readers, says a lot about how much respect we show them and how keen we are to present them with the best we have got, making it as effortless as possible for them to read. Consequently, this led to including focused citations inside *The Mirage* in a select number of its pages. Its citations have an intellectual abstract, bits of information or an idea that I wanted to highlight. At the same time, such citations are aesthetic assets, which are comfortable

Front cover of my book *From Tribe to Facebook: The Transformational Role of Social Networks*

to read because the proportions of 'mass and space' are well accounted for as an artistic and aesthetic value. Eventually, the Publications Department in the Center undertakes the printing of the book.

In the same context, I was keen that the books' covers and colors are attractive and appealing to the reader, and that they come off as a gateway that gives readers an idea about the content. Despite the undeniable effort made by designers and artists in the job, I used to envisage, while writing my books, one or more specific designs, which I would pass on to the specialists with all the details, leaving my ideas into their hands to implement. I used to get many suggestions to which I might add, delete or completely reject from the very beginning. I discuss these suggestions with them and my assistants and ask for their insights until we reach a point where I feel that the design really expresses what I have in mind.

There are no fixed or final rules in this respect, as the design might be brand new, or just inspired by a previous one that was used in the Center

At the signing ceremony of my book *Prospects for the American Age: Sovereignty and Influence in the New World Order* at Abu Dhabi International Book Fair, May 2, 2014

During discussion of the ideas of my books *Prospects for the American Age: Sovereignty and Influence in the New World Order* and *From Tribe to Facebook: The Transformational Role of Social Networks* at the Court of His Highness the Crown Prince of Abu Dhabi, March 5, 2014

and whose intellectual ownership lies with us. The latter was how we designed *From Tribe to Facebook: The Transformational Role of Social Networks*, where its main design theme was derived from previous activities of the Center. However, I found that this design is the best expression of the content of the book. Thus, I reused it with a simple modification to match what I had in mind.

The second book, *Prospects for the American Age: Sovereignty and Influence in the New World Order* rep-

Signing my book *Prospects for the American Age: Sovereignty and Influence in the New World Order* at the Fletcher School of Law and Diplomacy at Tufts University, USA, May 8, 2014

resents an important development on more than one level. While *From Tribe to Facebook: The Transformational Role of Social Networks* is 157 pages, *Prospects for the American Age: Sovereignty and Influence in the New World Order* contains 858 pages, with more than 160 pages of cross-references. About 500 references were used, spanning 42 pages in total. Moreover, the references contained Arabic and non-Arabic books, research papers published in academic periodicals, newspaper articles, international reports as well as a survey of a multistage random sample of 1,500 people in the United Arab Emirates, both citizens and expatriates.

With Dr. Abdulreda Assiri, former Dean of Social Sciences College, Kuwait University, at the opening of the signing ceremony of my book *Prospects for the American Age: Sovereignty and Influence in the New World Order* at Kuwait University, March 16, 2014

The nature of the book also entailed touching on political, economic, social and military issues as well as reliable statistics from credible international institutions

With Mr. Mohamed Kabbaj, President of Spirit of Fez Foundation and Dr. Omer Al Fasi Al Fahri, Permanent Secretary of the Hassan II Academy of Science and Technology, during my visit to Fez in Morocco to sign my book *Prospects for the American Age: Sovereignty and Influence in the New World Order*, April 11, 2014

about the United States of America and the other major powers. This whole process necessitated forming a specialized team to collect scientific material, which I tackled in the book and infused into the vision I had in mind of the new world order and the hierarchy of power and influence for the next 50 years; i.e., until end of the second third of the 21st century.

In *Prospects for the American Age: Sovereignty and Influence in the New World Order,* I was trying to offer a scientific response to many of our fellows in the Arab world who claimed that some global powers are set to overthrow the USA as a dominant power in the new world order. The problem is that this "wishful thinking" spreads into many Arabic writings, which completely

Signing ceremony of my book *Prospects for the American Age: Sovereignty and Influence in the New World Order* at Abu Dhabi University, April 21, 2014

Singing my book *Prospects for the American Age: Sovereignty and Influence in the New World Order* at the Bahrain International Book Fair, March 31, 2014

Signing a copy of my book *Prospects for the American Age: Sovereignty and Influence in the New World Order* at HCT, Abu Dhabi, May 28, 2014

Signing a copy of my book *Prospects for the American Age: Sovereignty and Influence in the New World Order* for Ali Saif Al Nuaimi, CEO, United Printing and Publishing, Abu Dhabi, during, my visit to United Printing and Publishing, April 28, 2014

ignore the facts, figures and evidence. This leads them to false conclusions, such as believing that countries like China, Russia or some blocs like the European Union might dominate the world order, or rival the United States of America in leading it. Such false conclusions would lead to wrong actions, as the Arab countries must build their policies on a clear understanding of the shape of the world order and the ranks of different countries within its hierarchy so as to preserve Arab interests.

Not so many years have passed since the book was published, but the events that took place after its publication support the ideas it proposed. Chinese expansion in the world is diminishing and the growth rate that China boasted for so many years is no longer maintained. On the other hand, the European Union is gradually losing much of its momentum and power on both the political and economic levels. The role played by Russia was originally based on weak foundations and prone to collapse at any time, as is the case now with the fall in oil prices. I think that the source of power of this

With Dr. Farhan Nizami (standing), Director of Oxford Centre for Islamic Studies, and another guest at the signing ceremony held for my two books *Prospects for the American Age: Sovereignty and Influence in the New World Order* and *The Transformational Role of Social Networks: From Tribe to Facebook,* at the University of Oxford, United Kingdom, April 7, 2014

At the signing ceremony of my two books *Prospects for the American Age* and *The Transformational Role of Social Networks: From Tribe to Facebook* at the University of Oxford, United Kingdom, April 7, 2014

book lies in its reliance on statistics and facts covering politics, economics, industry, military power, education, innovation and scientific research. Another advantage of the book is that it draws comparisons between the strengths of the United States of America and those of other countries. Thus, the core of the book becomes based on well-established and deeply-rooted evidence, bearing in mind whatever variables that may arise. However, I would not claim that there is a final say or an absolutely correct opinion.

My book *Prospects for the American Age: Sovereignty and Influence in the New World Order* was generously received by the Arab political and intellectual audience and I felt its message was clear to everybody. On June 16, 2014, in his article published by *Al-Jarida*, a Kuwaiti newspaper, Dr. Abdulhamid Al-Ansari said the book "presents ideas and information that, if understood and made use of, could help us understand the deepest interactions of our contemporary world, the new world order and its effects, and save us the misguided understanding of the global strategic reality. These ideas and information also would enable us to deal in a smarter way with nations and countries, ensuring that we maintain our interests. The book shows us

At the signing ceremony of my book *Prospects for the American Age: Sovereignty and Influence in the New World Order* at the Riyadh International Book Fair, March 14, 2014

At the signing ceremony of my book *Prospects for the American Age: Sovereignty and Influence in the New World Order* at Bahrain International Book Fair, March 31, 2014

At a lecture on my book *Prospects for the American Age: Sovereignty and Influence in the New World Order* at the Arab Thought Forum, in Amman, the Hashemite Kingdom of Jordan, June 9, 2014

the right path using a futuristic road map with clear-cut goals."

This description is important as it captures the objective of the book. Dr. Ammar Ali Hassan emphasized this in an article published in *Al-Ittihad* newspaper on March 7, 2014 saying "Thus, the book is not only for researchers and experts. It is also for decision makers, to be aware of the path to safeguard national interests based on an accurate understanding of the balance of power in the world with neither exaggeration nor underestimation, especially in this critical juncture in the history of the Arab region, as the USA changes its conceptions and tactics toward it without changing its strategies. It is important to understand the truth

Receiving a gift from Dr. Abdulreda Assiri, former Dean of Social Sciences College, Kuwait University, on the sidelines of the signing ceremony of my book *Prospects for the American Age: Sovereignty and Influence in the New World Order* at Kuwait University, March 26, 2014

With H.E. Dr. Mohammed Omran Al-Shamsi, Chancellor of the Higher Colleges of Technology, Abu Dhabi, while delivering a lecture at the signing ceremony of my book *Prospects for the American Age: Sovereignty and Influence in the New World Order* at HCT, May 28, 2014

concerning the American power now and in the future, in order to act in a manner that preserves our national interests, and how to expand the margin of our independent movement as much as possible."

With the late Egyptian Military and Strategic Expert Sameh Seif El Yazal, Dr. Nevine Massad, professor at the College of Economics and Political Science at Cairo University and former Director of Institute of Arab Research and Studies affiliated with Arab League; and Dr. Ammar Ali Hassan, Egyptian researcher and political analyst, at the signing ceremony of my book *Prospects for the American Age: Sovereignty and Influence in the New World Order*, in Cairo, June 11, 2014

I think that my book *Prospects for the American Age: Sovereignty and Influence in the New World Order* has provided me with more channels of communications with Arab and international intellectual and research communities than ever before; this time from the position of an author rather than that of the director of a research center. The book speaks to a wide segment of both specialized and non-specialized readers. Moreover, it received a tremendous number of reviews and opinion columns in almost all Arab countries. Also, I have received hundreds of messages, some of which agree while others disagree with what I had written. However, they all referred to the scientific effort exerted in the book, the solid foundations of its ideas, academic approaches and language that reached wider segments of readers.

In an article published in *Al-Ittihad* newspaper on June 24, 2014, the well-known academic Dr. Ahmad Yusuf Ahmad, referred to a discussion in Cairo related to the main idea of the book. In that article, which was solely dedicated to my book, the writer said "Most of the comments contained reservations or restrictions on such an idea. However, it is worth mentioning that Dr. Jamal Sanad Al-Suwaidi is completely convinced of his idea and absolutely prepared to defend it calmly and logically based on confirmed facts and numbers that entice us to believe in its correctness. His comments on such reservations are always clear and decisive. Thus, the disagreement in points of view always leads to rich and refined discussions. It seems to me that disagreement is a natural result of the difference between the standpoint of the objective analyst who refuses to see the naked truth, and the standpoint of those who hate to hear that the aggressive superpower, which disregards and even worse violates their rights if it contradicts its own interests, will remain in the world arena as an unwanted guest for at least two more decades."

I received numerous invitations to sign the book and discuss its ideas at intellectual and cultural institutions inside and outside the UAE. I was delighted to meet university students or fresh postgraduate students inside the UAE, and many Arab, Gulf and Western countries who discussed the ideas of the book indicating that they have thoroughly read it. This was not limited only to the Arab countries, where my scientific tours in Europe, the United States of America and some Asian countries confirmed that serious scientific effort will always find open arms. Translating the book into English was a gateway to expand its readership since reading an Arab research on international relations by foreign readers will enable them to realize that there are Arab researchers who have something to add.

I believe *The Mirage*, released in 2015, is the most influential among my latest books. This book is about political religious groups in terms of thought and practice. In the introduction, I wrote that: "I have found a striking resemblance between the condition of millions of citizens in some Arab and Muslim countries and that of someone who is exposed to the effects of a unique but common natural phenomenon—namely 'The Mirage'" (p. 13). I started writing the book at a time when such political religious groups seemed to be at the peak of their influence and success, after the so-called "Arab Spring." However, I knew that the end was near for them. The effort I exerted in writing the book was crowned with success by winning the Sheikh Zayed Book Award, the highest and most important Arab award in its field. I will discuss this award in the next chapter of the book.

What so many people do not really know about *The Mirage* is that about 300 out of its 815 pages are part of my PhD dissertation, which I completed in May 1990 in English. It has been translated into Arabic and some of its ideas and sections have been updated ever since. However, most of the content I included in the dissertation remained intact and can be built upon today. I think that touching on the issue of political religious groups needs some courage, since they sometimes resort to outright murder and by means of defamation, declaring people infidels and making up scandalous stories about anyone who dares to reveal the truth about them. Some Arab writers and intellectuals avoid criticizing those groups because they are afraid that they might get hurt, physically or emotionally. I have already received death threats through phone calls from ISIS (Da'esh) and my son, Dr. Khaled, also received threats. However, I never paid attention to them.

Members of the political religious groups and their supporters never provided any scientific response to the ideas laid out in the book. Instead, I was personally attacked. The matter is not personal, though. I do not bear any hatred toward any political movement. I started off from a simple idea: these movements, when they practice politics, seem to become more or less like many leftist or liberal movements, whose ideas and attitudes are subject to evaluation, criticism and refinement. The presence of political religious groups, such as the Muslim Brotherhood, among the key players in the political scene for decades, makes such criticism a duty and necessity. It is completely wrong that such groups consider themselves as representatives of God the Almighty on Earth, just as the church did in Europe during the 15th and 16th centuries.

After publishing my two books *Prospects for the American Age: Sovereignty and Influence in the New World Order* and *The Mirage*, I noticed that the media and many writers started calling me an "intellectual" rather than an "academic" or "researcher," which used to precede my name. This may be attributed to the fact that I included in those two books the essence of many years of thought, contemplation and research. The world order, as well as political Islam, has been one of my main concerns ever since I started to study political science in 1977. I had been through many battles against political-religious organizations even before I was 20 years old. For my PhD dissertation (1988–1990), I chose to write on the subject of Political Islam. I spent about 35 years, since I started my master's degree studies, piling up experiences enhanced by my work

A new edition of my book *The Mirage* after winning The Sheikh Zayed Book Award 2016

at the university, studies I published in prestigious journals and finally, my rich experience at the Emirates Center for Strategic Studies and Research, with all the books and studies I have edited and written. This is in addition to my close connection to politics through my position as a political adviser to His Highness Sheikh Mohamed bin Zayed Al Nahyan (may God protect him). I have experienced a period of "research stagnation" during which I used to store ideas, mentally linking them, while following up on events all over the world. Even the time I was sick created a human experience that added much to my knowledge. All this was manifested in these books, which represented the essence of a long journey of knowledge.

Along with the research mentality, experience is paramount. Some people might possess a great research mentality and capability, for example, when they are only 21 years old. However, would you find in their intellectual production at this very early age the all-encompassing and deep view you might be seeking? I do not think so! Simply, at this young age, they are

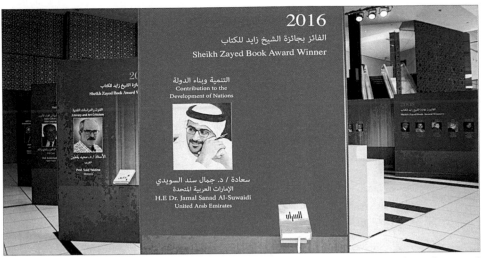

Photos of the winners of the Sheikh Zayed Book Award in front of the hall where the award celebration was held on May 1, 2016

H.H. Sheikh Mansour bin Zayed Al Nahyan, UAE Deputy Prime Minister and Minister of Presidential Affairs, at the Abu Dhabi International Book Fair, March 2015

inexperienced. It is probable that this aspect was why my books *Prospects for the American Age: Sovereignty and Influence in the New World Order* and *The Mirage* were highly received and appreciated. Just as *Prospects for the American Age: Sovereignty and Influence in the New World Order* was received with hundreds of articles written by highly distinguished professors and intellectuals, *The Mirage* was even more widely well-received, probably due to the importance of issues of terrorism and political religious groups in the intellectual, cultural and political reality and not only in the Arab world, but also all over the world. Many seminars and lectures have been held to discuss the book's ideas, and have turned into means to resist these groups and then dismantle their ideologies;

something that makes me feel that the book achieved its purpose.

The massive spread and wide readership of my book *The Mirage,* inside and outside the Arab world brought me huge fame, which took me by surprise. Recently, I have often been referred to as "The author of *The Mirage.*" The interest in my book extended beyond Arab countries and into foreign ones, as it earned "Five Stars" on Amazon Kindle, which means that its reading rate was very high among foreign readers. Today, the book is available in English, French, German, Spanish, Russian, Chinese and Urdu, in order to enable different Western and other foreign readers to get acquainted with an Arab view criticizing the political religious groups and explaining their nature, rationales, ideologies, practices and future prospects.

A coincidence relating to the views of writers and intellectuals about my book

With H.H. Sheikh Mohammed bin Rashid Al Maktoum, Vice President and Prime Minister of the UAE and Ruler of Dubai (may God protect him), while presenting His Highness with a copy of my book *The Mirage*, March 10, 2015

With H.H. Sheikh Humaid bin Rashid Al Nuaimi, Member of the Federal Supreme Council and Ruler of Ajman, when I presented H.H. with a copy of my book *The Mirage*, March 12, 2015

With H.H. Sheikh Hamad bin Mohammed Al Sharqi, Member of the Federal Supreme Council and Ruler of Fujairah, presenting H.H. with a copy of my book *The Mirage*, March 8, 2015

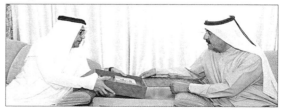

With H.H. Sheikh Saud bin Rashid Al Mualla, Member of the Federal Supreme Council and Ruler of Umm Al Quwain, presenting H.H. with a copy of my book *The Mirage*, March 16, 2015

With H.H. Sheikh Saud bin Saqr Al Qasimi, Member of the Federal Supreme Council and Ruler of Ras Al Khaimah, presenting H.H. with a copy of my book *The Mirage*, March 4, 2015

With H.H. Sheikh Hamdan bin Zayed Al Nahyan, Ruler's Representative in the Al Dhafra Region (formerly Western Region), presenting H.H. with a copy of my book *The Mirage*, January 6, 2016

With Lt. General H.H. Sheikh Saif bin Zayed Al Nahyan, UAE Deputy Prime Minister and Minister of Interior, presenting His Highness with a copy of my book *The Mirage* April 15, 2015

With H.H. Sheikh Mansour bin Zayed Al Nahyan, UAE Deputy Prime Minister and Minister of Presidential Affairs, presenting H.H. with a copy of my book *The Mirage*, November 2, 2015

The Mirage was that two important writers used an expression to describe me in two different articles separated by more than a year and a half. Dr. Abdullah Al-Awadhi wrote an article, published in *Al-Ittihad* newspaper on November 21, 2014, titled "Dr. Jamal: The Mirage Detector." Then, Mr. Kamal Abdul Hamid wrote an article, published in the same UAE newspaper on June 30, 2016, titled "Jamal Sanad Al-Suwaidi: The Comprehensive Detector of the Mirage." It is certain that Mr. Kamal Abdul Hamid did not see the title of the first article. I was delighted to see such a concurrence in the description between the two writers because it referred to a role I personally cherish and regard as one of the duties of the Arab intellectuals in particular; i.e., offering revealing insights that benefit the society as much as possible and distinguishing good from bad ideas among those currently floating around. Surely, theoretical thinking has its value, but priorities oblige us to move our effort toward a different direction. The Arab world needs those who provide scientific views that interact with reality and its issues, illuminating the scene to the masses as they can be easily misled by false hopes, especially the hopes that manipulate religious sentiments.

Many Arab intellectuals and academics showed interest in my book *The Mirage*, even before it received the Sheikh Zayed Book Award. Also, many articles were written to discuss one of its aspects or issues. The Moroccan academic Dr. Abdulhaq Azouzi described the book in an article he wrote on May 19, 2015 in *Al-Ittihad* newspaper, say-

With H.H. Sheikh Hamed bin Zayed Al Nahyan, Chairman of Abu Dhabi Crown Prince's Court, presenting H.H. with a copy of my book *The Mirage*, November 24, 2015

With H.E. Dr. Sheikh Khalid bin Khalifa Al Khalifa, Deputy Chairman of the Board of Trustees and CEO of Isa Cultural Centre and a number of writers and intellectuals during a seminar organized by the Isa Cultural Centre, on my book *The Mirage*, in the Kingdom of Bahrain, March 23, 2015

With H.E. Isa Al Hammadi, former Minister of Information Affairs, Shura Council and Council of Representatives Affairs in the Kingdom of Bahrain, at the signing ceremony of my book *The Mirage* on the sidelines of a seminar on its ideas in the Isa Cultural Centre in the Kingdom of Bahrain, March 23, 2015

With a number of writers and intellectuals on the sidelines of a seminar organized by the Isa Cultural Centre, on my book *The Mirage* in the Kingdom of Bahrain, March 23, 2015

ing "In terms of the content, it is an unmatched book. It explains the reality and uses compelling and rational arguments, adopting a forward-looking approach and recalling history, religious sciences, sociology and other sciences. Its aim is also to tackle a very sensitive issue of concern to the public and

With Dr. Mohammed Mukhtar Juma, Egyptian Minister of Awqaf; Mr. Makram Mohammed Ahmed, former Head of Egypt's Syndicate of Journalists; Consultant Khalifa Hamed Al Tunaiji, UAE Deputy Ambassador to the Arab Republic of Egypt, and Dr. Sharif Shaheen, Chairman of the Egyptian National Library and Archives, at a symposium on my book *The Mirage* held at the Egyptian National Library and Archives, October 18, 2015

experts alike, not only in our Arab world, but the entire world: Political Islam. *The Mirage* raises many questions, which take the form of comparative paradoxes approved in the literature of scientific methods in dissertations (such as PhD's) and adopted in the most prestigious universities in the world, and answers them in a professional and scientific way."

In an article on *The Mirage*, published in the Egyptian newspaper *Almasry Alyoum*, on May 15, 2016, the Egyptian poet Fatima Naoot wrote "I still hope that the book will be distributed in libraries across the Arab world, in social clubs and salons, forums of universities and institutes, so that young people may come to know the secrets of such violent ideology in order to prevent such groups from recruiting our uninformed youth. I also hope that excerpts from *The Mirage* would be included in preliminary curricula in order to develop within our children the rejection of such savage ideology, to defuse the potential opportunities to penetrate those innocent young people when they grow up. This is achieved by learning from an early age that all the slogans proclaimed by such organizations on justice, equality, piety and faith are purely a mirage. These terrorists are interested only in the spoils of power and stealing the reigns of authority in order to oppress people, humiliate men, enslave women and steal children and wealth, just as ISIS (Da'esh) is doing today."

I have been asked if I was thinking of Western readers

With Moaness Al Mardi, Chairman of Bahraini Journalists Association, during the signing ceremony of my book *The Mirage* on the sidelines of a seminar on the book's ideas, organized by Isa Cultural Center, Kingdom of Bahrain, March 23, 2015

With H.E. Mohammed Obaid Al-Mazrouei, Executive Director of the UAE General Authority of Islamic Affairs and Endowments, at the ceremony organized by the Authority for signing my book *The Mirage* and presenting copies to mosque preachers, November 23, 2015

Presenting a copy of *The Mirage* to H.E. Dr. Abdullatif bin Rashid Al Zayani, Secretary-General of the Cooperation Council for the Arab States of the Gulf (GCC), during a lecture delivered by H.E. at the ECSSR titled "Cooperation Council for the Arab States of the Gulf: Achievements and Aspirations," January 20, 2016 while I was writing this book or if I was targeting them with some of my ideas. My answer was No. Arab readers are my main concern. Western readers were never in my mind except when I wrote my master's and PhD dissertations, since the referees were Westerners. However, what makes my book *The Mirage* attractive to Western readers is its ideas and approach, as well as its findings about political religious groups' probable retreat. The majority of such groups have no political, economic or cultural programs. They only repeat loose slogans on the appli-

Presenting a copy of my book *The Mirage* in French to former French President Nicolas Sarkozy on the sidelines of a lecture given by him at the ECSSR titled "The World Today: A Conversation with Nicolas Sarkozy," January 13, 2016

Presenting a copy of my book *The Mirage* to Lord William Hague of Richmond, former Secretary of State for Foreign and Commonwealth Affairs, UK, on the sidelines of a lecture titled "Global Trends," delivered by him, at ECSSR, December 16, 2015

cation of Sharia without developing programs that indicate how to turn such slogans into applicable plans and to achieve the aspirations of the citizens of the Islamic countries to live in dignity, peace and stability.

In 2016, my book *Eternal Imprints: Figures that Made History and Others that Changed the Future of their Countries* was released. The book includes a thorough and intensive reading of the life of a group of Arab and foreign personalities that played a major role in the progress of their societies. Although most of these figures were leading politicians, there were others from various fields such as physics, cinema and computer

A cake prepared by the ECSSR staff at a ceremony they organized on the occasion of *The Mirage* winning the Sheikh Zayed Book Award, May 4, 2016

technology. A large part of the book was published in monthly articles in *Al-Ittihad* newspaper in 2015.

Although I always write in a language that endeavors to reach the largest possible number of readers, the nature of the topics that I deal with usually attracts an elite of intellectuals and researchers, or somewhat knowledgeable readers. However, my book *Eternal Imprints: Figures that Made History and Others that Changed the Future of their Countries*, with its ideas that are far less specialized and distant from difficult research treatments, is directed at a wider audience. In addition, writings that deal with public figures receive more attention from readers, especially as these figures belong to several Arab countries as well as renowned world leaders and icons. However, I wanted to include in the book's introduction the specific rules on which I have based the selection of these figures. This will allow readers to know in advance that the process of selection and exclusion was not random. Also, I was keen on clarifying the commonalities between the personalities that left "eternal imprints."

A short period of time after the book's release, reactions started coming in. Within a couple of months, many articles and reviews were published regarding the book and its ideas. Among them was an article by the Algerian writer Khalid Umar Binguega, published in *Al-Arab* newspaper, London, on February 14, 2016, which included

With H.E. Ahmed Abdul Rahman Al Jarman, Assistant Minister of Foreign and International Cooperation for Political Affairs, at the signing ceremony of my book *Eternal Imprints: Figures that Made History and Others that Changed the Future of their Countries* at the UAE Ministry of Foreign Affairs and International Cooperation, May 9, 2016

a smart vision of the book and its ideas. The writer described the book saying "It has its own special taste of knowledge. It clearly combines experiences that built countries, formed civilized awareness, contributed to history of mankind, leaving its grades engraved in the memory of time and transcending national border with creativity… it is a restoration of the ideas of the deceased innovators, and a recognition and thorough explanation of ideas of those that are still alive on all fronts. On the other hand, *Eternal Imprints: Figures that Made History and Others that Changed the Future of their Countries* represents an awareness of the need to encourage wider categories and more groups to read. Hence, the writer was careful to simplify visions without impairing the depth of ideas."

I think that changeability has become a standard that defines the ability of countries to develop and progress. In the past, we used to divide the world into developed and developing countries. However, countries are now divided into two categories: those that accept change and those who resist it. I am currently preparing to write a new book titled *Change*, which focuses on the idea that we live in a changing world. This change encompasses many areas, such as education, media, political participation,

With H.E. Ahmed Abdul Rahman Al Jarman, Assistant Minister of Foreign and International Cooperation for Political Affairs, and some of audience at the signing ceremony of my book *Eternal Imprints: Figures that Made History and Others that Changed the Future of their Countries* at the UAE Ministry of Foreign Affairs and International Cooperation, May 9, 2016

wars, communications, computer technologies and technology in general, medicine, therapy and all other aspects of life.

Such change will have its impact on life, societies and ideas. Therefore, we should be prepared for change by understanding its rules and courses. Unless the Arab world prepares accordingly, it will fall further behind. The theme of change, as is the case with previous books, has its origins that go back to my university years, and my teaching years at the university during which I taught a course on "change." I think the matter needs the contributions of other Arab intellectuals, given its multiple aspects and since one or even a group of books might not be sufficient to thoroughly cover it. This also applies equally to social media, the future of the world order, and ideologies of political religious groups and their future. All these issues need to be seriously addressed by Arab and foreign researchers. Writing on these issues stemmed from my interest in shedding light on their importance to encourage Arab researchers to tackle them from different perspectives.

Chapter 5

Travel, Awards and Honors

Chapter 5

Travel, Awards and Honors

(I): Travel

Travel has been an extremely important part of my life, so much so that I devoted a separate section of my autobiography to discuss my travel endeavors. I think that some aspects of my career can be understood through my travels, which I started at an early age. Probably, the inner desire to explore and gain more knowledge was one of the reasons that made me a "constant traveler" from 1977 to 1990. This continu-

During a trip to New York City, USA, in May 2013

ous travel was interrupted for only one year, when I joined the Ministry of Foreign Affairs. I traveled less during that year, and after 1993, I became a "semi-constant traveler," due to the nature of my work.

With my son Dr. Khaled in California, USA, in August 2014

During a trip to Sharm el-Sheikh, Egypt, October 21, 2015

With Major General Tariq Al-Mahdi Abdul-Tawab, former Governor of Alexandria, during a visit to Egypt on September 28, 2014

So far, I have visited more than 70 countries, dispersed all over the world's continents. These countries varied from the heart of Africa, with its jungles and primitive tribes, to the most civilized places on Earth. My journeys varied from hiking the peaks of mountains and hills, to touring nuclear reactors, and exploring the deep waters of seas and oceans. They also ranged from the most luxurious and extravagant hotels to refugee camps and hunting tents in the open air. My travels varied from areas where sun rays scorched overhead to places where temperatures dropped to minus 20° C; from hospital beds and operating-theaters to negotiation tables and honor ceremony podiums; from meetings with leaders, chiefs and business tycoons around the world to sitting with simple people in the alleys and streets of cities and enjoying their spontaneous conversations.

I experienced almost all types of travel. I traveled for tourism, leisure, education, medical treatment and work. I traveled by land and by air for hundreds of thousands of miles. I also traveled a lot by sea-cruises and one of those trips included many ports on the Mediterranean. During those journeys, I became familiar with most cultures of the world, both Eastern and Western ones. I became acquainted with many religions, creeds and beliefs embraced by hu-

During a trip to Brazil, July 5, 1995

man beings in various countries. In some of those journeys, death was hovering and lurking over us, and in other travels, there were some of the most glorious signs of appreciation waiting for me.

The outcome of these constant journeys was manifested in a wealth of human culture and knowledge, besides political, managerial and professional expertise, which influenced my character and my diligent professional performance.

Presenting a copy of my book *Prospects for the American Age: Sovereignty and Influence in the New World Order* to Muhammad Abdul-Salam, adviser to Dr. Ahmad Al-Tayib, The Grand Imam of Al-Azhar Mosque; at the premises of Al-Azhar Sheikhdom, Cairo, June 12, 2014

Be at the Airport within One Hour

Most of my travels were for work, while less than 10 percent were for tourism. Many of my official trips were in the company of His Highness Sheikh Mohamed bin Zayed Al Nahyan (may God protect him). They included negotiations and meetings, which I attended due to my position as Political Adviser to His Highness. This position required of me to be

With Dr. Liza Anderson, former President of the American University in Cairo, September 24, 2014

With Ret. Major General Suhail Shaheen Al-Marar, Ret. Major General Khalifa Al-Musafiri, and a number of officers from the UAE Armed Forces and the Moroccan Royal Army, during a visit to Morocco on July 1, 1995

perfectly prepared for anything that might be included in the talks and negotiations, in terms of ideas and topics. Being prepared means I had to have comprehensive understanding of data, figures and dates, alongside sufficient knowledge of a wide array of political, economic and social issues in many countries. I had to have the capabili-

During my trip to Brazil, July 5, 1995

ty to recall the information from memory or papers which should be readily available at the right moment. Therefore, each journey used to present me with a real test, and when that test was about to be over, another test would emerge in another part of the world.

From 1993 to 2003, I used to travel 50 or 60 times a year. Some of those travels were due to my position as the Director General of the Emirates Center for Strategic Studies and Research (ECSSR). They occurred to sign agreements of cooperation, to organize joint activities with other think tanks in various countries around the world, or to deliver some lectures, chair sessions and participate with research papers at

With H.H. Sheikh Mohamed bin Zayed Al Nahyan, Crown Prince of Abu Dhabi and Deputy Supreme Commander of the UAE Armed Forces (may God protect him), and His Majesty King Mohammed VI of Morocco, then Crown Prince, during a visit to the Kingdom of Morocco, July 1, 1995

conferences. I used to receive hundreds of invitations to either attend or participate in these conferences every year. However, I used to attend a reasonable number of such activities, which could be consistent with my constantly overloaded work schedule. Probably, this type of travel and visits was somewhat easier than the abovementioned type, as surprises were less and these trips were related to research, free from the complications of political meetings and the rounds of negotiations and dialogues. The latter ones naturally witnessed diversion of views and conflicts of interests and wills.

Accordingly, my briefcase and bags were always ready for traveling, or at least there were clothes ready and suitable for various types of tasks and variations of weather. Sometimes I would be informed that I should be ready for traveling within a few hours, or maybe even less. That frequently occurred while I was already occupied and busy performing another task. Therefore, I always had to delegate tasks to some of my aides who could perform them while I would be on my way home to find my suitcase ready, so I could pick it up quickly and rush off to the airport.

My memory is filled with many details from those trips. I recall now a trip to the USA in 1998, along with H.H. Sheikh Mohamed bin Zayed Al

With H.H. Sheikh Nahyan bin Zayed Al Nahyan, Chairman of the Board of Trustees of the Zayed bin Sultan Al Nahyan Charitable and Humanitarian Foundation, and H.E. Dr. Anwar Gargash, UAE Minister of State for Foreign Affairs and former Vice President Al Gore, during a visit to the USA, May 12, 1998

Nahyan (may God protect him) in a UAE delegation led by H.H. Sheikh Khalifa bin Zayed Al Nahyan, UAE President (may God protect him), who was then the Crown Prince of Abu Dhabi; alongside Sheikh Diab bin Zayed Al Nahyan and Sheikh Abdullah bin Zayed Al Nahyan. During that trip, H.H. Sheikh Khalifa bin Zayed Al Nahyan met with then US President Bill Clinton and Vice President Al Gore at the White House. After the meeting, we went to Texas to visit the area where F-16 fighters were being manufactured. The UAE would later buy those fighters through a deal known as the "Deal of the Century." Also during that trip, we visited the future US President George W. Bush, who was the Governor of Texas at the time.

Closing that deal was not an easy task. It was done after years of continuous hard effort. This effort included negotiations about state-of-the-art technologies, which the UAE insisted on having its fighters equipped with. At that time, there was not a single Middle Eastern country that possessed such technologies, due to the pressures of the Israeli lobby in the USA. The pro-Israel lobby, which has a significant influence on American decisions, tried its best to obstruct the deal through its political and media wings and its influential societies and institutions inside the USA. That lobby tried intensely to abort

H.H. Sheikh Khalifa bin Zayed Al Nahyan, UAE President (may God protect him), and H.H. Sheikh Mohamed bin Zayed Al Nahyan, Crown Prince of Abu Dhabi and Deputy Supreme Commander of the UAE Armed Forces (may God protect him), in a meeting with former US President Bill Clinton, in May 15, 1998

the delivery of those highly-advanced technologies to the UAE. On our side, we worked hard to neutralize these hostile forces, through coordinated and tightly-disciplined work, which resulted in achieving all the objectives of the UAE. The deal was closed and signed in the form, fulfilling all the terms and conditions demanded by the UAE. Thus, that deal became the cornerstone in the modernization process and the huge development trend witnessed by the UAE Armed Forces over the following two decades. The strategy of that development was devised by His Highness Sheikh Mohamed bin Zayed Al Nahyan (may God protect him) who had diligently and efficiently pursued that process.

Through that restructuring process, H.H. Sheikh Mohamed bin Zayed (may God protect him) has led major transformations inside the UAE Armed Forces, in terms of organization, training and weapon acquisition. He devoted more attention to enhance and raise the level of proficiency of commanders and troops to the best and most refined status of qualifying, and according to the most updated techniques and known methods at the best military academies and major armies in the world. The result of that transformation appeared clearly through the amazing military performance of the

UAE Armed Forces in the difficult tasks that were assigned to them. Through the "Deal of the Century" in 1998, the UAE's negotiation capabilities proved highly efficient and the capability to use all factors of strength possessed by the country. I feel proud that I was one of the team members who contributed to the delivery of that achievement.

With Ret. Lt. General Suhail Shahin Al-Murr, Ret. Lt General Khalifa Al-Musafiri, and H.E. former UAE Ambassador to the Kingdom of Morocco, Easa Hamad Bu-Shehab, during a visit to the Kingdom of Morocco, July 1, 1995

Throughout a full decade of extensive work (1994–2003), I was frequently assigned the task of organizing official visits. I had to set schedules, and to define the list of topics to be discussed in those talks and meetings, especially in the countries of significant importance such as the USA, UK, France and

With Dr. Jawad Al-Hamad, Director of Middle East Studies Institute, in Jordan, during my visit to Jordan to give a lecture about my book *Prospects for the American Age: Sovereignty and Influence in the New World Order*, June 8, 2014

several other European and Arab countries. Those schedules and agendas were prepared based on extensive research, which covered political, economic, military and security aspects. Moreover, our research explored the background and contexts of the related issues, and accordingly defined the objectives and interests that could be achieved. Needless to say that our research also covered points of convergence and divergence between the UAE and the country, or countries, that would be included in the visits, as well as defining the most important personalities and influential powers whose attitudes needed to be taken into consideration.

During the official visits, I met a large number of presidents, kings, leaders and dignitaries. The biggest gathering that I witnessed of those leaders was during my participation in the funeral ceremony of King Hussein bin Talal of Jordan in 1999. I was in the delegation accompanying H.H. Sheikh Mohamed bin Zayed Al Nahyan (may God protect him). There was a large crowd of official delegates attending the funeral ceremony of the late King Hussein. Presidents and kings walked on foot amid highly protective security procedures. I remember seeing at

With H.E. Dr. Al-Sadiq Al-Faqeeh, Ambassador of Sudan to Jordan (then Secretary-General of the Arab Thought Forum), in Jordan, June 9, 2014

With H.E. former UAE Ambassador to Jordan, Dr. Abdullah Naser Sultan Al-A'amiri, during my visit to Jordan on June 10, 2014

the airport the 40th plane land, from the list of official delegates' planes arriving to participate in the funeral.

The most annoying aspect of official trips that bother me is when they do not have a clear objective or a clear agenda. Probably this concern has something to do with my nature, as I like to know precisely what I aim to achieve, prepare the proper tools and means, and the suitable schedule and agenda of the trip would be set accordingly. As for the trips that do not have a clear objective and their timetables would not be fixed, they make me feel more exhausted. Unfortunately, confusion of schedules does happen in some official trips.

The large amount of official trips made me in most cases relinquish my right to choose the destinations of travel with my family for tourism and leisure. Therefore, I used to let my wife and children select a place of their choice, when circumstances allowed me to have a vacation to take some rest from the strain of continuous work. Fortunately, their choices conformed to my desires in most cases. Among the joyful leisure trips that I remember was a sea cruise in 2014. It came after a period of exhausting work. In terms of the quality of rooms, beds, service, and number of excellent restaurants and cafes, the cruiser on which we sailed was more like a luxurious hotel than a ship. They offered various options of food and drinks to satisfy different tastes. The

With Nicholas Normand, Deputy Director of the Institute of Graduate Studies for National Defense in Paris, on May 21, 2014. The table seen in the photo is the table which belongs to the renowned French leader Napoleon Bonaparte

With H.E. Muhammad Mir Abdullah Al-Raeesi, former UAE Ambassador to France, during my visit to France on May 21, 2014

ship used to sail at night, and during the day, it would dock at a European city or village on the route of its journey. We stopped in Italy, France, Monte Carlo, Spain, Greece and Turkey. This joyful variety of places would allow you to fall asleep to a certain view then wake up to another. You would also meet people different from those you have met just a few hours ago.

Among the reasons that made me enjoy that cruise was that the passengers were mostly adults and many of them were of old age. There were no teenagers or children who indulge in partying late at night and behaviors that might sometimes disturb adults. The quietness that characterized the cruise allowed us to meditate and think about what we were passing through, in terms of the captivating natural scenery. We became familiar with part of the character of the Mediterranean Sea, as we saw its traits in the sea-ports and cities located along its coastline. I also found time to read with a clear mind the final drafts of my book *The Mirage*, and to review it carefully so that the book would appear the way I wanted.

Seventy Thousand or More

There are some countries I always wanted to visit. These countries give me a deep feeling of comfort and enjoyment. Among them are the UK, Morocco, the Seychelles and Italy. The UK was the first European country that I visited during my undergraduate study at Kuwait University. The trip to the UK, in which I spent a full month, opened a door for me for reflection, knowledge and comparison at an important stage of

The cruise, which covered many seaports on the shores of the Mediterranean, was one of my most joyful leisure journeys. The photo was taken in Monte Carlo during the cruise in 2014

my life. As I mentioned before, the title of articles that I wrote in the student magazine *Free Forum* during my time at Kuwait University was "Memoirs of a Poor Man Who Traveled to London." It reflected the huge influence that was left in my mind by that journey. Since then, I have traveled to the UK more than 20 times, on official visits accompanying His Highness Sheikh Mohamed bin Zayed Al Nahyan (may God protect him), H.H. Sheikh Hamdan bin Zayed Al Nahyan, H.H. Sheikh Abdullah bin Zayed Al Nahyan; and on other visits related to the activities of the ECSSR.

The UK capital, London, hosted the conference titled "Gulf Security: A National Perspective II," at Whitehall on April 29–30, 1998, under the generous patronage and participation of His Highness Sheikh Mohamed bin Zayed Al Nahyan (may God protect him). The list of attendees included a number of the most important political and military leaders and decision makers in the

Gulf region. Among them were: the late Sheikh Salem Sabah Al-Salem Al-Sabah, former Defense Minister of Kuwait; H.H. Prince Salman bin Hamad Al Khalifa, Crown Prince of Bahrain; Sheikh Hamad bin Jassim, former Qatari Prime Minister; H.E. Yousuf bin Alawi bin Abdullah, Minister Responsible for Foreign Affairs in the Sultanate of Oman; and H.E. Staff Lt. General Hamad Ali Al-Atiyah, Adviser to the Emir of Qatar for Defense Affairs, who was then holding the post of Chief of Staff of the Qatari Armed Forces. During the conference, we also received Prince Charles, the UK's Crown Prince. A number of top British officials and military commanders as well participated in the proceedings of that conference. The opening speech was delivered by George Robertson, former UK Defence Secretary. In addition, two speeches were delivered by John Reid, UK Minister of State for the Armed Forces at the time; and Charles Guthrie, former UK Chief of the Defence Staff, during the conference sessions.

Moreover, in October 2014, Whitehall was the location for the ECSSR celebration to mark the 20th

With Prince Charles, UK Crown Prince, and the late Sheikh Salem Sabah Al-Salem Al-Sabah, former Defense Minister of Kuwait; on the sidelines of the conference: "Gulf Security: A National Perspective II," UK on April 29, 1998

With Prince Charles, UK Crown Prince, and H.E. Staff Lt. General Hamad Ali Al-Atiyah, Adviser to the Emir of Qatar for Defense Affairs, during the conference: "Gulf Security: A National Perspective II," UK on April 29, 1998

With Dr. Farhan Nezami, Director of Oxford Centre for Islamic Studies, and two attendees during the ceremony of signing my book *Prospects for American Age: Sovereignty and Influence in the New World Order*, at Oxford Centre, during a scholarly tour of the UK, April 7, 2014

With H.E. Dr. Ali Rashid Al-Nuaimi, Member of Abu Dhabi Executive Council, Director General of Abu Dhabi Education Council and Chancellor of UAE University; and Dr. Farhan Nezami, Director of Oxford Centre for Islamic Studies, during the symposium "Security in the Arabian Gulf," that was held at Ditchley Park in Oxfordshire, UK, October 30, 2014

During the celebration of the 20th Anniversary of the launch of the ECSSR, at Whitehall, UK. The photo shows H.E. Sheikh Mohammed Sabah Al-Salem Al-Sabah, former Minister of Foreign Affairs of Kuwait; Dr. Abdul Latif Al-Zayani, Secretary-General of the GCC, and Dr. Farhan Nezami, Director of Oxford Centre for Islamic Studies, October 30, 2014

Anniversary of its inception. That was at the sidelines of the Second International Symposium organized jointly by the ECSSR and the Oxford Centre for Islamic Studies, under the title "Security in the Arabian Gulf." Among the participants in the symposium were H.E. Sheikh Mohammed Sabah Al-Salem Al-Sabah, former Minister of Foreign Affairs of the State of Kuwait; Dr. Abdul Latif Al-Zayani, Secretary-General of the GCC; Dr. Farhan Nezami,

Director of Oxford Centre for Islamic Studies; General David Petraeus, former Director of the CIA; as well as a large number of Arab and foreign officials, academics and researchers.

Gulf security was also the topic of another symposium in the UK during July 12–14, 1999 in which I participated. Sandhurst College organized a symposium titled "Gulf Security: Opportunities and Challenges for the New Generation," in which I presented a paper on "Weapons of Mass Destruction: Threat Perceptions in the Arabian Gulf."

With H.H. Sheikh Hamdan bin Zayed Al Nahyan, Ruler's Representative in the Al Dhafra Region (formerly Western Region), (Minister of State for Foreign Affairs at that time); H.E. Eisa Saleh Al-Gurg, former UAE Ambassador to the UK, in 1997

The UK was also a familiar destination for our leisure trips with my family. The country has a wide variety of natural scenes and historical sites, ranging from old cities to the English countryside with its meadows spreading as far the eyes can see and majestic stone castles. London occupies a special place in my mind and in the minds of my family members, who enjoy being there whenever an opportunity arises. Among the visits that combined the official mission and leisure, was a visit to a wonderful mountainous area in Scotland, with the company of H.H. Sheikh Mohamed bin Zayed Al Nahyan (may God protect him). We stayed at a house located in the middle of a vast field, owned by H.H. Sheikh Mohammed bin Rashid Al Maktoum (may God protect him). During that tour, the 9/11 terrorist attacks took place, which shook the whole world.

The Kingdom of Morocco is another country that I am always delighted to visit, whether in an official capacity or for tourism and leisure. I visited Morocco for the first time in 1994, and I believe that Morocco is one of the best destinations for tourists. My visits were often limited to

With H.H. Sheikh Mohamed bin Zayed Al Nahyan; Crown Prince of Abu Dhabi and Deputy Supreme Commander of the UAE Armed Forces (may God protect him); the late King Hassan II of Morocco; and His Majesty King Mohammed VI of Morocco, then Crown Prince, during a visit to Morocco, July 1, 1995

In Morocco, 2013

Rabat, except for once or twice when I went to Casablanca. However, my visit to Morocco in 2013 was different. In addition to the usual stops in Rabat and Casablanca, I went to Tangier, Fez, Marrakesh and Ifrane. I witnessed the amazing variety of cultures, geography and people who live in this important Arab country, and I came closer to its historical richness. Ifrane was one of the cities which attracted my attention, and I consider it one of the most beautiful places in the world. Even though I had seen many luxurious hotels in my travels, I consider the hotel where I stayed in Ifrane the most beautiful of them all.

I believe if Ifrane was a European city, for example, it would have been in a better shape as an attractive destination for tourists from all over the world.

Although Morocco is among the successful tourism countries, the charming nature of Ifrane and the captivating beauty that God blessed it with qualify this city to be much more famous. I thought about this when I visited the Leaning Tower of Pisa in Italy in 2013. The number of visitors on that day was more than 70,000 tourists of different nationalities. I thought to myself that the Tower of Pisa is just one building, while there are many buildings that are thousands of years older in some Arab countries. Those sites could attract millions of tourists if their potentials were invested in and utilized properly, and if those countries built the required infrastructure for tourism.

Since my first visit there in 1994, Italy has been one of the countries that I love to visit and tour its cities. My first visit was to attend a conference held at Castel Gandolfo, a small town near Rome, that is home to the Pope's summer residence. The conference was part of The Gulf Project 2000, organized under the sponsorship of Columbia University, in the United States of America. That project held 10 conferences during the period 1994–2004, in various Arab and European cities. The ECSSR hosted the second conference in this series, in 1995. Within the framework of the same project, I went on my second visit to Italy to Bellagio near Lake Como, which is one of the most beautiful lakes that I

During a conference titled "Gulf Security Issues," hosted by the ECSSR on March 27, 1995, as part of a series of conferences under the title "The Gulf Project 2000 " organized by Columbia University, USA, with participation of Arab researchers and think tanks

With some officers of Moroccan Royal Army, during a visit to Morocco, July 1, 1995

With H.E. Dr. Anwar Gargash, UAE Minister of State for Foreign Affairs; the Kuwaiti Academic Mohammed Al-Rumaihi; and a number of experts and academics in the Italian Bellagio city, which hosted a conference titled "Future Perspectives for the Gulf" in July 1996, as part of a series of conferences under the title "Gulf Project 2000 "organized by US Colombia University, with participation of Arab researchers and think tanks

have ever seen during my travels around the world.

I have toured many Italian districts and cities, including, Rome, Venice, Milan and Florence. I also visited the Vatican for the first time, and met the Vatican Secretary of State, during a scholarly visit, which included discussion of the themes of my book *Prospects for the American Age: Sovereignty and Influence in the New World Order*, in June 2014. Rome was my destination for most of my visits to Italy. I will

With Vatican Secretary of State Cardinal Pietro Parolin, in the presence of Michele Capasso, Head of "Euro-Mediterranean Foundation," during my visit to Italy, June 22, 2014

With Michele Capasso, Head of "Euro-Mediterranean Foundation," and in the background appears the Colosseum Building, in the Italian capital, Rome, during my visit to Italy, June 22, 2014

never forget how much I enjoyed visiting the Colosseum, with its majestic Roman sights. I also enjoyed visiting the famous tourist landmark known as the Spanish Steps in the heart of Rome. It is surrounded by many cafes and shops. Shopping-lovers and crowds of people are always filling the place and giving it some of their liveliness. In November 2015, I visited Italy on my way to Switzerland to attend a ceremony on the occasion of being granted an Honorary PhD from the Swiss University of Lugano (USI). Even though Lugano is located in Switzerland, there have been no border checkpoints between the two countries for years.

Writing a word in the Visitors' Book, at the Italian Center for Defense Graduate Studies, during my visit to the premises of the center in Rome, to discuss the ideas and sign copies of my book *Prospects for the American Age*, June 20, 2014

During receiving the Honorary PhD. in political science and international relations, from Professor Antonello Martinez, Chancellor of the University of Lugano, and Professor Abdullah Raweh, Vice Chancellor of the University, November 17, 2015

Among my memories was also my first visit to Italy, which coincided with the 1994 Football World Cup in the USA. Italy and Brazil reached the final match in Los Angeles. We were watching the match in a theater with a huge screen fixed on the stage. The Italians, naturally, were supporting their national team, while I was supporting the Brazilian team. Finally, the game came down to a penalty shoot-out. The Italian star Roberto Baggio missed his penalty kick, handing the victory and the cup to Brazil.

France is one of the countries that I visited a lot, having been there more than 10 times on official visits and leisure trips with my family. The first visit was in June 1993, to participate in a conference hosted by Paris-Sorbonne University. There are several strong work ties and partnerships connecting the ECSSR with few French institutions, such as the Center for Strategic Affairs at the French Ministry of Defense, with which we organized an important symposium about strategic dialogue in 1999. The ECSSR also established strong bonds with the Observatory of Geopolitical Studies, which is an affiliate

With Nicholas Normand, Deputy Director of the Institute of Graduate Studies for National Defense, during a visit to France on May 21, 2014

With Jack Lang, President of the Arab World Institute in Paris, and former French Minister of Culture, during my visit to the French Capital, Paris, January 26, 2016

of the French Senate. I consider Paris one of the most beautiful cities, and its hotels are among the most beautiful hotels in the world, particularly the George V Hotel and Plaza Athénée. I felt terribly sorry about the terrorist attack that took place in Paris in November 2015, because this beautiful city and its residents do not deserve what they have suffered in the violent terrorist attacks that have targeted them in recent years.

With Florentino Pérez Rodríguez, President of Real Madrid FC, during a visit to the club in Spain, March 22, 2014

With Xabier "Xabi" Alonso, the former player for Real Madrid, during a visit to the club in Spain, March 22, 2014

With Cristiano Ronaldo, the famous Real Madrid footballer, during a visit to the club's home in Spain, March 22, 2014

Monaco is located near France, and while it is very small, it enjoys incredible beauty. I think our first visit to Monaco was on the occasion of New Year's Eve. We were on board a yacht that docked on a Monaco beach that night. On the second visit, we toured that small principality, which hosts a population of about only 37,000 citizens.

Spain is another of my favorite countries. I traveled to Spain many times, both on official and leisure trips. During my visit to Spain in March 2014, I watched a football match between Real Madrid and Barcelona in the stadium. Through a recommendation from the UAE, the President of Real Madrid, Florentino Pérez Rodríguez took us to watch a training session of the team, and we took photos with the players during their

With H.E. Yousuf Manei Al-Otaiba, UAE Ambassador to the USA, on the sidelines of my participation in "Zayed Charity Marathon" in New York city, May 19, 2014

Presenting a copy of my book *Prospects for the American Age: Sovereignty and Influence in the New World Order* to Dr. Charles Perry, Vice President of the Institute for Foreign Policy Analysis (IFPA), and Director of Studies at the IFPA, in Boston, USA, May 7, 2014

Scientific Discussion about my two books *From Tribe to Facebook: The Transformational Role of Social Networks* and *Prospects for the American Age: Sovereignty and Influence in the New World Order*, with Mrs. Robin Meili, Director of International Programs at RAND Corporation, in Los Angeles, USA, May 19, 2014

During the ceremony of signing my book *Prospects for the American Age: Sovereignty and Influence in the New World Order*, at University of Chicago, USA, May 14, 2014

practice and at the hotel where they were staying. Among those players were Cristiano Ronaldo and Xabier "Xabi" Alonso. We also took photos with Florentino Pérez and saw the trophies obtained by the club in European and international tournaments.

The exciting game ended with Barcelona winning 4–3 against Real Madrid. In a funny incident related to that match, I was sitting in the sector assigned for VIPs, and beside me was a person from the UAE delegation wearing a T-shirt bearing the emblem of Barcelona. In a place reserved for the supporters of Real Madrid, that scene made many Real supporters feel somewhat tense. If I had not been wearing a cap with the Real Madrid logo, that Emirati sitting next to me could have faced real trouble.

When I talk about the countries that I like to visit continuously, I will take a long pause when I mention the United States of America. I lived in the USA for eight years, during my graduate studies doing my master's and PhD degrees. I have visited the USA dozens of times for official tasks, as well as leisure trips. I also received treatment for cancer there. I believe I have visited all 50 states.

During the ceremony of signing my book *Prospects for the American Age: Sovereignty and Influence in the New World Order*, in New York, May 9, 2014

During the signing ceremony for my book *Prospects for the American Age: Sovereignty and Influence in the New World Order*, at Public and International Relations College, the University of Colombia, New York, on May 9, 2014. Beside me is Professor Dan McIntyre from the university

Discussing my book *The Mirage* and the situation of Political Islam, at the United Nations headquarters in New York, April 8, 2016

Since 1982, no year has passed without me paying the USA at least one visit.

I had a strong connection with the USA. All my children were born there. Based on my research interest, I found myself connected to most American universities and think tanks, as well as media organizations and official agencies. Through my position as the Director General of the ECSSR, I have developed connections with many American academics and politicians, whom have been hosted by the ECSSR in its various activities. Moreover, through my work as the political adviser to H.H. Sheikh Mohamed bin Zayed Al Nahyan (may God protect him),

Delivering a lecture about my book *Prospects for the American Age: Sovereignty and Influence in the New World Order*, at Massachusetts Institute of Technology (MIT) in USA, May 7, 2014

With Dr. Hilary Rantisi, at Harvard University, USA, during an academic discussion about my book *Prospects for the American Age*, May 9, 2014

I have undertaken the burdens of many other tasks that were closely connected to the centers of influence and decision making in the USA. Taking into consideration the USA's dominant role in many issues of the Gulf region and the world in general, I was deeply familiar with the details of the American political system, and what was going on within its daily events and actions.

The United States of America is still the greatest producer of ideas, and it is one of the most important fertile environments for scientific research and innovation, along with economic, cultural and military power. Regardless of our attitude toward American policy, I respect American work ethic and achievements. These values encourage creativity and innovation, thus making this country the land of opportunities for everyone who introduces a useful idea; the USA provides him with the means and requirements needed to transform the idea into a positive asset and a source of fortune, strength and further enhancement of his status.

Near the Pyramids, Cairo, in 1978

The Republic of Seychelles occupies a special place on the list of countries I love to visit. Most of my visits to the Seychelles were devoted to leisure and enjoying its beauty. Some visits were in the company of H.H. Sheikh Mo-

Presenting a copy of my book *The Mirage* to Dr. Jaber Jad Nassar, President of Cairo University, during my visit to Egypt, February 25, 2015

hamed bin Zayed Al Nahyan (may God protect him). Over the years, I had the opportunity to witness the development of the Seychelles, to which H.H. Sheikh Mohamed bin Zayed Al Nahyan (may God protect him) had contributed. Since my first visit in the early 1990s, I used to spend two or three weeks there every year. Everything in the Seychelles gives you the feeling of tranquility and peace. You can see the infinite expansion of the clear blue ocean, hills and plateaus covered with green plantations, and thousands of singing birds flying over the scenery. At sunrise and sunset, the glowing sun creates painting-like landscapes with lovely colors and shadows. All of that gives the Seychelles a special place in my heart, and makes me want to visit it constantly.

Egypt is another one of the countries that I visited at an early age. My first trip to Egypt was in 1978, while I was at the beginning of my university education. I climbed the pyramids and went inside them. I have also visited *Al Qanatir Al Khayriyah*, which hosted in the past a house for the late President Mohammed Anwar Al-Sadat. My visits to Egypt became more frequent after I came back from the USA. Most of my trips to Egypt were official visits with H.H. Sheikh Mohamed bin Zayed Al Nahyan (may God protect him). Some were to participate in conferences, research and intellectual activities. However, official visits frequently turned into leisure trips. Cairo is one of the cities that I love, and I believe that its tourism potential is strong.

Likewise, trips to Lebanon were also usually transformed from official to leisure visits. I have visited Lebanon many times on official visits, and the remaining trips were for tourism and recreation. During my last visit to Lebanon, I stayed with my family at Mua'awad Hotel in Broummana. The scene of the valley from the window of my room was unforgettable, and the weather was at its best. However, Lebanon is one of the countries that is deprived of its tourism value. The political and sectarian divisions in Lebanon ruin the chances for the country to earn billions of dollars that could flow from tourism.

My trips to Russia were important and interesting as well. I traveled to Russia more than six times for official visits. During one of these visits, I stayed as a guest at the residence of the UAE Ambassador to Moscow. I met the former Russian President Boris Yeltsin on one of the visits as I was among the team accompanying H.H. Sheikh Mohamed bin Zayed Al Nahyan (may God protect him). We visited the Kremlin and toured its museums, which contained rare treasures and art pieces made of gold and diamonds, an indicator of the combination of luxury and beauty. Our visits, however, were only limited to Moscow and we did not get to see any other cities.

The ceremony to receive my honorary PhD in political science and international relations from the Swiss University of Lugano, November 17, 2015

Buffalo Horn, Flamingo Portrait & Banned Books

The rhythm of events is usually faster during travel than the familiar pace when the person stays in his home country, where the individual goes to his work, meets people whom he is used to seeing and walks in streets familiar to him. The events of travel vary between what is humorous and what is terrifying. My memories of some countries are connected with the events that happened during those visits. The Netherlands is among those countries that bring me bad memories. I visited it once for an official visit, on which we met the Dutch Defense Minister and some other officials. During that visit, we were involved in a terrifying car accident when one of our cars overturned. Fortunately, none of its passengers were hurt. In general, the Netherlands did not leave a nice positive impression in my mind and I never wished to visit it again.

My first visit to Sweden in 1995 was connected with a strange event. The aim of the trip was to attend a conference organized by the United Nations Institute for Disarmament Research. H.E. Dr. Anwar Gargash accompanied me on that trip. We were forced to cancel the visit because of a terrorist threat, targeting to kill us, as we were warned by security agencies. The suspected

The Nobel Museum, in the Swedish capital Stockholm, which I visited during my trip to Sweden, in November 2015

perpetrator was arrested, and we came to know that he was of Arab origin and he previously worked at a pharmacy in Abu Dhabi. The second visit to Sweden was much better. I was honored by the United Nations Institute for Peace on the occasion of receiving an honorary PhD from the University of Lugano in November 2015. I had an interview with the Swedish newspaper, published in English, *The Local*, which is read by about eight million readers all over Europe. I also visited the Nobel Museum, which I consider one of the most marvelous museums around the world. Nevertheless, I would not recommend anyone to visit Sweden if they do not have work or business there because it lacks entertainment and leisure facilities, which are needed for the tourists; still, Sweden provides a good quality of life for its citizens.

Among the trips that were eventful due to their nature were the hunting trips. Some of these trips were in former Soviet republics such as Uzbekistan and Turkmenistan, while others were in Pakistan, Morocco, and some African countries, such as Kenya and Tanzania. From what I can remember from one of our trips in Turkmenistan, where we were traveling with H.H. Sheikh Mohamed bin Zayed Al Nahyan (may God protect him), accompanying His Highness Sheikh Khalifa bin Zayed Al Nahyan, UAE President (may God protect him), is that we drove about 300 kilometers along a rugged, unpaved road and the weather was extremely cold. The sand mixed with snowflakes and hit our faces, driven by the force of strong winds. We experienced that terribly gloomy weather for 12 continuous hours, from 8:00 am to 8:00 pm. It was very difficult to find the Houbara Bustard birds, as the freezing weather forced them to stay in their shelters.

On another hunting trip to Pakistan, we camped at the hunting area and not in the city. We were in the company of H.H. Sheikh Mohamed bin Zayed Al Nahyan (may God protect him) and H.H. Sheikh Hazza bin Zayed Al Nahyan; we were all accompanying H.H. Sheikh Khalifa bin Zayed Al Nahyan, the UAE President (may God protect him). What made that trip unforgettable for me was that I had such severe stomach pain at night that I needed a doctor to treat me. Even though hunting and falconry are important traditional sports that should be preserved as part of the Emirati identity, I am not one of those who practice them. My interests in life went in other directions. Pakistan is one of the countries that I visited many times. Some of those trips were official visits in the company of H.H. Sheikh Mohamed bin Zayed Al Nahyan (may God protect him) and H.H. Sheikh Abdullah bin Zayed Al Nahyan. During those trips, I was given the chance to visit the Pakistani Nuclear Reactor.

An unforgettable situation that I encountered in Pakistan was when H.H. Sheikh Khalifa bin Zayed Al Nahyan, the UAE President (may God protect him) had a conversation with me during one of those hunting trips. He asked me what I would like to eat for lunch during the journey, as His Highness knew already that I was a vegetarian, and getting a meat-free meal while on a hunting trip might not be easy. So H.H. Sheikh Khalifa the President, ordered those in charge of the kitchen to prepare a special vegetarian meal for me to have at lunch.

More interestingly, hunting in Africa left me with many special memories. I was among the team accompanying H.H. Sheikh Mohamed bin Zayed Al Nahyan (may God protect him) on about five hunting trips to Tanzania, the last of which was in 2002. Among participants were His Majesty King Abdullah II Ibn Al-Hussein of Jordan, and his brother Prince

Ali bin Al-Hussein. We stayed in a hunting camp that was erected on a piece of land owned by H.H. Sheikh Mohammed bin Rashid Al Maktoum (may God protect him) near the Serengeti National Park, which is the best natural reserve in Africa. It was the first time in my life that I saw animals like giraffes, lions, tigers, leopards, monkeys and crocodiles, moving freely in their natural environment. They were quite different from the animals that I had previously seen in zoos.

I still remember the huge ostriches and how we approached a large parade of elephants moving with their large bodies toward us. I kept thinking that our proximity to them might scare them or push them toward a reaction that could be terrifying. Despite these concerns, our presence in the heart of mother nature was a special kind of entertainment. On one of those trips, I was in the company of H.H. Sheikh Mohamed bin Zayed Al Nahyan (may God protect him) on board a helicopter, and we visited the famous Lake Victoria. From above the lake I saw an amazing scene that stretched as far as the eyes can see, with thousands of flamingos, proudly colored in a beautiful harmony between white and pink.

While hunting in Africa was done by hunting rifles, most of our hunting on these trips was with falcons. In Africa, and the Bu-Arfa region in Morocco near the border with Algeria, boars and geese were hunted on a private farm. On one of the trips to Tanzania we were in the company of H.H. Sheikh Abdullah bin Zayed Al Nahyan in a car that H.H. Sheikh Abdullah was driving. One of the employees in His Highness's office shot a bullet at a huge male buffalo, but the bullet missed the target. The furious beast blocked the narrow road between two mountains and rushed toward our car ramming us with its hard horns. Thus, H.H. Sheikh Abdullah hastily drove the car away from the beast, but the buffalo horn had already hit the car. When we reached a distant safe spot, I discovered that the buffalo horn had hit a spot only two centimeters away from my head. We were shocked by the amount of damage that beast had done to the car in that fast moment, and most of the damage was in the area where I was sitting.

With H.H. Sheikh Mohamed bin Zayed Al Nahyan, Crown Prince of Abu Dhabi and Deputy Supreme Commander of the UAE Armed Forces (may God protect him); the late South African President Nelson Mandela; former South African Minister of Defense; and former UAE Ambassador to South Africa, during a visit to Cape Town, South Africa, in 1997

During trips to Tanzania, I also saw the Massai tribes, who still preserve the traditional lifestyle of their forefathers from centuries ago. They did not allow modern life to change their habits. They dwell in the same ancient caves/homes, while they build their homes in the same way inherited from centuries ago, using materials from the natural environment. They feel proud of their traditional clothes of joyful bright colors. Their survival depends on cow grazing. I have seen children of eight years old tending their cows and carrying long sticks. Each child controls a big herd and guides the herd to penetrate the jungle amid predatory beasts. It seems as if those beasts are afraid to come close to members of Massai tribes. Massai shepherds rub their bodies with certain materials, such as milk, which make them smell disgustingly repulsive; this smell prevents beasts from coming close to them. Life in such circumstances obliges and trains human beings to adapt to the environment and face risks. We used to set up our tents high up from the ground, to avoid creeping snakes, scorpions and insects, which are abundant there.

I visited Nigeria only once when I spent a few days there in the 1990s. The African country that reserves a large place in my memory is South Africa, which I visited with H.H. Sheikh Mohamed bin Zayed Al Nahyan (may God protect him), in 1997, where we met the renowned African leader Nelson

At the moment of disembarking from the plane, on an official visit to Brazil, July 5, 1995

Mandela. The funny part is that when we went to Cape Town, albeit on an official visit, we were received by children who seemed to be the grandchildren of Mandela and they told us that he was sitting in his office. Then we entered the house to meet him. Our trip to South Africa also included visits to famous places, such as the spot where the Indian and Atlantic oceans meet. We flew over the area in a helicopter and watched how high waves from both oceans intertwine. We also flew over the prison inside which Mandela had spent a long period of his life. During our presence in Cape Town, we resided on the 28th floor in a hotel built of stone and I remember feeling the building swaying in the strong winds at night.

Among the risky situations that I still remember was the funny accident that took place at the Virgin Islands, which are a group of islands located south of the USA. I visited the Virgin Islands in the company of His Highness Sheikh Mohamed bin Zayed Al Nahyan (may God protect him) in 1995, on our way to Brazil on an official visit. In the Virgin Islands, we tried diving to a sizable depth under water. For me, it was the first time I had tried this sport, which needs some advanced training and knowledge. I asked for help from some of our trip companions who had experience in diving, and they gave me some instructions. After diving under water, something happened that made me laugh. I did not know that laughing would make most of the oxygen supplied to a diver escape from the cylinder. Therefore, I had to go up to the surface before losing the remaining amount of oxygen. One of our companions pushed the emergency button, which is designed for such situations. Finally, I succeeded in reaching the surface after a frightening few moments.

With H.H. Sheikh Mohamed bin Zayed Al Nahyan, Crown Prince of Abu Dhabi and Deputy Supreme Commander of the UAE Armed Forces (may God protect him), during an official trip to Brazil, July 5, 1995

After the difficult trials of diving, we went to Brazil, on an official visit accompanying H.H. Sheikh Mohamed bin Zayed Al Nahyan (may God

With Ret. Lt. General Saeed Khalaf Al-Rumaithi, and some members of the delegation during the visit to Brazil, July 5, 1995

protect him). This was my only visit to South America. During that visit, we settled in the capital, Brasilia, where the UAE embassy is located. We met a number of Brazilian political and military leaders in work meetings to discuss key political and military issues. H.E. Abdulaziz Al-Shamsi, UAE Ambassador to Brazil at the time, offered us a lunch banquet, during which very significant discussions took place. Then we went to Rio de Janeiro and stayed at a hotel there for a couple of days.

Sometimes, a traveler loses some personal items during their trips, and travelers usually keep remembering those lost items because they represent something special for them. During my work at the Ministry of Foreign Affairs, as the Editor in Chief of *The Diplomat* journal, I used to travel by my car, and I used to cross some of the Arab Gulf countries. I had in my car a set of books in English and in Arabic. At the border checkpoint of one of those countries, my books were confiscated because they were forbidden in that country. I still feel angry when I remember my lost books.

There are some countries that I have visited more than once, even settled in them without previous planning. I visited Thailand more than five times during the illness of my late mother (may God rest her soul in peace). I resided for a long time there, attending to my mother. I, myself, have received hydrotherapy for bone pain in Thailand. Healthcare is good there, but I have never visited it for tourism purposes. The only time in which I visited Thailand before the sickness of my mother was in October 2003, for one day to attend the finals of the Asian Football Champions League, which saw a match between the UAE's Al-Ain Club against a Thai club. Al-Ain were winners of the match, which took place at the "Rajamangala National Stadium" in the Thai capital Bangkok. The supporters of the Thai team got angry at their loss and threw stones, empty cups and cans at us.

The ironies of travel never end. On one of my visits to Germany, intended for treatment, I visited a center for physiotherapy in a town in the Black Forest, south of Frankfurt. I saw a Rolls Royce with a UAE plate, and so I expected the car to be owned by an Emirati citizen. However, I came to know that its owner was a wealthy Indian man staying at the same hotel as I was. I visited Germany many times on official visits accompanying H.H. Sheikh Mohamed bin Zayed Al Nahyan (may God protect him), and recently, I visited it as Director General of the ECSSR. I have received treatment sessions in Germany as well. However, I do not think that the German people are capable of attracting tourists; the Germans are mostly unwelcoming people and they do not make an effort to offer comfortable services for the visitor or the patient.

I Have Been Here for 2,000 Years, Who Are You?

With H.E. Juma Rashid Al-Zahiri, UAE Ambassador to Serbia, during the opening ceremony of the Belgrade Book Fair on October 21, 2016. The photo shows one visitor of the Fair asking me to sign a copy of my book *The Mirage*

Places and nations are like individuals: you either feel comfortable in some of them, to the extent that you do not feel like a stranger there anymore and you wish to extend your stay; or, some of them create a sense of distress inside you. Part of these feelings and emotions is related to the characteristics of the country itself. Another part of the feeling is related to your own experience in a certain country. There are two Arab countries that I have visited only once. I did not attempt to repeat the visits and I feel uncomfortable when the plane passes over the airspace of one of them. I was lucky enough that the official tasks and work missions did not force me to visit these two countries again.

I had the same feeling toward Iran, which was the place that marked the start of my travels abroad, as I previously mentioned. The trip was in 1977, during the Shah's reign and before the start of the Iranian Revolution, which changed many things. During that trip, I visited both Shiraz and Tehran, which were among the usual tourist destinations for travelers from the Arab Gulf countries. However, I did not feel the desire to repeat the visit. I believe the transformations that have affected Iran since 1979 have had negative impacts that made the country change into an unwanted destination on the travelers' list. Huge changes also occurred in the nature of places and the nature of people and transformed Iran into a repellent destination that deters visitors and is not attractive to them anymore. I do not think the issue is related to only political reasons. I had the same feeling of discomfort toward the Netherlands, which I went to on an official visit in 1994.

With H.H. Sheikh Abdullah bin Zayed Al Nahyan, UAE Minister of Foreign Affairs and International Cooperation, during a visit to a refugee camp established by UAE to shelter Kosovan refugees and supplying them with basic humanitarian aid, November 26, 1999

Greece was also among the countries that did not leave nice memories in my mind after my first visit. Behind that feeling, there are certain political circumstances connected with the nature of this visit in 1999. That year, the crisis of Muslim Albanians in the Kosovo province was at its peak. During the events in the wake of the collapse of the former Yugoslavia, the Serbs, who were known for their nationalist and religious fanaticism, were practicing brutal violence against the Muslim Albanians. The UAE wasted no time in performing its humanitarian role, with the brave men of the UAE Armed Forces participating in the relief effort to help Kosovans, building shelters and hospitals, and offering various services to refugees. To reach the UAE relief camp, as the UAE took part in peace-keeping missions there, we had to pass through Greece.

We flew in a military aircraft and we noticed that the Greek authorities had put in place obstacles to hinder our flight. We felt that there was a sense of deep hostility among the Greek people with whom we had to contact for crossing and reaching our destination. We realized later the motives behind that hostile behavior: the Greeks, who are Christian Orthodox like the Serbs, did not favorably view our mission to offer relief assistance to Kosovans because we are Arabs and Muslims. However, the UAE's record in donating humanitarian relief has never differentiated among the deprived people on the basis of religion, ethnicity or color of their skin. In order to continue our journey to the camp, we needed the interference of the UAE embassy in Athens and the help of goodwill people.

Presenting a copy of my book *The Mirage* to John Gatt-Rutter, Head of Counter-Terrorism Section at the European Foreign Act Agency, in the Belgian capital, Brussels, October 19, 2016

The strange thing is that I visited Serbia in October 2016, during a tour of Europe, that included Belgium and Montenegro. That visit left a positive impression on my mind, and I attended the opening ceremony of the Belgrade Book Fair, with H.E. Juma Rashid Al-Dhaheri, the UAE Ambassador to Serbia. A lot of time had passed, which changed the hostile sense that we faced in 1999, and Serbia has changed significantly after the turmoil that followed the dismantling of the former Yugoslavia. Serbia started to reshape its relations again with many countries in the world, including the UAE.

With Prof. Radmila Vojvodić, Vice-Chancellor of the University of Montenegro; and Her Excellency Hafsa Abdulla Al-Ulama, UAE Ambassador to Montenegro, during a lecture about my book *The Mirage*, at the University of Montenegro, October 23, 2016

That visit also included Montenegro, which is one of the states that emerged from the dismantling of Yugoslavia. I visited the University of Montenegro in the capital Podgorica, and held a ceremony for signing my book *The Mirage* there. I met with Prof. Radmila Vojvodić, Vice-Chancellor of the University of Montenegro, in the presence of Her Excellency Hafsa Abdulla Al-Ulama, UAE Ambassador to Montenegro, and her effort in that country gained my attention and appreciation.

The visit to Serbia and Montenegro came after an

With Dr. Fuad Kaiman Director of Istanbul Public Policy Center, in a ceremony for signing my book *Prospects for the American Age: Sovereignty and Influence in the New World Order*, at the Center, June 16, 2014

With H.E. Saif Abdulla Al-Shamsi, UAE General Consul in Turkey, at the premises of the UAE Consulate in Istanbul, during a scientific trip to discuss and sign my book *Prospects for the American Age: Sovereignty and Influence in the New World Order*, June 17, 2014

With Her Excellency Michèle Alliot Marie, Head of the Mission of Relations with Arab Peninsula at the European Parliament(former French Defence Minister); John Gatt-Rutter, Head of Counter-Terrorism Section at the European Foreign Act Agency; Antonio López-Istúriz White, Member of the European Parliament and Head of European-Emirati Friendship Society; and Mr. Nedal Shuqair, Head of the Association of European Press for the Arab World, during the forum How Can We Fight Terrorism Today? at the premises of the European Parliament, in Belgium, October 19, 2016 important visit to Belgium. I previously went to Belgium on a short visit, which did not leave any specific impression on my mind. However, the second visit, which lasted for few days, included an important seminar at the premises of the European Parliament titled "How Can We Fight Terrorism Today?" on October 19, 2016. The seminar focused on my book *The Mirage*. I also visited the premises of the European Commission and held an important work meeting with Quinn Metsou, Head of Counter-Terrorism Committee at the Belgian Parliament; John Gatt-Rutter, Head of Counter-Terrorism Section at the European Foreign Act Agency; Antonio López-Istúriz White, Member of the European Parliament and Head of European-Emirati Friendship Society; and a number of other officials. I also met Mrs. Michèle Alliot-Marie, Head of the European Parliament Mission for Relations with Arabian Peninsula and former French Defence Minister. I will discuss this meeting in a later section of this chapter.

With The late Air Commodore Jasjit Singh, during the symposium "Emirati-Indian Relations in the Coming Decade," which was held in New Delhi in collaboration with The Indian Institute for Defense Studies and Analyses (IDSA), April 13, 1999

With Krishnaswamy Subramanian, one of the speakers, during the symposium "Emirati-Indian Relations in the Coming Decade," April 13, 1999

I had the same feeling of discomfort toward Turkey, even though many people, particularly from Arab Gulf countries, view Turkey as an attractive place for tourism. In 2014, I had given a lecture about my book *Prospects for the American Age: Sovereignty and Influence in the New World Order*, organized by the Istanbul Center for Policies. I also visited some Turkish universities and think tanks in order to discuss the ideas of the book with a number of Turkish academics and researchers. I do not believe I would visit Turkey again unless there is something related to an official work or task. I felt the same discomfort during my sole visit to Iraq in 1979, and I have never visited it again.

With former Indian Minister of External Affairs, Jaswant Singh (standing at the podium); and the late Indian strategist and Air Commodore Jasjit Singh, during the symposium: "Emirati-Indian Relations in the Coming Decade," held in New Delhi in collaboration with Indian IDSA, April 13, 1999

India is also one of the countries that I would prefer not to go to for tourism if I was given the choice. I have visited India more than 10 times, most of them were official missions, and very few times for tourism. Nevertheless, I still keep pleasant memories from those visits. Moreover, India taught me a lot of useful lessons. The official visits were mainly in the company of H.H. Sheikh Mohamed bin Zayed Al Nahyan (may God protect him) and H.H. Sheikh Abdullah bin Zayed Al Nahyan. Furthermore, I visited India as Director General of the ECSSR

With the late Indian strategist and Air Commodore Jasjit Singh, during the symposium: "Emirati-Indian Relations in the Coming Decade," held in New Delhi in collaboration with Indian IDSA, April 13, 1999.

With the late Indian Strategist and Air Commodore Jasjit Singh, during the symposium: "Emirati-Indian Relations in the Coming Century," held in New Delhi in collaboration with Indian IDSA, April 13, 1999

With H.E. Dr. Anwar Gargash, UAE Minister of State for Foreign Affairs; the late Indian Strategist and Air Commodore Jasjit Singh; and a number of attendees during a dinner banquet at the sidelines of the symposium: "Emirati-Indian Relations in the Coming Decade," held in New Delhi in collaboration with Indian IDSA, April 13, 1999

and in April 1999, we organized a symposium in collaboration with the Indian Institute for Defense Studies and Analyses (IDSA) in the capital New Delhi, under the title "Emirati-Indian Relations in the Coming Decade." The outcome was an analysis of political, economic, military and security relations between the two countries, along with a future vision of those relations.

My visits included the capital New Delhi and Mumbai, which is connected with the Arabian Gulf region through ancient trade and cultural relations. I also visited Bangalore, which hosts a large number of technology companies and is viewed as "The Indian Silicon Valley." I visited the Taj Mahal and other cities. I had the chance to meet the late Indian President Dr. Avul Pakir Jainulabdeen Abdul Kalam, and Vice President Hamid Ansari. It is worth mentioning that both of them were Muslims in a Hindu majority country. I also met Indian State-Minister for Foreign Affairs, Jaswant Singh, who previously occupied two key positions, as Finance Minister, and Defense Minister. He is a highly-refined intellectual and a proficient politician. During those visits, I also met many military commanders, including Defense Minister, Commander of Indian Navy Forces and Commander of Indian Air Forces, at that time. I had a lot of dealings and connections with the late Air Commodore Jasjit Singh, Director of the IDSA at that time, and I recognized that he is a strategic thinker and a real military man. The late Air Commodore Jasjit Singh had visited us several times at the ECSSR, and there had been a friendly personal relationship between him and myself as well as a strong academic collaboration between the ECSSR and IDSA.

India is a vast country and it seeks to impress its visitors and to show them its points of strength. The reception organized by Indian officials to welcome us always carried a lot of hospitality, whether my visits were in the company of H.H. Sheikh Mohamed bin Zayed Al Nahyan (may God protect him) or as Director Gen-

The front cover of the Arabic version of the book *Empires of the Monsoons*

eral of the ECSSR. I remember that our Indian friends prepared an extravagant dinner banquet for us during the symposium, which was held by the ECSSR in partnership with IDSA.

What I also remember about that visit was that the Indian Navy Commander then told us a story with a very meaningful message. During a trip by some Indian navy ships, the Commander was about to enter the Arabian Gulf waters. At that moment he received a warning message from a battleship of the US Fifth Fleet deployed in the Gulf. The message said "Who are you? Introduce yourself." The Indian Commander responded quickly "I have been in this region for 2,000 years. The question is who are you?" This reply carries a reference to a former Indian influence in the Gulf region, and ancient trade, cultural and political bonds connecting India to the Arab Gulf countries. It also implies that the presence of the Americans in the Gulf is the issue that needs justification, as opposed to the Indian presence, which is considered natural. The Indian Navy Commander had not wasted the opportunity to convey the message to the Americans. The same message was meant to be conveyed to the Arabs as well.

In the same context, the ECSSR has published two highly important books presenting a refined scientific discussion on the issue of the civilizational and cultural exchange across the seaports of the Indian Ocean over 2,000 years. These two books provide a large reservoir of knowledge, built on historical, geographic, anthropological, sociological, literary and religious studies and research. These studies uncovered a treasure of common experiences, skills, habits, and traditions, which were accumulated through trade voyages across the Indian Ocean and the transfer of ideas,

The front cover of the Arabic version of the book *Dhow Culture of the Indian Ocean*

habits, goods and human beings among these seaports. Those activities created a unique cultural status, which deserves more analyses and studies.

The first book is titled *Empires of the Monsoons: A History of the Indian Ocean and its Invaders*, by Richard Hall. The book is a scientific classic over about 750 pages. It provides astonishing conclusions about the inevitability of economic integration of East Africa with Asia, rather than with Europe. This conclusion is based on historical, cultural and civilizational backgrounds. When those in the land extending from the Red Sea to the Cape of Good Hope achieve rapprochement with Asia today, this actually means they are echoing 1,000 years of rapprochement, which continued until it was undermined by the Western colonial intervention by means of coercion. Although this conclusion is debatable, the deep and enjoyable historical presentation, and the large number of references and sources included in the book, make it a unique work in this field of knowledge. The ECSSR published the Arabic version of the book in 1999.

The second book is titled *Dhow Culture of the Indian Ocean: Cosmopolitanism, Commerce, and Islam*, which has also been translated into Arabic. The author is a Tanzanian writer named Abdul Sheriff, one of the prominent African specialists in anthropology and history of civilization. Throughout a voyage traveling from seaports such as Lamu in Africa, to Sur in the Sultanate of Oman, Hadhramaut in Yemen, the shores of Persia, the Malabar coastline in India, to China and Indonesia, the author reveals the roles and deep influences left by dhows (sailboats) along the coastline of the Indian Ocean. He also reveals the prevailing trade and cultural system, which had remained characterized by freedom and tolerance until the Portuguese colonialists came and destroyed that system.

Dhow Culture of the Indian Ocean: Cosmopolitanism, Commerce, and Islam was published by the ECSSR, in 2013, about 14 years after publishing *Empires of the Monsoons*. This presents evidence of the wide variety of arenas that are covered by the publications of the ECSSR, and proof of the ECSSR's effort to cover the numerous fields and aspects in which the Arabic library suffers a grave shortage.

The Airport Closes at 9:00 pm

Iceland is also among the countries in which I did not find anything that would encourage me to return there. I went there at the end of a cruise during which I passed by a number of cities on the European coast. In Iceland, I stayed near the lake "Blue Lagoon," which attracts many tourists because of its hot water that is used to cure bone

In front of Universal Studios (Hollywood), Los Angeles, during my visit to the USA, in 2014

433

With Dr. Nevin Musaad, Professor at the Faculty of Economics and Political Science at Cairo University in Egypt and former Director of the Arab League's Institute of Arab Research and Studies; and a number of officials at the institute, in its premises in Cairo, June 14, 2014

pain. There, I met a large number of Germans and Japanese who came to the lake for treatment or to enjoy the natural landscapes. It was interesting to note that the temperature was around 9° C in September; how much colder would it be in December and January?

Receiving a gift from Major General Khaled Fouda, Governor of South Sinai, in Sharm el-Sheikh, Egypt, October 21, 2015

A variety of reasons compel me to decide not to repeat the visit to a certain country. Some countries lack tourism infrastructure such as roads, new facilities, hotels and places for entertainment, which everyone needs whether for work or pleasure. Moreover, stability and security are very important for tourist destinations. Except for treatment and some natural landscapes in Iceland, there was no other type of entertainment and

During the ceremony for receiving an Honorary PhD in political science and international relations from the University of Lugano, Switzerland, November 17, 2015

During my visit to Japan, 15 December 1997

leisure. More importantly, there should be the culture of hospitality and care for tourists. For example, in Barcelona or Madrid, the policeman offers you all the information you need and helps you to reach your desired destination because he realizes the importance of tourism. If you were in a certain country and someone treated you rudely, you would never think of going back there. I think the Americans come at the top of the people who take care of tourists and deal with them with kindness and hospitality. In this aspect, the Americans are generally better than the British, French, Germans and other Europeans.

The vital cities that are bursting with activity and movement attract me much more than the dormant cities. Therefore, I did not like Switzerland that much, although I have visited it more than five times accompanying H.H. Sheikh Mohamed bin Zayed Al Nahyan (may God protect him). On one of those visits, we spent 40 days there, with the late Sheikh Zayed bin Sultan Al Nahyan (may God rest his soul in peace). Also, I visited Switzerland in November 2015, on the occasion of being granted an honorary PhD from the University of Lugano. Lugano is a beautiful city, very different from Geneva and Zürich. It reminds me of the beautiful area around Lake Como in Italy, but in Switzerland, I feel constrained, and life is of a slow pace. Naturally, I favor the cities full of liveliness, which stay busy 24 hours a day, such as New

A memorial photo of the participants in the second round of a symposium titled "Storm of Thought," hosted by Isa Cultural Center in Bahrain, March 28, 2016

York, Los Angeles, Washington, D.C., and Cairo. However, in Switzerland, in its various cities, you are in front of a neutral people, whose day ends at 8:00 pm. Even the airport closes its doors and runways at 9:00 pm. Nevertheless, many people view Switzerland as an ideal place for luxurious and distinguished tourism; at the end of the day, it is an issue of personal taste.

I went to Japan in 1997; I was invited by the Japanese government to deliver a lecture on Arabian Gulf security at the Center for Middle East Studies, in the capital Tokyo. I noticed the skyrocketing prices that make it difficult for Japan to become a favored tourist destination. There are fine hotels and advanced infrastructure. The country tries to attract tourists; there are places for entertainment, but all that would not make Japan a tourism country, in my view, because it lacks the landmarks that attract tourists.

When I say there are countries that I have visited only once, that means I did not find anything attractive to lure me to visit them again. Among such countries are Libya and Algeria, which I have visited only once, on an official visit with H.H. Sheikh Mohamed bin Zayed Al Nahyan (may God protect him). During that visit, we met the Algerian President Abdelaziz Bouteflika. We traveled to Algeria and came back on the same day.

The same case occurred to me in the Philippines. I traveled there once with H.E. Ambassador Hassan Al-Suwaidi in 1982, during my service at the

With Mr. Issa Al Shayji, Editor in Chief of *Al-Ayam*, Bahraini newspaper, during my visit to the premises of the paper, March 23, 2015

UAE Ministry of Foreign Affairs. The trip was planned to attend a conference about racial discrimination sponsored by the United Nations, in the capital Manila. There were many things in the Philippines that shocked me. However, the most outrageous thing was seeing girls being exhibited behind the windows of shops. It was insulting, a violation of the sacredness of the human body, and disrespectful of human beings, contrary to what

During my attendance of the wedding party of Sheikh Abdullah bin Ahmad Al Khalifa in the Kingdom of Bahrain, March 25, 2015

is advocated by all philosophies, religions, norms of behavior and moral systems. Such sights were rooted in my mind during that visit, which made me dislike the Philippines and not want to willingly visit it. Fortunately, the requirements of my work after 1982 did not require me to visit it again, as sometimes, work tasks lead you to places and countries in which you do not feel comfortable.

The Most Important Lesson

I have visited all the GCC countries several times, and in all of them I feel as if I am still in my home country, the UAE. The most special among them are Bahrain and Kuwait. I have a real friendship and close scholarly and personal relationships with many prominent officials and intellectuals in the Kingdom of Bahrain.

Underwater, inside a submarine at 45 meters deep, near Jeju Island, South Korea, December 15, 2012

Evidently, Kuwait occupies a special place in my mind, as I lived in Kuwait during my undergraduate studies, while Kuwait was at the peak of its prosperity. I have also married a Kuwaiti woman. My mother

At Jeju Island, South Korea, December 15, 2012

and my sister lived in Kuwait. Similarly, every one of the GCC countries had a special place in my heart. Since the mid-1990s, I have met both former and current kings and emirs of the GCC countries many times. On one of those official visits to the Sultanate of Oman, we stayed at the palace of Sultan Qaboos. I visited all the Arab countries except Sudan and Yemen.

I still visit various countries in the world, based on the requirements and necessities of the work, and the need for some entertainment, whenever the opportunity presents itself. In December 2012, I visited South Korea for the first time, as Director General of the ECSSR, during a tour in Asia that included China and Vietnam as well. Although I enjoyed my visit to Jeju Island in South Korea, which is considered a tourist area as a symbol of heritage with plenty of beauty, and although I visited South Korea for the second time to attend a conference at the Ministry of Foreign Affairs, on Feb-

With H.E. former UAE Ambassador to Vietnam, Ahmad Al-Mua'alla, during my visit to that country, December 17, 2012

Wearing the traditional Vietnamese hat, during my visit to Vietnam, December 17, 2012

The mausoleum of the late Vietnamese leader Ho Chi Minh, during my visit to Vietnam, December 17, 2012

ruary 11, 2017, I do not consider it a tourist-friendly country. It resembles Japan, in terms of letting the practical side take over the nature of the country.

In China, I have visited the famous historical attractions. I have been to the Great Wall of China, but I did not stay long because of the severe cold. I have

Receiving an artistic painting from one of the Vietnamese scientific institutions, during my visit to Vietnam, December 19, 2012

In front of The Forbidden City, the Imperial Palace for the Chinese emperors; during my visit to China, December 19, 2012

In front of Sheikh Zayed bin Sultan Al Nahyan Centre for Arabic Language and Islamic Studies, in China, during my visit to China, December 19, 2012

also visited the Forbidden City, or the Imperial Palace, which was the residence of the Chinese emperors of both the Ming and Qing dynasties, the two families that ruled China for about 500 years. There, I strolled in the famous Tiananmen Square, in the capital Beijing. I stood for long moments in front of the gigantic photo of Mao Tse-tung and I visited his tomb. I have mentioned his career and achievements in one of my articles published in the Arabic-language *Al-Ittihad* newspaper, Abu Dhabi. My book titled *Eternal Imprints: Figures that Made History and Others that Changed the Future of Their Countries* included the career of this leader. I believe there are many things that can be learned by anyone who visits China. I was somehow surprised by the beauty of the Chinese cities, such as Beijing and Shanghai, with broad streets, and the wide variety of entertainment options, besides luxurious hotels, the promising touristic potentials and the interest of Chinese government to develop tourism. To some extent, I have seen the same trend and effort during my visit to Viet-

Standing by a car whose date of manufacture coincides with my birthday, at the Old Cars Museum, on Jeju Island, South Korea, 15 December 2015

At the tomb of the late Chinese Leader Mao Tsetung, during my visit to China, December 19, 2012

In front of a maquette (model) of the Sheikh Zayed bin Sultan Al Nahyan Mosque, at Sheikh Zayed bin Sultan Al Nahyan Centre for Arabic Language and Islamic Studies in China, during my visit to China on December 19, 2012

The Louvre Museum, in the French capital Paris

nam, where I have seen a number of its most important landmarks.

I have seen many museums that contain famous artistic works and ancient artefacts, from various civilizations. Among the most important visits to museums was my visit to the Louvre Museum in 1999. However, I am more interested in the landmarks and sites of attraction in cities when

New York Yankees Museum, in New York City, May 12, 2013

these sites constitute part of the city life and fill it with energy. For example, I preferred to visit the Egyptian Obelisk in Paris at the center of the square crowded with visitors, rather than seeing it in a museum isolated from the movement of life and human beings.

Travel is still interesting and a source of enjoyment for me, even if some journeys are long and exhausting. I remember that the longest flight for me was from the Gold Coast region in Australia to Al-Ain in the UAE. A private jet carried us after an official visit, where I was in the company of H.H. Sheikh Mohamed bin Zayed Al Nahyan (may God protect him). The flight lasted for about 17.5 hours. On another flight, we flew non-stop for 16 hours from Los Angeles to Abu Dhabi.

The list of countries that I have visited is still very long, as it includes Canada, which I had visited during my study in USA. I spent one week in Toronto. I have also visited the Maldives for tourism, and spent about five days there. I vis-

With Mr. Makram Mohammed Ahmad, former Head of the Egyptian Journalists' Union; and Mr. Usama Haikal, Chairman of Media Production City and former Egyptian Minister of Information; and the Egyptian journalist Nabil Fahmi, in Sharm el-Sheikh, Egypt, October 21, 2015

ited Austria, as I wanted to visit one of the UN agencies there, after my visit to Germany. I also spent about four days in Cyprus, which is a small Mediterranean island, but I did not find anything worth visiting. I have passed through Singapore airport as a transit passenger, but I did not have the chance to visit the country. I have visited Bangladesh once. Moreover, I have been to Tunisia once during my undergraduate studies, and I have mentioned some details of that journey through my talk about memories of that stage. We met the Tunisian Prime Minister then, Mohamed Mezali, and then Secretary-General of the Arab League, Chedli Klibi.

One of the problems that I was confronted with during the 1990s was the lack of vegetarian meals in some hotels and countries, as they were not yet used to fulfilling demands of this type. Workers in those hotels found it very strange to see a man from the Arabian Gulf who did not eat meat, chicken or even fish. I used to settle for having the available types of salads. Nevertheless, this problem is solved now; hotels all over the world became more aware of the idea that some guests have special requirements and habits for their food.

Finally, continuous travel had an effect on my private life and family, as work trips distanced me from my family and people in general, and deprived me from social activities and duties, which require constant presence among people. Nevertheless, as a researcher and a human being, travel has offered me an array of lessons and experiences. The most important lesson is probably tolerance. When you travel a lot, on every journey you have the chance to get to know different cultures, habits and religions. You can see the

Honoring of the late Mohammed Khalaf Al-Mazrouei, Adviser for Culture and Heritage at the Crown Prince Court (at that time), with the Federal Personality Award in its second round, which is offered by H.H. Sheikh Mohamed bin Zayed Al Nahyan (may God protect him), during the ECSSR's 42nd National Day celebrations, November 28, 2013

diverse heritage of nations, alongside different lifestyles in every place you go, thereby getting in the habit of accepting other people as they are. You get the aptitude to respect moral systems of societies and individuals, regardless of whether you are convergent with or divergent from them. Therefore, I assuredly say that tolerance, as a moral value, is the most important lesson I learned from traveling.

(II): Awards and Honors

The renowned American psychologist Abraham Maslow designed a hierarchal arrangement of human needs, known as Maslow's Pyramid. At the base of the pyramid, we find the basic physiological needs to secure survival for a human being, including food, water, reproduction and avoiding pain and physical harm. At the higher part of the pyramid, we find the need for security. Above that, Maslow puts the social needs or the need for belonging. This need is represented in the search for a family and society, in which the individual will be a member. On the fourth level, near the top of the pyramid, we see the need for respect and appreciation. From one aspect, this need is connected with self-esteem or the inner-self-respect. From the other, it is manifested in the recognition by other people and society of the excellence, accomplishments and status of the person, who attained these accomplishments through real dedicated personal effort. At the peak of the pyramid, Maslow put the need for self-fulfillment, or "transcendence needs," which are exclusively the merits of genius people and the architects of major creative and intellectual achievements.

Receiving the Order of Merit, First Class – Commander Rank – from His Majesty King Mohammed VI of Morocco (then Crown Prince) on July 1, 1995

The most interesting level for me is the fourth level of needs; that is, the need for appreciation. It represents a channel to understand and explain the human behavior and his balance or imbalance, as a result of fulfilling or not fulfilling this need.

The American psychologist William James expressed the importance of appreciation in a brief expression reading as follows "The deepest principle in human nature is yearning for appreciation." This expression became widely renowned after he wrote it on April 6, 1896, in the second volume of the book titled "The Letters of William James," which was edited by his son Henry James and published in 1920. Accordingly, societies and nations that experience and promote the culture of rewarding and appreciation, and offer to their members the respect they deserve, they do so to fulfill a pressing human need. This need actually supports the psychological safety of individuals and societies, and contributes to the advancement and development of both.

Throughout my life, I have received various types of honors and appreciation. That started at the moment I finished my university education, and continued up to the time of publishing this book. These honors and awards are related to my achievements in the field of my scientific specialization over almost three decades, alongside my work in directing the ECSSR toward a distinguished status on both Arab and international levels. The outcome of this effort was represented in the large number of local, regional and international awards, attained by the ECSSR, and attained by me personally, during a period full of extensive productive work, extending for more than 23 years.

I was 36 years old when I got my first considerable medal, from the esteemed Arab Kingdom of Morocco in 1995. That was an early recognition and appreciation of the scholarly role that I performed. That honor was very special to me, as it made me feel that I was on the right path. Later, awards flowed successively from different agencies; but the last five years have witnessed a significant increase in the number and quality of the awards that I have received. That is considered as an indicator that I have reached the stage of "reaping the fruits of my labor," while I am still continuing my job. The seeds that I have tried to plant during

Presenting H.H. Sheikh Hamdan bin Mohammed bin Rashid Al Maktoum, Crown Prince of Dubai, Chairman of Dubai Executive Council, with Sheikh Khalifa UAE Writer Award, which is offered by the ECSSR, for the book *My Vision*. Sheikh Hamdan received the Award on behalf of his father, H.H. Sheikh Mohammed bin Rashid Al Maktoum, Vice President and Prime Minister of UAE and Ruler of Dubai (may God protect him), who won this prize, March 31, 2008

Receiving Sheikh Zayed Book Award, for my book *The Mirage*, from H.H. Sheikh Mansour bin Zayed Al Nahyan, Deputy Prime Minister and Minister of Presidential Affairs of the UAE, at the ceremony of distributing the prize to winners, May 1, 2016

those long years are the seeds of persistence, diligence and faithfulness for scholarly research and service for my home country, as well as both local and Arab societies. Also among those seeds are: defending the key human val-

A group photo, with the winners of "Federal Personality Award" in its 3rd round, offered by H.H. Sheikh Mohamed bin Zayed Al Nahyan, Crown Prince of Abu Dhabi and Deputy Supreme Commander of the UAE Armed Forces (may God protect him), December 11, 2014

ues, with priority to cultural and intellectual openness, appreciation of science and respecting human intellectual accomplishments, wherever they were produced, and whoever were the producers; and more importantly, rejecting fanaticism and militancy in all its forms. Moreover, that included the seeds of exposing all types of extremism and ideological deviations, which hold back both the Arab and Islamic worlds from achieving development. One of the key objectives is securing better conditions for a satisfactory and decent life for ordinary people. Finally, those seeds included exposing the extremist rhetoric and confronting it with courage and resolve.

Encouraging Environment

I take pride in all the types of appreciation, awards and medals that I have attained. Yet, the honors received from my home country, the UAE, and from its leaders and main figures, are the most precious for me. I have won the Sheikh Zayed Book Award, in the category of Best Contribution to the Development of Nations, for my book *The Mirage,* and I consider it the crown of all other awards that made me happy.

Perhaps, among the aspects that distinguish the UAE from other Arab countries is that the culture of rewarding and appreciation is deeply rooted in this nation. That was based on a cultural, social and religious heritage, which was later transformed into an institutional effort sponsored and encouraged by the government through various departments and ministries. This culture has spread to the society, where you find businessmen, civic associations and private organizations offering respected awards.

The UAE offers a vast array of awards and prizes, including: Zayed International Prize for the Environment; Zayed Future Energy Prize; Sheikh Zayed Book Award; Khalifa Award for Education; Mohamed bin Zayed International Robotics Challenge (MBZIRC); Mohammed bin Rashid Government Excellence Award, which is affiliated with the Sheikh Khalifa Program for Government Excellence; Khalifa International Date Palm Award; Emirates Energy Award; Emirates Appreciation Award for Science, Arts and Literature; Emirates Appreciation Award for the Environment; Emirates Appreciation Award for Sports; UAE President's Appreciation Award; UAE AI and Robotics Award for Good; Emirates Award for Educational Excellence; Emirates Award for Innovative Teachers; Emirates Novel

Presenting the "Federal Personality Award," in its 2nd round, offered by H.H. Sheikh Mohamed bin Zayed Al Nahyan, Crown Prince of Abu Dhabi and Deputy Supreme Commander of the UAE Armed Forces (may God protect him), to H.E. Sheikh Nahyan bin Mubarak Al Nahyan, Minister of Culture and Knowledge Development (Minister of Culture, Youth, and Community Development at that time) during the ECSSR's celebration on UAE 42nd National Day, November 28, 2013

Presenting Dr. Abdullah Al-Raisi, Director General of the UAE National Archives, with the "Federal Personality Award" in its 4th round, offered by H.H. Sheikh Mohamed bin Zayed Al Nahyan, Crown Prince of Abu Dhabi and Deputy Supreme Commander of the UAE Armed Forces (may God protect him), March 21, 2016

A group photo with the winners of "Federal Personality Award" in its 4th round, offered by H.H. Sheikh Mohamed bin Zayed Al Nahyan, Crown Prince of Abu Dhabi and Deputy Supreme Commander of the UAE Armed Forces (may God protect him), March 21, 2016

Award; Emirates Award for Young Scientists; Mohammed bin Rashid Arabic Language Award; Mohammed bin Rashid Al Maktoum Award for World Peace; Mohammed bin Rashid Al Maktoum Knowledge Award; MBR Business Innovation Award; Hamdan bin Rashid Al Maktoum Award for Distinguished Academic Performance, Abu Dhabi Award for Excellence in Government Performance; Abu Dhabi Award for Statistical Excellence; Abu Dhabi Medical Distinction Award. All the above mentioned awards are just a portion of what the UAE offers in terms of prizes

Presenting H.E. Ambassador Ahmad Abdullah Al-Jarman, Assistant Minister of Foreign Affairs and International Cooperation for Political Affairs, with the "Federal Personality Award," in its 4th round, offered by H.H. Sheikh Mohamed bin Zayed Al Nahyan, Crown Prince of Abu Dhabi and Deputy Supreme Commander of the UAE Armed Forces (may God protect him), March 21, 2016

and awards in various fields. That trend makes the UAE the biggest and most important pioneer in terms of enhancing the culture of honoring excellence, along with humanitarian deeds, in the Arab world and the entire Middle East region.

With H.H. Sheikh Khalifa bin Zayed Al Nahyan, the President of the UAE (may God protect him), handing me The UAE Appreciation Award for Science, Arts and Literature in its 3rd round Humanities category – political science, December 2, 2008

These prizes and awards, many of which are given to prominent Arab and international personalities, not only to UAE figures, created some sort of tradition inside each institution, enhancing the practice of honoring its distinctive employees, aside from offering prizes to certain influential officials in society. We have practiced both types of prizes at the ECSSR. It became an annual familiar practice at the ECSSR; the administration offers prizes and financial and moral rewards to the staff of the ECSSR, who are deemed as examples for good performance, and demonstrate the spirit of initiative and creativity. During the celebrations organized annually by the ECSSR, on the anniversary of its inception, UAE National Day, or other various occasions, usually a number of the ECSSR staff from different categories, are selected to be rewarded. This appreciation includes high posts, specialized and assistant posts, and even office boys and cleaners. Everyone who performs their work

With H.H. Sheikh Khalifa bin Zayed Al Nahyan, the President (may God protect him), handing me The UAE President Appreciation Award, December 2, 2013

meticulously and diligently deserves to receive the financial and moral appreciation in front of his colleagues. I think this tradition has motivated all the ECSSR staff to spare no effort while performing their jobs. If the hard workers and innovators were treated as equally as lazy and sluggish people, this motivation would have never been created.

As for the awards related to community service, they include the *"Durrat Watan"* (Jewel of a Nation) competition, and the "Federal Personality Award." *"Durrat Watan"* is an annual research competition open for participants from inside and outside the country. It aims to encourage scientific research about various aspects of the UAE federation's experience and development effort being witnessed by the nation. In its third round in 2014, the competition focused on the accomplishments of the late Sheikh Zayed bin Sultan Al Nahyan (may God rest his soul in peace). In its fourth round in 2015, it focused on the achievements of H.H. Sheikh Khalifa bin

With H.H. Sheikh Mohammed bin Rashid Al Maktoum, Vice President and Prime Minister of UAE and Ruler of Dubai (may God protect him), while giving me the "Arab Social Media Pioneers Award, 2015" on March 17, 2015

Zayed Al Nahyan, UAE President (may God protect him). As for the "Federal Personality Award," it is an award usually granted to Emirati officials who played a significant role in terms of supporting the progress of the Union and reinforcing its pillars. During the past five rounds of the competition, a large number of figures who have left distinguished imprints in this field have won the award.

My Home Country Is Generous

To be honored by my home country is the most precious, most lasting appreciation in my heart. When the appreciation comes from H.H. Sheikh Khalifa bin Zayed Al Nahyan, the UAE President (may God protect him), it is engraved inside the soul forever, and becomes a source of positive energy and hope. When the appreciation is repeated twice from His Highness the President, it is an unparalleled honor. I feel that being honored twice by His Highness the President was evidence that no matter how much we give this gracious country, it will remain the most generous and the most giving.

With H.H. Sheikh Mohamed bin Zayed Al Nahyan, Crown Prince of Abu Dhabi and Deputy Supreme Commander of the UAE Armed Forces (may God protect him), on the occasion of granting me the Abu Dhabi Award 2011, January 24, 2012

In 2008, I won the UAE Appreciation Award for Science, Arts and Literature, in its third round, the Category of Humanities. I consider the moment I received this award as one of the most beautiful moments in my entire life. I received the award from H.H. Sheikh Khalifa bin Zayed Al Nahyan, the UAE President (may God protect him), and the prize was in my specialization, political science, in which I take pride.

The reasoning and assessments behind the committee's decision to give me this award focused on "the importance of his intellectual presence and eminent effort serving the political decision maker in the UAE, through prudent political analyses and his contributions as Director General of the ECSSR, toward organizing and managing numerous political and intellectual conferences that left a significant and positive effect." At that time, I had not yet published the important books that I authored later, such as *From Tribe to Facebook: The Transformational Role of Social Networks, Prospects for the American Age: Sovereignty and Influence in the New World Order,*

The Mirage and *Eternal Imprints: Figures that Made History and Others that Changed the Future of Their Countries*. Moreover, I was still struggling with the side-effects of cancer, and I was still receiving light chemotherapy doses called "maintenance therapy" for cancer. I believe that such an honor, increased my capability to resist pain and physical fatigue. This appreciation was followed by winning the UAE Appreciation Award. I was honored when I received the award from H.H. Sheikh Sultan bin Zayed Al Nahyan, Representative of His Highness the President, during the celebrations to mark the 40th UAE

A photocopy of the decree issued by H.H. Sheikh Mohamed bin Zayed Al Nahyan, Crown Prince of Abu Dhabi and Deputy Supreme Commander of the UAE Armed Forces (may God protect him), granting me the Abu Dhabi Award, received in January 2012

National Day. That celebration commemorated all the winners who were honored with that award between 2006 and 2010.

In 2013, I was chosen for another award that gave me great honor, from His Highness the President (may God protect him), for the second time. It was special for me, as I do not think there are many who have been granted such an honor. On December 2, 2013, I received the Head of State Merit Award. The decree, which declared the launch of this prize says "The prize is to be given to the genuine faithful individuals who generate a distinguished product, and innovators who give contributions that help to enhance the status of the UAE at the local, regional and international levels, or those who perform great services to the nation." What is considered of special importance in my opinion is receiving the award while I was still doing my research work. I wish that the practice of honoring those who are still active and making valuable research contributions to their nation was extended to other Arab countries. Actually, many awards are given to those who had made old contributions, or those who have left our world.

On March 17, 2015, as Director General of the ECSSR, I received the "Arab Social Media Pioneers Award" from H.H. Sheikh Mohammed bin Rashid Al Maktoum, Vice President and Prime Minister of UAE, and Ruler of Dubai (may God protect him). It was given to the ECSSR, in the category of Policy, granted to institu-

Receiving "Al-Owais Award for Innovation, 1995" from the late Businessman Sultan bin Ali Al-Owais, on June 12, 1996. The ECSSR also won the award of "Cultural Personality of the Year." The photo shows also H.E. Mohammed Al-Murr, former Speaker of the UAE Federal National Council

The Certificate of winning the "Cultural Personality of the Year" Award, received on June 2, 2015

With H.E. Abdul Rahman Al-Owais, Minister of Health and Prevention; and H.E. Sultan Saqr Al-Suwaidi, Chairman of Dubai Science and Culture Forum, during granting me the award of "Cultural Personality of the Year," June 2, 2015

tions. I received that prize during the "Arab Social Media Pioneers Summit." Shortly before the summit, I had published my book *From Tribe to Facebook: The Transformational Role of Social Networks*, which received extensive media coverage.

The third award I will never forget is the Abu Dhabi Award 2011, which I received in January 2012. It was delivered by H.H. Sheikh Mohamed bin Zayed Al Nahyan (may God protect him). The Abu Dhabi Award is usually given based on a special evaluation combining the public nomination, and the assessments of the nominees' achievements by the relevant committee. Therefore, the award is considered a combination of official and public appreciation. It is given, as per the applied rules posted on the website of the award, to all "Performers of charities who bring about benefit to the Emirate of Abu Dhabi," regardless of their ages and nationalities. The reason I won the prize referred to the contributions of my humble personality to "enrich the cultural and academic life on both local and Arab levels, through his articles published in a number of international periodicals and magazines; and his writings that address many of the significant local and Arab issues. His Excellency Al-Suwaidi has provided valuable contributions toward building cultural bridges among nations, and to nurture the culture of research and studies in Abu Dhabi and the UAE."

With H.H. Sheikh Mansour bin Zayed Al Nahyan, Deputy Prime Minister and Minister of Presidential Affairs of the UAE; H.E. Dr. Ali bin Tamim, Director General of Abu Dhabi Media Company and Secretary-General of Sheikh Zayed Book Award and Editor-in-Chief of the news portal 24 (www.24.ae); and the winners of the Sheikh Zayed Book Award, during the ceremony of distributing the award, May 1, 2016

With H.H. Sheikh Mohamed bin Zayed Al Nahyan, Crown Prince of Abu Dhabi and Deputy Supreme Commander of the UAE Armed Forces (may God protect him); and H.E. Dr. Ali bin Tamim, Director General of Abu Dhabi Media Company and Secretary-General of Sheikh Zayed Book Award and Editor-in-Chief of the news portal 24 (www.24.ae), in a group photo with the winners of Sheikh Zayed Book Award, May 2, 2016

With a number of the winners of Sheikh Zayed Book Award, during the ceremony of distributing the prize to winners, on March 12, 2008. The ECSSR won the prize in the category of Publishing and Technology for 2008

Every appreciation or honor that I receive from H.H. Sheikh Mohamed bin Zayed Al Nahyan (may God protect him) occupies a special place in my soul, particularly, if the honor was related to my scholarly and research work. However, what made this prize very distinguished was the behavior that H.H. Sheikh Mohamed showed while giving me the award. His actions manifested the ethics of great men, and how the charisma and nobility were combined together in his modest kindness. This merit gives him unrivaled status in the hearts of those who had the honor and chance to work with His Highness On that day, my steps toward the stage were somewhat slow, due to some health issues at the time, and I had to go up a few steps to

With H.H. Sheikh Hamdan bin Zayed Al Nahyan, Ruler's Representative in the Al Dhafra Region (formerly Western Region), (Deputy Prime Minister at that time) and Mr. Rashid Al-Araimi, former Editor-in-Chief of *Al-Ittihad* newspaper, while I was receiving the Sheikh Zayed Book Award, 2008 in the ceremony of distributing the award to winners, on March 12, 2008. The ECSSR was one of the winners of this prize, in the category of Publishing and Technology

reach the stage. However, His Highness Sheikh Mohamed surprised me and the audience by his initiative, when he moved toward me. He went down the few stairs and his face was shining with an encouraging and cordial smile. H.H. Sheikh Mohamed bin Zayed did not just shake my hand, rather he initiated a very emotional passionate hug. Instead of leaning on the hand of my escort, His Highness Sheikh Mohamed's generous hand extended to help me get up the stairs. He himself continued supporting me until he seated me in my place among the honored individuals. Above the award, there was a morality much more precious. This tender kindness was one of the merits that H.H. Sheikh Mohamed bin Zayed Al Nahyan (may God protect him) adds to everything he does. His acts are always abundant with value and sincerity, which give his deeds unforgettable uniqueness.

On June 2, 2015 I received another award with a significant status in my soul. It was "The Cultural Personality of the Year Award." It is the highest prize among the "Al-Owais Creativity Awards," which was founded by the Emirati poet and intellectual, the late Sultan bin Ali Al-Owais. That award is one of the proofs of the vitality of the UAE society and its initiatives that support creativity in all domains. This award has its traditions

Receiving the "UAE Pioneers" Award from H.H. Sheikh Mohammed bin Rashid Al Maktoum, Vice President and Prime Minister of UAE and Ruler of Dubai (may God protect him), November 28, 2016

and standards that have been established through-out more than 25 years. The referees and assessment committees for issuing that prize consist of the most prominent Arab and Gulf men of thought, who enjoy renowned scientific careers and eminent personalities.

Certificate of being awarded the "UAE Pioneers" Award, November 28, 2016

The Cultural Personality of the Year Award is granted to individuals and institutions that have produced important and useful cultural contribution during the related year. It was one of the coincidences that increased my joy as, in 1996, I stood on the same platform to receive the same notable award, Cultural Personality of the Year for 1995. However at that time, it was given to the ECSSR, which at two years old, was still in its infancy. That award constituted an immense moral boost for the ECSSR at the time it was still taking its early steps toward excellence. The award itself is evidence that UAE institutions, both public and private ones, perform their expected national role to enhance the pioneering initiatives. The UAE appreciates all the faithful effort made in the domain of culture, thought and innovation.

On April 1, 2016, I was honored with the most important Arab book award ever. It was the "Sheikh Zayed Book Award" granted to my book *The Mirage*. This award is open to Arab writers and researchers of all nationalities. It is known for its strict standards, conditions and procedures, which guarantee the highest level of integrity in the assessment process to select

UAE Medal for Voluntary Work awarded to me in recognition of the help I provided to UAE Conference for Community Volunteering, May 30, 2016

the winners. This award witnesses real competition among the best Arab authors and researchers, who dream of winning such a prize because of its high moral and financial value. Therefore, they seek to participate with the best and strongest products of their work in various categories. I take pride in being the first Emirati author to have won the prize in the category of "Best Contribution to the Development of Nations." It is worth mentioning that the ECSSR had already won this prize in 2008 in the category of "Publishing and Technology" due to its large amount of scientific refined, upscale publications.

This prize crowned the fine response and welcoming interest in my book *The Mirage*, in both the Arab world and the West. Somehow, however, I was surprised. I said during one of my meetings with the ECSSR staff that I felt that the effort made and the scientific vision in the book *Prospects for the American Age: Sovereignty and Influence in the New World Order* might

A collection of my writings and of ECSSR publications, which had been included within the syllabus of National Education in UAE schools, at the beginning of the academic year 2016/2017

be, in my opinion, better than the ones in *The Mirage*. However, the readers and the audience might have their own view that could well be different from the author's. This might be due to the fact that the Arab intellectual arena was in dire need for someone who dared to confront the extremist religious political groups, in a comprehensive battle in the domain of ideology and thought, to expose their trivial, collapsing logic.

On November 28, 2016, I was awarded the prize called "UAE Pioneers." It is very dear to my heart because of two reasons: First, I received the award from H.H. Sheikh Mohammed bin Rashid Al Maktoum, Vice President and Prime Minister of UAE and Ruler of Dubai (may God protect him). Second, it encourages reading, and I am one of those who believe that reading is the first door toward knowledge. The rise of any nation should inevitably start with reading. In my writings, I have expressed many times my dissatisfaction toward statistics that reveal a frightening regression in the average number of readers in the Arab world, compared to other nations around the world.

The moment I went up on the stage to receive my award nurtured hope. The place was radiating with the cheerful presence of H.H. Sheikh Mohammed bin Rashid Al Maktoum (may God protect him) and his distinguished ability to spread optimism, hope and positive attitude wherever he goes. Even nature responded to his optimism and bright feeling, as the soft breeze of November and the pristine blue seawater of the Arabian Gulf at Al-Saadiyat Island in Abu Dhabi, where the celebration was held, multiplied my delight and joy of winning.

Being honored by H.E. Sheikh Nahyan bin Mubarak Al Nahyan, Minister of Culture and Knowledge Development (Minister of Culture, Youth, and Community Development at that time) for my strategic partnership with Chartered Institute for IT (BSC), November 2, 2015

Some of the prizes that I have been awarded from UAE institutions were related to other fields covered by my work as well. For example, *Al-Ittihad* newspaper presented me with an honorary gift on November

With Dr. Abdullah Al-Neyadi, Chairman of the Al-Tawasol International Tent, during my visit to the Tent, in Al-Khatim, Abu Dhabi, May 25, 2015

9, 2015, as an appreciation of the effort I made in supporting the newspaper, as I explained in Chapter Three of this book, alongside the support I offered to the 10th round of the "Al-Ittihad Forum." That forum included the writers of *Wujhat Nazar*, the opinion page in *Al-Ittihad*. Also, the Red Crescent Society of the UAE awarded me the "Gold Medal," on September 16, 2008 due to "Your distinguished effort to support and serve our humanitarian message and spread its noble princi-ples." I received the prize from H.H. Sheikh Hamdan bin Zayed Al Nahyan, in a prestigious cere-mony. Seven years later, on July 2, 2015, the Zayed Humanitarian Forum, in its sixth round, grant-ed me the "Zayed Medal for Hu-manitarian Action," as an appre-ciation of the support I provided to that forum, along with my ac-tivities at the time, including the establishment of the Cancer Pa-tient Care Society (RAHMA).

On May 30, 2016, I was awarded the "UAE Medal for Voluntary Work" on the basis of my support for the UAE Con-ference for Community Volun-

With H.H. Sheikh Hamdan bin Zayed Al Nahyan, Ruler's Representative in the Al Dhafra Region (formerly Western Region), (Deputy Prime Minister at that time) at the ceremony for distributing the Sheikh Zayed Book Award, on March 12, 2008. The ECCSR has won the award, in the Publishing and Distribution Category

teering, as we hosted its eighth round at the ECSSR on that same day. Un-doubtedly, any honors in the field of humanitarian work carry a lot of value and meaning for me because they are connected to the values of giving and sacrifice. These values manifest the ideal image of humanity in the human being. I commented on this appreciation by saying "The bright example of the UAE in the domain of humanitarian work, and the spreading of the cul-ture of giving and voluntary work in the UAE society, are truly the results of the initiatives started by the late Father, Sheikh Zayed bin Sultan Al Na-hyan (may God rest his soul in peace). The late Sheikh Zayed was a symbol of giving and charity, and he had planted in the minds of the UAE popula-tion the culture of constant giving, without expecting anything in return."

During the ceremony to present me with the honorary PhD in political science and international relations and membership of the academic council at the University of Lugano, Switzerland, November 17, 2015

In the domain of education, I have been honored by the "Interim Committee for School Books" when they awarded me a Memorial Shield. The reason for this award was that the ECSSR had been a member in that committee. The members of the committee recognized that many of the ECSSR publications and a number of my writings were worthy of being included within the UAE school book syllabus for certain education stages and subjects. I think that is right, and can be true on one condition, the contents of these books should be re-edited to be fit for the school syllabus. The ECSSR actually worked with the Ministry of Education to prepare and edit these books to be fit for the school syllabus. As mentioned before, a number of the books I authored became part of the National Education syllabus, in the academic year 2016/2017.

I have also received appreciation in the field of Information Technology, considering that I have realized the importance of this domain early on. I always seek to have the most updated IT applications available for the staff working with me. Thus, I was honored by the "Chartered Institute for IT (BSC)," on April 21, 2013, for my effort in pushing the wheel of research and knowledge in the domain of IT. That was the onset of scientific cooper-

With H.H. Sheikh Mohamed bin Zayed Al Nahyan, Crown Prince of Abu Dhabi and Deputy Supreme Commander of the UAE Armed Forces (may God protect him); and Mrs. Michèle Alliot-Marie, Chairwoman of Delegation for Relations with the Arabian Peninsula at the EU Parliament (and former French Minister of Defense), after granting me the French Order of Merit, First Class, December 17, 2002

ation between the ECSSR and the Royal Institute. This appreciation was repeated by the Royal Institute on November 2, 2015, when H.E. Sheikh Nahyan bin Mubarak Al Nahyan awarded me a Memorial Shield.

One of the institutions that also honored me was the Emirates ID Authority, which gave me the

With Mrs. Michèle Alliot-Marie, Chairwoman of Delegation for Relations with the Arabian Peninsula at the EU Parliament (and former French Minister of Defense), granting me the French Order of Merit First Degree, December 17, 2002

award of "Unique Leadership and Futuristic Vision," in 2012. That was an appreciation of a joint work with the ECSSR. Moreover, Al Tawasol International Tent, headed by Dr. Abdullah Al-Neyadi, honored me in May 2015. It was a popular appreciation and I take pride in it, as it was granted by one of the Civil Society organizations. This "Tent" is active in important fields of social communication.

With Mrs. Michèle Alliot-Marie, Chairwoman of Delegation for Relations with the Arabian Peninsula (and former French Minister of Defense)at the EU Parliament, and Antonio Lopez, a Member of the European Parliament, October 19, 2016

I have also received awards in the domain of sports. Dubai's Al-Ahli Club honored me as a "Personality Supporting Sports Movement." In fact, I have had an interest in sports since my early childhood. I believe that sports help in building a balanced character. That prize gave me a lot of happiness, as there was a member of the ECSSR staff who was a player for Al-Ahli Club. I used to help him and facilitate his work hours to ensure he could take part in the training sessions with his team and help them win championships. I consider encouraging talent in sports one of my duties in society. The appreciation by Al-Ahli Club was a generous gesture because it came from the domain that I love, cherish and acknowledge its importance.

Binary Awards

Probably, it is a coincidence that I have been honored with some awards twice. In the UAE, I have been honored twice by H.H. Sheikh Khalifa bin Zayed Al Nahyan, the UAE President (may God protect him), with two special awards in 2008 and 2013. I have also been honored twice with the Al-Owais Award, in 1996 and 2015. Moreover, I have been honored twice with the Sheikh Zayed Book Award, in 2008 and 2016, as previously mentioned.

These double awards were applicable outside the UAE as well. I attained an honorary PhD from the International University in Vienna, the capital of Austria, in 2008. In 2015, I was granted an honorary PhD from the University of Lugano, Switzerland. The similarity is not just receiving these two honorary PhDs; rather, it extends to the fact that both universities were European, both countries share borders, and while German is the official language in Austria, it is also widely spoken in Switzerland. For me, this means the

Receiving the Key to the city of Fez, Morocco, from the Moroccan academic Dr. Abdul-Haq Azzouzi, and Prof. Mostafa Bousmina, President of the Euro-Mediterranean University, in Fez. The ceremony was held at the premises of the ECSSR, March 5, 2013

reasons for granting me this precious degree, which I take pride in, are compelling, and attaining this degree is not by chance. The similarity of cultures between both European countries, and the similarity of scientific and academic traditions constituted the reason that made the two universities agree to grant me an honorary PhD.

The Key to the city of Fez, Morocco, received on March 5, 2013

The other double awards that I have also received include the Order of Merit with the Rank of Commander from Morocco in 1995; and again the Order of Merit with the Rank of Commander from France, in 2002. I think the repetition of such an award is proof itself—the tangible cultural rapprochement between Morocco and France is manifested in many traditions, including the tradition of giving similar awards and medals. Receiving these two medals is similar to when I received the two PhD degrees from two similar neighboring nations. Both cases indicate the reliability and consistency of the reasoning upon which the medals were given. I have also been awarded these two medals in the presence of H.H. Sheikh Mohamed bin Zayed Al Nahyan (may God protect him), which multiplies my pride of these events.

The Royal Moroccan Medal has a special importance for me for many reasons. It was the first medal I received in my practical life after completing my graduate studies. I received that medal from the late

The Key to the city of Alexandria, Egypt, received on September 28, 2014

King Hassan II of Morocco. He was one of the persons toward whom I have the most respect. I wrote a chapter about him titled "The King of Wisdom and Balance," in my book *Eternal Imprints: Figures that Made History and Others that Changed the Future of their Countries*. I dedicated most of that book to leaders who changed the future of their nations positively. Moreover, I received that medal when I was 36 years old, a year after the inception of the ECSSR, when I had just started my long journey. That medal assured me that I was walking in the right direction, and the effort I make could find someone who would appreciate it in a brotherly nation.

The French medal, in its turn, was very important. It was presented to me by Michèle Alliot-Marie, when she was Minister of Defense; she later held the positions of Minister of Justice, Interior and Foreign Affairs. She then moved to work for the European Union. I had the chance to meet Mrs. Alliot-Marie again, about 14 years after our first meeting, at a symposium organized at the headquarters of the European Parliament in Brussels, Belgium. The symposium was held under the title "How Do We Fight Terrorism Today?" on October 20, 2016. During a tour in Europe that included the Belgian capital, Brussels, I participated in that event, along with a number of EU officials concerned with methods of countering terrorism. Now, Mrs. Alliot-Marie holds the position of Chairperson of the Delegation for Relations with the Arabian Peninsula at the EU Parliament. On the sidelines of that visit and symposium, I had an important meeting with her that resulted in fruitful and valuable discussions.

The French medal was an outcome of long cooperation with French research institutions concerned with defense affairs, including the French Center for Strategic Affairs, affiliated with the Ministry of Defense. The

The Certificate of Appreciation awarded to me by the Association of Economics and Political Science at Kuwait University for passing the Bachelor of Arts exams with Distinction with Honors, in the academic year 1981

Chief of Staff of the French Armed Forces, General Jean-Pierre Kelche, visited the ECSSR in 1998 in a collaborative framework. This type of effort was one of the ECSSR's tasks. The scientific meetings, which include academics and media officials, pave the way for a closer and stronger cooperation with many countries. All political and economic issues were addressed in an atmosphere of transparent scientific discussion. Thus, those meetings were an opportunity to establish personal relations and reach common perspectives with elites from various countries. This effort made the subsequent political understandings, based on a solid ground of knowledge and awareness. That was the context and reason for which I was granted the French medal.

Another double award, which held an important moral dimension, was handing me the key to Fez in Morocco in 2013, and to Alexandria in Egypt in 2014. Handing the key to a city to a certain person implies a great symbolic value. The city, with all its significance and expansion in geography, history and civilization, expresses the attitude that it grants part of the moral authority to a certain person, based on certain achievements from which that city and its population have benefited.

I was deeply moved by receiving the Key to Fez, as this city, with its doors, walls, palaces and mosques, represents the richness of Islamic architecture and its astonishing artistic variety. Moreover, Fez is an ancient scientific center. Fez's first university, the University of Al Quaraouiyine, was established around 12 centuries ago. It has produced many successive generations of scientists, students and researchers. Probably, that is what makes the Key to Fez an award that is harmonious with my interests, which are focused around scientific research and encouraging culture and thought. After Morocco, represented in its political authority, granted me the first honor in my life, it was the cultural and intellectual sides of Morocco that granted me an award with a special impression on my soul.

Certificate of the "Man of the Year" representing the UAE in 2010 from the American Biographical Institute

After the Key to Fez, I was also handed the Key to Alexandria, from its former governor, Major General Tariq Al-Mahdi. Alexandria is also a center

Receiving the Revolutionary Thinker Award from the US College of William & Mary, April 5, 2016

I have been honored by Striking the Bells in the oldest American Church, which was built in 1776, coinciding with the founding of the USA itself, College of William & Mary, USA, April 5, 2016

of learning and a beacon of thought. It was widely known throughout the world for its immense library, that dates back almost 23 centuries. It kept carrying a civilizational message throughout history. A Twinning Agreement was signed between ECSSR and the Library of Alexandria, which revived the cultural role of the city. This library is an ancient prominent sci-

Receiving the Naguib Mahfouz Award for Literature, in appreciation of my role in achieving World Peace, in New York. Also in the photo is Dr. Tareq Mahfouz(left), a nephew of the late novelist, April 8, 2016

entific landmark and we respect and appreciate its role. I believe that this joint effort played a role in granting me the key to the City. Furthermore, the attitudes of the UAE toward the brotherly nation, Egypt, during this period, contributed significantly as to why I was granted this appreciation.

Honors and Awards I Take Pride in

The first honor I received was related to my achievement when I came first in my bachelor's degree in political science from Kuwait University in 1981. The Association of Economics and Political Science at Kuwait University

With a number of professors at the University of St. Thomas, in Houston, USA; on the sidelines of my lecture titled "The Mirage: A Discussion of Extremism in the Middle East," which I delivered on April 12, 2016

honored me at the premises of Kuwait Airways, and presented me with an appreciation certificate, which I still take much pride in. The words of the certificate are handwritten and still remind me of that occasion. It gave me a great push and encouragement at the start of my professional life. Moreover, I was selected for an honorary membership of the American Phi Kappa Phi Society, based on strict standards during the years of my master's degree at Wisconsin University. The reason for this decision knows no bias, nor accepts any steps not based on strong and reasonable motives.

One of the factors that make me happy with the awards I have received is the fact that all of them were the results of work I had completed, and in compliance with clear realistic reasoning connected with the field of my political and research activity. Honoring me at Kuwait University was based on an achievement measured by numbers, as I came top of my class. Without underestimating the value of any award, or any person, there are some prizes that are distributed in a celebratory way, such as granting ministers or officials medals or awards as part of protocol during official visits accompanying commanders and leaders. It might also occur as a response to an honor offered by a certain country to certain personalities from another country. These practices are just courtesies, and I do not think that I have received any award or honor in this category. Most of the awards that I have received saw a real competition with other nominees, whom I respect and appreciate. Most of my awards came as a result of a certain achievement in which I had a considerable role.

Similarly, I have received numerous and consecutive awards from outside the UAE, and even from outside the Arab and Muslim world, and that naturally confirms the reliability and weight of the Emirati and Arab awards given to me. In 2010, The American Biographical Institute in North Carolina selected me as the "Man of the Year," even though I did not have any relations with that institute. I did not know much about the institute itself, but it is distinguished by following carefully what is published in important sources, regionally and internationally, about research and scientific achievements that attained certain status. Based on comparisons, and disciplinary standards, the

With Mr. Michele Capasso, Chairman of Euro-Mediterranean Foundation, in a ceremony for handing me Mediterranean Award for Diplomacy and Thought 2014," at the ECSSR on April 21, 2014

institute chooses someone viewed as a person that has accomplished bigger and more important achievements.

On April 6, 2016, the American prestigious College of William & Mary, which was founded in 1693, granted me the "The Revolutionary Thinker" award. I received that award during one of my scientific tours of the USA in April 2016. The tour included a discussion of my book *The Mirage*, at the UN headquarters in New York City on April 7, 2016. Also during that tour, I delivered a lecture at the University of St. Thomas, in Houston, titled "The Mirage: A Discussion about Extremism in the Middle East."

In the USA tour, I also won a medal that I take much pride in because it carries the name of the Arab novelist and Nobel Laureate, Naguib Mahfouz. On April 8, 2016, I was handed the "Naguib Mahfouz Award for Literature," from Dr. Tareq Mahfouz, the nephew of the late novelist, in a ceremony attended by members of the Mahfouz family. I also felt more pride because I was granted the Mahfouz medal as "an appreciation of my role in seeking world peace." The values of tolerance, coexistence and peace were always among my concerns ever since my research tendencies became clear. I devoted a lot of time and effort to these values because I consider them an indispensable foundation for putting an end to conflicts and wars, and realizing a better life for humanity all over the world.

The late prominent novelist Naguib Mahfouz represented the Arab genius when it is set free from restrictions. Mahfouz relied on genuine Arab roots, knowledge of the international intellectual products and creativity, alongside hard work and persistence, which continued ceaselessly for about 70 years. All of that was backed by an exceptional talent, which is viewed as a grace from God. The combination of all these factors resulted in making the novelist a Nobel Laureate in Literature. That achievement was the first of its kind in the Arab world. The importance of winning the Nobel Prize surpasses the personality of the winner, as it crowns the country to which the winner belongs, and the culture they represent. Therefore, the winning of the Nobel Prize by Mahfouz was considered a victory for Arab Islamic culture, and proof that this nation has something to offer to hu-

With Mr. Pietro Grasso, President of the Italian Senate, during my visit to Italy on June 20, 2014

With Senator Jean-Marie Bockel, Member of French Senate, from the Union of Democrats and Independents Party, during the ceremony of handing me the Award of European Press for the Arab World, 2015, in Paris, January 27, 2016

With Dr. Charles Saint-Prot, Executive Director of the Observatory of Geopolitical Studies at the French Senate, receiving the Award for Geostrategic Studies 2015, January 27, 2016

With Dr. Charles Saint-Prot, Director of French Observatory for Geopolitical Studies, during a ceremony for signing my book *Prospects for the American Age: Sovereignty and Influence in the New World Order*, in Paris, May 21, 2014

During a symposium organized by the French parliament in Paris and attended by a large number of members of parliament, academics and politicians, about my book *The Mirage*, on February 7, 2016, the sidelines of receiving the Award of European Press for the Arab World, 2015

manity—the Arab nation has a strong foundation that enables its citizens to become among the innovators in the history of humanity.

Winning the award of Naguib Mahfouz implies great significance, due to the illuminating role played by Mr. Mahfouz in countering extremism through his many novels and stories, which manifested the deepest human feelings and emotions. One of the most ironic moments in the history of Arab culture was when an extremist maniac stabbed Mahfouz with a knife in his neck when he was 85 years old. That despicable attack was based on a provocative *fatwa* (religious ruling) and accusations of blasphemy against Mr. Mahfouz by those radicals who promote *takfir* (excommunication) and killing.

With the former Egyptian Minister of Culture Dr. Jaber Asfour (left); and Mr. Ibrahim Abu Zikri, President of the General Union of Arab Producers, during handing me the "Knight of Arab Studies" Award, February 25, 2015

The appreciation awards I received have ranged from the United States of America to many European countries and institutions since 2002, when I was awarded the French Medal of Merit from the President of France, and an honorary PhD from two notable universities, as previously mentioned. In November 2012, the Europe Business Assembly in Oxford, UK, honored me due to "distinguished effort in supporting societal programs offered by ECSSR and pioneering role in educating the Emirati society particularly, and the Gulf society in general." This award was preceded by long cooperation with the prestigious Oxford

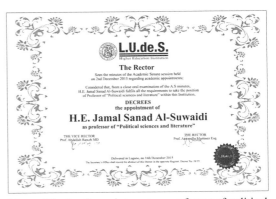

My certificate of appointment as professor of political science and literature from the University of L.U.de.S. (Switzerland) awarded to me on January 3, 2017

My certificate receiving title of "Ambassador for Peace" from the Universal Peace Federation on March 22, 2017

Receiving the certificate of "Ambassador for Peace" from the Universal Peace Federation on March 22, 2017

University, in constant joint scientific and research activities between the ECSSR and the Oxford Centre for Islamic Studies. Those activities also included many forums, meetings and conferences in the UAE and the UK. This cooperation started in 1999 and is still ongoing until today.

In 2014, an eminent European institution, the Euro-Mediterranean Foundation granted me the "Mediterranean Award for Diplomacy and Thought." In its reasoning, the foundation said "his tangible contributions and effort to build rapprochement among nations; and for his role in enhancing the concept of Culture Diplomacy, which is built on knowledge and thought production." I believe that I tried my best and saved no effort in the domain of promoting the culture of tolerance through knowledge and thought. I am quite certain that culture allows the world to see Arabs and Muslims in their real form, away from the unfair stereotypes that connect them to terrorism, militancy and hatred of others.

This prize came before my visit to Italy to sign my book *Prospects for the American Age: Sovereignty and Influence in the New World Order*, where I met Pietro Grasso, President of the Italian Senate at the time.

During handing me the GCC Excellence Award in the Field Research and Studies, by H.H. Sheikh Tamim bin Hamad Al-Thani, Emir of Qatar, on December 7, 2015. The photo shows also H.E. Rashid Al-Zayani, Secretary-General of the GCC

I also visited the Vatican and met Cardinal Pietro Parolin, Secretary of State for the Vatican. During the meeting with these two men and some other officials, the cultural, intellectual, religious and civilizational rapprochement was among the issues that were discussed expansive-

The GCC Excellence Award in Research and Studies which I received on December 7, 2015

ly. I believe these meetings were the basis for granting me the award from the Euro-Mediterranean Foundation, which is concerned with bringing both shores of the Mediterranean closer to each other. Moreover, the Chairman of the Foundation, Michele Capasso, devotes a lot of his time and effort to this issue. He works hard to create zones of understanding between the Arab and European countries. I visited Dr. Capasso at his office in Naples.

A group photo showing the winners of the GCC Excellence Award, with H.H. Sheikh Tamim bin Hamad Al-Thani, Emir of Qatar, December 7, 2015

On January 27, 2016, I was honored with two awards on the same day during my visit to France. The first was the "Award of European Press for the Arab World 2015," which is granted by the European Press Association for Arab World, in collaboration with the EU Institute for Strategic Studies of Prospects and Security in Europe.

The second was the Geopolitical Studies Award for 2015, granted by the Observatory for Geopolitical Studies at the French Senate. I received both awards in a ceremony on the sidelines of a symposium organized by the French Parliament about political Islam. The symposium was planned to discuss the ideas of my book *The Mirage*. It was an opportunity to present an Arab point of view about the risk of terrorism and the effort made by Arab countries and Arabian Gulf countries to counter it. This helped in providing the French Members of Parliament with an idea about the intellectual confrontation on the Gulf and Arab levels. This also revealed to them that Arab thinkers – whom I was representing at that event – are fighting an existential battle against terrorism and militancy to serve the progress and development of their countries.

On January 3, 2017, I was honored with a new European appreciation, as I obtained professorship in political science and literature from the University of L.U.de.S. (Switzerland). It is one of the universities that enjoy a prominent scientific and academic reputation, both in Switzerland and abroad. Likewise, the Universal Peace Federation granted me the title of "Ambassador for Peace" on March 22, 2017.

At the Arab level, The General Union of Arab Producers has honored me with a distinguished award "Knight of Arab Studies," on February 25, 2015. The Union of Arab Producers is an organization that works through the Council of Arab Media Ministers, which is an affiliate to the Arab League. The honoring ceremony was held in Egypt, and it was attended by a number of Arab and UAE officials, including the former Egyptian Minister of Culture Dr. Jaber Asfour, and Her Excellency Dr. Maitha Salim Al-Shamsi, UAE Minister of State, on behalf of Her Highness Sheikha Fatima bint Mubarak (Mother of the Nation), who was also one of those honored at the ceremony.

The year 2015 was another distinguished one in the course of honoring me for my work. During that year, I was honored with eight awards. The last one of 2015 gave me a special feeling. On December 7, 2015, I received from H.H. Sheikh Tamim bin Hamad Al-Thani, Emir of Qatar, in his capacity as President of the 35th Session of GCC Supreme Council Summit, the "GCC Excellence Award in the Field of Research and Studies," at the first honoring round of the award.

There are several reasons that gave the GCC Excellence Award a special status in my mind and soul. First, it was issued by the organization that manifested the most successful model of Arab collaboration and the most active performance in all fields. Second, selecting me among the honored people in the first round of the award – which is issued once every five years, and the nominees to be honored were nine people from each country member of GCC – enhanced my pride with the award. The third reason was that the award was granted to me in the field of research and studies, which I consider as my first home and my first identity, no matter how varied the other fields reached through the expansion of my responsibilities and tasks.

Being honored creates a turning point in the life of every person. I think everyone feels joy when they receive honors and awards, regardless if the process was simple or symbolic. Unfortunately, many Arab countries do not pay as much attention to honoring their creative citizens as they should. I guess that the UAE might urge other brotherly Arab countries to enhance and deepen the culture of appreciation and honors in their societies. Probably, the organizations of Arab collaboration, mainly the Arab League, should be the body to push this trend and practice, and should devote part of their effort for this mission. Taking into consideration that many cases of individuals and collective success could be enhanced simply by a word of appreciation, or a prize that does not cost much, but it may carry a huge moral value.

The moment when one stands to be honored is one of the unforgettable moments in the life of each and every human being. The desire to relive and repeat that moment represents one of the strongest motives for self-development, and urges the person to make strenuous effort to achieve success. Arab countries need to make use of this inherent human nature to invest in their human resources and benefit from them to achieve comprehensive progress.

Epilogue

Epilogue

While the writing of this autobiography was approaching its finishing stage, I was still persistently carrying on my usual way of work. I spend at least 10 hours per day in my office at the Emirates Center for Strategic Studies and Research (ECSSR). I follow up on and monitor the perfection of every single detail of work in the various sections and departments of the ECSSR. Even when I am outside the Center, I perform my tasks ceaselessly day and night. I have kept the same diligence with which I started my career. Needless to say, every single job or task I initiate, I perform as if I am doing it for the first time, with the same attentiveness and care, and not neglecting any small detail, as all details should be coherent and harmonious to create a product in the best possible shape.

This is one of the crucial notions that I want to discuss in the last few pages of this autobiography. As long as life keeps renewing itself in every moment, we should keep renewing and reshaping ourselves to keep up with its fast pace. In our body, thousands of cells die every seconds. However, thousands more cells are instantaneously generated to replace the dead ones. The human cognizance should have the same feature: renewal, movement and never surrendering to stagnation as this means death. Movement is a

A composite photo showing me with H.H. Sheikh Khalifa bin Zayed Al Nahyan, President of the UAE (may God protect him); H.H. Sheikh Mohammed bin Rashid Al Maktoum Vice President and Prime Minister of the UAE and Ruler of Dubai (may God protect him); and with H.H. Sheikh Mohamed bin Zayed Al Nahyan Crown Prince of Abu Dhabi and Deputy Supreme Commander of the UAE Armed Forces (may God protect him), during various honoring occasions

common feature of giant planets in all galaxies, and unicellular creatures in which biological functions never stop even for one second.

Such a perception was the factor that made creativity a characteristic and a target that I tentatively take care of and always try to ignite within staff working with me because yielding to old styles – no matter how successful they seemed – leads gradually to weariness of the mind. Meanwhile, reviewing things, contemplation, posing new questions and searching for their answers, lead to the improvement of performance and increasing proficiency. That does not mean wasting or neglecting former experiences; rather it means using them without allowing them to form a constraint curbing creativity and innovation, alongside constantly searching for new solutions. These ideas compel me to a talk about "success," and contemplate its meanings, reasons and aspects. This is what I prefer to conclude this autobiography with.

People and Events on the Road to Success

In addition to personal self-motivation, success in individual life is usually interconnected with the presence of people who influence that human being

During the visit of H.H. Sheikh Mohamed bin Zayed Al Nahyan, Crown Prince of Abu Dhabi and Deputy Supreme Commander of the UAE Armed Forces (may God protect him), to the ECSSR on July 6, 1997

positively. Such people pave the way for the success of the related human being at a certain moment, and through certain events, and that support gives the related person positive energy and strength required for facing hardships, even when some of them are painful. The three individuals whom I consider the most influential in terms of guiding my steps on this road are: H.H. Sheikh Mohamed bin Zayed Al Nahyan (may God protect him), my mother (may her soul rest in peace) and my wife. As for the events that influenced my career, they are: the birth of my son Khaled; getting a PhD; and falling ill with cancer. These three events brought with them a new perception of faith in God, and the relation between the human being and the Almighty Creator.

The first person that had the most significant effect on my life is His Highness Sheikh Mohamed bin Zayed Al Nahyan (may God protect him). My work under his command and direct supervision taught me numerous lessons, which any man needs to be successful. He has the talent and fore-

sight to recognize and select those who are high-
ly qualified and push
them to the center of the
scene. He has the merit
and willingness to pro-
vide all necessary capa-
bilities and overcome the
most formidable obsta-
cles. He is skilled in de-
vising ambitious objec-
tives and realizing them,
regardless of how tough
they appeared. I also be-
lieve that H.H. Sheikh
Mohamed bin Zayed Al
Nahyan (may God pro-
tect him) enable many

With my son, Dr. Khaled, during the celebration of the 22nd Anniversary of establishing the ECSSR, March 21, 2016

people who work with him to rediscover their potential. Supported by his foresight and inspiring personality, he extracts from them the potential and skills that they themselves do not realize that they own. Working with H.H. Sheikh Mohamed bin Zayed Al Nahyan (may God protect him) can be described as a "School for Success," as each person who enters that school will be provided with a rare chance to learn significant lessons about the arts of manufacturing and sustaining success.

The second person is my mother: she is my number one teacher in life. The tenderness, kindness and love she loaded me with were mixed with nurturing my sense of responsibility. She secured for me the surroundings of understanding and compassion. She provided me with optimism and self-confidence. She used simple, but highly prudent and rewarding educating techniques. In every situation I went through, she extracted a useful lesson, which she would transfer to me in a tender way, covered with great love. She would draw from the lesson any sense of coercion or obligation. She would always leave it up to me to make my choice. I believe when I strived for success, I had the desire to prove to this great woman that I was worthy of her trust. My success would be a message conveying love and gratitude for her and an acknowledgement of her favor and effort. The most pleasing moments of my life were the moments in which I realized

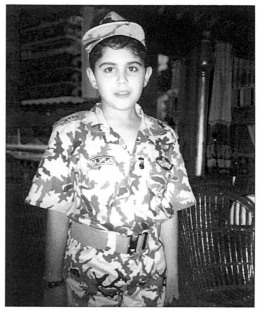

My son Khaled, wearing the uniform of the UAE Armed Forces, in 1991

that the success I achieved gave her tremendous happiness.

The third person is my wife, who provided me with all the factors that made success easier and smoother. We were married at an early age; however, her mental maturity was obvious ever since the first time we met at Kuwait University. Her educational and academic excellence and her persistence in seeking knowledge qualified her to accomplish major academic achievements. Nevertheless, she preferred to invest all the graces given to her by God, including maturity, wisdom, distinction and the strong personality capable of attaining achievements, in her role to prepare the tools, motives and environment for my success. I had received from her significant scientific and academic help while I was preparing the thesis for both my master's and PhD degrees.

I have been mindful to ensure that all critical decisions in my life are a product of discussion and agreement between my wife and I. She always chose whatever supported my career toward success, even if that choice brought us financial burdens, similar to those that we faced during my

With H.E. Dr. Anwar Gargash, the UAE Minister of State for Foreign Affairs and my academic and patriotic colleague, during his visit to the ECSSR pavilion at the Abu Dhabi Book Fair, May 1, 2016

graduate studies in the United States of America. She endured the exhausting family responsibilities happily and with full satisfaction. During my critical fateful confrontation with cancer, my wife was the one who helped me to resist the disease and to be unwavering while suffering pain—she encouraged me to forcefully cling to life. I was able to devote my time fully to work, while I felt secured and satisfied with what was offered to my children in terms of a proper upbringing. She knew how to build a balanced personality in our children; she mastered the ways of nurturing them to ensure when they leave her care to the outside world, they would be in the shape that we wished them to be.

The birth of my son Khaled was a turning point in my view toward life. No matter how others try to describe the feeling of fatherhood, no matter how much you have read about it, or how much you have imagined it, when you finally experience it in reality, you will actually discover that you had known nothing about it. As the Sufi aphorism goes "He who tastes, knows." When I experienced fatherhood, I discovered that the entire life of a human being could be manifested in a smile of a child; the gravest fear in life would not be regarding yourself, rather about your child. Your personal dreams take the back seat to create space for your dreams regarding the future of your child.

My son, Khaled, was born while I was overloaded with responsibilities, and amid hard financial circumstances during my graduate studies in the USA. I was exhausted because I would never accept an alternative to distinction, in spite of all these hardships. At that moment, when Khaled came into my life, I felt confident that these difficulties would be vanquished and that I was capable of confronting them easily. I felt an internal power suddenly emerge inside me and urged me to never surrender. I had

During the ceremony of the "Annual Forum for Information Technology" in which I was honored by H.E. Sheikh Nahyan bin Mubarak Al Nahyan, Minister of Culture and Knowledge Development (Minister of Culture, Youth, and Community Development at that time), November 2, 2015

discovered that happiness was a source of power inside me; I did not realize it existed in that way until the birth of my first son.

Receiving a PhD in 1990 was the major turning point in my career. It meant the end of living abroad and returning to my home country to undertake my duty toward my nation. This moment came after many years of being overwhelmed with strenuous effort and challenges. However, those years were full of lessons, on both the academic and human sides of life. I had the chance to see the world from a broader and more comprehensive perspective and to learn a lot about political and economic decision making and the factors affecting it. I started to believe with certainty and awareness during my graduate studies abroad that the Arab world desperately needed to enhance the

With H.H. Sheikh Mohamed bin Zayed Al Nahyan, Crown Prince of Abu Dhabi and Deputy Supreme Commander of the UAE Armed Forces (may God protect him),when His Highness received a delegation from the ECSSR, May 9, 2017

basics of scientific research, and to pay more attention to achieve what their nations aspire for in terms of decent living standards.

I believe that receiving a PhD degree from the University of Wisconsin, USA, was the first step toward "acknowledging" me as a researcher and an academic. With this scientific degree, the obstacles that had been created by the Muslim Brotherhood group in blocking my admission at United Arab Emirates University as a teaching assistant back in 1982 disappeared. It became clear to them that depriving me of my right to pursue my education with the support of government funds was pointless. I returned to the university against their will, to take part in exposing their viciousness and revealing their danger to the citizens of the UAE, students of its university and those in earlier education stages. I took part in disclosing their risk to the stability and security of the UAE.

As for being a cancer patient, it was the most critical test of my life. Undoubtedly, it is the same for any human being who falls ill to this disease. Cancer was the real test to measure the applicability of my principle "Never Give Up." Like everyone who has experienced this trial, I was haunted by moments of weakness, fear and despair, but they were transitory moments.

With H.H. Sheikh Mohamed bin Zayed Al Nahyan, Crown Prince of Abu Dhabi and Deputy Supreme Commander of the UAE Armed Forces (may God protect him), on the sidelines of a Forum titled "Yemeni War: Causes & Consequences" organized by the ECSSR, July 26, 1994

In the midst of pain, part of my soul was thinking of the future, which remained my primary concern in both research and humanitarian aspects. Contemplating the future and aspiring to it means that hope in the coming days is endless. Therefore, my faith in the future was a source of power and strength against pain, weakness and fear.

The issue that I consider very important is that I did not view my suffering from cancer, or recovery from the disease later on, as an excuse to stop working and cease performance of my national duty. There were many reasons allowing me to believe that I did my best and the health issues, which were facing me, justified for me to search for a comfortable life free of worries, without complicated and endless tasks that required a lot of effort from my mind to be followed and accomplished. However, I did not allow this alluring idea to enter my soul.

The unexpected gift that I gained from the cancer ordeal was the sweetness of being close to the Creator and the splendor of communicating with God, where the whole universe vanishes in front of my eyes and

With H.E. Sheikh Nahyan bin Mubarak Al Nahyan, Minister of Culture and Knowledge Development (Minister of Culture, Youth, and Community Development at that time); H.E. Dr. Mohammed Matar Al Kaabi, Chairman of the General Authority of Islamic Affairs and Endowments; Dr. Farouk Hamada, Religious Adviser at the Court of H.H. Crown Prince of Abu Dhabi, and Afra Al-Sabiri, Undersecretary of the UAE Ministry of Culture, during the signing ceremony of the Memorandum of Understanding; between the UAE Ministry of Culture, and Mohammed V University on October 29, 2015

the divine presence of God is all that remains. It was a communication that needed no words, as I frequently used to address Him in silence, overwhelmed by his divine grandeur and mercifulness. At those moments, physical pains faded away as if they had never occurred, and I used to feel light and free while my spirit was hovering in the heavens. That feeling gave me consolation and relief.

The Triumph of the Will

I searched the meanings and implications of the Arabic equivalent to the word "Success" and found the best explanation in a dictionary called *Maqayis Al-Lughah* (Language Criteria). The root of the word refers to: Triumph, Truthfulness and Goodness. When I extended the search, in the same dictionary, about the equivalent of the word "Triumph," which was repeated in all Arabic-Arabic dictionaries as a synonym for "Success," I found the explanation discussing the root word as representing two genuine origins. The first indicates Conquer, Winning and Predominance, and the other origin refers to: Strength. I believe these meanings and synonyms, to

A composite photo showing H.H. Sheikh Tamim bin Hamad Al Thani, Emir of Qatar, and His Majesty King Muhammad VI of Morocco during my receiving some Arab awards and medals, with me holding the Shield of "Knight of Arab Studies" Award

a large extent, portray Success as a combination of Triumph, Truthfulness, Goodness, Winning, Strength and Work Ethics. The existence of meanings, such as conquering and predominance, indicates that achieving success requires defeating hardships, and overcoming obstacles. It is a precise description of the difficulty of achieving success, as it is attainable exclusively to those who possess a fighting spirit, determination and willingness to challenge hardships.

The will is an essential element. However, the will alone does not guarantee achieving success, as it needs to be accompanied by awareness, knowledge and capability to understand and use the status quo, alongside the timely amendment of the courses. It also requires blessings from God. I believe that the experience of the ECSSR constitutes a manifestation of the combination of these elements. The financial and moral support from the leadership of the UAE was one of the conditions for the success of the ECSSR. That support was provided generously by H.H. Sheikh Mohamed bin Zayed Al Nahyan (may God protect him). Moreover, the ECSSR's success needed the talent of creativity to progress. Modestly, I believe that I possess a fair share of that talent, and I focus on it when I select employees to work at the ECSSR. Moreover, I seek to promote and encourage creativity among ECSSR

With H.H. Sheikh Mansour bin Zayed Al Nahyan, Deputy Prime Minister and Minister of Presidential Affairs of the UAE; and H.E. Dr. Ali bin Tamim, Director General of Abu Dhabi Media Company and Secretary-General of Sheikh Zayed Book Award and Editor-in-Chief of the news portal 24 (www.24.ae); and a number of winners of the Sheikh Zayed Book Award, during the ceremony of receiving the award, May 1, 2016

staff. The notion of supporting decision makers, based on a scientific basis and supporting scholarly research, was a brand new idea that was not found in the Arab world. It was neglected to the extent that some people believed that scientific research is only suitable for the West. However, the ECSSR succeeded in changing this notion, through persistent and long term effort, and it truly overcame many obstacles that faced its functioning. This allows me to consider the ECSSR a model for success.

Many friends and colleagues noticed that I simply offer an extract of my experiences and the essence of my know-how for everyone who demands it. For those who ask me for advice about work, I carefully explain the obstacles they might face and the ways they can overcome those emerging problems, as well as all the tools needed to perform the job as best as possible. Some of those who witnessed my attitude tried to advise me not to do this, on the pretext that the expertise I have gained – according to their perception – is a treasure that should be kept hidden and protected safely. They supposed

During the ECSSR's celebration on the 41st UAE National Day, November 28, 2012

that my expertise had been gained through a lot of hard effort, and it was not wise to waste it on every demanding person, especially as some of them were working in the same fields as I was. Accordingly, they might become competitors in achieving success. The advice I received by those friends used to make me laugh. On many occasions, I explained to them that I work particularly to offer an example to others. I feel happy when I see some of them benefitting from what I have accomplished; especially if their effort will eventually serve the interests of the institutions of the United Arab Emirates, or any GCC or brotherly Arab country.

The variety of honors and awards I received, or received by the ECSSR, was an indicator, proof and acknowledgment of this success. When the ECSSR was chosen, or when I was selected for the Cultural Personality of the Year award, that was a big sign of success. When the books published by the ECSSR, the events organized by the Center, or the books I authored won prominent awards and received attention from intellectual, academic and research communities as well as widespread readership among Arabs and non-Arabs, that was considered proof and acknowledgment of success. When I find my pupils and students and many people who worked under my

With H.E. Saqr Ghobash, UAE Minister of Human Resources and Emiratization, during a forum titled "Future of Printed Newspapers in Multimedia Age" organized by the ECSSR, January 18, 2003

command occupying the most important positions in the UAE and abroad, raising the Emirates' flag high, and praising the experience they received at the ECSSR or other places, that is a type of success as well.

Success is the fuel that drove me to persist and continue on the road. I consider myself lucky because I witnessed the results of this success early in my life. My success at a certain stage would motivate me to continue on the road to the next stage. When I achieved the first rank among students of the Political Science Department at the University of Kuwait, in 1981, and tasted the flavor of success after strenuous effort, I found what had urged me to continue my graduate studies in the same domain, and to maintain distinction in order to restore the moment of feeling successful. I have devoted all my effort to that target while I was pursuing my master's degree and PhD studies, as my objective beyond those studies was not only to get the diploma, but also to leave a distinguished imprint on everything I do. I believe this approach is a type of success as well.

The idea of conquering or overcoming, indicated by the linguistic sense of the word (conquer/defeat), does not necessarily mean the defeated party

During a forum titled "Iraq: Reconstruction and the Future Role" organized by the ECSSR on September 14, 2003

should be a person or an enemy; rather it also indicates defeating the negative factors within the self, and reviving the elements of power inside the related person. Nobody can achieve success if he surrenders to negative factors such as reluctance, lack of resolve, giving in to comfort and laziness, or following their personal whims and inclinations. Even if the individual achieved success one time, he would not continue on the road of success. Accordingly, I see that among the things that make success real and secure is the ability of that person to achieve it, in various positions and at various stages of his life. This requires a person to channel all the power and resolve he might possess, every time he needs to perform a certain job or task. Undoubtedly, the constant readiness and alertness could be exhausting for many people; as the human soul often opts for comfort and ease. However, those who tasted the feeling of success know quite well that it deserves the effort paid for achieving it. They seek to relive the moments during which they felt that their work had achieved its objective and realized its end.

Success gives human beings the strength that they need in critical stages of their lives. I believe that granted me this type of strength to fight cancer. The feeling that you have a significant aim in life and an important

During a conference titled "Gulf Security: National Perspective I" in Abu Dhabi, April 5, 1997

role to play, and that you had really accomplished good achievements and still have the capability and the chance to achieve more in the future, helps you to resist weakness and makes defeating the disease possible. I always had the certitude, even during the most difficult moments of the disease, that my existence in this life has an objective and a meaning; therefore, I will never surrender.

Probably, the feeling of success I had could be magnified by the fact that for my entire life I possessed nothing but diligence, persistence and hard work. I was not one of those who were born with a silver spoon in their mouth, as I detailed in previous parts of this autobiography. My road was neither smooth nor paved; the doors were not open for me. On the contrary, there were some people – such as influential Muslim Brotherhood members – deliberately trying to close those doors, like when I was supposed to be employed as a teaching assistant at UAE University, or when I traveled to study in the USA. I have also faced many attempts to obstruct my success during the first few years of the inception of the ECSSR. The only defensive tool I had was to motivate the spirit of a fighter who is engaged in a decisive battle and never surrenders.

Not giving up is a key condition for success; it could almost be the utmost condition. Life never offers success on a golden platter nor grants it to those who do not strive to have it. Anyone who reads the biographies of those who achieved certain levels of success will discover that they, without any exception, faced obstacles and problems throughout various stages of their lives. Those obstacles could have broken these people if they did not have the resolve and strength to overcome challenging moments.

During a meeting at the ECSSR, January 23, 2002

In the same context, the Arabic equivalent of the word "triumph" implies "goodness." I believe that this linguistic connotation speaks to the essence of success. The connection of triumph and success with goodness is attributable

With Dr. Abdulreda Assiri, former Dean of Faculty of Social Science at the Kuwait University and a number of young people who took part in the ECSSR 21st Annual Conference titled "Youth & Development" on March 9, 2016

Delivering my speech at the ECSSR's 7th Annual Conference titled "Developing Human Resources in Knowledge Economy," February 9, 2002

to the fact that people who are used to achieving success are positive people in most cases. They tend to reconcile with themselves, and with people surrounding them; consequently they spread an atmosphere of positivity around them and vice versa. Moreover, success itself contains goodness for the successful person and those around him. The good positive effects emanating from the success of some people in public positions might extend to thousands and tens of thousands of people benefitting from those good effects. The effect of this goodness may also be sustained for many years in the future.

Strong will is one of the key factors for success. It is part of psychology research that attracted the interest of specialists and created a lot of analysis and scientific arguments. The notion of strong will focuses on the tendency stemming from the person himself to achieve certain objectives. This tendency necessarily contradicts some other personal inclinations or desires. The inclination toward comfort and ease is an effective power on the other side of the human psyche. This power lures human beings to forfeit their desired goals because their achievement requires enduring various

With a group of primary students from the Emirates National Schools during their visit to the ECSSR, with the aim to deliver their donations to RAHMA (Cancer Patient Care Society) on December 13, 2016

hardships. In the absence of strong will, the tendency toward comfort would have been fulfilled and obeyed. Here we notice the importance of some elements related to strong will, such as determination, resolve and persistence to achieve the goal. These elements depend on certain capabilities; some of them are inherent and the human being cannot control them. Other elements – and these are the most important in my view – can be acquired, developed and grown. The inherent/subconscious part is the one that moves you automatically in a way that precedes thinking. Then, the conscious part puts mechanisms and procedures designed to achieve the goals. Your motivation will be based on the fact that the feeling of triumph – which completely depends on achieving the goal – realizes a level of psychological satisfaction much higher than the returns of comfort and laziness.

Strong will depends on high levels of enduring pressures, which obstruct realizing the desired goals. In many situations, failure could seem closer than success, and that feeling is connected with tensions and psychological burdens. In such situations, strong will plays its significant role to overcome frustration, which could be fatal if it found a gap inside your psyche. Strong will also helps you in choosing the right path and making the right decisions amid the moments of confusion and multiple options, as such moments are numerous. Strong will keeps the clarity and sharpness of the mind, helps it to avoid con-

During a symposium titled "The Future Relations Between the GCC and the EU" organized by the ECSSR on May 21, 2002

fusion. Strong will also supports another important merit—realism, which protects the mind against the dominance of illusion. Realism helps the mind to choose the temporary goals and then amend them according to the real developments and changes, without curtailing its ambition to achieve the best and the maximum gains available.

Self-Competition

Success for me is linked to self-competition. This does not mean to underestimate competitors or to assume their nonexistence or weakness, as this expression might be misunderstood. What I believe is meant by self-competition is a completely different issue. The notion of self-competition is based on insistence to accomplish everything you do in a better way than you did before. It is a very important indicator of sustainability of success, which I talked about previously.

I have always tried hard to ensure that every activity I perform, or take part in, is better than the previous one. For instance, the ECSSR has or-

A composite photo of some international award which I have received

ganized about 800 events including conferences, symposia and lectures during 23 years, and my objective has always been to ensure that every event is better than the previous one. I also ensured that the success of a conference, a seminar, a lecture or a workshop is not the

With H.E. Dr. Ali bin Tamim, Director General of Abu Dhabi Media Company and Secretary-General of Sheikh Zayed Book Award and Editor-in-Chief of the news portal 24 (www.24.ae), on the sidelines of a lecture titled "Moral Education as the Basis for Building Nations" H.E. delivered at the ECSSR on December 21, 2016

end of the road, or a reason to stop searching for and boosting the tools of success. The standard of success, in my view, is to make every conference, seminar and lecture better than the previous one, through avoiding short-comings, and enhancing the positive practices along with adding new things to them. Accordingly, self-competition means pledging every day to be better than the previous day, and to constantly perform tasks in a better way.

Through continuous relentless work-cycles, some deficiency or fail-ure might occur; this is part of human nature. Successful people are able to transform these deficiencies into a source of power, and they supply success with the needed fuel. The first inevitable condition to do that is the courage to confess deficiency and to admit the occurrence of defect besides avoiding self-deception and inventing excuses. The next condition is the realistic and precise assessment of the reasons behind this failure, and to

With H.E. Hussain Ibrahim Al-Hammadi, UAE Minister of Education, during a lecture titled "Moral Education as the Basis for Building Nations" delivered at the ECSSR by H.E. Dr. Ali bin Tamim, Director General of Abu Dhabi Media Company and Secretary-General of Sheikh Zayed Book Award and Editor-in-Chief of the news portal 24 (www.24.ae), December 21, 2016

work diligently to avoid them in all upcoming tasks. Accordingly, even the casual cases of failure could be part of the success system, if they are used properly, and if the relevant party benefited from their learned lessons.

Self-competition does not mean to neglect the success of others, refuse to learn from them, ignore the internationally recognized standards for success, or set simple, modest targets and convince yourself that you have achieved them. Self-competition starts after you have reached an equal level to those working in the same field, or surpassed them, and put an imprint referring to you and embedded to your name. Success basically means to set big ambitious targets, and to work toward attaining them. After that, you can start the stage of self-competition, which will transform your thinking and perceptions entirely.

Instilling Success

Frequently, I receive questions about the advice I offer to the younger generation in the UAE and the Arab world. Success can be summarized in one phrase, "the triumph of the will." I believe that the secret of success primarily dwells in the following process: the human being puts his foot on the right path; works to possess the required tools in terms of knowledge and persistence; then saves no effort to achieve self-development. After that, he should be patient and tolerant and never be in a hurry to reach results. It is like a seed sown which you must take care of, irrigate, protect from pests, supply with fertilizers and nutrients and be patient with until you harvest its first fruit. The same steps should be followed if you want to reap the fruits of success. You should not expect success to come easily and quickly. Accelerating the growth of success before providing its nutrients and tools will hinder it. Therefore, patience is an indispensable attribute for those who want to be successful.

Based on my experience, persistent hard work is the most important pillar for success. For years, I have kept doing my best to possess the tools that help me to realize my objectives. The process has been ongoing since I started studying political science at the University of Kuwait in 1977. I suffered financial hardship and pressures related to pursuing knowledge and graduate studies in the United States of America for eight years. Those tough years were followed by years of lecturing at UAE University, which were not free of difficulties. Had I conceded to despair or surrendered then, or had I tried to find an excuse by saying to myself that I am making an effort without reaping any results, I would not have achieved many of my objectives, which I feel proud of achieving now.

Patience and relentless work are the basis of success. However, success does not necessarily mean that you will find yourself famous, rich or receiving large monetary rewards. Rather, it means that you have attained significant achievements in your specialization, no matter what the nature of your profession is. Based on this notion, you could be a successful teacher, engineer or policeman. No matter the profession and the job, you could offer something to yourself, your family and your society, through improving your performance to the highest standard possible and doing your best to be better than others. You should follow everything new in your domain and you should develop the talents of creativity and innovation inside yourself. Eventually, you will receive appreciation in various ways; from society, your colleagues, your students and from all the people you deal with around you.

Arrogance is a brutal scourge that kills success and hurries its ending, even if it had been achieved in some previous stage. Modesty is one of the most-needed elements to achieve success and to guarantee its sustainability. Modesty always makes you realize that what you have achieved is still missing something, and that is the nature of any work by a human being. Modesty spreads a positive atmosphere in your personal and professional surroundings, which allows you to continue on the road of success. Meanwhile, inflating one's ego leads successful people to laziness, inactivity and sufficing with the fake self-admiration. Then, their personal and professional crises will multiply, and this consumes their energy uselessly. Arrogance prevents a person from seeing his true self. An arrogant man sees absolute perfection in his actions. Then gradually, his capability will be depleted and he becomes incapable of developing himself and his work. Usually, such people eventually resort to a feeling of being oppressed and start seeking fake and feeble excuses to justify their degradations and failures.

The revival and development that are achieved by any society are carried on the shoulders of successful people. Nations' progress can be accredited to the persistence of some successful people, the fruits of their toil and their pursuit toward the best. Therefore, the government should provide the means of success, or what I call the "success infrastructure" or the "fertile soil" to transplant success. Successful nations are the ones that discover the potentials for success in their children at an early stage. Then, the government should develop and nurture those potentials, in order to secure success for both the individual and the society. This formula is a win-win situation for both parties. Success should not be left to luck and chance as it has become an industry with its own standards and rules.

Good education is another pillar of success, according to my principles. It requires from the Arabian Gulf countries and other Arab countries greater, deeper and more wide-ranging effort to establish a sophisticated education system, which adopts the values of creativity, innovation and sincerity. These values should be nurtured in the students to enable them to reach their maximum potential and capabilities. Although education has progressed in GCC countries, it is still much lower than our ambitions. It is worth-mentioning here that the initiative launched by His Highness Sheikh Mohamed bin Zayed Al Nahyan, Crown Prince of Abu Dhabi, Deputy Supreme Commander of the UAE Armed Forces (may God protect him) to support the education process in the UAE by adding a subject called "Moral Education" into school syllabuses, aims to fight the ideas of radicalism, extremism, fanaticism, discrimination and hatred of others. These ideologies should be eradicated from the minds of children and youth. The new subject is expected to nurture in these young students the spirit of initiative, the willingness for competition, understanding of their surroundings, recognizing the limits of their rights and duties, and their responsibility toward themselves, their societies and their countries. Such an initiative is not strange in the UAE and its wise leadership that seeks to achieve a pioneering position in various fields.

Based on my personal experience, I feel terribly sorry when I find that graduates from foreign universities, who had obtained their scientific degrees from Western countries, are more capable of success and achievement, compared to graduates who studied at universities inside the UAE or other Arab countries. Unfortunately, postgraduate degrees have become widely available, as people can get those upon paying money to the universities that sell such degrees. This situation made us suspect the credibility of scientific degrees and view them with a lot of doubt. Even the branches of foreign universities existing in the UAE, no matter how famous and attractive their names are, do not provide the expected level of academic services. Their educational services are not much better than the services of the local universities. Consequently, my interest was focused

My meeting with the Grand Imam of Al-Azhar, Dr. Ahmed al-Tayyeb at the premises of Al-Azhar in Cairo on June 12, 2014, and my meeting with His Holiness Pope Francis of the Vatican at the papal headquarters on April 12, 2017, achieve the idea of tolerance and inter-faith dialogue between civilizations in which I believe and which reflects acceptance of the other without any racial, political or religious prejudices

on the scholarship offered by His Highness the President of the UAE to the distinguished students, and I take pride in my experience in managing the details of these scholarships from the beginning. I consider this scholarship one of the most important projects witnessed by the UAE in terms of developing human resources.

Promoting the Culture of Tolerance

I am quite sure that my home country, the United Arab Emirates, is one of the most tolerant countries in the world. Based on this deeply rooted conviction, I was, still am and will always remain, carefully keen in all my works, interviews, visits and meetings, to be compliant with the UAE's open-minded tolerant policy. I will always work hard to support the efforts of the wise leadership toward enhancing the status of the country as a beacon for tolerance for the entire world, which enjoys the prevailing spirit of love, harmony and peace, and rejects violence and hatred. The UAE diligently seeks to nurture the values of tolerance, cooperation, coexistence, conformity, collaboration, dialogue, centrism and moderation among people. The UAE advocates the acceptance of others, the freedom of practicing religious rituals, and fighting extremism and bigotry. These genuine values are deeply rooted in the heritage, habits and traditions of the UAE society, and derived from the true Islam.

In this context, I held many meetings in which I directed my effort to reassure the belief of the UAE leadership and people in these great humane values, and the openness of our local culture and willingness to accept the others, and coexistence among various cultures, races and identities. Among these meetings was the meeting with Dr. Ahmad al-Tayyeb, the Grand Sheikh of Al-Azhar, at the premises of Al-Azhar sheikhdom, in Cairo. Another meeting was with the His Holiness Pope Francis of the Vatican, at the papal headquarters in the Vatican. During these two meetings, I highlighted the immense persistent effort made by the UAE to enhance the value of tolerance and consolidate it within the country and beyond. I focused on the preeminence of the UAE in terms of its tolerant social and cultural atmosphere, which can be considered an ideal to be imitated, in the midst of horrible proliferation of the discourse of hatred and discrimination in the world.

During my visit to His Holiness Pope Francis of the Vatican, I remember that after I presented His Holiness with a copy of my book *The Mirage,* he took off his *zucchetto* (skull cap) and gave it to me.

The Future Is My Main Concern

I think successful people are characterized by possessing a forward-looking perspective, rather than sticking to the past. That does not mean forgetting the past, which we need to learn from and understand its lessons and experiences. However, we should not cling to it and allow it to control our minds and ideas. The future is always in front of my eyes. I look at it with optimism and hope. I get ready to meet whatever could happen in the future, based on understanding and awareness; therefore, futuristic studies occupy a major share of my interest and research. During the celebrations organized by the

ECSSR on the occasion of the 20th Anniversary of its inception, the theme selected was "Foreseeing the Future is our Task."

As I said before, I have planned projects to write many books, among them a book about Change. Change is naturally connected to the future. Understanding the nature of changes and their trends is an inevitable tool to plan for the future. Rapid change in all fields is the common characteristic of the world in the present time. I also intend to publish a book about the most important events that left significant impacts and contributed to create major changes in the world, whether political, economic or social ones; even though the political aspect will be dominant due to my specialization. This expected book originally consisted of a number of articles published in the UAE's *Al-Ittihad* newspaper.

Every day, I have a busy schedule, and I believe that my work serves my country and the Arab world. Currently, for example, I am busy with the issue of the ministries of information, which were canceled in the UAE and some other Arab countries over the last few years. I am not reluctant to say that disbanding ministries of information is a mistake. This decision was taken as a response to superficial insignificant issues, without taking into consideration the status quo in the UAE and other Arab countries. Particularly in the current period, media organizations in the Arab world need a controlling authority to supervise and organize their trends that should be far from oppression and compulsion. Rather, it should be in the form of correcting the directions and monitoring deviations, which impose increasing risks in the current period. These media organizations can be used as weapons to tear countries and nations apart and to spread hatred and divisions. The opportunistic conspirators seek to use media tools as some of the most important weapons in the fourth generation of wars (4GW).

The importance of the ministries of information is increasing with the need to establish a major and specialized agency having the experience and authority to face the challenges related to new media. It should take into consideration the increasing effect of social media tools and what they create in terms of new challenges on a daily basis. The ministries of information are capable agencies, on the managerial, research, technical and organizational levels, to mobilize effort in order to contain the problems emerging from these new developments. They have the capability to devise the required strategies and plans to confront the related challenges. Therefore, I call strongly to reactivate the ministries of information, and to make the Minister of Information or the Minister of State for Information Affairs an official spokesperson for the government. That will enable us to avoid a lot of problems and cases of misunderstanding, which could emerge from the multiplicity of agencies speaking in the name of the government.

A Series of Firsts in My Life

- The first person who taught me the real meaning of love was my mother (may God rest her soul in peace). That simple woman knew how to love. When I was a little child, I used to tell her I felt that I had come out of the far sea. She used to smile and hug me, saying "the most important thing is that you came." At that time, I did not recognize that her tender hands are my boat, and she is that far and very close sea. I did not know that she is my unmatched pearl. After her death, I became unwilling to recall things, because I remember that I did not know she was my shore of safety, and I realize I will never be able to return to that shore. I swallowed the bitterness of the loss of my mother in a way that no other human being did. That is what I felt upon her death, and I still feel that way. I did not know that her absence would be severely painful. The taste of joy changed after her passing. The colors of flowers faded in my eyes. With her demise, I lost a piece of my soul, and that piece will never return.

- The first person who offered me support and funding at the work level, and at the personal level, was His Highness Sheikh Mohamed bin Zayed Al Nahyan, the Crown Prince of Abu Dhabi, and the Deputy Supreme Commander of the UAE Armed Forces (may God protect him).

- The first meeting with His Highness Sheikh Mohamed bin Zayed Al Nahyan, the Crown Prince of Abu Dhabi, and the Deputy Supreme Commander of the UAE Armed Forces (may God protect him) was in late 1990, or early 1991.

- The first person who paved for me the road to success, excellence and distinction was my sister Aisha.

- The first person who gave me a new source of hope and vigor was my wife.

- The first event when I experienced the meaning of true happiness, rarely created by any other event, was the birth of my first child, Khaled.

- The first thing I did after the Almighty God granted me recovery from cancer was rush to work and achievement. I became more aware of the importance of time. I started to feel how important it is to use every second in life. I realized that an individual can accomplish a lot within a short time. This feeling gave me a new positive energy that mobilized within me multiple times more enthusiasm than that I had before sickness. I have used this positive energy in writing, research, studies, interviews, conferences, seminars and lectures. My schedule became much more hectic than ever before.

- The first time I smoked a cigarette was at the beginning of my secondary school, or a little bit earlier.

- The first release of the constraint to which I subjugated myself for more than 40 years was giving up smoking, on November 15, 2011.

- The first person to whom I told my decision to study political science, and with whom I discussed the issue, was my sister Aisha.

- The first of my close friends was my cousin Tariq, the son of my maternal uncle Ali.

- The first person who taught me how sacrifice could be practiced was my late brother Abdullah (may God rest his soul in peace).

- The first result of my genuine belief in science and knowledge was represented in obtaining my PhD degree in 1990.

- The first people who I think would be proud of me someday are my grandchildren and the next generation of my home country, the UAE. They will realize that I tried – and I will keep trying until the last day of my life – to offer my home country and my countrymen what can benefit and teach them and illuminate their path in the future.

- The first person who influenced me on a personal level during my undergraduate education was Dr. Faisal Al-Salim, former professor of political science at Kuwait University.

- The first TV set we possessed was a gift from my late maternal uncle Ali; it was a black-and-white Philips TV.

- The first sport that I liked and practiced passionately was football.

- The first trip abroad in my life was a tourism trip to Iran in 1977, and my sister Aisha paid all the expenses.

- The first magazine of which I was Editor-in-Chief was *The Diplomat*, issued by the UAE Ministry of Foreign Affairs, in 1982.

- The first political battle in which I engaged started during my undergraduate study at the University of Kuwait. It was the battle of confronting the ideologies of extremist religious political movements, which are still active until now.

- The first tornado I saw was in Wisconsin, USA, in 1984.

- The first time I traveled to the United Kingdom was during my undergraduate study, in 1978.

- The first visit to the United States of America was on August 12, 1982.

- The first step in my professional career was being appointed as a lecturer at the Department of Political Science at UAE University in 1990.

- The first attempt I had at writing was at the elementary stage (grades 8/9).

- The first time I managed a research institution was with the establishment of the ECSSR of which I have been Director General since 1994.

- The first board of directors I chaired was the Board of Directors for the Scholarship of His Highness the President of the UAE, part of the Ministry of Presidential Affairs, since 1999, under the supervision of H.H. Sheikh Mansour bin Zayed Al Nahyan, Deputy Prime Minister and Minister of Presidential Affairs.

- The first opinion page I improved was in *Al-Ittihad* newspaper, in 2001, assigned and supported by H.H. Sheikh Abdullah bin Zayed Al Nahyan, Minister of Foreign Affairs and International Cooperation (Minister of Information and Culture at that time).

- The first experience I had in establishing a school was with the Emirates National School, which opened in 2002, with support from H.H. Sheikh Mansour bin Zayed Al Nahyan, Deputy Prime Minister and Minister of Presidential Affairs.

Conclusion

When I contemplate my career, I feel overwhelmed by satisfaction with what I have achieved so far. I also feel that the blessings of the Almighty God have supported me most of the time, helping me to overcome many hard stages in my life, which were plentiful. I also thank and praise God for His mercifulness and kindness toward me, during my fight with cancer, which taught me the most crucial lesson in my life. Throughout this stage, I started to view life from a completely different perspective.

I am also satisfied that I have accomplished many of my objectives and I have been honored on many occasions. Winning the Sheikh Zayed Book Award in 2016 was a source of happiness and pride for me, considering its significance and academic position, and taking into account the high quality of books that won the prize in previous rounds.

Many of my colleagues and friends, from inside and outside the UAE, expected that *The Mirage* would win the award upon entering the long list of candidates. They submitted valid convincing reasons for that prediction, to the extent that some of them congratulated me in advance. Nonetheless, when they informed me that I had won the award, that moment was exceptional and unprecedented in my life. My heart was filled with appreciation and gratitude to the Almighty God, as my diligent effort over a long period of time, alongside health issues while writing *The Mirage,* were rewarded by honoring me with this prize, which carries the name of the late Sheikh Zayed bin Sultan Al Nahyan (may God rest his soul in peace). That is the ultimate honor and pride for me.

The Mirage has achieved wide proliferation since its publication. However, I believe that winning the Sheikh Zayed Book Award secured the book a great place with a wide range of readers, as they were attracted to the book due to its winning the reputed prize. Thus, they pursued reading the book and its reviews. Undoubtedly, the wide reach of the message and themes of the book to the largest number of readers is the source of my happiness. Regardless of the desire to have a broad base of readership, I want the ideas of this book to reach its Arab readers at this current moment, while the risks of extremism abound, alongside the risks of radicals trading and masquerading in religion with the aim to achieve political gains and power.

If there was one thing I would like and I wish to achieve, it would be winning one of the grand international awards. That would exceed in its moral value and weight of the honorary PhD, which I have received from more than one European university. Nonetheless, I take pride in every form of honor and appreciation I have received, and I am grateful to every one of the institutions that granted me awards in

It was an honor to receive the Sheikh Zayed Book Award

any of the various fields to which I contributed. Although I know that the nature of the international awards of this size tends to be subject to the choice of non-Arabs or non-Muslims, I never lose hope that it will happen someday. I will not surrender. My desire

My grandchildren Yasmeena and Rashid in 2012

to win such prizes is connected in my mind with the fact that it would be a Western acknowledgement of an Arab Muslim researcher. Winning such a prize would also be a boost for the Arab and Islamic cultures to which I belong, and it would be an enhancement of my identity, which I take pride in.

First and foremost, there is a sense of satisfaction when I look at my family and see that the Almighty God had blessed me with many graces. Despite all the responsibilities that kept me busy and away from them, and despite the pain I suffered during the period of cancer, my children have reached places I hoped and wished for them. After the blessing of God, their success is due to the effort of my gracious wife who has constantly sought to make our children ready to take responsibility. All of them had inherited from my wife and me the love of knowledge, independence and the desire for excellence and achievement.

The happiest and most beautiful moments are those when you see your children following in your footsteps. Each one of them is doing that in their own way, and leaving a special impression emanating from the merits that distinguish every one of them. The happiest moments are those when you see your grandchildren overwhelming your world with love, purity and light through their laughter, which is the most beautiful thing the universe gives

you as a gift. With these grandchildren, the loving memory recalls past days when their fathers and mothers were the same age. Thus, the joy of past days would be renewed and relived, and it would restore to my heart the brightness and glamour of those days, which the long years cannot erase.

If there would be one piece of advice to conclude these chapters of my autobiography with, it would be: no matter how tough the hardships and difficulties are, follow your dream and seek to achieve your goals with all the energy and capability you have. Equip yourself with the weapons of hope, optimism and confidence because life without these will lose its most beautiful essence. So I conclude the chapters of this autobiography with the same phrase that I chose to be its title and urge all readers to believe in *The Triumph of the Will*.

Appendix (1)

Photos with Leaders and Dignitaries

With H.H. Sheikh Khalifa bin Zayed Al Nahyan, the President of the UAE (may God protect him), handing me The UAE Appreciation Award for Science, Arts and Literature in its 3rd round Humanities category – political science, December 2, 2008

With H.H. Sheikh Khalifa bin Zayed Al Nahyan, the President (may God protect him), handing me The UAE President Appreciation Award, December 2, 2013

With H.H. Sheikh Mohammed bin Rashid Al Maktoum, UAE Vice President and Deputy Prime Minister, Ruler of Dubai (may God protect him), at the International Defence Exhibition (IDEX), March 19, 1995

With H.H. Sheikh Mohammed bin Rashid Al Maktoum, UAE Vice President and Deputy Prime Minister, Ruler of Dubai (may God protect him), at the International Defence Exhibition (IDEX), 19 March 1995

With H.H. Sheikh Mohammed bin Rashid Al Maktoum, UAE Vice President and Deputy Prime Minister, Ruler of Dubai (may God protect him), at the International Defence Exhibition (IDEX), 19 March 1995

With H.H. Sheikh Mohammed bin Rashid Al Maktoum, UAE Vice President and Deputy Prime Minister, Ruler of Dubai (may God protect him), and H.E. Juma'a Al-Majid, Chairman of Dubai Economic Council; and H.E. the late Lt. General Khmais Mattar Al-Mazina, former General Commander of Dubai Police, during my visit to His Highness, to present him with a copy of my book *The Mirage*, March 10, 2015

With H.H. Sheikh Mohammed bin Rashid Al Maktoum, UAE Vice President and Prime Minister, Ruler of Dubai (may God protect him), presenting him with a copy of my book *The Mirage*, March 10, 2015

With H.H. Sheikh Mohammed bin Rashid Al Maktoum, UAE Vice President and Prime Minister, Ruler of Dubai (may God protect him), presenting him with a copy of my book *The Mirage*, March 10, 2015

With H.H. Sheikh Mohammed bin Rashid Al Maktoum, UAE Vice President and Prime Minister, Ruler of Dubai (may God protect him), honoring me with the Arab Pioneers Award 2015, March 17, 2015

With H.H. Sheikh Mohammed bin Rashid Al Maktoum, UAE Vice President and Prime Minister, Ruler of Dubai (may God protect him), honoring me with the UAE Pioneers Award 2016, November 28, 2016

With H.H. Sheikh Mohammed bin Rashid Al Maktoum, UAE Vice President and Prime Minister, Ruler of Dubai (may God protect him), honoring me with the UAE Pioneers Award 2016, November 28, 2016

With H.H. Sheikh Mohammed bin Rashid Al Maktoum, UAE Vice President and Prime Minister, Ruler of Dubai (may God protect him), honoring me with the UAE Pioneers Award 2016, November 28, 2016

With H.H. Sheikh Mohammed bin Rashid Al Maktoum, UAE Vice President and Prime Minister, Ruler of Dubai (may God protect him); H.H. Sheikh Hamdan bin Mohammed bin Rashid Al Maktoum, Crown Prince of Dubai; H.H. Lt. General Sheikh Saif bin Zayed Al Nahyan, UAE Deputy Prime Minister and Minister of Interior; Her Excellency Dr. Amal Al-Qubaisi, Speaker of the UAE Federal National Council; and H.E. Zaki Nasibah, Cultural Adviser at Ministry of Presidential Affairs, at "Al-Ittihad Museum," Al-Ittihad publishing house, January 8, 2017

With H.H. Sheikh Mohamed bin Zayed Al Nahyan, Crown Prince of Abu Dhabi, and Deputy Supreme Commander of the UAE Armed Forces (may God protect him), at the First Edition of the International Defence Exhibition (IDEX), February 14, 1993

With H.H. Sheikh Mohamed bin Zayed Al Nahyan, Crown Prince of Abu Dhabi and Deputy Supreme Commander of the UAE Armed Forces (may God protect him), during His Highness visit to ECSSR, April 6, 1994

With H.H. Sheikh Mohamed bin Zayed Al Nahyan, Crown Prince of Abu Dhabi and Deputy Supreme Commander of the UAE Armed Forces (may God protect him), during His Highness visit to ECSSR, April 6, 1994

With H.H. Sheikh Mohamed bin Zayed Al Nahyan, Crown Prince of Abu Dhabi and Deputy Supreme Commander of the UAE Armed Forces (may God protect him), and the late Baroness Margaret Thatcher, former UK Prime Minister, June 20, 1994

With H.H. Sheikh Mohamed bin Zayed Al Nahyan, Crown Prince of Abu Dhabi and Deputy Supreme Commander of the UAE Armed Forces (may God protect him); H.E. Mohammed Al-Bawardi, UAE State Minister for Defense Affairs; Retired Lt. General Saeed Khalaf Al-Rumaithi; and Navy Retired Major General Suhail Shaheen Al-Murr, in Holland, during a discussion session, September 13, 1994

Presenting a gift to H.H. Sheikh Mohamed bin Zayed Al Nahyan, Crown Prince of Abu Dhabi and Deputy Supreme Commander of the UAE Armed Forces (may God protect him); during the first annual commemoration of the ECSSR, June 20, 1995

With H.H. Sheikh Mohamed bin Zayed Al Nahyan, Crown Prince of Abu Dhabi and Deputy Supreme Commander of the UAE Armed Forces (may God protect him); and the late King Hassan II of Morocco, July 1, 1995

With H.H. Sheikh Mohamed bin Zayed Al Nahyan, Crown Prince of Abu Dhabi and Deputy Supreme Commander of the UAE Armed Forces (may God protect him); and His Majesty King Mohammed VI of Morocco, and a number of UAE and Moroccan Armed Forces officers, during a visit to Morocco on July 1, 1995

With H.H. Sheikh Mohamed bin Zayed Al Nahyan, Crown Prince of Abu Dhabi and Deputy Supreme Commander of the UAE Armed Forces (may God protect him); and Dick Cheney, former US Vice President, during a visit to ECSSR, March 19, 1996

With H.H. Sheikh Mohamed bin Zayed Al Nahyan, Crown Prince of Abu Dhabi and Deputy Supreme Commander of the UAE Armed Forces (may God protect him); and His Royal Highness Prince Khalid bin Sultan bin Abdul-Aziz Al Saud, former Deputy Minister of Defense, Saudi Arabia; during a conference titled "Gulf Security: A National Perspective I," in Abu Dhabi, April 5, 1997

With H.H. Sheikh Mohamed bin Zayed Al Nahyan, Crown Prince of Abu Dhabi and Deputy Supreme Commander of the UAE Armed Forces (may God protect him); and His Royal Highness Prince Khalid bin Sultan bin Abdul-Aziz Al Saud, former Deputy Minister of Defense, Saudi Arabia; during a conference titled "Gulf Security: A National Perspective I," in Abu Dhabi, April 5, 1997

With H.H. Sheikh Mohamed bin Zayed Al Nahyan, Crown Prince of Abu Dhabi and Deputy Supreme Commander of the UAE Armed Forces (may God protect him); and His Royal Highness Prince Khalid bin Sultan bin Abdul-Aziz Al Saud, former Deputy Minister of Defense, KSA; during a conference titled "Gulf Security: A National Perspective I," in Abu Dhabi, April 5, 1997

With H.H. Sheikh Mohamed bin Zayed Al Nahyan, Crown Prince of Abu Dhabi and Deputy Supreme Commander of the UAE Armed Forces (may God protect him); during a visit to the ECSSR, July 6, 1997

With H.H. Sheikh Mohamed bin Zayed Al Nahyan, Crown Prince of Abu Dhabi and Deputy Supreme Commander of the UAE Armed Forces (may God protect him); and the late Dr. A'atif Obaid, former Prime Minister of Egypt, during a visit to ECSSR, November 2, 1997

With H.H. Sheikh Mohamed bin Zayed Al Nahyan, Crown Prince of Abu Dhabi and Deputy Supreme Commander of the UAE Armed Forces (may God protect him); and the late Dr. A'atif Obaid, former Prime Minister of Egypt; and former Egyptian Ambassador to the UAE, during a visit to ECSSR, November 2, 1997

With H.H. Sheikh Mohamed bin Zayed Al Nahyan, Crown Prince of Abu Dhabi and Deputy Supreme Commander of the UAE Armed Forces (may God protect him); and H.H. Sheikh Diab bin Zayed Al Nahyan, during the celebration on the 4th Anniversary of Launching ECSSR, March 15, 1998

With H.H. Sheikh Mohamed bin Zayed Al Nahyan, Crown Prince of Abu Dhabi and Deputy Supreme Commander of the UAE Armed Forces (may God protect him); H.E. Issa Saleh Al-Qurk, former UAE Ambassador to the UK; the retired Major General Suhail Shain Al-Murr; and the retired Major General Pilot Khalid al-Buainin, from the UAE, in the UK, April 29, 1998

With H.H. Sheikh Mohamed bin Zayed Al Nahyan, Crown Prince of Abu Dhabi and Deputy Supreme Commander of the UAE Armed Forces (may God protect him); and Prince Charles, Prince of Wales, UK Crown Prince, on the sidelines of a conference titled "Gulf Security: A National Perspective II," in UK, April 29, 1998

With H.H. Sheikh Mohamed bin Zayed Al Nahyan, Crown Prince of Abu Dhabi and Deputy Supreme Commander of the UAE Armed Forces (may God protect him); during a conference titled "Gulf Security: A National Perspective II," in UK, April 29, 1998

With H.H. Sheikh Mohamed bin Zayed Al Nahyan, Crown Prince of Abu Dhabi and Deputy Supreme Commander of the UAE Armed Forces (may God protect him); during a conference titled "Gulf Security: A National Perspective II," in UK, April 29, 1998

With H.H. Sheikh Mohamed bin Zayed Al Nahyan, Crown Prince of Abu Dhabi and Deputy Supreme Commander of the UAE Armed Forces (may God protect him); and Afghanistan Former President Hamid Karzai, during ECSSR's 7th Annual Conference, titled Human Resources Development in A Knowledge-based Economy, February 9, 2002

With H.H. Sheikh Mohamed bin Zayed Al Nahyan, Crown Prince of Abu Dhabi and Deputy Supreme Commander of the UAE Armed Forces (may God protect him); and Mrs. Michele Alliot-Marie, Head of the Commission for Relations with Arabian Peninsula (former French Minister of Defense at the time), December 17, 2002

With H.H. Sheikh Mohamed bin Zayed Al Nahyan, Crown Prince of Abu Dhabi and Deputy Supreme Commander of the UAE Armed Forces (may God protect him); and Mrs. Michele Alliot-Marie, Head of the Commission for Relations with Arabian Peninsula (French Minister of Defense at the time), after honoring me with the French National Order of Merit with Commandor Rank, December 17, 2002

With H.H. Sheikh Mohamed bin Zayed Al Nahyan, Crown Prince of Abu Dhabi and Deputy Supreme Commander of the UAE Armed Forces (may God protect him); honoring me with "Abu Dhabi Award 2011," January 24, 2012

With H.H. Sheikh Mohamed bin Zayed Al Nahyan, Crown Prince of Abu Dhabi and Deputy Supreme Commander of the UAE Armed Forces (may God protect him); while H.H. received a delegation from the ECSSR and a delegation from Cancer Patient Care Society (RAHMA), May 9, 2017

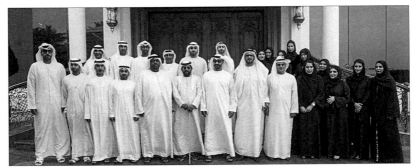

With H.H. Sheikh Mohamed bin Zayed Al Nahyan, Crown Prince of Abu Dhabi and Deputy Supreme Commander of the UAE Armed Forces (may God protect him); and H.H. Sheikh Tahnoon bin Mohammed Al Nahyan, Representative of the Ruler in Al-Ain region, amid a delegation from the ECSSR and a delegation from Cancer Patient Care Society (RAHMA), May 9, 2017

With H.H. Sheikh Mohamed bin Zayed Al Nahyan, Crown Prince of Abu Dhabi and Deputy Supreme Commander of the UAE Armed Forces (may God protect him); H.H. Sheikh Tahnoon bin Mohammed Al Nahyan, Representative of the Ruler in Al-Ain Region; and Ms. Nora Al-Suwaidi, Director General of Cancer Patient Care Society (RAHMA) carrying a t-shirt with the emblem of RAHMA signed by H.H. Sheikh Mohamed bin Zayed Al Nahyan, while H.H. received a delegation from RAHMA, May 9, 2017

With H.H. Sheikh Dr. Sultan bin Mohammed Al-Qassimi, Member of the Supreme Council of UAE Federation, Ruler of Sharjah, honoring the refereed periodical *Strategic Visions*, published by ECSSR, at Sharjah International Book Fair, November 6, 2013

With H.H. Sheikh Humaid bin Rashid Al-Nuaimi, Member of the Supreme Council of UAE Federation, Ruler of Ajman, during my visit to His Highness, March 12, 2015

With H.H. Sheikh Humaid bin Rashid Al-Nuaimi, Member of the Supreme Council of UAE Federation, Ruler of Ajman, presenting His Highness with a copy of my book *The Mirage*, March 12, 2015

With H.H. Sheikh Hamad bin Muhammed Al-Sharqi, Member of the Supreme Council of UAE Federation, Ruler of Fujairah, presenting His Highness with a copy of my book *The Mirage*, March 8, 2015

With H.H. Sheikh Saud bin Rashid Al-Mu'alla, Member of the Supreme Council of UAE Federation, Ruler of Um Al-Quawain, during my visit to His Highness at his palace, March 16, 2015

With H.H. Sheikh Saud bin Rashid Al-Mu'alla, Member of the Supreme Council of UAE Federation, Ruler of Um Al-Quawain, presenting His Highness with a copy of my book *The Mirage*, March 16, 2015

With H.H. Sheikh Saud bin Saqr Al-Qassimi, Member of the Supreme Council of UAE Federation, Ruler of Ras Al Khaimah, during a visit by His Highness to ECSSR, April 11, 2001

Presenting a gift to H.H. Sheikh Saud bin Saqr Al-Qassimi, Member of the Supreme Council of UAE Federation, Ruler of Ras Al Khaimah, during a visit by His Highness to ECSSR, April 11, 2001

With H.H. Sheikh Saud bin Saqr Al-Qassimi, Member of the Supreme Council of UAE Federation, Ruler of Ras Al Khaimah, during my visit to His Highness at his palace, March 18, 2013

With H.H. Sheikh Saud bin Saqr Al-Qassimi, Member of the Supreme Council of UAE Federation, Ruler of Ras Al Khaimah, presenting His Highness with a copy of my book *The Mirage*, on March 4, 2015

With H.H. Sheikh Saud bin Saqr Al-Qassimi, Member of the Supreme Council of UAE Federation, Ruler of Ras Al Khaimah, during my visit to His Highness at his palace, March 4, 2015

With H.H. Sheikh Hamdan bin Mohammed bin Rashid Al Maktoum, Crown Prince of Dubai; and H.E. Abdulrahman bin Hamad Al-Attiyah, former Secretary-General of GCC, during ECSSR's 13th Annual Conference titled "Arabian Gulf Between Conservatism and Change," March 31, 2008

With H.H. Sheikh Hamdan bin Zayed Al Nahyan, Ruler's Representative in the Al Dhafra Region (formerly Western Region), during my visit to His Highness, January 6, 2016

With H.H. Sheikh Hamdan bin Zayed Al Nahyan, Ruler's Representative in the Al Dhafra Region (formerly Western Region), while presenting H.H. with a copy of my book *The Mirage*, January 6, 2016

With H.H. Sheikh Suroor bin Mohammed Al Nahyan, UAE, during a Ceremony to honor ECSSR as one of the most prominent strategic partners of Abu Dhabi Police General Command, December 25, 2007

Presenting a copy of my book *The Mirage* to H.H. Sheikh Suroor bin Mohammed Al Nahyan, UAE, during H.H. visit to ECSSR, November 10, 2015

With H.H. Sheikh Hazaa bin Zayed Al Nahyan, former UAE National Security Adviser; and H.E. Mohammed Al-Murr, Former Speaker of the UAE Federal National Council, on the sidelines of ECSSR's 5th Annual Conference, titled "2000 The Making of The Future," October 9, 1999

With H.H. Sheikh Nahyan bin Zayed Al Nahyan, Chairman of the Board of Trustees of Zayed bin Sultan Al Nahyan Charitable and Humanitarian Foundation; former US Vice President Al-Gore, and H.E. Dr. Anwar Gargash, State Minister for Foreign Affairs, in the USA, May 12, 1998

With H.H. Lt. General Sheikh Saif bin Zayed Al Nahyan UAE Deputy Prime Minister and Minister of Interior; and His Royal Highness Prince Turki Al-Faisal bin Abdulaziz Al Saud, Chairman of the King Faisal Center for Islamic Studies and Research, Saudi Arabia, during ECSSR's 14th Annual Conference, titled "Human Resources and Development in the Arabian Gulf," February 2, 2009

With H.H. Lt. General Sheikh Saif bin Zayed Al Nahyan UAE Deputy Prime Minister and Minister of Interior; during my visit to H.H. at the Headquarters of AD Police General Command, to present H.H. with a copy of my book *The Mirage*, April 15, 2015

Presenting a gift to H.H. Lt. General Sheikh Saif bin Zayed Al Nahyan, UAE Deputy Prime Minister and Minister of Interior; during my visit to H.H. at the Headquarters of AD Police General Command, April 15, 2015

With H.H. Sheikh Saif bin Zayed Al Nahyan, UAE Deputy Prime Minister and Minister of Interior, during ECSSR's 7th Annual Education Conference titled "Education and Development, Investing in the Future," held at ECSSR, November 1, 2016

With H.H. Sheikh Saif bin Zayed Al Nahyan, UAE Deputy Prime Minister and Minister of Interior; and H.E. Ali Rashid Al-Nuaimi, member of AD Executive Council and Director of AD Education Council and Chancelor of UAE University; during ECSSR's 7th Annual Education Conference titled "Education and Development, Investing in the Future," held at ECSSR, November 1, 2016

With H.H. Sheikh Saif bin Zayed Al Nahyan, UAE Deputy Prime Minister and Minister of Interior; and H.E. Hussain Ibrahim Al-Hammadi, Minister of Education, on the sidelines of ECSSR's 7th Annual Education Conference titled "Education and Development, Investing in the Future," held at ECSSR, November 2, 2016

With H.H. Sheikh Mansour bin Zayed Al Nahyan, UAE Deputy Prime Minister and Minister of Presidential Affairs; during the ceremony of launching the refereed scientific periodical *Strategic Visions* by ECSSR, December 12, 2012

With H.H. Sheikh Mansour bin Zayed Al Nahyan UAE Deputy Prime Minister and Minister of Presidential Affairs; and H.E. Ahmad Al-Humairi, Secretary-General of the Ministry of Presidential Affairs; and H.E. Saif Sultan Al-Aryani, Secretary-General of the UAE National Security Council, during the ceremony of launching the refereed periodical *Strategic Visions* by ECSSR, December 12, 2012

With H.H. Sheikh Mansour bin Zayed Al Nahyan UAE Deputy Prime Minister and Minister of Presidential Affairs; and H.E. Sheikh Hamdan bin Mubarak Al Nahyan (UAE Minister of Higher Education and Scientific Research at that time), during the ceremony of honoring the graduates of the Distinguished Student Scholarship of His Highness the President of the UAE, January 22, 2014

With H.H. Sheikh Mansour bin Zayed Al Nahyan UAE Deputy Prime Minister and Minister of Presidential Affairs; presenting H.H. with a copy of my book *The Mirage*, November 2, 2015

With H.H. Sheikh Mansour bin Zayed Al Nahyan UAE Deputy Prime Minister and Minister of Presidential Affairs; H.E. Ahmad Juma Al-Zaabi, Deputy Minister of Presidential Affairs; and H.E. Ahmad Al-Humairi, Secretary-General of the Ministry of Presidential Affairs; during my attending the ceremony of honoring the graduates of the Distinguished Student Scholarship of His Highness the President of the UAE, April 19, 2017

With H.H. Sheikh Mansour bin Zayed Al Nahyan UAE Deputy Prime Minister and Minister of Presidential Affairs; H.E. Ahmad Al-Humairi, Secretary-General of the Ministry of Presidential Affairs; H.E. Dr. Abdullah Al-Raisi, Director General of the UAE National Archives; H.E. Mohamed Salim A-Zahiri, Executive Director of School Operations Sector at Abu Dhabi Education Council and Member of the Board of Student Scholarships affiliated with the Ministry of Presidential Affairs; H.E. Dr. Ali Al-Irri, Director of External Scholarships at the Scholarship Office affiliated with the Ministry of Presidential Affairs; and H.E. Dr. Abdullah Maghribi, Director of Studies and Research Sector at the Ministry of Presidential Affairs, during a ceremony for honoring graduates of the Distinguished Student Scholarship of His Highness the President of the UAE, April 19, 2017

Presenting a copy of my book *The Mirage*, to H.H. Sheikh Hamid bin Zayed Al Nahyan, Chairman of the Abu Dhabi Crown Prince's Court, November 24, 2015

With H.H. Sheikh Hamid bin Zayed Al Nahyan, Chairman of the AD Crown Prince's Court; H.E. Mohammed Al-Bawardi, UAE State Minister for Defense Affairs; and H.E. Ali Al Hashemi, Religious Adviser at the Ministry of Presidential Affairs; during a conference titled "The Fourth Generation of Wars (4GW), held at ECSSR, May 16, 2016

With H.H. Sheikh Diab bin Zayed Al Nahyan, UAE, during ECSSR's 3rd Annual Conference, titled "The Impact of the Information and Communication Revolution on Society and State in the Arab World," January 4, 1997

With H.H. Sheikh Diab bin Zayed Al Nahyan, UAE, during the 3rd Annual Energy Conference, titled "Privatization and Deregulation in the Gulf Energy Sector," organized by ECSSR, November 25, 1997

With H.H. Sheikh Diab bin Zayed Al Nahyan, UAE, during the Conference, titled "Gulf Security: A National Perspective II," held in UK, April 29,1998

With H.H. Sheikh Diab bin Zayed Al Nahyan; UAE, and H.E. Dr. Anwar Gargash, Minister of State for Foreign Affairs, on the sidelines of a conference titled "Gulf Security: A National Perspective II," held in UK, April 29, 1998

With H.H. Sheikh Abdullah bin Zayed Al Nahyan, Minister of Foreign Affairs and International Cooperation (Undersecretary of Information and Culture at that time), on the sidelines of a lecture by Dr. Edwin Feulner, titled "A New Conservative Internationalist Foreign Policy," organized by ECSSR, October 17, 1995

With H.H. Sheikh Abdullah bin Zayed Al Nahyan, Minister of Foreign Affairs and International Cooperation (Minister of Information and Culture at that time), during the conference: "Gulf Security: A National Perspective II," held in UK, 29 April 1998

With H.H. Sheikh Abdullah bin Zayed Al Nahyan, Minister of Foreign Affairs and International Cooperation (Minister of Information and Culture at that time); H.E. Dr. Anwar Gargash State Minister for Foreign Affairs; and H.E. Essa Saleh Al-Gurg former UAE Ambassador to the UK, April 29, 1998

With H.H. Sheikh Abdullah bin Zayed Al Nahyan, Minister of Foreign Affairs and International Cooperation (Minister of Information and Culture at that time); Algerian President Abdulaziz Butafliqa and Prof. Mark Tessler, professor of political science at the University of Michigan – Ann Arbor during ECSSR's 4th Annual Conference, titled "Challenges of the Next Millennium: Education and Development of Human Resources," May 24, 1998

With H.H. Sheikh Abdullah bin Zayed Al Nahyan, Minister of Foreign Affairs and International Cooperation (Minister of Information and Culture at that time); during ECSSR's 5th Annual Conference, "2000 The Making of the Future," October 9, 1999

With H.H. Sheikh Abdullah bin Zayed Al Nahyan, Minister of Foreign Affairs and International Cooperation (Minister of Information and Culture at that time); and the late Staff Major General Haiye Juma'a Al-Hamili, during ECSSR's 5th Annual Conference, "2000: The Making of the Future," October 9, 1999

With H.H. Sheikh Abdullah bin Zayed Al Nahyan, Minister of Foreign Affairs and International Cooperation; and His Royal Highness Prince Turki Al-Faisal bin Abdulaziz Al Saud Chairman of the King Faisal Center for Islamic Studies and Research, KSA; during a Dinner Banquet on the sidelines of ECSSR's 12th Annual Conference: "Arabian Gulf Security: Internal and External Challenges," March 6, 2007

With H.H. Sheikh Abdullah bin Zayed Al Nahyan, Minister of Foreign Affairs and International Cooperation; and H.E. Dr. Tariq Al-Haidan Assistant Foreign Minister for International Organizations Affairs, during ECSSR's 16th Annual Conference: "Global Strategic Developments: A Futuristic Vision," March 21, 2011

With H.E. Sheikh Nahyan bin Mubarak Al Nahyan, UAE Minister of Culture and Knowledge development (Minister of Higher Education and Scientific Research at the time), during the 6thAbu Dhabi International Book Fair, April 1, 1996

With H.E. Sheikh Nahyan bin Mubarak Al Nahyan, UAE Minister of Culture and Knowledge development (Minister of Culture, Youth and Community Development, at the time), during ECSSR's 4th Annual Education Conference: "The Future of Education in the UAE: Innovation and Knowledge Production," held at ECSSR, September 17, 2013

With H.E. Sheikh Nahyan bin Mubarak Al Nahyan UAE Minister of Culture and Knowledge development (Minister of Culture, Youth and Community Development, at the time), during "The First Arabian Gulf Public Health Research Conference," January 21, 2014

With H.E. Sheikh Nahyan bin Mubarak Al Nahyan UAE Minister of Culture and Knowledge development (Minister of Culture, Youth and Community Development, at the time), during the opening session of a conference titled "The Challenges of Nation-Building in Arab Countries that have Recently Witnessed Change," held at ECSSR, October 6, 2015

With H.E. Sheikh Nahyan bin Mubarak Al Nahyan UAE Minister of Culture and Knowledge development (Minister of Culture, Youth and Community Development, at the time), during a celebration: "The Annual Forum of the Royal Institute for Information Technology, 2015; on November 2, 2015

With H.E. Sheikh Nahyan bin Mubarak Al Nahyan UAE Minister of Culture and Knowledge development (Minister of Culture, Youth and Community Development, at the time), during a celebration: "The Annual Forum of the Royal Institute for Information Technology, 2015; on November 2, 2015

With H.E. Sheikh Nahyan bin Mubarak Al Nahyan UAE Minister of Culture and Knowledge Development (Minister of Culture, Youth and Community Development, at the time); retired Lt. General Mohammed Hilal Al-Ka'abi, Chairman of International Golden Group (IGG) in the UAE; H,E, Hashim Al-Qaysiyah, special adviser to H.H. Sheikh Tahnoon bin Zayed Al Nahyan, UAE; and the Filipino boxer Manny Pacquiao, during the charity marathon organized by RAHMA Society, at Bani Yas Island, March 7, 2015

With Sheikh Dr. Ahmad bin Saif bin Mohammed Al Nahyan, UAE, at the International Defence Exhibition (IDEX), March 14, 1999

With H.E. Sheikh Sultan bin Tahnoon Al Nahyan, Member of Abu Dhabi Executive Council, at the honoring gathering organized by ECSSR to offer a Memorial Service of the late Mohammed Khalaf Al-Mazrouei, Adviser for Culture and Heritage at the Abu Dhabi Crown Prince's Court, December 23, 2014

Presenting a gift to H.E. Major General Pilot Sheikh Ahmad bin Tahnoon Al Nahyan, Head of UAE National and Reserve Service Authority, during his visit to ECSSR to sign the agreement for gauging public opinion as a service to NRSA, December 8, 2016

With Sheikh Saeed bin Saif bin Mohammed Al Nahyan, Chairman of *Al Watan* newspaper (previously *Akhbar Al Arab*), during his visit to ECSSR, October 19, 1999

Receiving an appreciation letter from Sheikh Saeed bin Saif bin Mohammed Al Nahyan, Chairman of *Al Watan* newspaper (previously *Akhbar Al Arab*), during my visit to the headquarter of the paper, November 8, 2016

Receiving a gift from H.H. Sheikh Saeed bin Saif bin Mohammed Al Nahyan, Chairman of *Al Watan* newspaper (previously *Akhbar Al Arab*), during my visit to the premises of the paper, November 8, 2016

Presenting the UAE Federal Personality Award, at its 3rd edition, to Her Excellency Dr. Amal Al-Qubaisi, Speaker of the UAE Federal National Council, on December 11, 2014. This award is issued by H.H. Sheikh Mohamed bin Zayed Al Nahyan, Crown Prince of Abu Dhabi, and Deputy Supreme Commander of the UAE Armed Forces (may God protect him).

With His Majesty Hamad bin Isa Al Khalifa, King of Bahrain, during my visit to his majesty in Bahrain, December 5, 2013

With H.H. Sheikh Hamad bin Khalifa Al-Thani, former Emir of Qatar, October 27, 1998

With His Majesty King Abdullah II ibn Al-Hussain, of Jordan, during ECSSR's 6th Annual Conference "Leadership and Management in Information Age," November 5, 2000

With His Majesty King Mohammed VI of Morocco, and Ret. Major General Khalifa Al-Musafiri, UAE Armed Forces, during a visit to Morocco, July 1, 1995

With H.E. former US President George W. Bush Jr. during his visit to the UAE, January 13, 2008

With H.E. former US President George W. Bush Jr. during his visit to the UAE, January 13, 2008

With H.E. Mikhail Gorbachev, former President of the Soviet Union and Nobel Peace Prize Laureate, during his visit to the ECSSR, December 4, 1994

With H.E. former French President Nicolas Sarkozy on the sidelines of a lecture he delivered at the ECSSR, titled "The World Today: A Conversation with Nicolas Sarkozy," January 13, 2016

Presenting a gift to H.E. former French President Nicolas Sarkozy on the sidelines of his lecture that he delivered at the ECSSR, titled "The World Today: A Conversation with Nicolas Sarkozy," January 13, 2016

With H.E. former French President Nicolas Sarkozy, while presenting him a French copy of my book *The Mirage* on the sidelines of his lecture he delivered at the ECSSR, titled "The World Today: A Conversation with Nicolas Sarkozy," January 13, 2016

With Her Excellency the late Baroness Margaret Thatcher, Former British Prime Minister, during her visit to the ECSSR, June 20, 1994

Presenting a gift to H.E. former British Prime Minister Tony Blair on the sidelines of a lecture he delivered at the ECSSR titled, "The Opportunities and Challenges of Globalization," August 17, 2016

A conversation with H.E. former British Prime Minister Tony Blair about my book *The Mirage* on the sidelines of a lecture he delivered at the ECSSR titled "The Opportunities and Challenges of Globalization," August 17, 2016

With His Holiness Pope Francis of the Vatican, when I presented him with a copy of my book *The Mirage*, in Spanish, April 12, 2017

With H.E. former President of Finland and Nobel Peace Prize Laureate, Martti Ahtisaari, on the sidelines of a lecture he delivered at the ECSSR titled "Conflict Resolution as a Tool for Egalitarian Politics," February 9, 2014

Presenting a gift to H.E. former President of Finland and Nobel Peace Prize Laureate, Martti Ahtisaari, on the sidelines of a lecture he delivered at the ECSSR titled "Conflict Resolution as a Tool for Egalitarian Politics," February 9, 2014

With H.E. Dr. Ólafur Ragnar Grímsson, former President of Iceland, on the sidelines of his lecture titled "The Clean Energy Economy: A Road to Recovery from a Financial Crisis," organized by ECSSR, March 5, 2014

Presenting a gift to H.E. former President of Iceland, Ólafur Ragnar Grímsson, on the sidelines of his lecture "The Clean Energy Economy: A Road to Recovery from a Financial Crisis," organized by ECSSR, March 5, 2014

Presenting a gift to H.E. former President of Poland and Nobel Peace Prize laureate, Lech Walesa, on the sidelines of a lecture he delivered at the ECSSR titled "The Challenges of Globalization and the Need for Solidarity," March 9, 2014

Presenting a gift to H.E. former President of Poland and Nobel Peace Prize laureate, Lech Walesa, on the sidelines of a lecture he delivered at the ECSSR titled "The Challenges of Globalization and the Need for Solidarity," March 9, 2014

With Her Excellency Ms. Julia Gillard, former Prime Minister of Australia, on the sidelines of a lecture she delivered at the ECSSR titled "The UAE and Australia: A Roadmap for Future Cooperation," January 15, 2014

Presenting a gift to H.E. John Howard, former Prime Minister of Australia, on the sidelines of a lecture he delivered at the ECSSR titled "Current Socio-Political Developments in the Middle East," October 21, 2014

Presenting a copy of my book *Prospects for the American Age: Sovereignty and Influence in the New World Order* in English, to H.E. John Howard, former Prime Minister of Australia, on the sidelines of a lecture he delivered at the ECSSR titled "Current Socio-Political Developments in the Middle East," October 21, 2014

Presenting a gift to H.E. Dr. Mahathir Mohamad, former Prime Minister of Malaysia on the sidelines of a lecture he delivered at the ECSSR titled "The Global Financial Crisis: Lessons Learnt and the Way Forward," May 5, 2010

With the late Dr. Kurt Waldheim, former Secretary-General of the United Nations and former President of Austria, during his visit to the ECSSR, December 1, 1997

With the late Dr. Kurt Waldheim, former Secretary-General of the United Nations and former President of Austria, during his visit to the ECSSR, December 1, 1997

Presenting a gift to H.E. former President of South Yemen, Ali Nassir Muhammad, during his visit to the ECSSR, February 13, 2000

With His Royal Highness Prince Salman bin Hamad Al Khalifa, Crown Prince of the Kingdom of Bahrain, during a conference titled "Gulf Security: A National Perspective I" in Abu Dhabi, April 5, 1997

With His Royal Highness Prince Salman bin Hamad Al Khalifa, Crown Prince of the Kingdom of Bahrain, during a conference titled "Gulf Security: A National Perspective I" in Abu Dhabi, April 5, 1997

With His Royal Highness Prince Salman bin Hamad Al Khalifa, Crown Prince of the Kingdom of Bahrain; and His Royal Majesty Prince Charles, Crown Prince of the United Kingdom, on the sidelines of a conference titled "Gulf Security: A National Perspective II" held in the UK, April 29, 1998

With His Royal Highness Prince Salman bin Hamad Al Khalifa, Crown Prince of the Kingdom of Bahrain; His Royal Majesty Prince Charles, Crown Prince of the United Kingdom; H.E. Hamad bin Ali Al-Attiyya, Adviser to the Emir of Qatar for Defense Affairs; and the late Hisham Nazer, Saudi Arabia's former Oil Minister, on the sidelines of the conference "Gulf Security: A National Perspective II" held in the UK, April 29, 1998

With His Royal Highness Prince Salman bin Hamad Al Khalifa, Crown Prince of Bahrain, and H.H. Sheikh Hamad bin Jassim bin Jaber Al Thani, former Qatari Prime Minister and Minister of Foreign Affairs, at the conference "Gulf Security: A National Perspective II" held in the UK, April 29, 1998

With His Royal Highness Prince Salman bin Hamad Al Khalifa, Crown Prince of the Kingdom of Bahrain at the conference "Gulf Security: A National Perspective II" held in the UK, April 29, 1998

With His Royal Highness Prince Salman bin Hamad Al Khalifa, Crown Prince of the Kingdom of Bahrain, during my visit to His Highness, in Bahrain, March 24, 2015

With His Royal Highness Prince Salman bin Hamad Al Khalifa, Crown Prince of the Kingdom of Bahrain, during my visit to His Highness, in Bahrain, March 24, 2015

With Casper Weinberger, former US Secretary of Defense, during his visit to ECSSR, April 16, 1994

With Kuwaiti Academic Dr. Mohammed Al-Rumaihi, the late Kuwaiti writer Mohammed Musaed Al-Saleh and Kuwaiti writer Anwar Al-Yassin, during their visit to the ECSSR, October 9, 1994

With Saudi journalist Othman Al-Omeir, during his visit to the ECSSR, April 16, 1995

With Staff Brigadier Mohammed Ahmed Atiq Al-Bakiri, former Commander of Zayed II Military College, during the visit of a delegation from that College to the ECSSR, May 28, 1995

With the retired Staff Major General Hazza Sultan Al-Darmaki, UAE, during a visit to the ECSSR, May 29, 1995

With H.E. Ahmed Al-Humairi, Secretary-General of the UAE Ministry of Presidential Affairs; the late Mr. Nemir Kirdar and Mr. Nizar Al-Saeei from Investcorp, Bahrain, during a visit to the ECSSR, June 6, 1995

With H.E. Zaki Nusaibah, Cultural Adviser at the UAE Ministry of Presidential Affairs, during a visit to the ECSSR, July 1, 1995

With H.E. Dr. Hasan Muratovic, former Prime Minister of Bosnia, during a lecture titled "The Future of Bosnia: Peace or War?" organized by the ECSSR, November 20, 1995

With the late Kuwaiti thinker Dr. Khaldoun Al-Naqeeb, during the ECSSR 2nd Annual Conference titled "Gulf Security in the Twenty-First Century," January 6, 1996

With Dick Cheney, former US Vice President, during his visit to the ECSSR, March 19, 1996

With Dick Cheney, former US Vice President, during his visit to the ECSSR, March 19, 1996

With H.E. Mohammed bin Khalifa Al-Habtoor, former Speaker of the UAE Federal National Council (FNC), during a visit to the ECSSR by a delegation from the FNC, June 11, 1996

With H.E. Sir Malcolm Rifkind, former UK Secretary of States for Foreign and Commonwealth Affairs, on the sidelines of a lecture he delivered at the ECSSR titled "Britain and the Middle East: Into the 21st Century," organized by ECSSR, November 4, 1996

With Lt. Gen. Dr. Nasser bin Abdulaziz Al-Arfaj, former Chief of Staff for Intelligence and Security of the Saudi Armed Forces, during his visit to the ECSSR, June 3, 1997

With Gen. Georg Meiring, former South African Chief of Staff, during his visit to the ECSSR, October 1, 1997

With Gen. Georg Meiring, former South African Chief of Staff, during his visit to the ECSSR, October 1, 1997

With French Commodore Stephane Le Grix De La Salle, during his visit to the ECSSR, October 28, 1997

With the late Dr. Atif Ubaid, former Prime Minister of Egypt, during his visit to the ECSSR, November 2, 1997

With Sheikh Abdulrahman bin Saud Al Thani, former Chairman of the Emiri Court in Qatar, during his visit to the ECSSR, November 3, 1997

With Sheikh Abdulrahman bin Saud Al Thani, former Chairman of the Emiri Court in Qatar, during his visit to the ECSSR, November 3, 1997

With the late Prince Turki bin Sultan bin Abdul Aziz, former Deputy Minister of Information for External Media in the Kingdom of Saudi Arabia, during his visit to the ECSSR, March 2, 1998

With the late Prince Turki bin Sultan bin Abdul Aziz, former Deputy Minister of Information for External Media in the Kingdom of Saudi Arabia, during his visit to the ECSSR, March 2, 1998

With Jean-Claude Mallet, former Adviser for Minister of Defense and Commissioner for Strategic Planning, French Ministry of Defense, during his visit to ECSSR, April 4, 1998

With His Royal Majesty Prince Charles, Crown Prince of the UK; H.E. Dr. Anwar Gargash, UAE Minister of State for Foreign Affairs; and the late Hisham Nazer, Saudi Arabia's former Oil Minister, on the sidelines of the conference "Gulf Security: A National Perspective II" held in the UK, April 29, 1998

With His Royal Majesty Prince Charles, Crown Prince of the United Kingdom; H.E. Dr. Anwar Gargash, UAE Minister of State for Foreign Affairs; and the Bahraini thinker, Dr. Mohammed Jabir Al Ansari, on the sidelines of the conference "Gulf Security: A National Perspective II" held in the UK, April 29, 1998

With His Royal Majesty Prince Charles, Crown Prince of the United Kingdom, and the late
H.H. Sheikh Salim Sabah Al-Salim Al-Sabah, former Kuwaiti Minister of Defense, on the
sidelines of the conference "Gulf Security: A National Perspective II" held in the UK, April
29, 1998

With the late Sheikh Salem Sabah Al-Salem Al-Sabah, former Kuwait's Defense Minister, and
H.E. Yousuf bin Alawi bin Abdullah, Minister Responsible for Foreign Affairs in the Sultanate
of Oman, on the sidelines of a conference titled "Gulf Security: A National Perspective II,"
UK, April 29, 1998

With Professor Kjell Eliassen during the visit of the delegation from the Centre for European and Asian Studies, in Norway, to the ECSSR, June 16, 1998

With Dr. James J. Zogby, President of the Arab American Institute, USA, during his visit to the ECSSR, June 20, 1998

With His Royal Highness Staff General Khalid bin Bandar bin Abdul Aziz Al Saud, former Commander of the Armored Corps, Kingdom of Saudi Arabia, during his visit to the ECSSR, October 4, 1998

With His Royal Highness Staff General Khalid bin Bandar bin Abdul Aziz Al Saud, former Commander of the Armored Corps, Kingdom of Saudi Arabia, while presenting His Highness a gift at the ECSSR, October 4, 1998

With Sheikh Ahmed Zaki Yamani, former Saudi Arabian oil minister, during the ECSSR's 4th Annual Energy Conference titled "Caspian Energy Resources: Implications for the Arab Gulf," organized by the ECSSR, October 25, 1998

With Dr. Michael Mooney, President of Lewis and Clark University, USA, during his visit to the ECSSR, November 2, 1998

With Her Excellency Deborah Jones, former US Chargé d'Affaires to the UAE, during her visit to the ECSSR, November 8, 1998

With Air Marshal Ray Funnell during the visit of a delegation from the Australian College of Defense and Strategic Studies to the ECSSR, November 10, 1998

With General Jean-Pierre Kelch, former French Army Chief of Staff, during his visit to the ECSSR, December 13, 1998

With H.E. Ural Latypov, former Deputy Prime Minister and Minister of Foreign Affairs of the Republic of Belarus, during a visit he made to the ECSSR, January 17, 1999

With Richard J. Danzig, the US Undersecretary of the Navy, and Ambassador Theodore Kattouf, former US Ambassador to the UAE, February 20, 1999

With Dr. Abdelbaki Hermassi, former Minister of Culture of Tunisia, during a visit he made to the ECSSR, February 24, 1999

With Dr. Abdelbaki Hermassi, former Tunisian Minister of Culture, during a visit he made to the ECSSR, February 24, 1999

With Major General Mahmoud Moawad Abdel-Aal, during the visit of a delegation from the Egyptian Armed Forces' Strategic Studies Center to the ECSSR, April 3, 1999

With H.E. Major General Mu'did Hareb Al-Khaili, former Commander of Zayed II Military College, UAE Ambassador to France, during his visit to the ECSSR, April 7, 1999

With Jaswant Singh, former Indian Minister for External Affairs, and the late Air Commodore (retired) Jasjit Singh, at a symposium titled "The UAE-India Relations in the Next Decade" held in New Delhi, April 13, 1999

With Dr. Ajit Nagpal, former Adviser on Health Policy & Hospital Affairs, at UAE Ministry of Health, during his visit to the ECSSR, July 13, 1999

Presenting a gift to Dr. Joseph Moynihan, Chairman of the National Council on US-Arab Relations, October 9, 1999

With media personality Jassim Al Azzawi, during his visit to the ECSSR, October 18, 1999

With H.E. former Syrian Ambassador to the UAE Ahmed Al Hallaq and H.E. Ambassador Ali Saif Sultan Al-Awani, UAE ambassador to Yemen, during their visit to the ECSSR, November 13, 1999

With Staff Lt. General Abdul Rahman Sir Al-Khatim, Sudan's former Minister of Defense, during a visit he made to the ECSSR, November 17, 1999

With Her Royal Highness the Jordanian Princess Aisha bint Al Hussein, during her visit to the ECSSR, November 21, 1999

With Staff Brigadier Mufleh Ayedh Al-Ahbabi, during the visit of a delegation from the UAE Armed Forces Command and Staff College to the ECSSR, November 26, 1999

With Prof. Abdul Ghani Maa al-Bared, former President of Damascus University, during his visit to the ECSSR, February 2, 2000

With Prof. Abdul Ghani Maa al-Bared, former President of Damascus University, during his visit to the ECSSR, February 2, 2000

With Khalid Ghalib Al Muhairi and Mike Tooth from Abu Dhabi Distribution Company, during their visit to the ECSSR, February 14, 2000

With Dick Cheney, former US Vice President, during (defence exhibition) TRIDEX 2000, March 5, 2000

With Marc Perrin de Brichambaut, former Secretary-General of the Organization for Security and Co-operation in Europe, during his visit to the ECSSR, May 2, 2000

With Dr. Ludger Volmer, former Minister of State for Foreign Affairs, Federal Republic of Germany, during a visit he made to the ECSSR, May 27, 2000

With H.E. Saeed Saif bin Jabr Al-Suwaidi, former Chairman of Abu Dhabi Chamber of Commerce and Industry, during his visit to the ECSSR, July 10, 2000

Presenting a gift to H.E. Saeed Saif bin Jabr Al-Suwaidi, former Chairman of Abu Dhabi Chamber of Commerce and Industry, during his visit to the ECSSR, July 20, 2000

With H.E. Ambassador Salim Ullah, former Ambassador of Pakistan to the UAE, during his visit to the ECSSR, July 11, 2000

With General Yves Crene, Commander of the French Land Forces, during his visit to the ECSSR, October 21, 2000

With General Yves Crene, Commander of the French Land Forces, and the accompanying delegation members during their visit to the ECSSR, October 21, 2000

With General Jehangir Karamat, former Pakistani Chief of Staff, during his visit to the ECSSR, October 24, 2000

With the late Indian Strategist Air Commodore Jasjit Singh, at the ECSSR, November 18, 2000

With the late Staff Major General Huyai Juma Al-Hamili, UAE and Shaikh Saif bin Hashel Al-Maskari, former Assistant Secretary-General for Political Affairs at GCC, during a symposium titled "The Future of the GCC Countries," organized by ECSSR, November 24, 2000

With H.E. Abdullah Bishara, former Secretary-General of the GCC, and Sheikh Saif bin Hashil Al-Maskari, former GCC Assistant Secretary-General for Political Affairs at GCC, during a symposium titled "The Future of the GCC Countries," organized by ECSSR, November 24, 2000

With H.E. Yousef Mana Al-Otaiba, UAE Ambassador to the USA, during his visit to the ECSSR, January 20, 2001

With the late Palestinian thinker Dr. Ahmed Sidqi Al Dajani; Dr. Bahgat Korany, professor of political science at the American University in Cairo; the late Dr. Abdulhadi Al Johari, Dean of Literature College at Minia University Egypt; Dr. Nevine Massad, Professor at the College of Economics and Political Science at Cairo University and former Director of the Institute for Arab Studies and Research affiliated with the Arab League; Dr. Talal Atreesi, Professor of Sociology at the Lebanese University; and Her Excellency Sheikha Najla Al Qasimi, former UAE Ambassador to Portugal, on the sidelines of a symposium held at the ECSSR, February 5, 2001

With Rear Admiral Shami Mohammed Al Dhaheri, former Commander of the Command and Staff College, Saudi Arabia, during his visit to the ECSSR, March 21, 2001

With Dr. Mohammed Al Majzoub, President of the Arab Association of Political Science, during his visit to the ECSSR, March 31, 2001

Presenting a gift to Dr. Edmund Ghareeb, Professor of International Relations, American University, Washington, during his visit to the ECSSR, March 31, 2001

With Dr. Wamid Jamal Nazmi, former professor of political science, at Baghdad University, during his visit to the ECSSR, April 2, 2001

With Gordon Olson, former US Chargé d'Affaires to the UAE, during his visit to the ECSSR, September 26, 2001

With Dr. Maha Qanout, former Syrian Minister of Culture, during her visit to the ECSSR, October 23, 2001

With Her Excellency Marcelle Wahba, former US Ambassador to the UAE, during her visit to the ECSSR, October 24, 2001

With H.E. Dr. Hanif Hassan, former UAE Minister of Health at a symposium titled "Islamic Perspective on Terrorism," organized by ECSSR, October 28, 2001

With H.E. Dr. Hanif Hassan, former UAE Minister of Health, and Staff Brigadier General Rashid Mohammed Al-Mualla, former Commander-in-Chief of Umm Al-Quwain Police, at a symposium titled "Islamic Perspective on Terrorism," at ECSSR, October 28, 2001

With H.E. Ahmad Al-Humairi, Secretary-General of the Ministry of Presidential Affairs; H.E. Mohamed Salim A-Zahiri, Executive Director of School Operations Sector at Abu Dhabi Education Council and Member of the Board of Student Scholarships affiliated with the Ministry of Presidential Affairs, at an event held by ECSSR, December 4, 2001

With Dr. Amin Saikal, former professor of political science and director of the Center for Islamic and Arabic Studies at the Australian National University, during his visit to the ECSSR, January 13, 2002

With Counselor Abdul Aziz Al-Rawwas, Adviser on Cultural and Heritage Affairs to His Majesty the Sultan Qaboos bin Said of Oman, during his visit to the ECSSR, January 23, 2002

With Mr. Fahmi Huwaidi, Egyptian writer and researcher in Contemporary Islamic Issues, on the sidelines of a lecture delivered by him, at ECSSR, March 12, 2002

With Abdul Qadir Abdul Rahman Bajamal, former Prime Minister of Yemen, during his visit to the ECSSR, October 26, 2002

With Dr. Nihad Awad, Director General of the Council on American-Islamic Relations (CAIR), during his visit to the ECSSR, November 23, 2002

With Abdul Alim bin Mustahail Rakhyoot, Chairman of the Omanization Committee, at the Diwan of the Royal Court, Sultanate of Oman, during his visit to the ECSSR, December 17, 2002

With French diplomat and journalist Eric Rouleau, at a symposium titled "The Future of Journalism in the Age of Multimedia," January 19, 2003

With US diplomat William Rugh, and French diplomat and journalist Eric Rouleau, at a symposium titled "The Future of Journalism in the Age of Multimedia," January 19, 2003

With Mike Bawden, Chairman of Ecco International, during his visit to the ECSSR, March 25, 2003

With Dr. Azmi Bishara, Director General of the Arab center for Research and Policy Studies, during his visit to the ECSSR, April 28, 2003

Presenting a gift to Dr. Ahmed Al-Qubaisi, Head of the Association of Muslim Scholars in Iraq, during his visit to the ECSSR, April 29, 2003

With Mr. Hamid Ansari, Vice President of India, during his visit to the ECSSR, September 10, 2003

With H.E. William Cohen, former US Secretary of Defense, and my son Dr. Khaled, on the sidelines of the ECSSR's 11th Annual Conference titled "Current Transformations and Their Potential Role in Realizing Change in the Arab World," March 12, 2006

With H.E. Mohammed Dhaen Al Hamli, former UAE Minister of Energy at the ECSSR's 12th Annual Energy Conference titled "China, India and the United States: Competition for Energy Resources," held at ECSSR, November 19, 2006

With Condoleezza Rice, former US Secretary of State, during her visit to the United Arab Emirates, January 13, 2008

With His Royal Highness Prince Turki Al-Faisal Al Saud, Chairman of the King Faisal Center for Islamic Research and Studies, KSA, on the sidelines of the ECSSR's 14th Annual Conference titled "Human Resources and Development in the Arabian Gulf," February 2, 2009

With His Royal Highness Prince Turki Al Faisal ibn Abdul Aziz, Chairman of the Board of Directors of King Faisal Center for Research and Islamic Studies in Saudi Arabia, on the sidelines of the ECSSR's 22nd Annual Conference titled "The Future of the Region: Oil Price Challenges," March 21, 2017

With Michael Martin, Speaker of the British House of Commons, during his visit to the ECSSR, April 6, 2009

With H.E. José Botelho de Vasconcelos, Angola's Minister of Petroleum, at the ECSSR's 15th Annual Energy Conference titled "Energy Security in the Gulf: Challenges and Prospects," held at ECSSR, November 16, 2009

With H.E. Mohammed Al-Shaali, former UAE Minister of State for Foreign Affairs, at a symposium titled "Thirty-Eighth Anniversary of the UAE Federation," November 24, 2009

With Majeed Al-Alawi, Kingdom of Bahrain's former Minister of Labor, during the ECSSR's 15th Annual Conference titled "Education and the Requirements of the GCC Labor Market," February 1, 2010

With H.E. Sheikh Fahim Al-Qasimi, former Secretary-General of the GCC, and other participants at the ECSSR's 15th Annual Conference titled "Education and the Requirements of the GCC Labor Market," February 1, 2010

Presenting a gift to Hélène Pelosse, former Director General of International Renewable Energy Agency (IRENA), on the sidelines of a lecture she delivered at the ECSSR, titled "Renewable Energies: A New Energy Paradigm," April 28, 2010

Presenting a gift to H.E. Dr. Majid bin Ali Al Nuaimi, the Kingdom of Bahrain's Minister of Education, on the sidelines of the ECSSR's 1st Annual Education Conference, October 5, 2010

Presenting a gift to H.E. David Miliband, former UK Secretary of State for Foreign and Commonwealth Affairs, on the sidelines of a lecture he delivered at the ECSSR titled "New Coalitions for A Changing World," November 8, 2010

With Major General (Retired) Khaled Abdullah Al Buainain, former Commander of the UAE Air Force and Air Defense, during the ECSSR 16th Annual Conference titled "Global Strategic Developments: A Futuristic Vision," March 21, 2011

With H.E. Dr. Ali Fakhro, Bahrain's former Minister of Education, at the ECSSR's 16th Annual Conference titled "Global Strategic Developments: A Futuristic Vision," March 21, 2011

With Charles W. Freeman, former US Ambassador to the Kingdom of Saudi Arabia, May 16, 2011

With H.E. Humaid Al-Qatami, former UAE Minister of Education, at the ECSSR's 2nd Annual Education Conference titled "Essentials of School Education in the United Arab Emirates," October 3, 2011

Presenting a gift to Dr. Abdulsalam Al-Majali, former Prime Minister of Jordan, during his participation in the ECSSR's 2ⁿᵈ Annual Education Conference titled "Essentials of School Education in the United Arab Emirates," October 3, 2011

With Mr. Hans Blix, former Swedish Minister for Foreign Affairs and Honorary Director General of International Atomic Energy Agency, and former Executive Chairman of the United Nations Monitoring, Verification and Inspection Commission; on the sidelines of the ECSSR's 17ᵗʰ Annual Energy Conference titled "Global Energy Markets: Changes in the Strategic Landscape," organized by ECSSR, November 1, 2011

With Mr. Hans Blix, former Swedish Minister for Foreign Affairs and Honorary Director General of International Atomic Energy Agency, and former Executive Chairman of the United Nations Monitoring, Verification and Inspection Commission; and Dr. Ali Al-Yabhouni, Chief Executive Officer of UAE Ruwais Fertilizer Industries (FERTIL), during the ECSSR's 17ᵗʰ Annual Energy Conference titled "Global Energy Markets: Changes in the Strategic Landscape," organized by ECSSR, November 1, 2011

With Reggie Jackson, former New York Yankees baseball player, while visiting me, December 11, 2012

With Hasan Shehata, former Egyptian football coach, while visiting me, December 11, 2012

With British footballer David Beckham, while visiting me, December 12, 2012

With British footballer David Beckham, at the launching ceremony of *Strategic Visions* journal, December 12, 2012

With British footballer David Beckham; American tennis player Serena Williams; and Reggie Jackson, former New York Yankees baseball player, at the launching ceremony of *Strategic Visions* journal, December 12, 2012

With American tennis player Serena Williams at the launching ceremony of *Strategic Visions* journal, December 12, 2012

With American tennis player Serena Williams at the launching ceremony of *Strategic Visions* journal, December 12, 2012

With one of the senior officials in the Chinese Communist Party (to my left) during my visit to The Central Party School in China, December 19, 2012

With Dr. Saad Eddin Al-Hilali, Professor and Chair of the Department of Comparative Jurisprudence at the Faculty of Sharia and Law, Al-Azhar University, Egypt; on the sidelines of a lecture organized by ECSSR, titled "Sharia and Islam," March 6, 2013

With H.E. Leon Panetta, former US Secretary of Defense, on the sidelines of a lecture he delivered at the ECSSR titled "The US Defense Budget: Repercussions for US Global Commitments," April 22, 2013

With H.E. Leon Panetta, former US Secretary of Defense, on the sidelines of a lecture he delivered at the ECSSR titled "The US Defense Budget: Repercussions for US Global Commitments," April 22, 2013

With H.E. Mohammed Salem Al Dhaheri, Executive Director of School Operations Sector in Abu Dhabi Education Council and Member of the Board of Student Scholarships at the Ministry of Presidential Affairs, during the opening of Ramadan Football Tournament, July 14, 2013

With UAE National Team footballer Omar Abdulrahman at the opening ceremony of the Ramadan football tournament, July 14, 2013

With Islamic scholar Sheikh Al-Habib Ali Al-Jifri, Director General of "Tabah" Foundation, at the ECSSR's Ramadan Tent activities, July 16, 2013

With the late Egyptian strategic expert Major General Samih Saif Al-Yazal, at the ECSSR's Ramadan Tent activities, July 16, 2013

With Dr. Ridwan Al Sayyid, Professor at the Lebanese University, at the ECSSR's Ramadan Tent activities, July 23, 2013

With Saudi journalist Turki Al-Dakheel, at the ECSSR's Ramadan Tent activities, July 23, 2013

Honoring the late Mohammed Khalaf Al-Mazrouei (Adviser for Culture and Heritage Affairs at the Abu Dhabi Crown Prince's Court, at the time) with the The Federal Personality Award, in its second edition, which is issued by H.H. Sheikh Mohamed bin Zayed Al Nahyan, Crown Prince of Abu Dhabi and Deputy Supreme Commander of the UAE Armed Forces (may God protect him), during the ECSSR's celebrations of the 42nd UAE National Day, November 28, 2013

Presenting Aysha Al-Hamili, the UAE's permanent representative to the International Civil Aviation Organization (ICAO), with the Federal Personality Award in its second edition, which is issued by H.H. Sheikh Mohamed bin Zayed Al Nahyan, Crown Prince of Abu Dhabi and Deputy Supreme Commander of the UAE Armed Forces (may God protect him), November 28, 2013

With Dr. Abdulreda Assiri, former Dean of Sociology College at Kuwait University; and the Kuwaiti singer Nabil Shuail at the ECSSR's celebrations of the UAE 42nd National Day, November 28, 2013

With Dr. Abdulreda Assiri, former Dean of Sociology College at Kuwait University; and the Kuwaiti singer Nabil Shuail at the ECSSR's celebrations of the UAE 42nd National Day, November 28, 2013

With Dr. Muhammad Yunus, Nobel Peace Prize laureate, on the sidelines of a lecture he delivered at the ECSSR, January 8, 2014

With General David Petraeus, former Director of the Central Intelligence Agency, during a visit to ECSSR, January 29, 2014

Presenting a gift to Hekmat Karzai, Founding Director of the Centre for Conflict and Peace Studies, on the sidelines of the lecture he gave at the ECSSR, February 3, 2014

With Lord Hindlip, former Chairman of London's auction house Christie's, February 3, 2014

With Javier Solana, former EU High Representative for the Common Foreign and Security Policies, on the sidelines of a lecture he delivered at the ECSSR titled "2014: A European View," February 19, 2014

Presenting a gift to Javier Solana, former EU High Representative for the Common Foreign and Security Policies, on the sidelines of a lecture he delivered at the ECSSR titled "2014: A European View," February 19, 2014

Presenting a gift to H.E. Dr. Nabil Elaraby, former Secretary-General of the Arab League, on the sidelines of a lecture he delivered at the ECSSR titled "The Future of Collective Arab Action," February 26, 2014

Presenting a gift to H.E. Dr. Nabil Elaraby, former Secretary-General of the Arab League, on the sidelines of a lecture he delivered at the ECSSR titled "The Future of Collective Arab Action," February 26, 2014

Receiving a gift from H.E. Jabr Ghanem Al-Suwaidi, Director General of the Court of His Highness Abu Dhabi Crown Prince, March 5, 2014

With Dr. Abdulla Nasser Al Suwaidi, Vice Chairman of the Abu Dhabi Vocational Education and Training Institute, at the signing ceremony of my book *Prospects for the American Age: Sovereignty and Influence in the New World Order*, at Kuttab Cafe, Dubai, March 06, 2014

With His Royal Highness Prince Faisal bin Salman bin Abdul Aziz, Governor of Madina province, KSA, during my visit to the Saudi capital Riyadh, March 14, 2014

Presenting a copy of my book *Prospects for the American Age: Sovereignty and Influence in the New World Order* to His Royal Highness Prince Faisal bin Salman bin Abdul Aziz, Governor of Madina province, KSA, during my visit to the Kingdom of Saudi Arabia, March 14, 2014

Presenting a gift to writer and journalist Jihad Al-Khazen, on the sidelines of his lecture titled "The Press: Arab and Western Perspectives" at the ECSSR, March 13, 2014

With the journalist Mr. Jihad Al-Khazen on the sidelines of the ECSSR's 22nd Annual Conference titled "The Future of the Region: Oil Price Challenges," March 21, 2017

Presenting a gift to H.H. Sheikh Nassir Al-Muhammad Al-Sabah, former Prime Minister of Kuwait, during my visit to His Highness in Kuwait, March 16, 2014

Presenting a copy of my book *Prospects for the American Age: Sovereignty and Influence in the New World Order* to H.H. Sheikh Nassir Al-Muhammad Al-Sabah, former Prime Minister of Kuwait, during my visit to His Highness in Kuwait, March 16, 2014

With Dr. Abdulreda Assiri, former Dean of the College of Social Sciences, Kuwait University, during the signing ceremony of my book *Prospects for the American Age: Sovereignty and Influence in the New World Order* at Kuwait University, March 16, 2014

With Her Royal Highness Princess Rym Al-Ali, Founder of "Media Institute" in the Hashemite Kingdom of Jordan, during the opening session of the ECSSR's 19th Annual Conference titled "Technology: Impacts, Challenges and the Future," March 18, 2014

Presenting a copy of my book *Prospects for the American Age: Sovereignty and Influence in the New World Order* to Mr. Abdul Rahman Mohammed Saif Jamsheer, President of Alumni Club of the Kingdom of Bahrain, in the presence of H.E. Dr. Majid bin Ali Al-Nuaimi, the Kingdom of Bahrain's Minister of Education, during the signing ceremony of my book held at InterContinental Regency Bahrain, March 29, 2014

With H.E. Dr. Majid bin Ali Al Nuaimi, Bahrain's Minister of Education; Abdul Rahman Mohammed Saif Jamsheer, President of Alumni Club of Bahrain; and Moaness Al-Mardi, Head of Journalist Association in Bahrain; at the signing ceremony of my book *Prospects for the American Age: Sovereignty and Influence in the New World Order* in the Kingdom of Bahrain, March 29, 2014

With H.E. Dr. Majid bin Ali Al Nuaimi, Bahrain's Minister of Education; Abdul Rahman Mohammed Saif Jamsheer, President of Alumni Club of Bahrain; and Moaness Al-Mardi, Head of Journalist Association in Bahrain; at the signing ceremony of my book *Prospects for the American Age: Sovereignty and Influence in the New World Order* in the Kingdom of Bahrain, March 29, 2014

Receiving a gift from H.E. Dr. Majid bin Ali Al Nuaimi, Bahrain's Minister of Education, on the sidelines of the signing ceremony of my book *Prospects for the American Age: Sovereignty and Influence in the New World Order*, at InterContinental Regency in the Kingdom of Bahrain, March 29, 2014

Presenting a copy of my book *Prospects for the American Age: Sovereignty and Influence in the New World Order* to Bahraini thinker Dr. Mohammed Jaber Al-Ansari at his home in Bahrain, March 30, 2014

With H.E. Sheikh Khalid Bin Ahmed Al Khalifa, the Kingdom of Bahrain's Minister of Foreign Affairs, during my visit to His Highness in the Bahrain Capital Manama, March 31, 2014

Presenting a copy of my book *Prospects for the American Age: Sovereignty and Influence in the New World Order* to H.E. Sheikh Khalid Bin Ahmed Al Khalifa, the Kingdom of Bahrain's Minister of Foreign Affairs, during my visit to His Highness in the Kingdom of Bahrain, March 31, 2014

Presenting a copy of my book *Prospects for the American Age: Sovereignty and Influence in the New World Order* to H.E. Sheikh Khalid bin Ahmed Al Khalifa, Minister of the Royal Court in the Kingdom of Bahrain, during my visit to H.E. in the Kingdom of Bahrain; with Mr. Abdul Rahman Mohammed Saif Jamsheer, President of the Kingdom of Bahrain's Alumni Club appearing in the photo, March 31, 2014

With H.E. Lt. General Sheikh Rashid bin Abdullah Al Khalifa, the Kingdom of Bahrain's Minister of Interior, while presenting His Excellency with a copy of my book *Prospects for the American Age: Sovereignty and Influence in the New World Order*, during my visit to Bahrain, March 31, 2014

With Bahraini writer and businessman Khalid bin Rashid Al-Zayani, during my visit to the Kingdom of Bahrain, March 31, 2014

Presenting a copy of my book *Prospects for the American Age: Sovereignty and Influence in the New World Order* to H.E. Ali Saeed bin Harmal Al-Dhaheri, Chairman of the Abu Dhabi University's Executive Board, April 21, 2014

Presenting a copy of my book *Prospects for the American Age: Sovereignty and Influence in the New World Order* to Dr. Radwan Al-Jarrah, Dean of the College of Arts and Sciences, Abu Dhabi University, April 21, 2014

Presenting a copy of my book *Prospects for the American Age: Sovereignty and Influence in the New World Order* to H.E. Dr. Tariq Al Haidan, Assistant Foreign Minister for International Organizations Affairs, at a signing ceremony of my book held at the UAE Ministry of Foreign Affairs and International Cooperation, April 23, 2014

With Mr. Michele Capasso, Chairman of Euro-Mediterranean Foundation, in a ceremony for handing me the Mediterranean Award for Diplomacy and Thought 2014," at ECSSR on April 27, 2014

With Mr. Ali Al Nuaimi, CEO, United Printing and Publishing, during my visit to the UPP, April 28, 2014

With H.E. Tamer Mansour, former Ambassador of the Arab Republic of Egypt to the UAE, and his wife, during the signing ceremony of my book *Prospects for the American Age: Sovereignty and Influence in the New World Order* at Abu Dhabi International Book Fair, May 2, 2014

Signing a copy of my book *Prospects for the American Age: Sovereignty and Influence in the New World Order* to Staff Colonel Yasser Sabri, former Defence Attaché at the Egyptian Embassy in the UAE, during Abu Dhabi International Book Fair, May 2, 2014

With captain Hasan Shehata, former Egyptian football coach, and captain Ahmed Suleiman at the signing ceremony of my book *Prospects for the American Age: Sovereignty and Influence in the New World Order* at Abu Dhabi International Book Fair, May 02, 2014

Discussing with Dr. Charles Ebinger, Director of the Energy Security and Climate Initiative at Brookings, the main ideas of my book *Prospects for the American Age: Sovereignty and Influence in the New World Order* during my visit to Brookings Foundation as part of my scholarly visit to the USA, May 5, 2014

With Her Excellency Marcelle Wahba, former US Ambassador to the UAE, and Mr. Dan Churchill, Chairman of the School of Policy and International Affairs, University of Maine, during a scholarly visit to the USA, May 6, 2014

Discussing the main ideas of my books *Prospects for the American Age: Sovereignty and Influence in the New World Order* and *From Tribe to Facebook: The Transformational Role of Social Networks* with Professor Richard Shultz, Director of the International Security Studies Program at the Fletcher School of Law and Diplomacy, United Atates of America, May 7, 2014

Presenting a copy of my book *Prospects for the American Age: Sovereignty and Influence in the New World Order* to Her Excellency Ambassador Lana Zaki Nusaibah in New York city, United Atates of America, May 9, 2014

With Lieutenant General (retired) Mohammed Hilal Suror Al-Kaabi, Chairman of International Golden Group, in UAE, during my participation in the "Zayed Charity Marathon," in New York City, May 10, 2014

With Rear Admiral (Ret.) Suhail Shaheen Al-Marar, from UAE, on the sidelines of the "Fourth-generation Warfare Conference," ECSSR, May 16, 2016

Presenting a copy of my book *Prospects for the American Age: Sovereignty and Influence in the New World Order* to Francesco Bandarin, head of the UNESCO World Heritage Centre, during my visit to Paris, May 21, 2014

With Dr. Gretty Mirdal, Director of the Paris Institute for Advanced Studies, during my visit to France, May 21, 2014

With Dr. Tayeb Kamali, Vice Chancellor of the Higher Colleges of Technology in the UAE, during the signing ceremony of my book *Prospects for the American Age: Sovereignty and Influence in the New World Order* held at the Higher Colleges of Technology, May 28, 2014

Presenting a copy of my book *Prospects for the American Age: Sovereignty and Influence in the New World Order* to Dr. Tayeb Kamali, Vice Chancellor of the Higher Colleges of Technology in the UAE, during the signing ceremony of the book held at the Higher Colleges of Technology, May 28, 2014, with H.E. Dr. Mohammed Omran Al-Shamsi, Chancellor of the Higher Colleges of Technology, appearing in the photograph

Presenting a copy of my book *Prospects for the American Age. Sovereignty and Influence in the New World Order* to H.E. Dr. Ali Rashid Al-Nuaimi, Member of the Abu Dhabi Executive Council and Director General of the Abu Dhabi Education Council and Chancellor of UAE University, July 3, 2014

With Dr. Mohammed bin Huwaiden, Professor of International Relations at UAE University during a discussion of my book *Prospects for the American Age: Sovereignty and Influence in the New World Order* at UAE University, June 3, 2014

Receiving a gift from Professor Ekhleif Al-Tarawneh, President of The University of Jordan, during my visit to the University, June 9, 2014

With H.E. Dr. Mohammad Al-Momani, Jordan's Minister of State for Media Affairs and Communications, during my visit to Jordan, June 10, 2014

With Dr. Ahmed El Tayeb, the Grand Imam of Al-Azhar, at Al-Azhar, Cairo, June 12, 2014

Presenting a copy of my book *Prospects for the American Age: Sovereignty and Influence in the New World Order* to Dr. Ahmed El Tayeb, the Grand Imam of Al-Azhar, at Al-Azhar, Cairo, June 12, 2014.

With H.E. Dr. Nabil Elaraby, former Secretary-General of the Arab League, during my visit to Cairo, June 12, 2014

Presenting a copy of my book *Prospects for the American Age: Sovereignty and Influence in the New World Order* to Dr. Ahmed Elsayed Elnaggar, Chairman of Al-Ahram Foundation, during my visit to Cairo, June 13, 2014

Presenting a copy of my book *Prospects for the American Age: Sovereignty and Influence in the New World Order* to Mr. Diaa Rashwan, Director of Al-Ahram Center for Political and Strategic Studies and former chairman of the Press Syndicate in Egypt, during my visit to Cairo, June 13, 2014

With Prof. Saad Eddin Ibrahim, director of the Ibn Khaldun Center for Development Studies, at the signing ceremony of my book *Prospects for the American Age: Sovereignty and Influence in the New World Order*, at Ibn Khaldun Center for Development Studies, Cairo, June 13, 2014

Receiving a gift from the journalist Yasser Rizk, Chairman of the Egyptian "Akhbar El Yom" foundation, during my visit to Egypt, June 14, 2014

With H.E. Saif Abdullah Al Shamsi, the UAE's Consul General in Turkey, at the Consulate during my visit to Turkey, June 17, 2014

With Salvatore Calleri, President of Fondazione Caponnetto, at the signing ceremony of my book *Prospects for the American Age: Sovereignty and Influence in the New World Order* in Italy, June 19, 2014

Presenting a gift to Mr. Pietro Grasso, President of the Italian Senate, during my visit to Italy on June 20, 2014

Presenting a copy of my book *Prospects for the American Age: Sovereignty and Influence in the New World Order* to H.E. Abdul Aziz Al-Shamsi, former UAE Ambassador to Italy, June 20, 2014

Presenting a copy of my book *Prospects for the American Age: Sovereignty and Influence in the New World Order* to Admiral Rinaldo Veri, President of the Center for Advanced Defense Studies in Italy, in the presence of Michele Capasso, President of the Fondazione Mediterraneo, June 20, 2014

With Pierfrancesco Sacco, Head of Policy Planning Unit, Italy's Ministry of Foreign Affairs, during my visit to Italy to discuss and sign my book *Prospects for the American Age: Sovereignty and Influence in the New World Order*, June 20, 2014

With Vatican Secretary of State Cardinal Pietro Parolin, in the presence of Michele Capasso, Head of "Euro-Mediterranean Foundation," during my visit to Italy, June 22, 2014

With H.E. Dr. Ali Rashid Al-Nuaimi, member of the Abu Dhabi Executive Council and Director General of the Abu Dhabi Education Council and Chancellor of UAE University, during his visit to the ECSSR, July 1, 2014

Presenting a gift to Mr. Mohammed Al-Hammadi, Editor-in-Chief of the UAE's *Al-Ittihad* newspaper, during his visit to the ECSSR, July 1, 2014

Presenting a gift to Dr. Fatima Al-Shamsi, Deputy Vice Chancellor for Administrative Affairs, Paris-Sorbonne University Abu Dhabi, July 8, 2014

Presenting a gift to H.E. Dr. Mohammed Mokhtar Gomaa, Egyptian Minister of Religious Endowments (Awqaf), on the sidelines of a lecture he co-delivered at the ECSSR titled "A Culture of Coexistence: Towards a New Vision," July 15, 2014

Presenting a gift to Lebanese University Professor Ridwan Al Sayyid, July 15, 2014

With Staff Colonel Yasser Sabri, Military Attaché at the Egyptian Embassy in the UAE, on the sidelines of the lecture titled "A Culture of Coexistence: Towards a New Vision," at the ECSSR, July 15, 2014

Presenting a copy of my book *Prospects for the American Age: Sovereignty and Influence in the New World Order* to Dr. Lisa Anderson, President of the American University in Cairo, September 24, 2014

With Dr. Bahgat Korany, professor of political science at the American University in Cairo, on the sidelines of signing ceremony of my book *Prospects for the American Age: Sovereignty and Influence in the New World Order* in Cairo, September 24, 2014

With Dr. Ismail Serageldin, Director of the Library of Alexandria, during my visit to Egypt, September 28, 2014

Presenting a gift to H.E. Dr. Rashid Ahmad Mohammed bin Fahad, former UAE Minister of Environment and Water, October 14, 2014

Presenting a gift to Dr. Jaber Al-Jabri, Deputy Secretary-General of the Environment Agency–Abu Dhabi, at a conference titled "Climate Change and the Future of Water," held at the ECSSR, October 15, 2014

Signing a copy of my book *Prospects for the American Age: Sovereignty and Influence in the New World Order* for H.E. Hussain Ibrahim Al-Hammadi, UAE Minister of Education, during a book signing ceremony held at Khalifa University, Abu Dhabi, October 16, 2014

Presenting a gift to Dr. Tod Laursen, President of Khalifa University, October 16, 2014

Receiving a gift from Dr. Ahmad Alawar, Director of the Institute of Applied Technology, UAE, October 20, 2014

With Lieutenant General (Ret.) Terry A. Wolff, Director of the Near East and South Asia Center for Strategic Studies, US National Defense University in Washington, during his visit to the ECSSR, October 21, 2014

Presenting a gift to Mr. Nayef Hawatmeh, Secretary-General of the Democratic Front for the Liberation of Palestine, on the sidelines of a lecture he gave at the ECSSR, November 10, 2014

With H.E. Mohammed Al-Murr, former Speaker of the Federal National Council (FNC), at the signing ceremony of my book *Prospects for the American Age: Sovereignty and Influence in the New World Order* held at the Sharjah International Book Fair, November 12, 2014

With Dr. Abdulla Nasser Al-Suwaidi, Vice Chairman of the Abu Dhabi Vocational Education and Training Institute, browsing through my book "Islamic Political Movements and Authority in the Arab World: The Rise and Fall" at the Sharjah International Book Fair, November 12, 2014

With H.E. Mohammed Al-Murr, former Speaker of the UAE Federal National Council (FNC); and H.E. Eng. Suhail Mohamed Faraj Al-Mazrouei, UAE Minister of Energy, November 18, 2014

Presenting a gift to H.E. Eng. Suhail Mohamed Faraj Al-Mazrouei, UAE Minister of Energy, November 18, 2014

With Dr. Habib Ghuloom, Director of Cultural Activities at the UAE Ministry of Culture, Youth and Community Development; Sultan Humaid Al-Jasmi, Director General of the UAE International Award for Poets of Peace; Dr. Aisha Al-Busmait; UAE poet Karim Matouq; and Sameh Kaoosh, Award's Media Adviser, November 23, 2014

Her Excellency Dr. Amal Al-Qubaisi, Speaker of the UAE Federal National Council (FNC); Ahmed Al-Hemeiri, Secretary-General of the UAE Ministry of Presidential Affairs; H.E. Mohammed Al-Murr, former Speaker of the UAE Federal National Council (FNC); and Moroccan academic Dr. Abdelhaq Azzouzi, during the ECSSR's celebration of the UAE 43rd National Day, December 11, 2014

With H.E. Mohammed Al-Murr, former Speaker of the UAE Federal National Council (FNC), during the ECSSR's celebration of the UAE 43rd National Day, December 11, 2014

Presenting the son of Lieutenant General (Ret.) Khalfan Matar Al-Rumaithi, escort of the late Sheikh Zayed bin Sultan Al Nahyan (may God rest his soul in peace), on behalf of his father, with the "Federal Personality" Award in its 3rd round, offered by H.H. Sheikh Mohamed bin Zayed Al Nahyan, Crown Prince of Abu Dhabi and Deputy Supreme Commander of the UAE Armed Forces (may God protect him), December 11, 2014

With H.E. Dr. Abdullah Nasser Sultan Al-Amiri, former UAE Ambassador to the Hashemite Kingdom of Jordan, upon his receipt of the "Federal Personality" Award in its 3rd round, offered by H.H. Sheikh Mohamed bin Zayed Al Nahyan, Crown Prince of Abu Dhabi and Deputy Supreme Commander of the UAE Armed Forces (may God protect him), December 11, 2014

With the UAE poet Salem Al Mansouri, winner of the 6th round of the Million's Poet, during his receipt of the "Federal Personality" Award in its 3rd round, offered by H.H. Sheikh Mohamed bin Zayed Al Nahyan, Crown Prince of Abu Dhabi and Deputy Supreme Commander of the UAE Armed Forces (may God protect him), December 11, 2014

With my son, Dr. Khaled; Moaness Al Mardi, Chairman of Bahraini Journalists Association; and Dr. Ali Qasim Al Shuaibi, UAE Media Personality and Academic, during the ECSSR's celebration of the UAE 43rd National Day, December 11, 2014

Presenting H.E. Ibrahim Al-Abed, Adviser to the Chairman of the Board of National Media Council in the UAE, with the "Federal Personality" Award in its 3rd round, granted by H.H. Sheikh Mohamed bin Zayed Al Nahyan, Crown Prince of Abu Dhabi and Deputy Supreme Commander of the UAE Armed Forces (may God protect him), December 11, 2014

With Prof. Saad Eddin Ibrahim, Chairman of the Ibn Khaldun Center for Development Studies in Cairo, during the ECSSR's celebration of the UAE 43rd National Day, December 11, 2014

With Eng. Ibrahim Mahlab, former Prime Minister of Egypt, and the late Egyptian Military Expert and strategist Major General Samih Saif Al-Yazal, while presenting a copy of my book *The Mirage* to Eng. Ibrahim Mahlab, on the sidelines of a conference titled "Against Terrorism," organized in Cairo by *Al-Jumhuriya* newspaper, December 14, 2014

With Dr. Jabir Asfour, former Egyptian Minister of Culture, during the launching ceremony of my book *The Mirage* in Cairo, December 14, 2014

With the Egyptian actor Izzat Al-Alaili during the launching ceremony of my book *The Mirage* in Cairo, December 14, 2014

With Ms. Azza Yahya, Deputy Editor-in-Chief of the Egyptian *Al Masaa* newspaper, during her visit to the ECSSR, January 4, 2015

With Dr. Zeina el-Tibi, President of the Observatoire d'Études Ggéopolitiques [Center for Geopolitical Studies] (OEG) in Paris; Dr. Charles Saint-Prot, the Director of the OEG; and Dr. Jean-Yves de Cara, Chairman of the OEG Scientific Committee, during their visit to the ECSSR, February 15, 2015

With Mr. Osama Haikal, Chairman of Media Production City in Egypt and former Egyptian Information Minister; and Mr. Makram Mohammed Ahmed, former Head of Egyptian Press Syndicate, during my visit to Media Production City in Egypt, February 24, 2015

Receiving a gift from Mr. Osama Haikal, Chairman of Media Production City in Egypt and former Egyptian Information Minister, during my visit to Egypt, February 24, 2015

With Her Excellency Dr. Maitha Salem Al Shamsi, Minister of State and Chairwoman of the Marriage Fund in the UAE; Ibrahim Abu Zekri, Head of the Arab Producers Union; Dr. Jabir Asfour, former Egyptian Minister of Culture; and the Egyptian actor Izzat Al-Alaili, during the 'Thank You UAE' celebration in Cairo, Egypt, February 25, 2015

With Her Excellency Dr. Maitha Salem Al Shamsi, Minister of State and Chairwoman of the Marriage Fund in the UAE; and Dr. Jabir Asfour, former Egyptian Minister of Culture, during the 'Thank You UAE' celebration in Cairo, Egypt, February 25, 2015

With President of Cairo University, Dr. Jaber Jad Nassar, during my visit to Egypt, February 25, 2015

With Lebanon's Grand Mufti, Sheikh Abdul-Latif Derian, during his visit to the ECSSR, March 10, 2015

With Staff Major General Khalid Al Fadhala, Chairman of the Board of Trustees of Bahrain Center for Strategic, International and Energy Studies (DERASAT) during his visit to the ECSSR, March 10, 2015

With Staff Major General Khalid Al Fadhala, Chairman of the Board of Trustees of Bahrain Center for Strategic, International and Energy Studies (DERASAT) during his visit to the ECSSR, March 10, 2015

With Rodi Kratsa, President of the Konstantinos Karamanlis Institute for Democracy and former European Parliament Vice President, during her visit to the ECSSR, March 10, 2015

With H.E. Dr. Sheikh Khalid bin Khalifa Al Khalifa, Vice Chairman of the Board of Trustees and Executive Director of Isa Cultural Center in the Kingdom of Bahrain, during his visit to the ECSSR, May 16, 2015

With Sheikh Rashid bin Isa bin Ali Al Khalifa during a visit by a delegation from Isa Cultural Center in the Kingdom of Bahrain, to the ECSSR, March 16, 2015

With Mr. Nabil Yakoub Al-Humur, Media Affairs Adviser to His Royal Majesty King Hamad bin Isa Al Khalifa, King of Bahrain, during the launch of my book *The Mirage* at Isa Cultural Center in the Kingdom of Bahrain, March 23, 2015

With H.E. Field Marshal Sheikh Khalifa bin Ahmad Al Khalifa, Commander-in-Chief of the Bahrain Defense Force, during my visit to His Excellency in Manama, the capital of the Kingdom of Bahrain, March 25, 2015

With H.E. Lt. General Sheikh Rashid bin Abdullah Al Khalifa, the Kingdom of Bahrain's Minister of Interior, presenting His Excellency with a copy of my book *The Mirage*, March 25, 2015

With H.E. Sheikh Khalid bin Ahmad Al Khalifa, Minister of the Royal Court in the Kingdom of Bahrain, during my visit to His Excellency in Manama, the capital of the Kingdom of Bahrain, March 25, 2015

Presenting a gift to H.E. Sheikh Khalid bin Ahmad Al Khalifa, Minister of the Royal Court in the Kingdom of Bahrain, during my visit to His Excellency in Manama, the capital of the Kingdom of Bahrain, March 25, 2015

Receiving a gift from H.E. Dr. Sheikh Khalid bin Khalifa Al Khalifa, Vice Chairman of the Board of Trustees and Executive Director of Isa Cultural Center in the Kingdom of Bahrain, during the launch of my book *The Mirage* in the Kingdom of Bahrain, March 25, 2015

With Staff Major General Khalid Al Fadhala, Chairman of the Board of Trustees of Bahrain Center for Strategic, International and Energy Studies (DERASAT) during my visit to the Kingdom of Bahrain, March 26, 2015

Signing a research cooperation agreement with the Bahrain Center for Strategic, International and Energy Studies (DERASAT) during my visit to the Kingdom of Bahrain, March 26, 2015

With H.E. Dr. Tariq Al Haidan, UAE Assistant Foreign Minister for International Organizations Affairs, during an interactive symposium on my book *The Mirage* held at the UAE Ministry of Foreign Affairs and International Cooperation, April 13, 2015

With H.E. Dr. Tariq Al Haidan, UAE Assistant Foreign Minister for International Organizations Affairs, during an interactive symposium on my book *The Mirage* held at the UAE Ministry of Foreign Affairs and International Cooperation, April 13, 2015

With Mr. Muammar Essa Al Mannai, Cultural Attaché at the Embassy of the Kingdom of Bahrain in United Arab Emirates, during his visit to the ECSSR, May 12, 2015

With H.E. Ali Al Hashimi, Religious Adviser in the UAE Ministry of Presidential Affairs, during a lecture held at the ECSSR titled "The GCC and Arab National Security: Roles and Challenges," May 13, 2015

Presenting a gift to H.E. Dr. Sheikh Khalid bin Khalifa Al Khalifa, Vice Chairman of the Board of Trustees and Executive Director of Isa Cultural Center in the Kingdom of Bahrain, during a visit he made to the ECSSR, May 13, 2015

With H.E. Dr. Sheikh Khalid bin Khalifa Al Khalifa, Vice Chairman of the Board of Trustees and Executive Director of Isa Cultural Center in the Kingdom of Bahrain; and H.E. Dr. Abdullah Al-Raisi, Director General of the National Archives, on the sidelines of a lecture at the ECSSR titled "The GCC and Arab National Security: Roles and Challenges," May 13, 2015

With H.E. Dr. Sheikh Khalid bin Khalifa Al Khalifa, Vice Chairman of the Board of Trustees and Executive Director of Isa Cultural Center in the Kingdom of Bahrain, on the sidelines of the ECSSR's 22ⁿᵈ Annual Conference titled "The Future of the Region: Oil Price Challenges," March 21, 2017

With Mr. Fawwaz Suleiman, International Relations Adviser at Isa Cultural Center, Kingdom of Bahrain, on the sidelines of the lecture at the ECSSR titled "The GCC and Arab National Security: Roles and Challenges," May 13, 2015

With Lt. General Dhahi Khalfan Tamim, Deputy Chief of Police and General Security in Dubai; and Mr. Saeed Mohammed Al-Raqbani, Special Adviser to His Highness the Ruler of Fujairah, during a symposium at the ECSSR titled "The Mirage: Enlightened Thought in Countering Terrorism," May 19, 2015

With Makram Mohammed Ahmad, former Head of the Egyptian Press Syndicate, during his visit with a delegation from Egypt to the ECSSR, May 21, 2015

With Mr. Jabir Mohammed Nasser Salem Al Shuaibi, Researcher at the Abu Dhabi Systems and Information Centre, during his visit to the ECSSR, May 26, 2015

Receiving a gift from Dr. Abdullah Al-Niyadi, Chairman of Al-Tawasol International Tent in the UAE, May 28, 2015

With Dr. Mustafa Salama, Secretary-General of the Arab Producers Union, May 31, 2015

Presenting a gift to His Eminence Mohammed Ali Al-Husseini, Secretary-General of the Islamic-Arab Council, on the sidelines of his lecture at the ECSSR titled "The Dangers of Sectarian Conflicts and Means to Confront Them," June 3, 2015

Presenting a gift to H.E. Dr. Abdullah Al-Raisi, Director General of the UAE National Archives, during a signing ceremony of my book *The Mirage* held at the National Archives, Abu Dhabi, June 4, 2015

Receiving a gift from H.E. Dr. Abdullah Al-Raisi, Director General of the UAE National Archives, during a signing ceremony of my book *The Mirage* held at the National Archives, Abu Dhabi, June 4, 2015

With Lieutenant General Ahmad Shafeeq, former Prime Minister of Egypt, during his visit to the ECSSR, August 30, 2015

With the consultant Eng. Aiyed Wahhab Al-Dhafeeri, Director General and Chairman of the Board of the Australian Arab Institute for Strategic Affairs, during his visit to the ECSSR, August 31, 2015

With the Kuwaiti media personality Dr. Ayed Al Manna on the sidelines of a symposium at the ECSSR titled "Storm of Thought," September 1, 2015

With Staff Brigadier Dr. Ahmed bin Daifallah Al-Qurani, Adviser at the Office of His Royal Highness Deputy Crown Prince of Saudi Arabia at the "Storm of Thought" symposium, held by the ECSSR, September 1, 2015

With H.E. Dr. Mohamed Mokhtar Gomaa, Egyptian Minister of Awqaf; and H.E. Ali Al-Hashimi, Religious Adviser at the Ministry of Presidential Affairs, on the sidelines of a lecture titled "Deconstructing Extremist Ideology" delivered by Dr. Gomaa at the ECSSR, September 2, 2015

With H.E. Dr. Mohamed Mokhtar Gomaa, Egyptian Minister of Awqaf, on the sidelines of the lecture titled "Deconstructing Extremist Ideology" he delivered at the ECSSR, September 2, 2015

With Mr. Saif Al-Marri, former Director General and Editor-in-Chief of Dar Al-Sada Press, UAE, September 13, 2015

With Nidal Shokeir, President of the European Press Association for the Arab World, during his visit to the ECSSR, September 13, 2015

With Adam Krzymowski, former Polish ambassador to the UAE; and H.E. Hashim Al-Qaysiyah, special adviser to H.H. Sheikh Tahnoon Bin Zayed Al Nahyan, at the launching ceremony of the Cancer Patient Care Society (RAHMA), September 15, 2015

With Her Excellency Grace Princesa, former Philippines Ambassador to the UAE, at the launching ceremony of the Cancer Patient Care Society (RAHMA), September 15, 2015

With H.E. the Jordanian Diplomat Muwaffaq Al-Ajlouni during his visit to the ECSSR, September 17, 2015

Presenting a gift to H.E. T. P. Seetharam, Ambassador of India to the United Arab Emirates, during his visit to the ECSSR, September 29, 2015

Presenting a gift to Mr. Andre van de Venter, Deputy Head of Mission at Embassy of the Republic of South Africa in the UAE, during his visit to the ECSSR, September 29, 2015

With the Egyptian Counselor Motee' Mamdouh and Egyptian Journalist Nabil Fahmi at a business lunch, October 1, 2015

With Mr. Tariq Al Bahr, Procurement Manager at the Emirates National School, October 3, 2015

With Major General Staff Pilot Rashad Salim Al-Saadi, Commandant of the UAE National Defense College, at the "Political Islam" conference, held by the National Defense College, October 5, 2015

Receiving a gift from Major General Staff Pilot Rashad Salim Al-Saadi, Commandant of the UAE National Defense College, at the "Political Islam" conference, held by the National Defense College, October 5, 2015

With H.E. Dr. Ali bin Tamim, Director General of Abu Dhabi Media Company and Secretary-General of Sheikh Zayed Book Award and Editor-in-Chief of the news portal 24 (www.24.ae); and the Saudi writer Mansour Al-Nigaidan, on the sidelines of the conference on "Political Islam" held by the UAE National Defense College, October 5, 2015

With Edward Mortimer, former Director of Communications in the Executive Office of the United Nations Secretary-General, at the signing ceremony of my book *The Mirage*, Oxford University, UK, October 12, 2015

With H.E. Mr. Hilmy Al-Namnam, Egyptian Minister of Culture, during my visit to Egypt, October 17, 2015

Receiving a gift from Dr. Sharif Kamel Shaheen, Director General of the Egyptian National Library and Archives, on the sidelines of a symposium on my book *The Mirage* held at the premises of the Egyptian National Library and Archives, October 18, 2015

With Major General Khaled Fouda, Governor of South Sinai, and Makram Mohammed Ahmed, former Head of the Egyptian Press Syndicate, during the laying down of the foundation stone for the Sheikh Zayed bin Sultan Al Nahyan Road in Sharm el-Sheikh and completing H.H. Sheikh Mohamed bin Zayed Al Nahyan Complex for UAE-Egyptian Culture and Friendship, Sharm el-Sheikh, Egypt, October 21, 2015

With Dr. Farouk El-Baz, Director of the Center for Remote Sensing, Boston University, during the ECSSR's 6th Annual Education Conference titled "Education and Development: Towards a Modern Education System in the UAE," October 28, 2015

Presenting a gift to Her Excellency Dr. Maitha Salem Al-Shamsi, Minister of State and Chairwoman of the UAE Marriage Fund, November 1, 2015

With Dr. Hassan Qayed Al Subaihi, professor of mass communication at UAE University, during his visit to the ECSSR, November 3, 2015

Presenting a gift to Dr. Stephen Hanson, Director of the Reves Center for International Studies at the College of William & Mary; with Dr. Davison Douglas, from the Reves Center, appearing in the photo, during their visit to the ECSSR, November 3, 2015

With Dr. Stephen Hanson, Director of the Reves Center for International Studies at the College of William & Mary, and Dr. Davison M. Douglas, from the Reves Center, during a visit to the ECSSR, November 3, 2015

With H.E. Dr. Mohammed Matar Al-Kaabi, Chairman of the UAE General Authority of Islamic Affairs and Endowments, and Dr. Farouk Hamada, Religious Adviser at the Court of His Highness the Crown Prince of Abu Dhabi, during a signing ceremony of my book *The Mirage* at Mohammed V University, Abu Dhabi, November 4, 2015

Presenting a copy of my book *The Mirage* to Dr. Farouk Hamada, Religious Adviser at the Court of His Highness the Crown Prince of Abu Dhabi, during a book signing ceremony held at Mohammed V University – Abu Dhabi, November 4, 2015

With Dr. Farouk Hamada, Religious Adviser at the Court of His Highness the Crown Prince of Abu Dhabi and President of Mohammed V University – Abu Dhabi, on the sidelines of the signing ceremony of my book *The Mirage* held at the University, November 4, 2015

Presenting a French copy of my book *The Mirage* to Dr. Farouk Hamada, Religious Adviser at the Court of His Highness the Crown Prince of Abu Dhabi and President of Mohammed V University – Abu Dhabi, on the sidelines of the signing ceremony of my book *The Mirage* held at the University, November 4, 2015

Presenting an English copy of my book *The Mirage* to international Filipino boxer Manny Pacquiao on the sidelines of the RAHMA charity marathon, organized by the Cancer Patient Care Society (RAHMA) on Yas Island, November 07, 2015

With Dr Xue Qing Guo (Bassam), Dean of the Sheikh Zayed bin Sultan Al Nahyan Centre for Arabic Language and Islamic Studies in China, during his visit to the ECSSR, November 10, 2015

With Italian Senator Roberto Formigoni, during my visit to Milan, Italy, November 16, 2015

Presenting a copy of my book *The Mirage* to Dr. Manuela Di Martino, President of the Swiss Lugano University, at the ceremony held to confer on me the Honorary Doctorate and membership of the Academic Council, Lugano University, Switzerland, November 17, 2015

Presenting a gift to Italian Politician Roberto Maroni, President of Lombardy, Italy, during my visit to Italy's Milan city, November 19, 2015

Presenting a copy of my book *The Mirage* to H.E. Dr. Mohammed Matar Al-Kaabi, Chairman of the UAE General Authority of Islamic Affairs and Endowments, on the sidelines of a book signing ceremony organized by the General Authority, November 23, 2015

Presenting a gift to H.E. Dr. Sultan bin Ahmed Sultan Al-Jaber, Minister of State and Chief Executive of the Abu Dhabi National Oil Company (Adnoc), November 26, 2015

With Ms. Nora Al Karbi, Member of the Executive Bureau and UAE Representative to the Arab Youth Council, during her visit to the ECSSR, December 13, 2015

With Dr. Farhan Nizami, Director of the Oxford Centre for Islamic Studies, at a symposium held as part of co-operation with the ECSSR titled "Security in the Arabian Gulf: Migration, Technology, Media and Change," December 15, 2015

With Lord William Hague of Richmond, former UK Secretary of State for Foreign and Commonwealth Affairs and current member of the UK House of Lords, on the sidelines of a lecture he delivered at the ECSSR titled "Global Trends," December 16, 2015

Presenting a gift to Lord William Hague of Richmond, former UK Secretary of State for Foreign and Commonwealth Affairs and current member of the UK House of Lords, on the sidelines of the lecture he delivered at the ECSSR, December 16, 2015

Presenting a gift to H.E. Mohammed Rashid Al-Zaabi, Assistant Undersecretary at the Abu Dhabi Accountability Authority, during his visit to the ECSSR, December 20, 2015

With H.E. Rashid Abdullah Al-Nuaimi, former UAE Minister of Foreign Affairs, and Dr. Abdul-Hamid Al-Ansari, former Dean of the College of Sharia at Qatar University, December 30, 2015

With Dr. Abdul-Hamid Al-Ansari, Former Dean of the College of Sharia at Qatar University, on the sidelines of his lecture at the ECSSR titled "Do Political Religious Groups Possess Applicable Development Plans? The Case of the Muslim Brotherhood," December 30, 2015

Presenting a gift to H.E. Wael Gad, Ambassador of Egypt to the UAE, during his visit to the ECSSR, January 5, 2016

Presenting a gift to H.E. Mohammed Al-Karib, Ambassador of the Republic of Sudan to the UAE, during his visit to the ECSSR, January 5, 2016

With H.E. Abdul Latif bin Rashid Al Zayani, Secretary-General of the GCC, on the sidelines of a lecture he delivered at the ECSSR titled "Cooperation Council for the Arab States of the Gulf: Achievements and Aspirations," January 20, 2016

Presenting a gift to H.E. Abdul Latif bin Rashid Al Zayani, Secretary-General of the Cooperation Council for the Arab States of the Gulf (GCC), on the sidelines of a lecture he delivered at the ECSSR titled "Cooperation Council for the Arab States of the Gulf: Achievements and Aspirations," January 20, 2016

With Lt. General Dhahi Khalfan, Deputy Chief of Police and General Security in Dubai, on the sidelines of a lecture titled "Cooperation Council for the Arab States of the Gulf: Achievements and Aspirations," January 20, 2016

With Irina Bokova, Director-General of UNESCO, during my visit to Paris, January 26, 2016

Presenting a gift to Irina Bokova, Director-General of UNESCO, during my visit to Paris, January 26, 2016

Presenting a copy of my book *The Mirage* to Dr. Ammar Ali Hassan, the Egyptian Writer and Political Analyst, on the sidelines of a lecture organized by the ECSSR titled "The Intellectual Similarities between the Muslim Brotherhood and Jihadi Organizations: Insights from The Mirage," February 3, 2016

With Moroccan Academic Dr. Abdelhaq Azzouzi, on the sidelines of a lecture organized by the ECSSR titled "The Pioneers of Reform and Renewal of Religious Thought in the Arab and Islamic worlds: Insights from The Mirage," February 10, 2016

Presenting a gift to H.E. Dr. Riyadh Yaseen, former Yemen's Minister of Foreign Affairs and Yemen's Ambassador to France, on the sidelines of a lecture he delivered at the ECSSR titled "Yemen Crisis Developments," February 17, 2016

Presenting a copy of my book *Eternal Imprints: Figures that Made History and Others that Changed the Future of their Countries* to H.E. Dr. Ali bin Tamim, Director General of Abu Dhabi Media Company and Secretary-General of Sheikh Zayed Book Award and Editor-in-Chief of the news portal 24 (www.24.ae), during my visit to "24.ae" news team, February 17, 2016

Presenting a gift to H.E. Dr. Ali bin Tamim, Director General of Abu Dhabi Media Company and Secretary-General of Sheikh Zayed Book Award and Editor-in-Chief of the news portal 24 (www.24.ae), during my visit to "24.ae" news team, February 17, 2016

Presenting a gift to Mr. Makoto Ohashi, Senior Fellow, Mitsui Global Strategic Studies Institute, Tokyo, Japan, during his visit to the ECSSR, March 6, 2016

Presenting a gift to H.E. Umej Bhatia, Ambassador of the Republic of Singapore to the UAE, during his visit to the ECSSR, March 15, 2016

Presenting a gift to H.E. Vasilis Polemitis, Ambassador of the Republic of Cyprus to the UAE, during his visit to the ECSSR, March 15, 2016

With Dr. Aref Al-Sheikh, writer of the words of the UAE national anthem, at the ECSSR's 22nd Anniversary, March 21, 2016

With Dr. Aref Al-Sheikh, writer of the words of the UAE national anthem, during his receipt of the "Federal Personality" Award in its 4th round, granted by H.H. Sheikh Mohamed bin Zayed Al Nahyan, Crown Prince of Abu Dhabi and Deputy Supreme Commander of the UAE Armed Forces (may God protect him), March 21, 2016

Presenting a gift to Her Excellency Joanna Wronecka, Poland's Undersecretary of State for Development Cooperation and African Affairs, during her visit to the ECSSR, March 22, 2016

During my attendance of the signing ceremony of the book *Abu Dhabi: Glimpses from the History of a City* by the UAE Media Personality and Writer Murad Abdullah Al-Baloushi, April 29, 2016

With H.E. Ahmad Abdul Rahman Al-Jarman, Assistant Foreign Minister for Political Affairs, UAE, at the signing ceremony of my book *Eternal Imprints: Figures that Made History and Others that Changed the Future of their Countries* held at the UAE Ministry of Foreign Affairs and International Cooperation, May 9, 2016

With H.E. Liborio Stellino, Ambassador of Italy to the UAE, during his visit to the ECSSR, May 22, 2016

With Dr. Farouk Hamada, Religious Adviser at the Court of His Highness the Crown Prince of Abu Dhabi; and H.E. Mohamed Ait Ouali, Ambassador of Morocco to the UAE, on the sidelines of a lecture delivered by Dr. Farouk Hamada at the ECSSR titled "The Concept of Caliphate: A Dialectic Model between the Past and the Present," June 14, 2016

Presenting a gift to Major General Khaled Fouda, Governor of Egypt's South Sinai, on the sidelines of a lecture he delivered at the ECSSR titled "Development and its Role in Confronting Terrorism," August 10, 2016

Receiving a gift from Major General Khaled Fouda, Governor of Egypt's South Sinai, on the sidelines of his lecture titled "Development and its Role in Confronting Terrorism" at the ECSSR, August 10, 2016

Presenting a gift to H.E. Dr. Mohammed Ateeq Al Falahi, Secretary-General of the Emirates Red Crescent Authority, on the sidelines of signing a Cooperation Agreement with the Authority, August 17, 2016

With Dr. Abdullah Al-Niyadi, Chairman of Al-Tawasol International Tent; and Dr. Abu Bakr Mohamed Hussein, environmental media expert, who presented me with a copy of his book *The Khalifa bin Zayed Initiative: the Knight of Environment and Sustainability* during his visit to the ECSSR, August 28, 2016

Receiving a gift from H.E. Dr. Riyadh Yaseen, Yemen's Ambassador to France and former Yemen's Minister of Foreign Affairs, on the sidelines of honoring me in the "Thank you Emirates of Benevolence" campaign where I received him at the ECSSR, September 4, 2016

Presenting a gift to H.E. Dr. Anwar Gargash, UAE Minister of State for Foreign Affairs, during his visit to the ECSSR, September 19, 2016

With representatives of the research centers taking part in the 3rd "Storm of Thought" Alliance Symposium, hosted by the Royal Institute for Strategic Studies in Rabat, Kingdom of Morocco, September 26, 2016

Receiving a gift from Mr. James Morse, President of Rabdan Academy, UAE, during his visit to the ECSSR, October 9, 2016

Receiving a gift from Her Excellency Sheikha Lubna Al-Qasimi, UAE Minister of State for Tolerance, during my visit to her at her office, 10 October 2016

Presenting a gift to Her Excellency Dominique Mineur, Ambassador of the Kingdom of Belgium to the UAE, during her visit to the ECSSR, October 11, 2016

With Mr. John Gatt-Rutter, Head of Counter Terrorism Division at the European External Action Service (EEAS); Mr. Nidal Shoukeir, President of the European Press Association for the Arab World; and the EEAS's overseas managers, during my visit to the Belgian capital, Brussels, October 19, 2016

With H.E. Hussain Ibrahim Al-Hammadi, UAE Minister of Education, and a number of participants in the ECSSR's 7th Annual Education Conference titled "Education and Development: Investing in the Future," November 1, 2016, with participants holding some of my books and the ECSSR's publications which have been included as part of civic education curriculum in the country

With the ECSSR staff raising the UAE flag in front of the ECSSR premises in celebration of the Flag Day, November 3, 2016

With H.E. Hussain Ibrahim Al-Hammadi, UAE Minister of Education, on the sidelines of the opening ceremony of the Abu Dhabi International Petroleum Exhibition and Conference "ADIPEC 2016," November 7, 2016

With H.E. Dr. Sultan bin Ahmad Sultan Al-Jaber, Minister of State and Chief Executive of the Abu Dhabi National Oil Company (Adnoc), on the sidelines of the opening ceremony of the Abu Dhabi International Petroleum Exhibition and Conference "ADIPEC 2016," November 7, 2016

Receiving a gift from H.E. General Tan Sri Dato' Sri Zulkifl bin Muhammad Zain, Chief of Defence Forces of Malaysia, during his visit to the ECSSR, November 7, 2016

With H.E. Dr. Mohammed Ateeq Al-Falahi, Secretary-General of the Emirates Red Crescent Authority and H.E. Rashid Mubarak Al-Mansoori, Deputy Secretary-General of the Emirates Red Crescent, during the ceremony held by the Cancer Patient Care Society (RAHMA) in cooperation with the UAE Red Crescent, to honor breast cancer female patients, November 10, 2016

Presenting a gift to H.E. Saleh Attia, Ambassador of the People's Democratic Republic of Algeria to the UAE, during his visit to the ECSSR, November 13, 2016

With H.E. Dr. Ali Rashid Al-Nuaimi, member of the Abu Dhabi Executive Council and Director General of the Abu Dhabi Education Council and Chancellor of UAE University; and Dr. Mohamed Albaili, Vice Chancellor of UAE University, during my visit to the University, November 22, 2016

Presenting a gift to Dr. Diaa Rashwan, Director of Al-Ahram Center for Political and Strategic Studies and former Head of the Egyptian Press Syndicate, during his visit to the ECSSR, November 23, 2016

With Mr. Bernardino León, Director General of Emirates Diplomatic Academy (EDA); and Mr. Omar Al-Bitar, Vice President of EDA, during my visit to the Academy, November 27, 2016

Presenting a gift to Dr. Khalifa Al-Suwaidi, Media Personality and Professor at UAE University, on the sidelines of a lecture he delivered at the ECSSR titled "Commemoration Day and the Federation Journey: Reflections on the Values of Gratitude and Generosity," November 28, 2016

With Dr. Khalifa Al-Suwaidi, Media Personality and Professor at UAE University; and the Jordanian Major General (Rtd) Dr. Saleh Al-Mayteh, faculty member at the UAE National Defense College, on the sidelines of a lecture he delivered by Dr. Khalifa Al-Suwaidi at the ECSSR titled "Commemoration Day and the Federation Journey: Reflections on the Values of Gratitude and Generosity," November 28, 2016

Receiving a gift from Dr. Noor Aldeen Sobhi Atatreh, Chancellor of Al Ain University of Science and Technology, during his visit to the ECSSR, November 29, 2016

With Sheikh Abdullah bin Mohammed bin Khalid Al Nahyan and H.H. Sheikh Faisal Bin Saqr Al Qasimi, Chairman of the Board of Gulf Pharmaceutical Industries (Julphar), during a symposium titled "Mohamed bin Zayed and Education" organized by the ECSSR, with attendance of an elite of officials, experts and specialists in education, January 12, 2017

With Lieutenant General Ahmad Shafeeq, former Prime Minister of Egypt, during his visit to the ECSSR, January 24, 2017

During an event organized by the Cancer Patient Care Society (RAHMA) under the title "World Cancer Day 2017," February 8, 2017

With Hazim Imam, former Egyptian Footballer and member of the Egyptian Football Association, during the event organized by the Cancer Patient Care Society (RAHMA) under the title "World Cancer Day 2017," February 8, 2017

During my participation in the 3rd International Korean-European Conference on Middle Eastern and North African, South Korea, February 14-15, 2017

With lieutenant general (Rtd) Mohammed Hilal Suroor Al-Kaabi, Chairman of Board of Directors of the International Golden Group (IGG) in the UAE, during my visit to the International Defence Exhibition (IDEX) in Abu Dhabi, February 21, 2017

During my visit to the International Defence Exhibition (IDEX) in Abu Dhabi, February 21, 2017

With H.E. Dr. Anwar Gargash, Minister of State for Foreign Affairs, during his receipt of the "Federal Personality" Award in its 5th round, granted by H.H. Sheikh Mohamed bin Zayed Al Nahyan, Crown Prince of Abu Dhabi and Deputy Supreme Commander of the UAE Armed Forces (may God protect him), March 14, 2017

With H.E. Mohammad Al Gergawi, Minister of Cabinet Affairs and the Future, during his receipt of the "Federal Personality" Award in its 5th round, granted by H.H. Sheikh Mohamed bin Zayed Al Nahyan, Crown Prince of Abu Dhabi and Deputy Supreme Commander of the UAE Armed Forces (may God protect him), March 14, 2017

With H.E. Staff Major General Abdullah Mohair Al Ketbi, Commander of the Shooting Support Units at the UAE armed forces, during his receipt of the "Federal Personality" Award in its 5th round, granted by H.H. Sheikh Mohamed bin Zayed Al Nahyan, Crown Prince of Abu Dhabi and Deputy Supreme Commander of the UAE Armed Forces (may God protect him), March 14, 2017

With Major General Dr. Ahmed Naser Al-Raisi, Inspector General of the UAE Ministry of Interior, during his receipt of the "Federal Personality" Award in its 5th round, granted by H.H. Sheikh Mohamed bin Zayed Al Nahyan, Crown Prince of Abu Dhabi and Deputy Supreme Commander of the UAE Armed Forces (may God protect him), March 14, 2017

With H.E. Dr. Ali bin Tamim, Director General of Abu Dhabi Media Company and Secretary-General of Sheikh Zayed Book Award and Editor-in-Chief of the news portal 24 (www.24.ae), during his receipt of the "Federal Personality" Award in its 5th round, granted by H.H. Sheikh Mohamed bin Zayed Al Nahyan, Crown Prince of Abu Dhabi and Deputy Supreme Commander of the UAE Armed Forces (may God protect him), March 14, 2017

With Brigadier-General Ali Ahmad Hassan Al-Tunaiji, from the UAE Presidential Guards, during his receipt of the "Federal Personality" Award in its 5th round, granted by H.H. Sheikh Mohamed bin Zayed Al Nahyan, Crown Prince of Abu Dhabi and Deputy Supreme Commander of the UAE Armed Forces (may God protect him), March 14, 2017

With Sultan Rashid Al Shamsi, Executive Director of the Private Affairs at the Abu Dhabi Crown Prince's Court, during his receipt of the "Federal Personality" Award in its 5th round, granted by H.H. Sheikh Mohamed bin Zayed Al Nahyan, Crown Prince of Abu Dhabi and Deputy Supreme Commander of the UAE Armed Forces (may God protect him), March 14, 2017

Appendix (2)
Résumé

Appendix 2

Résumé

I have held the position of Director General of the Emirates Center for Strategic Studies and Research (ECSSR) since 1994. I was born in 1959 and received my bachelor's degree in political science from Kuwait University in 1981 and my master's and PhD degrees in political science from the University of Wisconsin, USA, in 1985 and 1990, respectively. I worked as a visiting professor at the University of Wisconsin in 1992 where I taught a course on political systems in the Middle East and North Africa. I also served as a teacher of political science at United Arab Emirates University (1991/2000) where I taught various courses including Scientific Research Methodology, Contemporary Problems of the Islamic World, Arab Political Systems, Theories of Political Change, Contemporary International Issues, in addition to seminars and courses on Latin America, politics of the Middle East, United States of America and Europe.

I have written a number of books including *Eternal Imprints: Figures that Made History and Others that Changed the Future of their Countries* in 2016, *The Mirage* in 2015, *Prospects for the American Age: Sovereignty and Influence in the New World Order* in 2014, and *From Tribe to Facebook: The Transformational Role of Social Networks* in 2013 which was classified by the Emirati newspaper *Al-Imarat Al-Yawm* among the best-selling books in the UAE's 'book exchange'. I also wrote *The United Arab Emirates*

Society: A Future Perspective which was published as part of the Emirates Lectures Series, No. 71, (Abu Dhabi: ECSSR, 2003), and also appeared as a chapter under the title "Future Perspective" in the book *United Arab Emirates Society*, published by United Arab Emirates University in 2004.

I co-authored *Democracy, War and Peace in the Middle East* with Prof. David Garnham and Prof. Mark Tessler in 1995 where I contributed a chapter titled "Arab and Western Conceptions of Democracy: Evidence from a UAE Opinion Survey." I co-edited *Islamic Political Movements and Authority in the Arab World: The Rise and Fall* in 2014, and participated in the preparation and editing of *Air/Missile Defense, Counter Proliferation and Security Policy Planning* in 2000. I also compiled and edited *The Yemeni War of 1994: Causes and Consequences* in 1995, and compiled, edited and wrote the Introduction and a chapter titled "The Gulf Security Dilemma: The Arab Gulf States, the United States of America and Iran" for *Iran and the Gulf: A Search for Stability* in 1996, which won prizes for Best Publisher, Best Arabic Book in the Humanities and Social Sciences, and Best Writing at the 16th Annual Sharjah International Book Fair, held in 1997. In 1998, I edited *The Gulf Co-operation Council on the Eve of the 21st Century;* I also edited *Gulf Security in the 21st Century*, which won the Ibn Turki Award for Research and Future Planning in 1998, awarded by the Ibn Turki Foundation for Poetic Originality and Intellectual Research and Heritage, in the Kingdom of Saudi Arabia. I wrote a chapter titled "An Outlook for the Gulf Co-operation Council" for *The Future of the Gulf Co-operation Council*, which was published as part of the Emirates Lectures Series, No. 29, in collaboration with a group of intellectuals (Abu Dhabi: ECSSR, 1998).

I have published studies on various topics, such as: Arabian Gulf Security, Conceptions of Democracy in Arab and Western Societies, Women and Development, UAE Public Opinion on the Gulf Crisis, Religious Extremism and other topics in a number of world-known journals and periodicals, including *The Journal of South Asian and Middle Eastern Studies*; *Journal of the Social Sciences* published by Kuwait University; *Security Dialogue*; *Whitehall Series* by RUSI; *Indian Journal of Politics*, and many others.

I have published, and still do, articles in various UAE, Gulf and Arab newspapers. I also write a series of articles titled "Personalities and Accomplishments" in the UAE's *Al-Ittihad* newspaper since 2015, and I am the founder of the *Wujhat Nazar* (Perspectives) section in the same newspaper in 2001. I am the Editor-in-Chief for the ECSSR's scholarly, refereed Arabic periodical *Strategic Visions* which was launched in 2012, and I write regular articles for the ECSSR's *Aafaq Al-Mustaqbal* Arabic magazine. I am frequently interviewed by newspapers inside and outside the UAE such as the Egyptian newspapers *Al-Ahram* and *Al-Messa*, and the Bahraini *Al-Ayam* in addition to the interview in the Belgian *New Europe* titled "The Mirage: Tackling Terrorism with Education and Security," on October 24, 2016. The interviews are mainly about vital issues related to the Arabian Gulf region and the world. Interviews conducted by media and TV channels include one to the French *Euronews* titled "Supporting the Muslim Brotherhood," on October 23, 2016.

I have participated, and still participate, in many national and international conferences and seminars. I am a member of several political science associations such as the Midwest Political Science Association and the American Political Science Association, and also an affiliate member of a number of international studies entities and associations including the Middle East Studies Association of North America. I am a former board member of Georgetown University's Center for Contemporary Arab Studies (CCAS) in the USA, in addition to my membership of the board of research consultants of the Institute for Foreign Policy Analysis (IFPA) in the USA. I am a member of the Board of Advisors at the School of Policy and International Affairs (SPIA), University of Maine in the USA, and a member of the Arab Thought Forum in the Hashemite Kingdom of Jordan and a former member of the Advisory Board of the Center of Excellence for Applied Research and Training (CERT) at Higher Colleges of Technology in the UAE, as well as a former Board Member of the Emirates Diplomatic Institute in the UAE and a former member of the National Media Council in the UAE.

I have been the Chairman of the Board of Directors for the Scholarship of His Highness the President of the UAE, which is affiliated to the Ministry of Presidential Affairs, since 1999. I am also a former Chairman of the Board for the Emirates National Schools and a former Council Member at Zayed University in the UAE. In September 2009, I was appointed Chairman of the Higher Committee for the preparation of the National Strategy for Childhood and Motherhood in the UAE upon a decision by Her Highness Sheikha Fatima bint Mubarak (Mother of the Nation), Chairwoman of the General Women's Union, Supreme Chairwoman of the Family Development Foundation and President of the Supreme Council for Motherhood and Childhood.

I was granted membership of the International Advisory Board of The E-City for His Majesty the King of the Kingdom of Bahrain in January 2010. I am a member of the Board of Trustees of the Emirati–Swiss Friendship Council and a member of the Advisory Board of Casa Arabe of Spain. I am also a former member of the Advisory Board of Translation Studies at United Arab Emirates University. In 2012, I was named as a member of the Supreme Council for the National Defense College in the UAE. On May 19, 2015, I was appointed Chairman of the Founding Committee for the Cancer Patients Care Society (RAHMA) by Decree No. (13) for the year 2015, issued by His Excellency the Secretary-General of the Abu Dhabi Executive Council. On January 22, 2016, I was appointed as a member of the Advisory Council of the Center for International Studies at the University of St. Thomas in Houston, Texas, USA.

I have been awarded a number of national and international awards and medals. I received the Emirates Appreciation Award for the Sciences, Arts and Literature in Humanities (Political Sciences), in its 3ʳᵈ edition, in 2008, presented by His Highness Sheikh Khalifa bin Zayed Al Nahyan, President of the United Arab Emirates (may God protect him). Also in 2013, His Highness Sheikh Khalifa bin Zayed Al Nahyan, President of the United Arab Emirates (may God protect him), presented me with the "Head of State Merit Award" in recognition of my patriotism and sincere achievements and as a role model for upholding the "Values of Giving."

On March 17, 2015, I received the "Arab Social Media Influencers Award 2015 – Politics Category for Institutions" granted by His Highness Sheikh Mohammed bin Rashid Al Maktoum, Vice President of the UAE and Prime Minister of the UAE and Ruler of Dubai (may God protect him), to the Emirates Center for Strategic Studies and Research. On November 28, 2016, His Highness Sheikh Mohammed bin Rashid Al Maktoum, Vice President of the UAE and Prime Minister of the UAE and Ruler of Dubai (may God protect him), honored me in the 3ʳᵈ session of the UAE Pioneers Initiative.

In 2012, I was awarded the Abu Dhabi Medal by His Highness Sheikh Mohamed bin Zayed Al Nahyan, Crown Prince of Abu Dhabi and Deputy Supreme Commander of the UAE Armed Forces (may God protect him), after I received Abu Dhabi Award in 2011. On April 7, 2016, my book *The Mirage* won the "Sheikh Zayed Book Award for Contribution to the Development of Nations" at the award's 10ᵗʰ edition (2015/2016). On May 1, 2016, I was presented with the "Sheikh Zayed Book Award for Contribution to the Development of Nations" for my book *The Mirage* by His Highness Sheikh Mansour bin Zayed Al Nahyan, UAE Deputy Prime Minister and Minister of Presidential Affairs.

In 1995, I was awarded the Legion of Merit (Commander Degree) from the late King Hassan II of the Kingdom of Morocco. In 2002, I was awarded the French Order of Merit (First Class) by the President of the French Republic. In 2006, I received the Executive Personality Award for Young Leaders from the Middle East Excellence Awards Institute in Dubai, and an Honorary Professorship from the International University, Vienna, in 2008.

In 2012, I received the "Unique Leadership and Futuristic Vision Award" from the Emirates Identity Authority, and was honored in the same year by the European Business Association in recognition of my distinguished effort in supporting community programs offered by the ECSSR. In 2013, I was awarded the "Key to the Moroccan City of Fez" in an appreciation from the Kingdom of Morocco of my role in deepening the relations between the UAE and the Kingdom of Morocco. In 2014, I received the "Mediterranean Award for Diplomacy" from the Fondazione Mediterraneo, in recognition of my contributions and effort toward bringing nations closer and my role in promoting the concept of "cultural diplomacy" based on knowledge production and thought.

On September 28, 2014, I received the "Key to the City of Alexandria" in recognition of my effort in supporting culture. On February 25, 2015, I received the "Knight of Arab Studies Award" from the Arab Producers Union, which is an affiliate of the Arab League, in recognition of my vast intellectual and cultural contributions promoting the value of research. On May 28, 2015, the Abu Dhabi-based Al-Tawasol International Tent gave me an Appreciation Certificate in recognition of my pioneering and outstanding role in spreading and entrenching the culture of research. On June 2, 2015, the Culture and Science Forum and Sultan Bin Ali Al Owais Cultural Foundation honored me and the Foundation gave me the "Cultural Personality of the Year Award" in its 22nd edition.

On July 2, 2015, I was awarded the "UAE Medal for Humanitarian Work" by the 6th Zayed Humanitarian Forum in recognition of my effort in the field of social and humanitarian work at the Arab and international levels. On July 29, 2015, I was nominated by the senior leadership of the UAE Ministry of Foreign Affairs and International Cooperation to represent the country in the GCC Award for Excellence in the Field of Studies and Research. In September 2015, the UAE Interim Committee on Textbooks honored me in recognition of my effort in the Committee. On November 2, 2015, I was honored by His Excellency Sheikh Nahyan bin Mubarak Al Nahyan, Minister of Culture, Youth and Community Development, at the 2015 British Computer Society (BCS) Networking Forum, for my strategic role and fruitful partnership I forged with the BCS – the Chartered Institute for IT.

On November 9, 2015, the UAE's *Al-Ittihad* newspaper honored me and presented me with the "Honoring Shield" in recognition and appreciation of my role in supporting *Al-Ittihad's* 10th Annual Forum. On November 17, 2015, I was awarded an honorary doctorate in political science and international relations from the University of Lugano, Switzerland, and was also elected member of the University's Academic Council. On December 7, 2015, I was honored by His Highness Sheikh Tamim bin Hamad Al Thani, Emir of Qatar and Chairman of the 35th session of the GCC Supreme Council, on the occasion of my receiving the "GCC Award of Excellence in Research and Studies" in its first honoring edition. On December 13, 2015, I was awarded a Certificate of Appreciation from the Arab Youth Council for Integrated Development, Cairo, the Arab Republic of Egypt, in recognition and support of my effort in authoring my book *The Mirage*.

On January 27, 2016, I received the "Award of European Press for the Arab World 2015" from the Association of European Press for the Arab World in collaboration with the Institute for Prospects and Security in Europe for strategic studies. I was also awarded the "Geopolitical Studies Award 2015" from the Observatory of Geopolitical Studies at the French Senate, and was also granted membership of the Observatory's Scientific Council.

On April 5, 2016, I was awarded the "Revolutionary Thinker Award" from the College of William & Mary, the United States of America. On April 8, 2016, I was awarded the "Naguib Mahfouz Award for Literature" in recognition of my role in international effort serving world peace, by Dr. Tariq Mahfouz, the nephew of the writer Naguib Mahfouz, during the first annual ceremony of the award, organized by Naguib Mahfouz's family in New York, USA.

On May 30, 2016, I was awarded the "UAE Medal for Voluntary Work" in appreciation of the support I have given to the events and activities of the "Zayed Giving Initiative" as well as my support for the social, voluntary, and humanitarian initiatives of the pioneers of volunteer work. On June 4, 2016, I was awarded the "Arab Eagle Award for Public Management" by Tatweej Academy for Excellence Awards in the Arab Region. On September 4, 2016, I was honored in appreciation of my effort in supporting the Yemeni people in the face of aggression and was awarded an "Honoring Shield" by His Excellency Riyadh Yaseen, Ambassador of Yemen to France (former Yemeni Foreign Minister), and Feras Farouq Al-Yafae, head and coordinator of the "Thank You Emirates of Benevolence" campaign and of the "Thank You Kingdom of Firmness" campaign.

The UAE Ministry of Education chose a collection of my books, including *The Mirage*, to be taught as part of the curriculum for secondary students for the academic year 2016/2017. The Ministry also chose another collection of ECSSR publications to be taught at the elementary and secondary stages. On January 3, 2017, L.U.de.S University, in Switzerland, awarded me professorship in political science and literature.

On March 12, 2017, the Emirates Conference for Volunteering honored me by awarding me the Emirates Volunteer Medal and Award in appreciation of my rich career in giving, achievement, excellence and creativity. On March 21, 2017, the "Universal Peace Federation" awarded me the title of

"Ambassador for Peace," in recognition of my great and continuous effort to promote the culture of tolerance, moderation and acceptance of 'the other' among different nations and cultures of the world.

On May 1, 2017, I was awarded the title of the Ambassador for Loyalty and Happiness, and membership of the Higher Committee organizing the "Happiness Register to Delight the Leadership" in recognition of my leading role in promoting the culture of happiness and tolerance through my humanitarian and creative activities in service of humanity.

In 2014, I conducted a cultural and intellectual tour around the world to create an academic discussion regarding my book *Prospects for the American Age: Sovereignty and Influence in the New World Order* with the most prominent leaders of thought and culture in the world. This tour included Arab and Western countries, notably the Kingdom of Bahrain, the Kingdom of Saudi Arabia, the State of Kuwait, the Kingdom of Morocco, the Hashemite Kingdom of Jordan, the Arab Republic of Egypt, the United Kingdom, the United States of America, the French Republic, the Federal Republic of Germany, the Republic of Italy and the Republic of Turkey.

In 2015 and 2016, I conducted seminars and cultural and intellectual world tours in order to create an academic dialogue with the most prominent symbols of culture and thought in the world around my book *The Mirage*. These tours included Arab and Western countries, notably the Kingdom of Bahrain, the State of Kuwait, the Kingdom of Morocco, the Arab Republic of Egypt, the United States of America, the French Republic, the Kingdom of Belgium, the Republic of Serbia, and the Republic of Montenegro. On April 12, 2017, I met with His Holiness Pope Francis of the Vatican in Rome, and presented His Holiness with a copy of my book *The Mirage*.

I have provided consultations to several entities and councils inside and outside the United Arab Emirates such as: the Federal National Council;

Ministry of Foreign Affairs; Ministry of Education; and Ministry of Culture, Youth and Community Development in the United Arab Emirates, in addition to the numerous military and political consultations as the political adviser to His Highness Sheikh Mohamed bin Zayed Al Nahyan, Crown Prince of Abu Dhabi and Deputy Supreme Commander of the UAE Armed Forces (may God protect him).

I am married with four children. I am an art collector and enjoy watching and practicing sports. On November 28, 2003, I was diagnosed with T-Cell Lymphoblastic Lymphoma. I am now in remission and recovered well, by the grace of God the Almighty, strong will and unwavering resolve, after receiving intensive treatment at the MD Anderson Cancer Center in Houston, Texas, USA, until the summer of 2004 with continued treatment until the summer of 2012. In 2009, I underwent pelvic reconstruction surgery in the Federal Republic of Germany.